INDIVIDUALIZING PSYCHOLOGICAL ASSESSMENT

INDIVIDUALIZING PSYCHOLOGICAL ASSESSMENT

CONSTANCE T. FISCHER
DUQUESNE UNIVERSITY

Brooks/Cole Publishing Company
Monterey, California

Brooks/Cole Publishing Company
A Division of Wadsworth, Inc.

Printed in the United States of America

10 9 8 7 6 5 4 3 2 1

Library of Congress Cataloging in Publication Data

Fischer, Constance T., [date]
  Individualizing psychological assessment.

  Includes index.
  1. Personality assessment. 2. Personality tests.
3. Report writing. 4. Psychology—Authorship.
I. Title.
BF698.4.F56 1985   155.2'8   84-7796
ISBN 0-534-03981-2

Sponsoring Editor: *Claire Verduin*
Editorial Assistant: *Pat Carnahan*
Production Editor: *Penelope Sky*
Manuscript Editor: *Carol King*
Permissions Editor: *Carline Haga*
Interior and Cover Design: *Charles Carter Design*
Design Coordinator: *Jamie Sue Brooks*
Typesetting: *Omegatype Typography, Champaign, Illinois*
Printing and Binding: *Fairfield Graphics, Fairfield, Pennsylvania*

Preface

ASSESSMENTS by psychologists, educators, and other human-service professionals too often *end* with the client being reported in terms of scores, bell-shaped curves, traits, psychodynamic forces, or diagnostic labels. This book is about using these classification devices in ways that facilitate *returning* from them to the individual's life, both during the assessment session and in written reports.

Individualizing Psychological Assessment presents an approach and procedures through which a person's actual life becomes the subject matter of assessment. Within this framework an assessor uses training in psychometrics, personality theory, and research findings, and standardized tools such as objective tests, projective techniques, and behavioral assessment. This is *not* a book about using the "individual tests" requiring one-on-one administration; rather, it was written with the assumption that the reader has already acquired or is in the process of acquiring such training. *Individualizing Psychological Assessment* may be used with diverse test data, life situations, and direct observations. The wide range of cases presented as illustrations should be clear even to persons who have not yet completed formal courses in assessment, or whose work requires different instruments. The individualized approach is the fundamental concept that the reader should retain.

Within this individualized approach, the primary data are life events, both as reported and as directly witnessed during assessment sessions. Comportment during testing is regarded as a specialized instance of other life events. Data derived from testing, such as scores and statistical profiles, are tools to help revise and refine one's direct impressions of the client. Together, client and assessor explore the ways the subject moves through situations, shaping as well as being shaped by them. They collaboratively investigate both the client's experience and others' reactions to his or her ways of doing things. Tailored recommendations result from the client trying out personally viable alternative approaches within the assessment. En route, the assessment has addressed process as well as its products, and has explored not only how the client exemplifies categories but also how he or she exceeds them. This focus on life events rather than on derived data also facilitates effective communication with the client's other helpers. Moreover, because the written assessment describes actual comportment that has already been explored with the client, he or she may read the report and provide commentary on it.

This book will thus serve advanced undergraduates as well as graduate students, and will be helpful to practicing professionals who are looking for rationales and ways to individualize their own or their supervisees' assessments. Earlier versions and portions of this text have proven relevant not only for psychological assessors, but for therapists, counselors, teachers, rehabilitation specialists, school psychologists, child-care workers, parole officers, community mental-health center intake workers, and related human-services professionals.

Individualized assessment provides touchpoints with depth therapy and the human potential movement, and also serves as an effective preparation and framework for the diverse behavior-oriented therapies, including behavior modification, systems approaches, and cognitive psychology. My own theoretical orientation is human-science psychology, which is grounded in the European existential-phenomenological philosophy of science. I believe that a human-science approach is integrative; that is, it helps us combine our hard-earned status as reputable scientists with our recently renewed efforts to deal directly with human consciousness and purposefulness, which do not lend themselves to study via the methods of the natural sciences. With regard to psychological assessment, a human-science approach is not so much an alternative to our established paradigm as it is a spelling-out and systematizing of what many psychologists have been doing implicitly or inconsistently during these changing times.

Each chapter of this text is self-contained; readers may skip about to suit their requirements. In Part One, Chapter 1 describes the historical context of the individualized approach. Chapter 2 presents an overview of the assessment process, including a sample report and some guiding principles for individualizing assessments. Chapters 3 and 4 talk about "how to do it," and include tables showing the functions of tests, counterproductive assessor inclinations, and excerpts illustrating ways of involving clients in exploring their situations and options.

Part Two focuses on writing individualized reports. Chapter 5 contains tables that address the organization of reports, general writing principles (with sample excerpts and revisions), and individualized writing (with excerpts and alternative wording); there is also a do-and-don't checklist for reviewing the drafted report. Chapters 6, 7, and 8 offer sample reports for adults and children in counseling and clinical contexts. Besides being samples of report-writing styles, these examples further illustrate the assessment processes.

In Part Three, some traditional assessment topics are discussed in relation to the human-science approach and procedures presented earlier in the book. Chapter 9 examines the difference between interventional assessment and therapy, the integration of qualitative and quantitative data in program evaluation, how to free the meanings of words, human-science qualitative research, and the relations among rapport, privacy, and intimacy in an assessment setting. Chapter 10 is concerned with ethical dilemmas in standardized testing. Chapter 11 explores the nature of assessment descriptions through a comparison with Andrew Wyeth's art. The final chapter is the most explicitly theoretical; by stating often-asked questions and offering detailed responses to them, Chapter 12 addresses such issues as objectivity, dynamics, free will, projective theory, intelligence, the relations between environment and experience, unconscious motivation, pathology, and the human-science psychology out of which this particular individualizing of assessment developed.

Concrete examples abound throughout the text. Each chapter ends with a section of questions and responses that address issues that are often raised in classes and workshops. Major themes overlap from chapter to chapter, deliberately returning the reader to them by varying routes and situations. The appendixes offer two observation checklists for students who are learning to use tests: one for the WISC-R, and one for testing in general.

Acknowledgments

The psychology department of Duquesne University has specialized for twenty years in the development of theoretical foundations, research methods, and clinical applications of psychology as a human science. It has been in the company of fellow faculty members over years at Duquesne that I have developed this individualized approach to assessment. In the formative years I worked with Anthony Barton, William Fischer, Amedeo Giorgi, Richard Knowles, Charles Maes, Edward Murray, David Smith, and Rolf von Eckartsberg. For a brief time, former faculty member Jay Greenfield brought a stimulating version of Merleau-Ponty's later works into our jointly taught classes. Throughout, I have benefited from the special support, scholarship, and originality of my husband, William Fischer. At home, Michael's bemused patience with his mother has made its own contribution. The long-term interest of departmental staff members Tillie Cohen, Mary Fran Lerch, and Virginia Rago have been important, as has Virginia's special clerical assistance.

Graduate teaching assistants who have worked with me in assessment courses in recent years have also contributed to the development of individualized assessment. These colleagues are Susan Spilman, Christine Callahan, Arden Henley, Mary Hart, Bruce Levi, Donald Moss, Mary Anne Murphy, Marlene Mosca Goldsmith, Christopher Mruk, Charles Brice, Ellen Ormond, Teresa Kirchner Sherry, Kevin Jones, Donna Krotman, Rebecca Miles, and Cynthia Magistro. The students in these classes also participated in my formulations, and through the years other graduate assistants have reviewed drafts and made suggestions: although unnamed here, these people are appreciated. Finally, I would like to thank Michael Daehn, Louise Riscalla, and Emily Stevick, colleagues who offered comments on hefty portions of this book, as well as the following reviewers: Fred L. Adair, College of William and Mary; James E. Kantner, University of Southern Illinois at Carbondale; Dennis S. Klos, University of Michigan; Harold Murai, California State University, Sacramento; Lucile P. Saylor, Florida Agricultural and Mechanical University; Leona Tyler, Florence, Oregon; and Leon Vandecreek, Indiana University of Pennsylvania. Kenneth Starkey's conscientiousness in preparing the indexes is also appreciated.

Permission to present revised material from earlier writings is appreciated. Chapter 2 includes revised sections from a chapter on "Personality and Assessment" in *Existential-Phenomenological Alternatives for Psychology,* edited by Ronald S. Valle and Mark King, Oxford University Press, 1978. The structure of "Being Criminally Victimized" is from a chapter on "Empirical Phenomenological Analyses of Being Criminally Victimized," by Frederick J. Wertz and myself, in *Duquesne Studies in Phenomenological Psychology,* Vol. 3, edited by Amedeo Giorgi, Richard Knowles, and David Smith, Duquesne University Press, 1979. Part of Chapter 9 is a revision and expansion of a chapter on "Dilemmas in Standardized Testing," from *Working for Children: Ethical Issues beyond Professional Guidelines,* edited by Judith Mearig, Jossey-Bass, 1978.

Brooks/Cole has been a superb publisher. Jim Harrison's encouragement to undertake the project and to stick to it is deeply appreciated, as are Claire Verduin's steadfast integrity, patience, humor, and wisdom, and Penelope Sky's caring involvement and professionalism, and Jamie Sue Brooks's responsive, creative approach to design.

Constance T. Fischer

Contents

How Do Physical Environment, Bio-Neurology,
and Experience Interact?

Do You Have a Theory of the Relations
between Society and the Individual?

Does Individualized Assessment Require
a Different Model of Clinical Training?

INDIVIDUALIZING PSYCHOLOGICAL ASSESSMENT

PART ONE

THE CONTEXT AND PRACTICES OF INDIVIDUALIZED ASSESSMENT

THESE FIRST four chapters overview the entire process of individualizing psychological assessments and of writing reports, then describe the course of assessment sessions in detail. Each chapter ends with answers to questions often raised by students and practitioners.

Chapter 1 tells about the changing times during which this author adopted a human-science framework that supported development of procedures for individualizing psychological assessments. This chapter also describes touchpoints with the independent work of like-minded psychologists. It briefly indicates that major movements within psychology, such as behavior modification, have become more holistic and more accepting of the active roles of experience and consciousness.

Chapter 2 begins with an individualized assessment report, which illustrates both the spirit of the assessment practices and ways of describing the assessee in terms of his or her individuality. The rest of this chapter overviews the entire assessment and report-writing process. Following this glimpse of practices, the chapter includes a list of guiding principles for individualizing assessments.

Chapter 3 takes the reader through the "nitty gritty" of the beginning phases of an assessment: for example, preparing materials, taking notes, typical ways in which beginners stumble in their attempts to relate to clients. A table summarizes the positive functions of test materials. Chapter 4 shows how one can see the client shaping and being shaped by his or her world—that is, how the assessor can observe process. Tables of excerpts illustrate collaborative exploration with the client, both of his or her present style of moving through situations, and of personally viable options.

CHAPTER 1

A History of the Individualized Approach

INDIVIDUALIZING PSYCHOLOGICAL ASSESSMENT presents ways to explore and describe a person's life in process. Going beyond normative data and classifications, it addresses a particular person's situation as he or she experiences it and simultaneously contributes to it. Hence the client can collaborate throughout the psychological assessment, and may read and comment on the report, which is written in everyday language. That report summarizes ways the client and the assessor have discovered that the client can recognize movement into problematic terrain, and then pivot into an alternative, but still personally viable, course.

This individualizing of assessment is not always necessary. For many recording and decision-making purposes, a brief account of the person's standing in comparison to various criterion groups is sufficient. On other occasions it may be appropriate to individualize the assessment process but to write only a brief normative report or to individualize only descriptions of selected issues. Thorough familiarity with individualizing practices allows the assessor to employ them whenever it would be useful for the client and the client's other helpers to understand this person's situation as he or she lives it out.

During the process of presenting procedures and rationales for individualizing psychological assessment, this book touches on many issues and practices that also pertain to standardized assessment. However, this book is *not* intended to be a textbook on standardized testing. These chapters all assume that the reader already has such training or is in the process of receiving it. *Individualizing Psychological Assessment* is one more cornerstone, to be used with others on tests and measurements (Anastasi, 1982; Cronbach, 1984), projective techniques (Rabin, 1981), the history of testing (DuBois, 1970; Tuddenham, 1963), multimethod assessment (Nay, 1979), and clinical psychology as a profession (Garfield, 1983; Korchin, 1976).

The theoretical orientation of *Individualizing Psychological Assessment* will be referred to as "human-science psychology." This orientation within contemporary psychology wants our discipline to remain scientific but also to recognize human characteristics that are not particularly amenable to the traditional methods of the natural sciences. These characteristics include humans' simultaneous shaping of their environments even as they are shaped by them, behaving in accordance with their experience rather than just responding to external determinants, and being purposive. The term "human science" is a label for many movements that are trying in different ways to develop this paradigm. It is not opposed to our natural science methods and findings. Rather, its purpose is to integrate those achievements with others that emerge from recognition that humans are at once physical, biological, and psychological—related to their environments through consciousness, action, and goals, as well as through history and unconscious behavior.

A human-science approach is not essential for conducting individualized assessments. Most clinicians have carried out such practices to one degree or another, at one time or another, through principles of practicality and concern for clients. The practices presented in this book, however, were developed within a human-science orientation, and in the absence of some such explicit framework, most practitioners have found it difficult to individualize their assessments as thoroughly and consistently as possible. But this book is not a text on human-science psychology. Rather, it focuses on individualizing assessments; rationales and theory are presented only as they pertain to that project.

My Own Development

My own history may help readers to see the context in which this book's approach to individualized assessment arose and within which principles and practices were spelled out as alternatives. Although my particular route and theoretical foundations are not necessary for development of individualized practices, they may help readers to identify similarities and differences in their own experience. Readers may thereby be encouraged to take up this book's principles and practices in accordance with their own reading of changing times. Other psychologists who have traveled different routes to similar assessment innovations are considered later in this chapter.

Like many graduate students then (1960–1966) and now, I supplemented my reading of natural scientific psychology with novels and course-unrelated works such as those of Camus (1942, 1955), Sartre (1943, 1975), and May, Angel, and Ellenberger (1958). The natural science psychology was intriguing because of its rigor, its clear if overly simplified logic, and its ingenuity in devising laboratory experiments. Moreover, psychology departments were beginning to convert from cash-register style calculators to computers, with the exciting promise of information storage and analysis, which has now materialized. In addition, psychologists, inspired by diverse theories of learning, were beginning to apply laboratory research with animals to patients in mental hospitals and to institutionalized children. It was the birth of what has since become known as behavior modification. My private reading, however, was at least as necessary as my academic training when I attempted to understand my own life and the lives of the patients with whom I worked during practica and throughout my five-year traineeship with neuropsychiatric Veterans Administration hospitals.

At the university, graduate students were trained extensively in research design, statistical analysis, psychometric testing, and learning theory. Cognitive and associative theories of learning were giving way to the behavioral theories of Watson, Skinner, and Hull in courses taught by younger faculty members. From some of the older faculty members we learned psychoanalytic theory and projective testing. The latter were valued by supervisors in our clinical settings, but were regarded with disdain by the majority of the faculty. Most of us discovered that both realms of knowledge were helpful in our clinical work. We variously allowed them to co-exist, or relied on psychoanalytic understandings but reached into behaviorism and objective testing to fill gaps, or in the manner of Dollard and Miller (1950), incorporated psychoanalytic concepts into learning theory. Many of us accepted this dual framework for our testing and diagnostic activities, but also looked to Rogers' (1951, 1961) work on client-centered counseling to guide our therapy.

However we made peace with our university training, a major activity of psychologists in those days was testing. There, performance expectations were clear. The tester was a scientist whose task was to identify the patient's traits, defenses, symptoms, and diseases through measurement. Testing was a unilateral enterprise. The psychologist administered a battery of tests in a standardized manner, dismissed the patient, scored the tests, analyzed these scores along with other productions, drew conclusions from these data, and wrote a laboratory report. In fact, in those days, the VA hospital referral form requesting "psychologicals" was the same form used to request blood tests and other laboratory procedures. Psychologists, like physicians and lab technicians, wore white coats (and trainees wore blazer-length white jackets). Nursing aides escorted the patient into a testing cubicle that contained a table, two straight-backed chairs, and a wall clock that was in fact a stopwatch operated by a foot pedal. The psychologist conducted a clinical interview, administered the tests, wished the patient well, called an aide to return the patient to his[1] ward, and went back to the Psychology Service to score the tests. The language of the ensuing report was that of psychometrics (deciles, IQs, trait clusters) and of psychoanalytic psychiatry (symptoms, psychodynamic defenses, diseases). We were provided with checklists of such possibilities, alphabetically arranged: "anhedonia, anxiety, ataxia . . ." to jog our memories and enrichen our reports. There were no positive terms. Only with the advent of DSM II in 1968 were we allowed to diagnose "318.00—No Mental Disorder."

Besides arrival at a diagnostic label and the naming of psychoanalytically conceived dynamics (for example, "compulsive defensives decompensating," "unresolved Oedipal strivings"), these procedures were intended for psychology to make a scientific contribution to the case conference. The hallmark of science was objectivity; hence the distanced, unilateral approach to patients. Prior to the case conference, the psychologist carefully avoided the patient's charts and other sources of information that might bias the testing conclusions. The tests were supposed to stand on their own. At the case conference, a social worker presented the patient's social history, and the psychologist reviewed the testing and presented a diagnostic impression. The patient was brought in for a brief interview by the presiding physician, who then prescribed medications and told the ward nurse what attitude the staff should take toward the patient (for example, supportive or strict). The patient was then assigned to group and perhaps individual therapy, and to hospital activities.

---

[1]Only males occupied this Veterans Administration hospital during the sixties.

This format afforded superb training for the professionals and trainees. We learned to recognize a wide range of pathology, and we came to appreciate the relationships between social history and pathology, as well as the power of psychological tests to predict behavior from psychodynamics and levels of ability. Supervision of psychotherapy was also superb. Nevertheless, I was decidedly uncomfortable about the testing/diagnosing enterprise. Often we found that we had written the entire psychological evaluation, based exclusively on an array of test forms and productions (Bender-gestalt, House-Tree-Person drawings, and so on) spread across a desk, without recalling the patient—what he looked like or how we had interacted with him. In those lab reports, there was no person, neither veteran nor psychologist. Instead, the infrastructure of psychodynamics, traits, and abilities, along with schedules of reinforcement, extinction, and secondary reinforcement, presumably accounted for all else.

It seemed to me that the style of our psychological evaluations perpetuated the belief that for patients, trait equals fate. Patients—who indeed were called patients, not clients or residents—were treated kindly but with the general assumption that only external intervention could change their unconscious and conditioned maladaptions. To me, it seemed that we thereby were stultifying these persons' sense of purpose, responsibility, and esteem. The reports became self-fulfilling by contributing to the fatalistic, deterministic attitude toward the veteran on the part of the staff and the counselled family. In particular, since the report focused on explaining what was wrong with the patient, readers and hearers of the report then related to that patient as someone who was diseased, dumb, damaged, or deficient. My reading of existential authors strengthened my observation that we are our relationships. Insofar as mental health professionals treated veterans as sick, they were so. Because patients and family were not allowed to see the psychiatric records or psychological report, these "medical" charts seemed to be unquestionable, authoritative. The patient had no opportunity to confirm, question, qualify, or contradict the documents. The reason for secrecy was the assumption that only experts could understand these highly technical documents, but the effect was that patient and family were totally dependent upon the experts. The other side of this circumstance was that we professionals were locked into our own system, with little room for confrontation, correction, or growth.

Secrecy and distance on the part of the professionals seemed to engender guardedness and secrecy on the patient's part. It was no wonder that the prominent revelations of our tests were repression and other defenses. I wondered further if the mechanistic aspects of psychoanalysis, behaviorism, and psychometrics were not both a function of our materialistic, production-oriented society and a construction of our pragmatic "do something" helping professions. At the time, these concerns were mostly "in back of my mind," as I went about learning at the hospital, studying for comprehensive exams, writing a dissertation, and so on. In retrospect, I realize that if I had had the courage or confidence, I could have engaged at least several of my professors and many of my supervisors in extended discussions of these doubts. Instead, I began my progress by decrements—that is, I progressed toward an alternative understanding of psychological evaluation by dropping out the aspects of testing with which I disagreed. Gradually, and depending upon circumstances, I found that an evaluation's purposes were served just as well when I deleted IQs (a standard part of all reports), diagnoses, and jargon. These deletions were not accepted at my university, but they did not occasion the least disturbance at the Lexington VA hospital, where many of the psychologists had gathered to study with the phenomenological psychiatrist Erwin Straus, or through his influence had become interested in existential-phenomenological psychology. Among these psychologists were Erling Eng, William Fischer, Richard Griffith, Leonard Lipton, and Joseph Lyons. Although I do not recall phenomenological discussions of testing, there were numerous discussions and seminars about the philosophy of psychology.

After we had finished our internships and received our doctoral degrees, most psychologists of my generation chose, when they could, to engage in activities other than testing. We preferred activities like psychotherapy, consultation, supervision, and administration, which allowed for both collaboration and direct help in bringing about positive change. Increasingly, trainees and master's level psychometrists were delegated to do any necessary testing. Concomitantly, testing came to be remunerated at a lower level than other activities.

At the same time the literature criticizing testing, from several angles, began to grow. Szasz's (1960) naming and critique of the implicit medical model of mental illness, along with the humanistic movement's criticism of power elites, led to a widespread rejection not only of diagnostic labeling but of the evaluation process that had typically concluded with such labels. The Community Mental Health system was established in the midst of this changing climate. Many, perhaps most, CMH centers eschewed testing, and instead promoted community involvement by nonprofessionals ("paraprofessionals") or immediate assignment to a therapist. The therapist was typically a person with an M.A. degree in one of a wide range of programs—such as English, speech, or psychology—with little or no training in psychopathology or psychodiagnostic evaluation. In response to both diminished demand and a compelling literature demonstrating the nonreliability of diagnostic labels and of projective techniques, university graduate programs increasingly dropped from their curricula all assessment courses except intelligence testing and interpretation of the Minnesota Multiphasic Personality Inventory (MMPI). Other literature complained that psychological reports were rarely useful for planning interventions or for discussing them with patients or clients. (By the time the CMH centers had become well established, "patients" had become "clients.") Finally, many authors urged fellow psychologists not to perpetuate our identity as the testing profession, because that was the image of technicians, ancillary to physicians, who made referrals for such technical services and remained the professionals in charge of patient care.

Through history and happenstance, I sustained an interest in this realm and set about to develop an alternative approach. From Amedeo Giorgi, who had attended one of the Lexington Conferences on Phenomenology arranged by Straus and Griffith, Bill Fischer and I (soon to be married) learned that

Adrian van Kaam had begun an existential-phenomenological graduate psychology curriculum at Duquesne University. In 1965 Bill joined Duquesne's faculty, and I transferred my VA traineeship to the Pittsburgh VA Neuropsychiatric Hospital. The next year I too joined Duquesne's faculty. It was an exciting time and place. All the faculty had gathered there, at financial losses and at some risk to their credentials, to work together to develop "foundations for psychology as a human science." We had all come from traditional, mainstream graduate programs, and for the most part had been out of step with colleagues in our concerns about the inappropriateness of adopting natural-science philosophy as our own philosophy of science without adapting it to take into account that humans differ in many regards from other objects. Having at last found kindred spirits, we sat in on one another's classes, attended the Philosophy Department's graduate courses on Kant, Husserl, Heidegger, and Merleau-Ponty, and held our own seminars on Ricoeur, Schutz, Straus, Gurwitsch, and so on.

With those interests, no one wanted to teach the testing courses, which we nevertheless felt obliged to offer in order to give our students a broad background in psychology. This circumstance was presented to me as an opportunity to teach graduate courses on a consistent basis and thereby to stake out an area of my own within the department. I accepted that circumstantial opportunity, and began to work more systematically at "progressing by decrements," reexamining my earlier reservations about psychodiagnostic testing, and developing alternatives. I had no objection to teaching the "testing" sequence because I construed it as an "assessment" sequence, a series of courses developing and teaching ways in which client and psychologist could take stock of the client's situation. I saw using test materials as one means of such assessment, but not as a goal in itself. From my prior experience, I felt that with a shift of effort the assessment project could be directed toward understanding the person's world and toward jointly exploring his or her options.

Thus, at a time when many psychologists held reservations about the way we were doing psychological evaluations, I had come to work at a place where I could concentrate on examining our underlying assumptions, and where I could articulate foundations and develop practices more suitable to psychology as a human science. My colleagues at Duquesne were decidedly uninterested in assessment, but their shared efforts at developing theoretical foundations and specialized practices for research and psychotherapy were an invaluable resource. Graduate students, who came from far and wide during the 1960s to participate in the development of an alternative to mainstream psychology's natural-science allegiance, were equally invaluable for their enthusiasm, insistence on integrity and constancy, creative flair, and the comradery that evolved through sharing assessment, teaching, and research projects. In short, a major reason that I happened to publish the first calls to include clients as full participants within the assessment process (Fischer, 1970) was that such writing was consonant with my work environment, where I also could develop theoretical underpinnings for collaborative practices. Presentation of those underpinnings helped editors to take the calls for change more seriously. The Duquesne environment similarly supported later efforts to address behavior as process, as comportment which includes actional, reactive, decisional, bodily, dynamic, stylistic, habitual aspects.

My personal history had prepared me to believe that we must build our society, including our science, through informed, responsible choices, rather than allowing precedent to dictate our course. As military dependents, my mother, brother, and I had joined my father in Germany at the end of World War II. The stench of rotting bodies unearthed from beneath the rubble of bombed buildings was in the air. In a nine-year-old's way, I saw clearly that adults should not have allowed wars to happen. Over the next few years, I came to know many Germans and witnessed their struggles to rebuild their lives and to make sense of recent history. Adults from both sides of the war offered explanations, usually unsolicited, in terms of personal helplessness in the face of powerful forces, comparative national character, willingness to die for democracy or for Hitler. Clearly, it was adults who made our world the way it was and then made up explanations. Then in the late forties and early fifties, my father was stationed in Georgia. No one felt called on to explain whites' treatment of "the colored," but I soon understood that treatment as a variation of what I had observed in Germany. By then I was also beginning to realize that constructing a positive world was an uncertain and difficult project, but in the terminology of later decades, I knew that it is people who construct social reality. In high school, it became apparent that civics and history texts also were inevitably constructions; that is, authors had to adopt some perspective or other in order to organize and make sense of material. The same was true of the sciences.

By the time I had finished college, I had attended 17 schools in three countries and ten states and hence had developed a respect for parochialism—for richness found within differences, for the transcendent universality of which all the differences were constituents, and for the difficulty of communicating across differences of background and purpose. In short, my respect for perspectivity and its contribution to reality prepared me to appreciate philosophical phenomenology, and later to dare to try to influence the course of assessment psychology. Related background factors were: majoring in political science, with minors in philosophy and psychology as an undergraduate; maintaining for a while a double graduate major in social and clinical psychology; reading many of Piaget's and Freud's case studies and seeing case method as rigorous and viable. Finally, by the time I was teaching at Duquesne (1966), those of us who sympathized with the black civil rights movement in particular, and the sixties' societal critique in general, were heartened by the expansive changes that had been accomplished in an incredibly short period. The humanistic psychology movement similarly had gained momentum during this span, and had contributed to a sense of hopefulness—a sense that one could personally help to bring about positive change.

These were some of the circumstances out of which this book's approach to assessment arose. By now I encounter very little objection to the approach. Readers are still often surprised that reports can be written so descriptively and nonesoterically, but they usually find them consonant with their requirements. Many contemporary societal concerns are well served by individualized, collaborative assessment practices. The citizenry feels that it should be provided with consumer protections. The government now insists on accountability, and the quality assurance standards of accreditation associations insist that client treatment plans make everyday sense, and for that matter, be approved by the client. Federal legislation and court decisions have diminished obstacles for citizens who wish access to and explanations of student records, and of medical, personnel, and credit files. The antipsychiatry movement has been absorbed into a broader anti-elitism wherein we demand that our now admittedly fallable and limited leaders and experts be answerable to us and answer in nonesoteric language. Bureaucrats, insurance companies, attorneys, and journal editors are encouraging their colleagues to write straightforwardly, without technologese. Finally, several schools of thought within psychology are moving closer to positions consonant with a human-science orientation.

Nevertheless, just 10 to 15 years ago, manuscripts dealing with collaborative practices were frequently rejected by reviewers and editors as being "too controversial," "irresponsible," "unethical," "nonscientific," and "unprofessional." Having no one else's work to cite did not help. Once I could cite my own 1970 "The Testee as Co-evaluator," published in a journal of the American Psychological Association, reviewers and editors seemed more open to the approach. There were numerous occasions, however, when well-meaning editors tried to clarify my writing, and erroneously instructed typesetters to substitute "reinforce" for "co-constitute," "experimental" for "experiential," "subject" for "collaborator," and so on. The editorial policy of deleting hyphens for the sake of streamlining played havoc with efforts to convey mutual participation; *coauthor* and *coevaluator* just do not say the same thing as *co-author* and *co-evaluator*. On several occasions, at national conventions and in books and journals, colleagues presenting themselves as behaviorists actually invented quotations, complete with quotation marks, and then took me to task for that contrived content rather than addressing what in fact I had published.

Most psychologists, however, were struggling to reconcile what we were beginning to see as inconsistencies in our assumptions about human nature. For example, the American Psychological Association's 1963 code of ethics affirmed the individual's right to decide not to be tested. But it also assumed that consent to be tested was consent for the testers to decide who would receive the "results"—which were assumed to be natural-science findings reserved for the eyes of other scientist-professionals only. Today's *Ethical Principles* (1981) at least reserves to the client the right to determine who will receive copies of assessment reports.

For a period of about ten years, mostly during the seventies, however, objections were the prevailing response to proposals of collaborative and individualized assessment. In the early seventies, 88% of a sample of psychologists reported that they rarely or never allowed clients access to reports; half said that even upon direct request, they would not consider providing so much as a verbal account (Vane, 1972). Among the more frequent objections were the following: Clients could not be expected to understand either the technical content or their own personalities; clients are necessarily persons for whom things have gone awry and they are too fragile to learn certain facts about themselves; collaboration with clients would dilute the scientific/professional status of psychologists; individualized assessment takes too much time and energy; clients might argue with our findings and conclusions, perhaps even to the point of lawsuits.

Such objections gradually receded, primarily because of a changing social climate, in which the humanistic movement played a large part. Today, when assessors can be shown how to adapt their own assessment styles toward collaborative, individualized activity, they typically are open to such adaptations. Indeed, it is my impression that by now most assessors are forthrightly open with many clients. Still, however, the sharing most often occurs after the fact; after testing, the assessor explains his or her conclusions. Written reports are rarely read by the client.

This book is addressed into a largely receptive climate, to provide a theoretical framework accompanied by concrete practices and examples, so that interested clinicians might, when appropriate, more consistently and thoroughly individualize their assessment work.

Early Critiques of Assessment

Even from the beginning of the American psychometric and diagnostic movements, there were major theorists who urged practitioners to be mindful of human complexity, and to reject simplistic ways of characterizing their subjects. Gordon Allport (1937, 1961) is well known for his distinctions between nomothetic and idiographic procedures—that is, between research and data pertaining to general laws on one hand and attempts to understand a particular event or individual on the other. Robert Holt (1978a, 1978b) wrote extensively from the 1950s onward on such issues as values in science and the clinical versus statistical prediction controversy. Although he has remained firmly in the natural-science tradition, he helped to maintain cognizance of intuition, clinician influence on the testee, and the importance of remaining open to ambiguity.

George Kelley (1955) wrote that the purpose of testing ought to be to "survey the pathways along which the subject is free to move." He described that "freedom to move" in terms of the person's "constructions"—one's personal construals of the world. Kelley thus emphasized the relativity of knowledge, and the positive possibility of clients' channeling their lives differently through reflection on how they have anticipated (and thus channeled) events in the past. He also underlined the limitation of standardized tests in regard to describing personal constructs. He designed a Role Construct Repertory Test, which was intended to capture the "mathematical structure of psychological space," while beginning with the subject's own system of constructs.

Despite such writings by these and other well-known theorists, testing was often a laboratory-type activity, with testees regarded and treated as subjects to be scientifically processed, measured, and catalogued. During the 1960s several characterizations of this circumstance were published along with calls for breaking out of that artificial, restricted, and often damaging approach. George

Rosenwald (1963, 1965a, 1965b, 1968) described this physicalistic tradition of testing, and criticized its technological reliance on predetermined categories. He encouraged clinicians to pursue patients' individuality, and to develop novel means rather than automatically applying old tests and categories to all testees. At that time he found it necessary to point out that testing should be a means rather than an end in itself, and that testers should use their empathic sensitivities to patients rather than attempting to exclude such responsiveness. He argued that it cannot be "assumed that every person will have either a given trait or its opposite, or that a person cannot exhibit both traits simultaneously" (1965a). Alan Towbin (1964) pointed out that we had come to regard ourselves as "super technicians" whose projective techniques provided x-rays of personality. We regarded patients as passive respondents to stimuli, and ourselves as unobserved observers. He proposed that instead of either continuing in this manner or rejecting testing altogether, we could actually talk to both the referring person and the patient about the purpose of testing, discuss certain responses directly with the patient, and regard the test taker as a purposeful being whose test behavior is not fundamentally different from his or her other behavior.

Theodore Leventhal and his colleagues (Leventhal, Gluck, Slepian, & Rosenblatt, 1962) reviewed a growing research literature in order to make the case that the testing situation involved tester, environment, and transference variables in addition to the targeted testee variables. They then proposed that tests be regarded as only part of the diagnostic process, and that the patient be invited to discuss his or her view of the problem, both during an interview and during testing. The authors advocated explaining the test results to the patient, and pointed out that with "active handling of the test relationship," the patient is more productive, the productions are useful for "penetrating the defenses" *during* testing, and the patient is introduced to a therapeutic relationship.

A few practitioners also published atheoretical calls for engaging the client more actively in the assessment enterprise. Molly Harrower (1956) described her development of projective counseling, in which the Rorschach was used within a psychotherapeutic context. The client's associations to the inkblots were discussed openly, with the client gaining insight while contributing to the psychologist's psychodynamic explorations. Harrower (1966, 1968) called for a more systematic combination of psychodiagnostic and therapeutic insights, especially through inclusion of mental health potential, and through testing of persons closely associated with the patient. In particular, married couples were "jointly confronted with their own and their partner's test findings." The joint discussion of test records, from a descriptive profile form, was an "insight-giving experience." Gertrude Baker (1964) suggested that a patient's therapist could be present while the psychologist discussed the testing results with the patient. Joseph Richman (1967) pointed out, "Clinical psychologists have been concerned about proper presentation of their test results to everyone but the patient." He argued that "patients and their families can tolerate a great deal more information and hard facts than is generally recognized." Elsa Strauss (1967) called on assessors to have the courage to report their subjective impressions (as such) even when the source and full meaning of those feelings were obscure. She argued that it is better to admit that you cannot identify the source of your impression than to leave it out or to pretend that it is grounded in technical data.

Such calls may seem commonplace to us today, but they were isolated voices at the time. There was, however, a steady publication of articles criticizing the manner in which reports failed to tell the reader much about the particular individual or what to do for him or her. For instance, Norman Tallent (1958) characterized ways in which psychologists typically failed to "describe the client so that the reader knows how he differs from other people and in what important ways he is similar to others." The failures were variations of truisms (for example, "the patient is sometimes anxious") and biased totalizations, such as reporting only negative traits. In addition, many authors mentioned parenthetically that technical, filed-away reports were not of direct use to clients. However, when Tallent (1966) summarized the criticisms published throughout the 1950s and 1960s, there still were no calls to move beyond our use of the laboratory as our inspiration for writing assessment reports.

A significant shift away from the objectivistic, measurement approach to assessment awaited the trenchant critiques of humanistic psychologists. J. F. T. Bugental (1964, 1965), one of the most influential, criticized psychodiagnostics as a misguided "quest for certainty." He called for encounters between therapist and client, for meeting the whole person rather than measured parts—habits, instincts, and traits. Bugental stressed that it is important for a therapist to meet the patient as an individual, rather than as a class representative. He felt that putting a person through testing was a manipulation that transformed the patient into an object, played into the patient's dependency, and undercut efforts toward responsibility. Diagnostic testing emphasized powerful forces that were mysterious to the patient, and which gave therapists an overly certain sense of explanation. Carl Rogers (1951) in the meantime had said consistently that testing was unnecessary as a prelude to client-centered therapy.

Authors of the 1970s

Foundational arguments like those of Bugental were readily elaborated by the humanistic psychology movement. Humanistic psychologists characterized academic influence on testing as objectivistic, simplistic, and deterministic, and berated medical influence on diagnostics for its implicit disease model, determinism, and maintenance of a medical hierarchy. The allegiance to technology with which most assessors did their work was roundly castigated. The majority of humanistic psychologists found testing so antithetical to their beliefs that they simply turned away from it, and instead pursued therapeutic and growth activities.

Earl Brown (1972), at Georgia State University, argued that to proceed psychometrically violates the major tenets of humanistic psychology. Specifically, he charged that tests create an artificial situation, present an impersonal barrier, are based on deception and subterfuge, are pathology-oriented and depersonalizing, and place the testee in a one-down power relationship. Brown described the ideal assessment relationship as an encounter between persons of "equal humanity," as a personal friendship in which the participants would spend time together at all hours, with the psychologist always on call. His unpublished symposium proposal, "Replacing the Psychological Report with Existential Experiencing," emphasized that assessment participants should trust the healing power of love. Although patently unrealistic, Brown's proposed remedy did challenge practitioners to examine their ways of relating to assessees.

A more philosophically grounded but less publicized position on testing was presented by Timothy Leary (1970) in a book on new approaches to personality classification:

> Dynamic psychology is based on scientific philosophies which are outdated, ineffective, one-sided, and in terms of human values—dangerous. The outmoded philosophies to which I refer are the impersonal, abstract, static, externalized, control-oriented conceptions of nineteenth-century physics which led men to classify the elements and processes of a depersonalized subject matter and to determine the general laws which governed these elements and processes [p. 211].

Leary's alternative was to "study natural data, events as they occur, rather than artificial situations which *we* arrange in our offices." He suggested that we "use a conceptual language which arises from the data rather than imposing our own favorite, prefabricated variables upon the situation." Leary was interested in developing ways and models "for describing inner events" and relating "these with separate models and measures for describing external behavior."

Leary also proposed an "existential, transactional," open attitude between the psychologist and the person studied. The patient should help develop record-collecting devices or test forms. The patient's viewpoints, according to Leary's notion of "phenomenological equality," should be treated as equal to one's own. "The aim of psychodiagnosis should be to make the patient feel wiser and feel good." "Accurate diagnosis, collaboratively worked out with the patient, is effective therapy for both patient and doctor." These latter proposals, like Brown's, were not practical, but such challenges to psychology's grounding in natural-science philosophy encouraged practitioners to reflect about their own assumptions and practices.

In 1972, Ray Craddick, also a humanistic psychologist at Georgia State University, published a rebuttal to Brown's position, arguing that Brown's demands for humanism could be met in the testing situation. Craddick called for creative use of assessment techniques combining humanism and empiricism and permitting clients to be authentic, spontaneous, and genuine. He regarded interaction as one focus of assessment, and asked testees for feedback on how they had experienced him during the assessment. Craddick interpreted tests directly to the client and to the latter's therapist simultaneously, sometimes dictating a summary in the presence of both. In 1975, Craddick elaborated

some of these practices, emphasizing "mutuality in terms of trusting and allowing for a dialogue of questions and answers between the two people involved in the [assessment] process."

In 1978, Alan Sugarman, at Yale, returned to the question of whether assessment could be humanistic. His article implicitly reminds us that assessment's purpose is assessment, not encounter or therapy, and that clients can be respected even while being assessed for their limitations, disorders, and unconscious motivations. Sugarman explicitly argues that assessment can be consistent with a humanistic orientation *if* "the examiner attempts actively to engage the patient in the assessment process and is aware of the interpersonal context of the test responses and behavior."

Earlier in the 1970s several authors had independently based their work on the same conclusion. Charles Dailey, in *Assessment of Lives* (1971), attacked our bureaucratic system for evaluating people and making decisions about them almost entirely on the basis of paper documents such as diplomas, previous job titles, and IQs. He proposed a humanistic alternative, using a narrative account of an individual's life, and studying that person in his or her own habitat. Dailey emphasized that the person could participate fully in such an assessment.

A few psychologists developed tests which, although psychometric, addressed areas of life that had been neglected by our assessment tradition. One of the earliest, Everett Shostrom's Personality Orientation Inventory (1966), was designed to show the degree to which one's attitudes and values compare with those of self-actualizing people. Another example is the Existential World Inventory, which A. Moneim El-Meligi and Humphrey Osmond (1970) developed to allow patients to report changes in their perceived worlds, regardless of psychologists' and psychiatrists' theories and diagnostic systems. Frederick Thorne and Vladimir Pishkin published a monograph on "The Existential Study" (1973), a "200-item objective questionnaire designed to measure Self-concepts, Self-status, Self-esteem, Self-actualization, existential morale and demoralization, meanings of life, attitudes toward the human condition, and destiny, suicide, and existential success-failure" (p. 5).

All of the above contributions were solitary, both in the sense that the authors worked by themselves, unsupported by mainstream psychology, and in the sense that their contributions awaited the evolution of a systematic, comprehensive alternative approach to assessment. Rather than incorporating or challenging these contributions, however, most psychology departments during the 1960s and 1970s simply dropped the projective techniques courses from their assessment sequence. This action was variously in response to the above sorts of humanistic criticisms of testing, and at the opposite theoretical pole, to empiricist criticisms of testing's being too subjective and of unproven validity.

Counter to this trend, Richard Dana, at the University of Arkansas, continued to develop ways of teaching assessment to graduate students. In particular, he developed teaching methods to show would-be assessors how their personalities were at work in any systematic errors of interpretation (1966). He asked each member of a class to write a report from the same set of test data, and then presented client feedback to the class on these interpretations. Dana's textbook (1982) on assessment with projective techniques includes examples of such methods.

In much of his work, Dana has integrated traditional tests, research publications, and the few available writings on alternative approaches. In 1974, Dana and Leech reviewed articles consonant with "existential assessment." Through the years, Dana has been a consistent advocate of honoring subjective experience while using tests and their norms systematically. He has recommended contracting with assessment clients in regard to purpose, form, and use of results. He, too, has suggested three-way meetings to include the referring person. Finally, Dana has pointed out that feedback from the client during this process may affect the final report.

During this same decade I began publishing my own criticisms of the laboratory model of testing and my own constructive proposals, which I variously characterized as existential-phenomenological, structural, contextual, or collaborative (Fischer, 1969a, 1970, 1971a, 1972b, 1973b, 1978a; Fischer & Rizzo, 1974). As the times changed, I characterized my approach as human-science psychology (1978b), and my goal as individualized assessment (1974, 1979). Recently I have returned my attention to ways of researching and describing patterns of problematic comportment, and to theoretical exploration of how tests work. But at first I was more concerned about increasing clients' opportunities for active participation in the decisions that their professional helpers were making for them. In 1971, Stanley Brodsky and I brought together some kindred spirits for a symposium on "Shared Results and Open Files with the Client," held at the American Psychological Association annual convention. My paper, "Paradigm Changes Which Allow Sharing of Results" (1972a), was published in an APA journal along with the other papers, although two years earlier a similar version had been candidly rejected by the same journal as "too controversial." These few years were indeed dramatically transitional in terms of informed participation by human services clients.

Client Participation in Human Services: The Prometheus Principle (Fischer & Brodsky, 1978) called for a shift in the power structure, allowing "recipients" of services to share in decision making. Douglas Biklen addressed "Mental Retardation and the Power of Records"; I wrote on "Collaborative Psychological Assessment"; Donald Bersoff wrote on "Reciprocity and Coercion in Psychotherapy"; Rosemarie Parse addressed "Rights of Medical Patients"; Stanley Brodsky described "Prometheus in the Prison"; Mary Chisholm and Rolf von Eckartsberg described "The Prometheus Principle in the Classroom"; Leo Goldman posed "School Records: Whose and for What?"; Leslie Krieger wrote about "Informed Participation in Industrial Consultation"; and Robert Sardello described "The Subject as a Person in Psychological Research." Even though the Buckley Amendment and other "right of access" legislation had been enacted during the three years it took our small university press to bring out *Prometheus Principle,* the volume is still contemporary in its practical, nonbureaucratic illustrations of ways to actualize laws and ideals.

In the meantime, Riscalla (1972a) argued for open files and sharing information with rehabilitation patients and more generally urged psychologists to reject the historical pattern of secrecy from clients (1972b). Arcaya (1973) illustrated how a probation officer could share information and concerns directly with a probationer, and how they could then "generate a unique solution to the problem which is favorable for both viewpoints but is the result, also, of a flexible compromise." Janzen and Love (1977) reported on involving delinquent adolescents as active participants in developing their own treatment plans and in evaluating their own progress. Dinoff, Rickard, Love, and Elder (1978) described a similar process at a camp for emotionally disturbed children. There, the children and counselors came to agreement on the reason for the camp referral, contracted a treatment plan, and wrote the final evaluation and recommendations together.

Other assessors have developed innovative approaches that allow clients to use assessment devices to carry out their own explorations. Loo's self-puzzle (1974) encourages self-expression and reflection as the individual draws "a puzzle with parts that are labelled that best describe you, as you see yourself now." Brown (1975) has involved parents in the observation and assessment of their children, thereby minimizing the need for later one-way interpretation of "results" to the parents. The assessor shifts from "diagnostic 'star' to professional facilitator," and "diagnosis can be intertwined with intervention." Hammond and Stanfield (1977) have adapted Lazarus' (1976) multimodal-therapy approach to a systematic mapping, with the client, of problem areas (for example, behavior, affect, sensation, ideation). Client and counselor together follow an interview form to record their planned interventions for each area. McReynolds and DeVoge (1978) have developed a test consisting of twelve standardized improvisational role-plays and two sets of rating scales. The subject participates by evaluating his or her own role-play performance and comparing it to his or her real-life behaviors. Assessment is directly connected with the client's participation in therapy or self-help. Erdberg (1979) presents MMPI feedback simultaneously to the client and to the referring professional. The assessor serves as a consultant to client and therapist at once, facilitating their discussion of how MMPI data (described in everyday terms) might be relevant to their understanding of the treatment process. Progoff (1975) has developed guidelines for keeping "intensive" journals, which aid users both in getting to know themselves and in discovering broader horizons. Journal-keeping also is an example of techniques that clients can expore on their own with or without counseling.

Assessors also have been writing about the desirability of collaboration with clients, emphasis on life-world data, and use of everyday, shared language. Shevrin and Shectman (1973), after reviewing the usual complaints about diagnostic assessment, argued that they need not pertain, and that in fact "diagnosis can be conducted in a clear, empathic, and useful manner." They encouraged concurrent involvement of assessor and patient, through a personal relationship in which the patient is "emotionally involved and actually struggling with the issues and not simply talking about them." Rather than aiming the assessment at historical causes or underlying dynamics, they recommended finding a "middle level" of significant issues—"a point at which past factors are currently active." Within this framework, assessors can formulate "the issues close to the level of the clinical interaction, as a way of involving the patient and thereby sample actual functioning." Blatt (1975) also wrote about engaging the patient in an "active transaction," in which he or she "can begin to share the clinician's attempts to recognize and understand the patient's thoughts and feelings." He emphasized that in this way, and through using five to six diagnostic testing sessions, "the diagnostician serves as a bridge between therapist and patient . . . encouraging the patient to deal with these issues in more detail with his therapist." In this process, all three parties appraise the patient's present readiness for the candor and introspection that would be called for in therapy. Blatt is also representative of psychologists who believe that when assessment is conducted in this transactional manner, there is no reason why therapists should not conduct their own diagnostic evaluations with their patients.

Pruyser and Menninger (1976), in an article titled "Language Pitfalls in Diagnostic Thought and Work," are strong spokesmen for the growing conviction that prior to classification, persons should first be faithfully portrayed in their own right in "common unpretentious language." They point out that, for example, "Many patients are described not as sad, tearful, somber, or downhearted, but right away as depressed." Such terms are "categorical words that make verification difficult and thwart communication." They point out that classificatory diagnostic language puts the user in a "forced choice situation" before a "very small table of permissible words, guided by narrow rules for combination." Consonant with a human-science approach to assessment, they, too, remind us that "scientific data are always a function of the perspective in which they are spotted and formulated," and they, too, encourage us to look beyond classificatory nouns and other "word choices" that "freeze a condition into a fixed state." They encourage ordinary English as the language appropriate for description of persons. Finally, they, too, recommend use of verbs for describing the action and process of individual lives.

In addition to the emergence of innovative individualized assessment techniques and calls for greater collaboration and personalizing within assessment, publications in the 1970s also reported research on client acceptance of test interpretations. Snyder (1974) was among the first to devise these studies, which he characterized as "Barnum effect" research since his experiments involved giving every subject in an experimental group the same general and high-probability "interpretations" of his or her scores. He then compared levels of accepting the feedback as personally true under different conditions, such as being told variously that the typed interpretations were written by a Ph.D. or by an M.A. psychologist, or that the interpretations were based on the MMPI or on the Rorschach. Reviews of more than 50 studies in this area have been published by Snyder, Shankel, and Lowery (1977), Snyder, Ingram, and Newburg (1982), and Dana (1982). These reviews conclude that many of the findings have not been replicated consistently, and that further research is needed. Some of the inconsistencies probably are due to the artificial nature of these early experiments, in that most were conducted with college students enrolled in psychology courses and required to participate in the studies. These students had not requested assessment, did not bring personal concerns to it, and did not have an opportunity to discuss the test "interpretations." Moreover, the "interpretations" were not in fact about any particular individual. The "Barnum effect" studies are welcome as evidence that sharing results with clients has come of age, and as the beginning of systematic research on relevant conditions and outcomes. At this point, however, we are ready to go beyond this preliminary, artificial research design to study how clients participating in actual assessments experience and respond to the process.

In the meantime, trends within the above "client acceptance of interpretations" research are already relevant for individualized assessment. Among these trends. Subjects' acceptance of "interpretations" varies with how well-credentialed the source is, with the claimed scientific status of the test, with subjects being told that they have been very self-disclosive, and with heightened insecurity and "other" orientation (external locus of control). In addition, subjects who receive positive feedback rate their "diagnosticians" as more skilled and report themselves as desirous of further feedback. In the above research, subjects have not been particularly accurate in differentiating between bona fide interpretations and bogus, randomly generated "interpretations." Assessors would do well to bear in mind that the more confidently and positively they present themselves, their assessment materials, and their impressions, the more likely our clients are to consider our impressions as accurate, whether or not they are, and whether or not our clients have correctly understood our communications. The collaborative, contextualizing, and interventional aspects of individualized assessment are essential to assure that findings are in fact true of a particular individual and that initial findings are corrected or refined to provide better descriptions of the individual. The above "client acceptance" research encourages us to go beyond general discussion to explore concrete instances and contexts with clients. In this process, I refine my own initial impressions, and the client and I begin to understand when the client's particular style does and does not work. When it does not, I encourage the client to try out alternatives during the assessment.

In sum, the 1970s was a decade of growing interest in finding ways to address assessment techniques directly to clients' lives and to encourage clients to be active participants in that exploration. But even in the realm of so-called individual assessments, presumably for purposes of understanding and helping the client, it is still the exception when the client works with the assessor throughout the assessment process, consistently and jointly developing understandings and questions. Clients rarely read their reports or write commentaries on them. Most graduate courses on assessment continue to be test-oriented, stressing products rather than process. Research on self-disclosure continues to regard it as a dependent variable that can be jacked up and down by manipulation of other variables. Recently published textbooks continue to list test signs and traits, such as "drawings with visible teeth are evidence of aggression." On the other hand, test batteries are no longer automatically administered to new clients, and assessment findings are now utilized as much for understanding clients and for planning as for arriving at a diagnostic label. Moreover, the general attitude of North American theoreticians and practitioners is becoming progressively less technological and scientistic, and more open to concepts and methods that vary from those of the early physical sciences.

Contemporary Shifts in General Theory and Practice

The social sciences in general and psychology in particular have come of age during the last two decades. Our scientific accomplishments speak for themselves. We are now sufficiently mature and secure to question our own assumptions and methods, and to be more open to developments in neighboring disciplines. It is also increasingly difficult to be doctrinaire in the face of both rapid changes in knowledge and public demands that our work have practical value. In addition, there are so many universities (producing nearly 3000 Ph.D.s in psychology each year) where professors develop their own versions of psychology, that the field no longer can be dominated by just a few major figures. The electronic media remind us of the interrelatedness of nations, of the relativity of perspective, and of both the vulnerability and inevitability of human constructions of reality. The psychological literature of the last decade shows a clear shift away from the phase in which we were narrowly technocratic, scientistic, and behavioristic, and toward an interest in holistic structure and context, the mutuality of environment and behavior, the process of change, and the ways people shape not only their own lives but what we see as reality. The development of individualized assessment is part of this shift.

The following authors and trends are representative of the broad array of psychologists' concerns with their discipline's foundations and practices:

Sarason's 1980 presidential address to the American Psychological Association's Division of Clinical Psychology called for greater attunement to the social order in which our clients live and in which we practice. He likewise called for us to stop analyzing individuals as though they were self-contained, and to desist from treating them in isolated settings. He reminded us of our responsibility for the shape of the social order, and for developing a preventative clinical psychology. The Braginskys (1971, 1974) have documented "that implicit extra-scientific commitments guide much of the activity of the practitioners of the normal science of psychology, that research and practice in psychology are directed by implicit principles and premises that have their origins in politics, in morality, and in bureaucracy" (T. R. Sarbin in the Foreword of Braginsky & Braginsky, 1974). Buss (1979) has called for the development of a psychology that will study individual-society dialectics, thereby encouraging psychologists to become more aware of the broader social context of our work, the relativistic nature of problems studied and interpretations offered, and the value-laden nature of science. Riegel (1978, 1979) developed philosophical foundations for psychology conceived as a dialectical discipline. He viewed interviewer and subject as dialogue partners, addressing change and transformation. He described behavior as occurring in a cultural–societal context, and at a particular juncture of biological, personal, and physical dimensions.

Numerous textbooks and articles on "behavioral assessment" now present ways to address behavior directly, in its usual contexts (Hersen & Bellack, 1976; Ciminero, Calhoun, & Adams, 1977; Cone & Hawkins, 1977; Keefe, Kopel, & Gordon, 1978). "Behavior" now includes thoughts and beliefs, as well as overt motor acts. Thus far, behavioral assessors continue to stress observation at the expense of dialogue with clients, but at least assessees are being observed directly, in their own environments. And the observers are addressing "personality of situations" (Bem & Funder, 1978), rather than assuming environments to be constant across time, people, and circumstances. Mischel (1968) has long questioned our simplistic trait × environment models of personality and behavior, and now (1977) calls for a new image of the human being, acknowledging the role of context and the multiple determinants of behavior. He suggests that the subject could be included as an "expert and colleague" in an assessment, even to the point of making predictions about his or her own behavior.

As psychology acknowledges that behavior includes all of comportment, textbooks on assessment become much broader. Nay, for example, in *Multimethod Clinical Assessment* (1979), reviews four areas from which assessment information may be gathered in the interest of planning interventions: interview, observation in natural and clinical settings, written self-reports, and psychophysiological assessment. The last area traditionally belonged to experimental, not to assessment, psychology. Delprato (1979), writing as an "interbehaviorist," describes a "holistic view of behavior that recognizes that neural processes cannot be separated from behavior, but instead are integral, participating factors in all psychological behavior. An emphasis on organism–environment interactions and the interbehavioral field rules out classical mechanical, cause-effect, deterministic versions of causation" (p. 409). Ornstein (1977) goes further to say that when we choose tests to assess comparative functioning of the hemispheres, we should bear in mind that which hemisphere the person relies on depends not so much on the nature of the task we present as on which hemisphere the person chooses to use as consonant with his or her customary style of thought. On the other end of the behavior spectrum, McLemore and Benjamin (1979) argue that the emphasis on individual behavior, especially in the latest formal diagnostic system (DSM III), ought to be filled out with an interpersonal nosology. They review and extend existing pertinent psychosocial classificatory systems, enroute reminding us of Leary's (1957) classification of the interpersonal behaviors (reflexes) and the type of behaviors they tend to pull from the other person. Each category of reflex may be moderate/adaptive or extreme/pathological. All of these developments are consonant with individualized assessments' efforts to go beyond test scores to take into account persons' life contexts.

Authors who were earlier associated with psychodynamic assessment are also calling for revisions in our ways of thinking about our tests and our clients. Schafer (1976), in *A New Language for Psychoanalysis,* calls for description and conceptualization in terms of action, using adverbs to characterize process. Weiner (1977) and Exner (1980) have both urged that the Rorschach be regarded as an opportunity to sample behavior. Exner says that "the Rorschach answer is created by the 'routine' psychology of the person, or stated differently, the manner in which the person has been accustomed to dealing with stimuli, and especially those stimuli that require translation and decision operations" (p. 566). Exner and Weiner both encourage researchers to forego the old studies in which Rorschach validity was sought through correlating test scores and ratios with diagnostic labels and scores from other tests. Instead, they encourage exploration and validation against comportments in various actual life situations. Schwartz and Lazar (1979) further argue that the proper method for approaching human behavior via the Rorschach is through description and understanding of human meanings on their own terms, since it is in terms of these meanings that people conduct their lives.

The "assessment of cognitive style," a resurgent major development in assessment literature, at least to a point is consonant with individualized assessment. In one way or another the authors in this area hold that organisms respond to their cognitive construction of the environment rather than to objective reality. Contemporary authors here include Goldstein and Blackman (1978), Tyler (1978), and Witkin (1978). The positive touchpoint with individualized assessment is that knowledge of general conceptual styles (for example, authoritarian, field dependent, crystallized) can help us to understand individuals and help them to modify their approach, when advisable. Thus far, however, most researchers regard cognitive style as a way of organizing and processing "objective reality" as such. The processing is often regarded as a computer-like "mediating variable," rather than as a dialectical encounter with a world that researchers, too, necessarily construct in their own ways.

Cognitive therapy (for example, Beck, Rush, Shaw, & Emery, 1979), through an independent evolution, regards pathology as a product of the inaccurate thoughts with which one assesses his or her situation. For example, the thought "I won't pass my test anyway" results in immediate despair, failure to study, poor grades, further self-devaluation, and so on. Cognitive therapy is intended to help the client identity self-defeating thoughts and substitute more productive ones. The points of consonance with individualized assessment are the collaborative identification of those times that the person shapes his or her world counterproductively, and the joint development of alternative thoughts and actions. The theory may seem overly linear, but as people alter their comportment, the fuller structure of their lives alters also. The field of cognitive assessment (Merluzzi, Glass, & Genest, 1981) evolved to assess clients' cognitions and their progress in therapy. Theoretical orientations here range from information processing to cognitive-social learning. Again, although this approach retains a natural science framework and at least in its publications oversimplifies comportment, it deals much more directly than our traditional approaches did with the ways people construct their worlds, with personal meaning, with clients' ability to reflect, and with the possibilities of personal change.

The field of behavior modification as a whole has steadily followed the calls by Lazarus (1971) and London (1972) for a moratorium on theorizing, especially in terms of laboratory learning theory, while exploring first "what works." Mahoney, Kazdin, & Lesswing (1974) summarized the position of many colleagues in saying that "there is, indeed, no unified learning theory. . . . In many ways [behavior modification] . . . represents a powerful technology in search of a theory." They also noted a growing acknowledgment that "while borrowing from the laboratory model, the language and techniques frequently used in behavior modification are admittedly metaphorical." Meichenbaum (1977) explicitly describes the subject as an "active contributor to his own experience," who can "gain a sense of control of his emotional states, thoughts, and behaviors." Goldfried (1980) calls for a broader integration of theories, while Lazarus' (1976) multimodal behavior therapy is explicitly intended to transcend any particular system or school of therapy. Increasingly, behavior modifiers' techniques are useful to practitioners from a human-science orientation, individualized assessments are useful to behavioral practitioners, and both are exploring ways of remaining open to the complexity of human comportment while also being systematic and practical.

Consciousness is regaining respectability in academic circles as a legitimate realm for study (Pope & Singer, 1978; Lieberman, 1979). Psychology is becoming involved in holistic medicine and health (Riscalla, 1975), and in what is variously known as behavioral medicine, medical psychology, and health psychology. That is, we are taking a more holistic, integrative approach to biology/psychology/behavior. Journals are once again accepting case studies for publication, reflecting recognition that statistical presentations, despite their positive contribution, necessarily bypass a critical level of reality. Both public and professional organizations are calling increasingly for everyday language in documents, for access to one's own files, and for informed consent to participate in studies and treatment. Finally, as our society has changed, psychopathologies no longer seem to require symbolic interpretation so much as identification of habitual patterns and self-deceptions, and restructuring of social systems and environments. Collaborative, interventional, individualized practices are increasingly suitable for our changing times. These are also exciting, challenging times, in which persons interested in taking an individualizing, collaborative approach with their assessment clients are faced with rapidly evolving resources for further developing both theory and practice.

Questions and Responses

Question: Hasn't the idea of assessment always been to help the individual? Don't assessors already go beyond test scores in dealing with clients?

Response: No, the goal has not always been personal understanding and assistance. Rather, it has often been prediction via classification. But yes, most assessors intend their evaluations to be helpful to particular persons. Certainly most assessors are increasingly aware of the limits and potential abuses of tests.

Because we have not had an explicit alternative to the natural science model to guide our efforts at individualizing, we often unwittingly slip back into thinking in terms of traits, abilities, and causality. Indeed, going beyond these to an understanding of the particular person has been widely referred to, more or less derisively, as "subjective" and as an "art."

Question: But isn't your human-science terminology (comportment, co-create, shaped/shaping) *just a matter of semantics? Aren't common sense and regular language adequate?*

Response: No. The point is that natural science has formalized an everyday Western explanatory attitude toward reality, namely that things are made up of separate parts, that change is a series of discrete reactions, that there is an autonomous reality which we perceive in degrees of accuracy. To help us become systematically attuned to what and how we perceive prior to explaining things to ourselves, we must use a language that highlights this different way of looking. Language is not just something we use; it helps to create new ways of seeing—new visions. Indeed, the continuing struggle to develop appropriate terms is also an exploration and creation of a different reality. But yes, there is a danger that the special terminology can become esoteric on one hand and a fixed jargon on the other; both should be avoided.

Question: If you're trying to break out of the older, scientific psychology, why don't you jettison its tests, like the Wechsler intelligence scales and the Bender?

Response: There is nothing inherently objectifying or reductive about such test materials; it is the system of interpretation that can be objectifying. I like to say that I "use test materials" rather than "administer tests," thereby indicating that tests are in my service rather than the other way around. However, I am not starting out from scratch. I take very seriously the accumulated experience of 75-or-so years of clinical psychology, even while understanding it from a particular perspective. When we have developed the subject side as well as the object side of psychology, then we can adapt or custom-design our assessment/education/growth materials accordingly.

Question: Can behaviorally or psychoanalytically oriented assessors, eclectics, and so forth also be human-science practitioners?

Response: Yes. I personally draw heavily on my earlier training in behavioristic and psychoanalytic psychology. I advocate pluralism—knowing several theories of personality in depth, so one can draw from their different insights in a circumspect manner. However, absolute determinists and believers in a single truth would not have room in their systems for personal meanings or active participation. We should note, though, that major contemporary theorists of neurology (Smith, 1970; Ornstein, 1972), medicine (Thomas, 1974), psychoanalysis (Schafer, 1978), and behavior modification (Mahoney, 1977; Meichenbaum, 1977) all take into account cognition, if not consciousness, and its participation in constructing personal reality.

Question: Is human-science psychology scientific? Wouldn't science require strictly empirical, objective data?

Response: All facts are facts from particular perspectives; there are no facts apart from perspective. Objectivity is best served when the personal and theoretical perspectives are spelled out as much as possible. Objectivity does not take people out of the picture; it ensures that facts are inter- (or cross-) subjective—not merely one person's private view. Empirical assessment facts are always an interface of client, assessor, assessment materials, and readers.

Question: But how do report-readers know exactly what's referred to when description is in terms of personal "lived worlds," varying situations, assessor's "presence," and so on? Aren't IQs, MMPI profiles, and diagnoses much more precise?

Response: Certainly it is helpful to compare people on a common measure. These measures are useful starting places for further assessment; but as conclusions their clarity is false. That is, the numbers themselves are precise, but whatever they refer to does not come in equal interval units—or units at all, for that matter. Describing in terms of magnitude begs the question of what it is that is being measured, aside from answers in terms of still other measures. True, a single score may easily be agreed upon, but beyond that report, readers know less about what is being referred to than when they are provided with situated descriptions. Remember that for all their mathematical qualities, scores are derived data. Remember too that there is no single truth "out there," to be somehow pinned down by either measurement or qualitative description.

Question: I gather that individualized description, as well as openness and collaboration with clients, are all increasingly common. Are there any sources of explicit opposition to individualized practices, as there were in earlier years?

Response: No. So long as the assessor can share the grounds for conclusions and suggestions, the individualizing is usually appreciated by all concerned. Of course the individualizing is rightfully criticized if it is not necessary for answering the referral, or if its relevance has not been made clear. Many theoretically oriented psychologists see no need for a human-science amendment to their own natural-science theoretical tradition, but for the most part they maintain a "live and let live," or "to each his/her own" stance in regard to individualized assessment's theoretical foundations. I do have some concerns, though, that in the absence of formal training in psychology as a specifically human science, individualized practices may fall out as practitioners turn increasingly to printouts and desk-top computer terminals to increase their productivity.

Question: If there is a general openness to individualized practices, and if mainstream psychology and human-science psychology are growing closer anyway, what need did you see to write this book? Aren't practices evolving on their own toward collaboration with clients and awareness of the importance of context?

Response: I want to be part of the effort to become more thorough-going and consistent in our attention to clients *as individuals*. This effort has been much more difficult in assessment activities and reports than in our psycho-therapeutic activities. Acceptance of other practitioners' individualized practices often co-exists with continuation of one's own emphasis on psychometric norms, trait names, categories of pathology, and so on. Beyond that, openness to individualizing one's own assessment approach is not automatically actualized. This book's many examples and discussion of principles are intended to encourage comparison with the reader's practices so that the reader can more readily develop specific variations compatible with his or her own understandings and work setting.

CHAPTER 2

Overview of Individualized Practices and Report Writing

Assessments typically describe where a person fits within general trends, such as achievement percentiles, intelligence quotients, degrees of interest in career areas as compared with interests of persons already in those occupations, and similarities to testees already identified in terms of personality structure or diagnostic category. Individualized assessment also makes use of such information, but goes on to describe the person's particular situation and the ways in which he or she influences outcomes, both positively and problematically. Individualized assessment encourages the client to participate actively in developing these understandings, in tailoring and carrying out any suggestions for change, and in writing commentary on the typed report.

Although many, if not most, experienced practitioners do individualize their assessments to some extent, such practices have not been widespread, consistent, or thorough. University courses and textbooks for the most part have continued to stress quantitative, standardized practices, which historically have been our way of ensuring scientific, objective findings. The most explicit model for assessors has remained that of laboratory research and research reports. In its classical form, this model does not readily accommodate efforts to describe an individual's ways of living his or her life. Today, however, our discipline is looking for scientific ways to take into account aspects of being human and of being individual that have not lent themselves to positivist methods. During this phase, each practitioner has had to develop his or her own rationales and procedures for individualizing.

Of course, not all assessments need be individualized. The need for individualizing depends upon the purposes of the particular assessment. Individualizing is appropriate to the extent that familiarity with the client's particular ways of coping with life situations better enables the client's helpers to assist that person to help himself or herself.

Individualizing practices are as feasible with various kinds of clients as our more usual nomothetic assessments are. Greatest flexibility and ingenuity are required with limited clients such as retarded children or chronic schizophrenics, and with persons referred against their will, such as prisoners or "problem children." The report below is of a youngster with whom an individualized assessment approach was appropriate and easily feasible.

A Sample Individualized Report

The following report illustrates many individualized assessment and report-writing practices. It is an actual report, complete with the inelegance of field work, about a ten-year-old boy. Only the names and other identifying information have been altered. It is written in the form of a letter (on my private stationery) to the parents. After they had read it, we talked on the phone, discussed some points further, and agreed that I should forward a copy to the boy's new school, with a note saying that the parents had reviewed the report and asked for this action. In the meantime I had enclosed a copy of the report's suggestions to the boy, in a separately addressed envelope, as his own record.

I have chosen this report in part because there are no esoteric issues involved. However, even complex cases can be presented in this same form.[1]

Psychological Assessment of Robbie March

August 9, 19 ____

Mr. Henry March and Mrs. Joan March
421 Richardson Street
Pittsburgh, Pennsylvania

Dear Mr. and Mrs. March:

The following is a review of the observations, understandings, and suggestions we arrived at together last Thursday. Since there are also a couple of afterthoughts, please telephone me not only with any corrections of fact or additions but also for clarification or possible disagreement. I will then include these in a cover letter with this report to Sister Marion at Ebel School. I have also enclosed an additional note just for Robbie, excerpted from this report. The report is written primarily in third person form to facilitate reading by the Ebel staff.

The Referral and Assessment Situation
By the time Robbie completed fourth grade this past Spring with grades of D and F, his parents had decided that patience with the school system and with Robbie was not succeeding. They enrolled Robbie in a local parochial school (Ebel) for the coming Fall with hopes that he would benefit from its concern with the individual child, together with its tradition of consistent discipline. They were pleased by their visit to the school, especially by what they heard of

[1]Some notes about this particular report: (a) My reports to mental health specialists usually are briefer and more schematic than this one, which was written for the clients and for Robbie's teachers. I chose to reproduce this lengthy report because it describes many aspects of individualizing an assessment. (b) I rarely include IQ scores as I do here; in this case the parents and school personnel had already been given an IQ that was drastically discrepant from my findings, and I wanted to counter its earlier impact. (c) I do not typically remark to a client, as in my concluding note to Robbie, that I like or dislike him or her; in this case the former was true and seemed important to affirm to Robbie. (d) Telephone follow-up at two months and four months found Robbie taking initiative, making friends, and achieving well in school except for mathematics. Robbie created his own pseudonym for this chapter.

its use of small-group instruction. I imagine that they also may hope that a Catholic setting might minimize prejudices against a black student.

Mrs. March works in a personnel office, where Robbie has met the staff socially. These persons assured the Marches that Robbie seemed like a bright, untroubled, energetic boy, whose school difficulties probably were mostly situational. Nevertheless, during the summer the Marches contacted me, as an independent clinical psychologist, to conduct a formal assessment of Robbie's poor academic achievement.

Mrs. March's overview of the background, which she gave me over the phone, was essentially the same picture I came to through examination of Robbie's report cards and school papers and through my visit in the Marches' home. Robbie's kindergarten records describe a regular youngster getting along fine. His first grade report card describes a likable boy who meets academic expectations but who is overly "talkative" for the classroom setting. The second grade report indicates that the talkativeness and activity level probably are frustrating to the teacher and are interfering with school achievement. Robbie's third grade class had a series of substitute teachers, who assigned him grades of B and C. During that year the school reported that Robbie's Otis IQ was 90 (from which teachers would not expect higher achievement than Cs and Bs). During the past year (fourth grade), Robbie's teacher had described him as "quarrelsome" with and a "nuisance" to other students, as a daydreamer, and as overly talkative. She regarded him as not being serious about school, and as not being "motivated." She seems to have provided little if any positive response to Robbie's efforts. Her comments on his papers are of this sort: "This is not as bad as before."

My meeting with Robbie took place on August 7 in his home from 10:30 to about 3:15. Mrs. March intercepted me at a nearby crossing and guided me to their house. We entered through the recreation room, where my first view of Robbie was at his full set of drums, enthusiastically and loudly producing what seemed to me as high quality music. Turning off the amplifier, he looked me over and grinned broadly during a comfortable introduction. That image of an alert, energetic but relaxed, smiling youngster has remained with me as representative of Robbie. He led the way upstairs to the kitchen where Mr. March met us. (Both parents had taken the day off from work to be available during the assessment.)

My first impression of the Marches held up through our five hours together: straightforward, perceptive, unpretentious parents, with high aspirations for their son, eager to help him but also able to confront his limits and difficulties. Physically, all three are slim and evenly featured; all three were dressed neatly in slacks and shirts. I imagine that they are generally seen as being attractive persons.

My representative images of Mrs. March are of her leaning forward over the kitchen table (where most of our work took place), waiting for Robbie to have his own say but with eyebrow raised and mouth almost forming what she knew that he knew (despite his roundabout way of getting there). My image includes Mrs. March's catching herself in this posture, reflecting, and sitting back. My second representative image of Mrs. March is of her at the sink preparing our lunch: flowing but efficient movement, quietly and quickly carrying out her earlier plan for a light, attractive, refreshing lunch that all of us would be likely to enjoy.

As Mrs. March had mentioned on the phone, her husband was the quieter of them. He sat back into his kitchen chair, eyes following attentively/alertly, but his features otherwise composed for observation rather than interruption. When he did speak or otherwise take initiative it was done gently but firmly, flowing smoothly and helpfully into the proceedings. The parents deferred equally to one another, giving me the impression of a long-married couple that has come to terms with differences.

With other families I have asked to be left alone with the child after the initial group interaction, later bringing the parents back into a discussion of what I observed. In this case, finding no disruptive tension among the participants, and finding that all four of us were able to observe Robbie's test performance and to try out its implications for alternative approaches as we went, I wound up working with the entire family for almost all our time. (Actually, the "entire" family would have included Robbie's married sister, 15 years older than he.) Our discussions centered on Robbie's comportment through the Bender-Gestalt, the Wechsler Intelligence Scale for Children, a drawing, Thematic Apperception Test stories, and responses to selected Rorschach cards. Robbie also showed me his room and several of his drawings and projects.

Robbie as Seen through the Test Materials

Before beginning the Bender, I asked Robbie (who sat across from me at first, and later catty-corner, with a parent at each of the other table sides) to tell me what his folks had said about my coming. He sat tall but loosely, with glances at his parents being the only indication of wariness. He hesitated for a moment as though not sure of how to start, and then grinned with what struck me as a self-conscious and somewhat playful, "I forgot." As we gave hints, Robbie seemed both to be relieved and to take pleasure in our knowing that he knew more than he appeared to. Eventually, he announced that I was a "psychologist to help understand school." Again he hesitated to elaborate, looked for affirmation from us that his guess would be correct, and then launched into an account of school, confidently sending his mother out to bring in documents from time to time. I found myself appreciating his open enjoyment of our attention and his confidence that his parents would not let him down. But it also seemed that he looked to them rather than to himself for direction.

As Robbie talked about school, he seemed to wish that he did have better grades, but otherwise didn't know quite what to think about them. He was indignant about being blamed for trouble he didn't start and about students' taking his pencil or other belongings. Otherwise he seemed to regard his school career simply as the way things are.

When I asked Robbie to copy some geometric designs freehand (the Bender-Gestalt), he started right away and then had to erase part of the first design. Similarly, he scattered the designs on his paper without regard for the total number that would have to go on the page. Midway I interrupted to identify this continuing pattern. Robbie agreed that <u>starting without planning</u> is what leads to the messy papers that are so dissatisfying to his teachers. We explored the possibility that he could <u>stop and think before beginning</u>. For example, he could have counted the dots beforehand instead of midway as he had done. I suggested that he also could have made each figure smaller. Then he enthusiastically volunteered to start over. This time he numbered the figures, arranged them sequentially, corrected an error from the original sheet, and pronounced that the second sheet was much better (as it indeed was, although both were adequate for a 10-year-old).

Nevertheless, the same pattern of getting started first and <u>then</u> reflecting showed up through all of our activities. On the WISC, Robbie tossed out associations first, sometimes stopping there, sometimes (as when I just waited without writing down his answer) working his way to the most appropriate answer. For example, question: "What do we celebrate on the Fourth of July?"

Answer: "Fireworks. Parades. It's independence of America." During our discussions Robbie readily accepted hints and employed them with practice items, but his older pattern came to the fore as we began a new subtest.

A second theme is that of looking to adults. Instead of relying on himself for direction, Robbie habitually looked to one of us for guidance once he had jumped in. Examples: "Do I color in the dots?" "Did I do that one [acceptably]?" "Should I start over?" This turning to us was matter-of-fact and not self-conscious or helpless. But even as he took advantage of our responses, Robbie did not look for principles or an overview as such, but instead worked his way cumulatively to success. During the Bender and the WISC, the three Marches and I pursued the notion of Robbie placing himself "in charge," "being the quarterback," "being the captain" (of a hockey team, or in the navy). We were trying to help him to try taking responsibility for making overall plans and for deciding when his criteria had been met; but in part Robbie confused these features with "choosing whatever I want." He did proudly bring out a complicated plastic model ship he had built by following the printed instructions and checking only once with a cousin for help. (He also proudly explained that his Dad had been in the navy.) Both parents recognized these themes as already familiar ones. For example, his mother has been encouraging Robbie to set out all the ingredients and to read the entire recipe on his own before he begins to cook.

The third theme is perhaps a variation of the first two. As Robbie made up stories to the TAT pictures, we adults noted independently (and later discussed) that his characters did not have long-range goals or plans; they rarely took initiative, instead reacting to events or waiting for resolutions to happen. Examples: A man climbs down a rope to escape a fire, a boy goes inside a house only to get out of the heat, a boy doesn't like a gift violin. But on the blank card (where Robbie had to make up a picture as well as a story), he launched enthusiastically into a Flash Gordon adventure. He laughingly agreed to my suggestion that the character be called Robbie Gordon, and consistently used that name throughout. Later, when I asked what his three wishes (for anything at all) would be, he named a two-way radio, a Kenmor truck, and finally, after hesitating, said he would like to be a hero. The latter would be like "saving a spaceship from blowing up," or "stopping two trains from hitting each other." I added , "hitting a home run that wins a tournament," and Robbie agreed, happily instructing me to "write that down too."

At this point I tried to open a middle ground between Robbie's mundane TAT stories and his fantastic heroes. I asked if he could think of less dramatic ways of "being important." Here Robbie came up with "stopping the innocent from going to jail," "stopping the ocean from flooding a city," and "being an executive" (which turned out to mean being a research scientist concerned with ecology, inventing a phonograph record that doesn't wear out, or developing new ways of transporting things from country to country). It seems to me that at present Robbie does not conceive himself as able to work his way through the everyday to his own important contributions.

Robbie's TAT stories also contained several references to false blame that eventually is cleared up by authorities—parents, police, and "Robbie Gordon." Examples: lying about the main character, others assuming the boy was a killer, "calling him a name." Mr. and Mrs. March and I later agreed that Robbie's being in effect an only child, and one with no age-mate on his street, probably has contributed to his sensitivity to false (and accurate) blame. That is, he hasn't had a chance to "build immunity" through give and take with siblings and neighbors. This fourth theme is related to the next one:

During our time together Robbie made <u>few references to peers</u>. Out of concern for his relative isolation, the Marches had enrolled Robbie in Cub Scouts (but the troop has since folded), and this summer he went on an overnight camp and he played on a Little League baseball team . . . right into an all-star tournament. Robbie proudly showed me a photo of his team, as he had showed me his fourth-grade class picture, his portable tape recorder, encyclopedia set, and camp awards. But he did not speak of special friends. His other prized possessions were related to his parents: a newspaper clipping of the three Marches waiting for Pirate autographs, his autograph book filled with a range of sports figures contacted through his father or through the family's waiting together at sporting events, and crafts projects he has brought home to his mother. When I asked directly if he had any buddies (most 10-year-olds are into fast, if shifting, friendships), he mentioned two youngsters "up the hill" with whom he does sometimes play. I know that Robbie is sensitive to criticism from peers, but otherwise I can only report this much of his social relations. He also did not mention his grandmother, with whom he spends his free time while waiting for his parents to come home from work.

Concluding Remarks

From the above sorts of observation, it seems to me that Robbie's "lack of motivation," poor grades, and low achievement scores can be understood in terms of: (1) His confidence in his parents' respect for him and in a world in which authorities see to it that things eventually will be taken care of; (2) Fourth-grade (and in September, fifth-grade) work requires initiative, planning, and relatively independent follow-through, which are contrary to Robbie's current style (In retrospect I wonder whether this style has developed in the face of the Marches doing too much for Robbie while he feels that he has to maneuver them into paying attention directly to him . . . ??); (3) Standardized tests do not allow Robbie to check with adults or to correct himself after he leaps in; also, although Robbie works quickly, on my tests he seemed oblivious to being timed; and (4) At that critical fourth-grade stage, Robbie's adults apparently failed to evoke the school-related hero in him or to show him how to get from "jumping in" to being a "captain" with his school assignments.

On the WISC, where the individual administration allowed Robbie to work his way through initial approximations to the correct answer, his IQ (conservatively scored) was 122, placing him within the upper 10% of his age peers. Performance levels on the various subtests were remarkably consistent—an indication of the reliability of the IQ score. Moreover, Robbie worked steadily at these tests for more than four hours with only a few detours (to tell me about or show me his various other successes). Robbie clearly is not deficient in "intellectual ability" or in "motivation."

Although I probed for a range of possible psychological conflicts, I found none. No doubt, as the Marches and Robbie's teachers begin to work more systematically to help him toward "captaining" his way to achieved importance, then whatever interpersonal family struggles exist for Robbie would come into focus. I suspect these would be related somehow to Robbie's being the sole nonadult in a working family. I also anticipate that the Marches will be much more perceptive and constructive than many parents in recognizing and working with these developments.

Suggestions

The following suggestions are grounded in the above themes. The individualized groupings of suggestions for the parents, teachers, and Robbie are overlapping.

Mr. and Mrs. March

1. Your own ideas seem sound to me (such as encouraging Robbie to set out all his cooking ingredients in advance). Also recall our idea about helping Robbie to set up a prominently placed homework chart that would show goals, homework progress (scores on practice tests, checks for finishing assignments, and so on), grades, and other school accomplishments. Remember that the purpose is to help Robbie build up (over time and many activities) his own sense of how he can project achievement and then work his way toward it. It is important that he see his own progress and that he see continuity among school, home, and his adult future. Perhaps his progress with his drums could be included on the chart. Robbie should participate in drafting the chart, with you guiding him to include small enough units to demonstrate progress. If redrafting seems necessary, Robbie can help to plan that too.

2. Perhaps if Robbie felt that you openly affirmed and enjoyed his more child-like interests (horseplay, "being bad, cool," drums, "Robbie Gordon" fantasies), then he might seek his own council in those instances where he now seeks adult attention in the form of help with what he already knows . . . ??

3. Continuing to provide the warm support Robbie now receives while at the same time encouraging him to be a captain can be tricky. During projects (homework, cooking, building models), perhaps you could tell Robbie outright that one of you will stay in the same room with him to be readily available, but that he should present his questions in the form of "Here's what I think; does that sound right?" Other forms of request that are based on prior reflection should also be honored. Of course sometimes a 10-year-old needs to know that Mom and Dad will help out just because he's himself; standoffs should be avoided in favor of some give and take.

4. As you continue to look for occasions for Robbie to be with age peers (such as the YMCA programs), you might keep one eye on opportunities for Robbie to bring his acquaintances home. This might promote a sense of closer friendship.

Ebel Teachers

1. Robbie seems eager to get started at Ebel, but he has also mentioned being afraid that he'll be "different"—that he won't know the prayers, that he is black, that he may be called names, that he might goof up through not knowing the rules. Since it is especially important that Robbie get off to a good start, perhaps if reprimanding is necessary it could be in the form of: "Robbie, here we all do thus-and-so" (group model information rather than blame-placing). The Marches would be appreciative of any early calls you think might help them to explain or reinforce school principles.

2. Judging from his standardized achievement scores, Robbie may start out in the lower part of his class. This makes it all the more critical that whenever possible he receive positive feedback on what he has done correctly. Similarly, acknowledgment of how far he's come in any area goes a long way with Robbie. I anticipate that with such assistance Robbie will be in very good standing by the end of the school year.

3. I don't know how it might be done in a fifth-grade class, but it is important that Robbie be assisted to envision final products, to think ahead, to look for principles before plunging in. One general strategy might be to encourage Robbie to ask his questions in the form of "Is this right?" rather than open-endedly eliciting your assurance that he does know.

4. Similarly, an occasional two-some (teaming with another child) assignment (preparing a class presentation, cleaning blackboards) might help Robbie to enjoy planning and accomplishing. As the semester gets under way, perhaps you could identify areas of strength in which Robbie could assist

another child. Here too he could enjoy taking on responsibility, planning, and seeing his accomplishment, as well as developing friendships.

Robbie

When I scored those tests you took, I found out that you know enough and are smart enough to be making Bs and As in the fifth grade. Of course at first you'll have to work very hard to catch up with your new class. Your Mom and Dad will help you every night with homework and practicing for tests. Maybe you can even make a big "progress chart" together to keep track of what you practice and how well you're doing. Where would be the best place in which to keep it? —on your bedroom door, in the kitchen, or where? Anyway, if you practice hard in school and at home, I think you'll learn a lot—enough to be a research scientist—and you'll earn good grades too.

I think that your Mom and Dad and your teachers will be trying to help you to plan ahead, to stop and think before you get started, like you did on the second sheet of paper with those designs you copied. That means you have to know how you want something to come out before you start, like Robbie Gordon planned his attack on the enemy ship, or like a hockey captain plans his team's strategy. That's the best way to be "cool"—to know who you are and who you want to be, and what you want to do. To help you to be cool that way (to think for yourself), your parents and teachers sometimes will ask you to figure out what you think before you ask for help.

I think you're going to have a good year, Robbie. And I think your new teachers and classmates will like you, especially if you work hard and help other people. I know that I liked you very much.

Sincerely,

Constance T. Fischer, Ph.D.

Individualized Report Writing

Most textbooks on report writing properly admonish assessors to avoid jargon, to include only information directly relevant to the referral, and to write with the background and interests of particular readers in mind. Assessors are encouraged to describe what is specific to the particular client, and to avoid meaningless "Barnum" statements like "this patient is sometimes anxious" (we're all sometimes anxious). Similarly, report writers are urged to provide practical suggestions rather than rhetorical generalities like "therapy could be helpful." However, these standards have been difficult to meet while also trying to model our assessments in the form of laboratory research and reports. Huber (1961) provides sample reports from an earlier tradition; Tallent (1976 and 1983) presents criticisms of traditional reports and some sample reports from a variety of theoretical approaches.

The above report-writing standards were more easily met in Robbie's report because the assessment was intended from the beginning to focus on Robbie as a particular experiencing person. Quantification and categorization were regarded as helpful, but as adjunctive rather than basic.

The individualized report focuses on life comportment as primary data, with test performance being presented as specialized instances of such comportment. This word, "comportment," is purposely used to evoke the Latin and French meanings: the way one carries one's self. The idea is to evoke the simultaneously actional, decisional, stylistic, and habitual aspects of "behavior." The report represents the individual through selected examples of experience and action taken both from test performance and from his or her daily life. The examples are chosen to evoke for readers the assessor's sense of both how the individual experienced those situations and how the individual acted.

People always act in accordance with their experience, yet their experience evolves in accordance with their action. Experience and action are so intrinsic to each other, that I use von Eckartsberg's (1971) term *experiaction* in order to remind us of this mutuality. Early in a report I provide physical descriptions of the client, in part so that the reader can picture the client throughout the written assessment. I try to describe the client in motion rather than statically, so the reader will be attuned to the ways the person moves through and shapes and is shaped by his or her environment.

This description via representation serves two interrelated purposes: (1) The reader's own past experience is called into play through the vividness of the description and through the inclusion of my own presence as assessor and as a (necessarily) autobiographically rooted and involved observer. (2) Objectivity, in its broader and more basic sense, is served. The reader is aware that no description is independent of the observers, and that we are all referring to the same publicly observable events while respecting the variability-within-generality found in our "participant observations." The reader can see who I was while I was with the client and then can also imagine how the client might be somewhat different with him or her or with others. In part to encourage the reader to imagine me as a particular individual (with whom the client appears as he or she does in the report), I use first person ("I" rather than "the examiner") and active rather than passive voice. I also refer to reported events in the past tense to evoke a sense of situatedness rather than of pervasiveness (for example, "John worked slowly with the blocks" instead of "John works slowly").

The goal of the report is not merely to classify, but also to present individualized suggestions, already partly tried out and carefully adapted to the client's available ways of moving through situations. By the time the formal report is written, clients often have already begun to adapt the suggestions made during the assessment, and in that process have further refined their understandings of the assessment issues. The written report thus is regarded as a progress report—the current state of understandings and suggestions, always subject to further refinement through additional perspectives, and always in a sense out of date since events have continued to evolve.

Clients are told by the end of the assessment session what will be in the report. They may later read the report and write commentary on it directly. This recorded continuation of the collaborative assessment is a final reminder to readers of the client's status as a responsible, informed participant. The commentary also highlights any unresolved disagreements between the client's understandings and my own. Readers are thereby encouraged to maintain a continuing openness to the question of who the client is. Besides, although the assessor's professional impressions are useful, in order to engage the client directly, a helper must know the client's own views.

The length of the report varies with its purpose and with the complexity of the issues. If a basic decision is at stake (such as placement in special education or determination of legal competency), the report can answer the question in one or two pages. But usually the individualized report continues on to give the reader a sense of the client's world and style of moving through that world, and points where the client could pivot into an alternative course. This additional description is helpful both when the client is a primary reader, for whom the report is a reminder of understandings and suggestions developed during the assessment session, and when the reader is a person who will be working directly with the client. Experience with writing in individualized terms can be helpful even when the author chooses not to include such detail in a particular report. In this instance, experience helps the author to bypass unnecessary constructs and jargon.

Although my reports may include diagnostic, psychodynamic, or behavioristic parallel statements where called for by principal readers, these always refer back explicitly to the events described in the report. Personality, ability, and other constructs are not allowed to become more real than the situated, complex, interpersonal events that comprise the report.

The Process of Individualizing Assessment

Familiarity with standardized tests and their administration, norms, diagnostic systems, research data, and so on, is essential for all assessors. Individualized assessment provides a particular attitude with which our traditional tools may be used, along with some procedures for tailoring assessments to the individual, but it is not intended to be a freestanding activity. Some features of individualized assessment do differ from our more traditional practices.

Upon receiving a referral for an assessment, I first consult the referring person to find out what actual events and circumstances have led to the request. Three typical referrals are: "establish IQ," "differentiate between schizoid personality and group delinquent reaction," and "provide a personality picture." Exploring the context of such referrals is easier said than done, however, because most often the referring person has focused on an end result rather than the process that led to it. This result is conceptualized in abstract, sometimes mechanistic terms. For example, when I asked the teacher to explain the "establish IQ" referral, I was told, "Daniel didn't score at grade expectancy on social studies achievement tests, and I thought it might be because his IQ is not as high as we thought." An example from the second referral: "Well, this fellow has an arrest record, and I don't know whether it's because he's identifying with street leaders or whether he's schizoid." And from the third referral: "The patient was admitted as a depressive neurotic with suicidal preoccupations, but she has not responded to antidepressants [medication]; so I wondered if this could be simply a passive-dependent personality on one hand, or on the other, if the admissions staff failed to recognize an underlying agitation."

To get back to primary data (life events rather than numbers, categories, and constructs) I ask the referring person what decisions he or she is confronted with. In the above examples, the teacher told me that he does not know whether to encourage his student to try harder or to congratulate him for doing as well as he has; the Community Mental Health worker said she did not know whether to recommend group therapy or a behavior modification program to her client (the delinquent); and the psychiatrist was trying to decide whether to prescribe tranquilizing drugs and whether his staff should be supportive or demanding with the patient.

At this point it usually is easier for the referring person to recall events that would support one side or the other of the decision. I asked the teacher for examples of when the student (Daniel) *has* met or exceeded grade-level expectations, and we discovered that he holds his own on group projects, on homework assignments that he can check with his mother, and in classroom discussions. It turned out that he does not do as well when left totally on his own; for example, writing an independent book report or taking a standardized test. The teacher and I agree that the assessment referral, thus contextualized, should be revised to "Explore with Daniel Sanders the meanings of working by himself, and develop ways for him to extend his active participation in groups to independent work." Notice that IQ as such was no longer an issue. Even had Daniel been working below grade expectancy across the board, the assessor would try to describe the contexts of Daniel's performance in order to expand whatever already is working for him into other contexts. This is the realm of life events, to which scores are relevant; but they are not revelatory of anything more fundamental than the life events.

Often, after such preliminary contextualizing of the referral, the person who initiated it decides to defer or cancel further action by the assessor until he or she (the referring person) has further investigated the focal events directly with the subject and with the latter's other helpers. The assessor is not a test technician, but a consultant, one who integrates knowledge of relevant literature (within psychology, special education, or whatever) with an understanding of a particular subject's experience and action, and who then assists the referring person and subject to help themselves. In the preliminary consultant role, the assessor may bring the subject and referring person together so that all three collaborate at one time. Daniel Sanders (the student), for example, helped to identify times when he felt more comfortable working by himself. With that information, he and his teacher agreed that they would work systematically at expanding from workbook assignments (checking answers in the back of the book) to assignments that he could check with the teacher in the morning before class.

When the client is self-referred, client and assessor work together directly from the beginning. Often the client, much in the manner of the above teacher, mental health worker, and psychiatrist, initially talks about himself or herself in objectifying, totalizing terms: "I'm an intelligent person, but my inferiority complex blocks me from getting ahead," or "There's nothing wrong with me—it's all these establishment types who are uptight," or "When this impulse breaks out, I can't do anything about it; I wonder if it's hereditary." So here too the assessor inquires into critical situations that the client is facing, and asks for concrete examples of the "inferiority complex," the "impulse," and so on. The major difficulty in such efforts to discover and contextualize referents is that the clients, like all persons who are in defensive or problem-oriented modes, recall in terms of *object*ifications—persons or events now categorized in terms that imply mechanical causation of the problematic outcome. Especially in problematic situations, unless we make particular efforts to be open to other perceptions, we all (client and practitioner alike) perceive and think in terms of objects and forces. Thus Daniel's teacher had said, "I often think that he has more potential, but when he doesn't score well on the achievement tests, I think maybe he's just not intelligent enough after all." At first this teacher was unable to say just what he had experienced as Daniel's "potential." Eventually, as I encouraged focusing on actual events, the teacher shook off earlier conceptions and discovered recollections of Daniel leaning forward in his seat during lectures, asking questions in an excited manner, and requesting extra resources for a class project. Later, as the teacher watched Daniel in class, his vision was attuned to process and context. This is a significantly different vision.

Sometimes clients find that initial discussion has differentiated the problems and options adequately for further work by themselves. More often in my experience, however, discussion only circumscribes the issues, bringing client and myself into agreement about them but still in a rather vague, global way. At this point I turn to test materials. I do not necessarily "administer tests," but I do "use test materials." In the case of Link, who was referred by the mental health worker (for a diagnostic decision between schizoid personality and group delinquent reaction), I asked that he copy freehand the nine Bender-Gestalt geometric designs.

Link and I had been trying to understand how he gets into trouble even when he intends to stay clean. We both witnessed the first design's starting on the upper left corner of the paper, and the second design's completion in the middle of the page. I realized that although Link intended to do a good job, he was going to run out of space. Sure enough, at the seventh design Link looked up at me, puzzled that there was no space left. I just looked at him noncommittally, and Link smashed the pencil point on the sheet, angrily shouting that I had tricked him. "Yes," I said, "the same way Mr. Wilkins 'tricked you' into missing your appointment Tuesday."

We stared in silence for a while at the torn Bender sheet and its implicit history of our encounter. Then I asked Link to tell me about other times he had gotten himself into being "tricked." It appeared that sometimes he had in fact been used as a scapegoat by his sisters, father, and street group. But there were also times more like the Bender incident. For example, Link recalled that his shop teacher had promised to introduce him to a potential employer if Link would come to class on time, dress neatly, and clean up his area satisfactorily for the entire month. Link had kept his part of the bargain for two weeks while the shop teacher congratulated him regularly, but when these reminders stopped, Link began lapsing into prior habits. At the end of the month Link was told that he had lost his chance. Link accused the teacher of tricking him, and threw a shaving plane through a (closed) shop window.

With this and other recalled instances in mind, we returned to the Bender. I asked Link to retrace the figures as he had originally done them, but to look ahead for a way to solve this dilemma as he approached design seven. As he began, he asked, "Like what?" I replied, "Well, where else could the designs go?" In what I took as a defiant tone, Link announced that he could take another sheet of paper. As I smiled and nodded, and gestured for still more options, Link itemized more, gradually beginning to laugh as he elaborated his options into absurdities (from "using the back of this page" to "cutting down a forest to make my own paper"). Later in our session, I suggested that Link start from scratch with the Bender designs; I again gave the standard instructions, and he began with the first design. This time, though, as he recognized the feeling of what we came to name "just going along," he stopped to check his progress against the stimulus cards and his remaining space. When there nevertheless was not enough room for the last design, Link snorted and thumped the eraser end of his pencil on the desk, but recognizing this situation as also pivotal, he grinned sheepishly and asked, "So it's okay for me to put this one on the back—right?"

We proceeded in a similar manner through selections of the Wechsler Adult Intelligence Scale, some Thematic Apperception Test cards (ambiguously drawn scenes for which the subject makes up stories), and the Rorschach (inkblots). As we continued, variations of the Bender experience occurred, which we came to call "going along versus thinking for yourself." Each new occasion led to a re-understanding of prior instances as well as a different chance to try out "thinking on your own." Other themes emerged too, of course, and they modified each other. For example, to my initial surprise, Link did not become angry when I left him on his own, with no detailed instructions, to tell me what he could see in the inkblots. Later, when we talked about my puzzlement, Link replied, "Well, I knew right from the beginning that I was supposed to do this by myself—it didn't have much to do with you" (with my passing judgment each step of the way).

Link is equally independent when, all by himself, he takes care of his little brother, with whom he does not become angry and with whom he works hard without quitting. Thus, the answer to the earlier referral question was that although Link's difficulties have been the outcome of characterological patterns of experience and action, he is not always out of touch with other persons' perspectives, and his problems are not merely those of peer influence. My report described Link's trouble-making in terms of those circumstances in which he has and has not thought for himself, and in which he has and has not become angry. The assessment report went beyond these descriptions to include both summaries of our attempts at intervention and related suggestions for how the mental health specialist might work with Link to consolidate and further these efforts.

Using tests as access to process

Using test materials in the above individualized manner allows clients and me *together* to observe their "tracks" as they move through the materials, (for example, *Bender designs, failed and passed WAIS–R items*). Because we are working together to see what new understandings might emerge, clients do not feel they are being *object*ified or having their privacy invaded. To these ends, my preferred seating arrangement is not 180° across a desk, but about 100° and about six feet apart, so that we each can see all of the other. I do not use a pencil and pad until we are well into a collaborative relationship. And I do not begin with a question–answer period. Instead, I first briefly present the referral issue, and quickly ask the client to tell me his or her version of how the referral came about. As I say little, and gesture for the client to continue, the person finds himself or herself shifting from a standard, packaged version to an explication that begins to recognize gaps, seeming inconsistencies, and many ambiguities. The client himself or herself begins to qualify earlier absolute statements, and to consider new perspectives. When we reach the limits of this reflective exploration, I turn to the tests.

The test materials allow us to continue breaking through old conceptions and expectations. They help both of us to move out of conventional social modes and speech. As clients cope with some particular test, they find themselves in a context similar to others with which they are familiar; the test situation evokes structurally similar past events. Link's smashing his pencil into the evolving Bender is experiactionally nearly the same as his throwing the plane through the shop window. Through the test activity we find touch points with phenomena that were previously unavailable for reflection. Sometimes these phenomena are simply habitual patterns that the person has taken for granted. For example (from a different client), "Well, I guess I do typically ask a lot of questions to be sure what's expected of me; I guess what we're seeing is that sometimes that gets me into trouble—at least when supervisors think I'm not independent enough." The person's past is always present in the ways he or she co-creates the environment; and this co-creation also contains all the levels and complexity of what traditionally is known as "the unconscious." I sometimes compare my approach with psychoanalytic "depth" psychology by saying that "the unconscious is horizontal"—visible in the ways a person traverses his or her own terrain with its personal physiognomies, invitations, and danger signs.

This travel imagery (lived world, pathways, goals, territory) allows us to see more clearly how the person participates in bringing about what "happens to" him or her. For example, a paranoid fellow suspects that people may belittle him or worse, and his self-protection is aggressive. He maintains a social distance, stares penetratingly, out-argues authorities, and publicly accuses people of outrageous motives. In this way he shapes the world he travels; he shapes it into one in which people avoid him, talk behind his back, and do indeed experience outrageous feelings in regard to him. Sometimes I refer to this differentiation/shaping of one's traversed and future territory as one's "style" of moving through particular situations. The phrase acknowledges this highly contextualized, limited, but active process (which cannot be known in itself but only through the multiple perspectives of observers, including the client) that is at the heart of individualized assessment. Seeing style is a different vision.

Understanding situated style as a factor in the evolution of end-products (test scores, broken windows, and so on) is necessary if the assessor is to help the client to recognize the landmarks that call for a change in direction. And the assessor and other helpers must deal with style for the most productive and comprehensive intervention. When specific interventions are successfully tried out during the assessment, then the client can be guided toward these new alternatives that he or she has already discovered to be personally viable. Constructive intervention is possible even when the clients are guided into living out new variations without cognitive insight of their own.

Additional features

To illustrate additional aspects of individualized assessment, let us consider the psychiatric referral to distinguish the depressive neurotic from passive dependent personality. These additional aspects occur to some degree in any thorough clinical assessment. In the section that follows, I want to emphasize that fact and to describe some of the particular ways in which an individualized assessment regards the person's actual life as the point of departure into secondary data (such as test scores or diagnosis) *and* as the point of return from reflections on that data. Secondary data should be used only to help us understand actual events in their own right. The assessee is in an ideal position to collaborate in this effort.

During the initial contextualizing, I listen for what the client understands as the reasons for the assessment, but I also check on the client's understanding directly from time to time during the assessment as the client becomes progressively more open and reflective during our work together. For example, Mrs. Smyth (the psychiatrist's patient) at first told me, "The doctor wants to know if he should change my medicine." Later she clarified that he wanted to establish whether or not she was suicidal. Much later, in response to my direct inquiry, Mrs. Smyth acknowledged that she thought my job was to find out if she were "crazy." She herself had wondered if this could be true because in fact she was now in a mental hospital. Moreover, she had often been bewildered and frightened at her own sudden anger when people she usually counted on now expected too much of her. She had indeed wondered whether this meant she was crazy and if this craziness could cause her to kill herself. Early in our session she had been intent on disproving this possibility to both of us. In other words,

I did not look for constancies of personality or perception, but instead explored and took into account Mrs. Smyth's changing possibilities, which varied with her perceptions of her circumstances.

Even in the early stages of an assessment, collaborative analysis of a test profile can lead to the whens and when-nots of problematic events (that is, of when they do and do not occur). Mrs. Smyth's Minnesota Multiphasic Personality Inventory (MMPI) answers were scored and graphed prior to our meeting, and I tabbed my reference books for descriptions of persons with profiles like hers. I read relevant sections aloud to Mrs. Smyth and asked her in what ways these people were and were not like her. Even though she was not a particularly introspective or reflective person, she participated effectively. For example, she resolved the seeming contradiction between descriptions of her as "dependent" and as "knowing [her] own mind" in the following ways: "I know what I want, it's just that I shouldn't be expected to do everything by myself. Besides, I do lots by myself—I tend the house and do all the cooking. And when the kids were little, it was my husband [who] was lost. I was in charge of everything about them." This discussion eventually led us to see that Mrs. Smyth had functioned at her best when she could depend on her husband to be the master of the house and to look after her, even while he and the children acknowledged that she was the major caretaker of the children.

Like all assessors, I integrate test profiles and background information as a means of formulating my own preliminary understandings. For example, in this case, the nursing staff felt that Mrs. Smyth was still depressed because they had seen her moody isolation on the unit and her occasional crying spells. They felt that she was too immobilized to be considered suicidal at the time. But on the MMPI she scored relatively high on scales that usually reflect energized resentment, which led me to suspect that she might indeed make a suicidal effort, out of desperation but also in retaliation against those who were failing her. Without fairly explicit awareness of alternative possibilities, the assessor cannot make full use of comportment that occurs during the use of performance tests and projective materials.

Similarly, I identify any actual events in the client's life that are similar to patterns reported in our literature; in this instance, our suicide literature. For example, I noted that in Mrs. Smyth's case there were indeed "precipitating events," especially "losses" that precluded continuation of her prior "identification" and way of relating to her family. Specifically, her two children were now approaching adolescence. They no longer let her "mother" them, and instead maintained a charged distance from which they made demands and derogatory judgments. In addition, Mr. Smyth recently had accepted trucking jobs that took him away from home for weeks at a time. Because Mrs. Smyth could not see a viable alternative way of being and because she was rather nonreflective, I felt that she might "impulsively" kill herself. This possibility was consonant with her report that she had gained rather than lost weight. That is, she did not fit the pattern of those depressed clients who eat little, lose weight, and either plan a suicide or allow themselves to be "accidentally" killed. Rather, she fit the pattern of distressed persons. Thus, the assessor can answer the general referral question while also answering how that general finding is true of this particular person. On the other hand, individualized assessment is not only about an individual, but is also about that person in comparison with others.

Another resource that I consulted along with my direct observations of Mrs. Smyth was research on phenomenological structures. As I experienced her as anxious, I was reminded of W. Fischer's (1970) writings on being anxious, and I then became attuned to Mrs. Smyth's feeling that she must continue to be the mother she had been, and her desperate doubt that she could do so. My own qualitative research on crying alerted me to observe that Mrs. Smyth's tears were those of protest as well as tears of resigned sorrow. Reflections such as these helped me to see the possibility of an angry and despairing suicide attempt, which was more pertinent than the differential diagnosis that the psychiatrist had requested. These integrations of my direct observations with qualitative research findings allowed me to answer the referral by describing Mrs. Smyth as a generally dependent but giving person, diagnostically more distressed than depressed. Because my primary focus had been Mrs. Smyth, however, I was able to formulate individualized suggestions. Specifically, I suggested that the unit staff should meet her where she is, offering compassion and support, but in addition pulling her into helping out with tasks and projects around the ward. Group therapy might focus on ways she could maintain her old routines despite her children's turbulence. Older members might hold out the probability that once the children are past adolescence, they will not only once again allow their mother to care for them, but also encourage her to depend on them for support. Finally, my report emphasized the importance of working with the entire Smyth family to further assess and collaboratively alter Mrs. Smyth's dilemma; her difficulty was both "environmental" and "psychodynamic."

A collaborative approach does not preclude disagreements between client and assessor; each of us is the ultimate authority on his or her own opinion. Mrs. Smyth and I disagreed about my impression that she was resentful of her husband's leaving her on her own with the growing children. My report included this disagreement, and our respective grounds, thereby telling readers not only my understanding but the client's as well. Her helpers would have to approach her through both understandings.

Very often the client cannot directly assist the assessor in finding other instances of experience and comportment observed during the assessment. In these cases, I consult the client's involved others (family, employer, institutional staff), sharing an observation from the assessment and asking them for similar examples and exceptions. When I mentioned to the nursing aides that Mrs. Smyth had cried in a choking way, protesting that "life isn't fair," and that I had sensed an angry resentment at that moment, an aide recalled that Mrs. Smyth had glared at him and then yanked a broom from his hand when he had sternly insisted that sick or not, she was responsible for cleaning her own cubicle.

Access to everyday life events that occur outside the assessor's office is of course facilitated when the assessment takes place in the clients' home environment. In Mrs. Smyth's case, I saw her in several of the hospital's settings (her cubicle, the dayroom, the canteen). I worked with Daniel in his school setting, but I saw Link only in my office. I conducted my interviews with Robbie and his parents entirely in their home.

Finally, because the client has been involved throughout the assessment—during which test comportment has been regarded as a specialized instance of other, everyday behavior—the psychologist has no reason to keep his or her observations and report secret from the client. The client's comment on the written report increases the accuracy of its portrayal of his or her perspective. This focus on life events, rather than on presumed underlying conditions or technical categories, also enables the client to continue the assessment's explorations of new understandings and personal options.

Six Guiding Principles

The above practices are based on six guiding principles of a human-science approach to assessment. These principles are all interrelated. Our individualized approach to assessment is:

Descriptive.   Our primary data are particular life events. Test scores, theoretical constructs, and research literature are all derived, secondary data through which the assessor modifies and refines his or her perception of life events—both those that are reported by the client and those that occur during the assessment. Description via primary data, rather than by interpretation of personality traits, defense mechanisms, and the like, is "representational description." The client's comportment is sampled (represented) by re-presenting particular instances relevant to the referral, along with their meanings to the assessor.

Contextual.   Events within the assessment session as well as those outside of it are described not only as behaviors, but also in terms of their contexts. Contexts include (1) the physical setting or condition—such as blood levels of various chemicals, (2) the location within a temporal sequence, (3) the assessor's relation to the client, both as influence and as access to the client, and (4) the meanings of the situation for the client (as comprehended by the assessor but presented as much as possible in the client's words and actions). Description, then, may include evolved comportment, physical context, immediate meanings to the client, and the assessor's understandings and observations. For example: "At first she smoothed the fresh paper, lined up the two pencils, and leaned back expectantly, reminding me of an eager student with new supplies."

The contexts of similar behaviors, also described and discussed, enrich the initial understandings of an event. Exploration of times (the "when nots") when a problematic event did *not* occur can lead to discovery of positive comportment, which the person may then extend in the future, perhaps bypassing the old problem.

Collaborative.   We recognize that people participate in what happens to them; they shape as well as are shaped by their worlds. So we encourage the client to be an informed, active participant throughout the assessment, and to comment on any written documents. As a co-assessor, the client is acknowledged as partly responsible for his or her past and future and as capable of participating in his or her own redevelopment. *Client Participation in Human Services: The Prometheus Principle* (Fischer & Brodsky, 1978) presents principles and practices of informed participation in a variety of facilities.

Interventional.   Assessment, even of the traditional sort, always affects the client—who inevitably finds the experience meaningful in one way or another. The human-science assessor acknowledges this and tries to make sure that the inevitable interventions are constructive. These interventions into the client's ways of moving through situations are intended both to evaluate the client's current possibilities, and to try out different ones. Current limitations are not considered final. By way of contrast, recall that in the past assessment too often has been based on the beliefs that the client *has* a particular set of abilities and personal characteristics and that the interviewer should record these without influencing them. Also bear in mind that historically a major function of assessment was to classify the individual into already established group norms. Psychologists too often have acted as though individualized understanding and intervention should be reserved totally for a separate enterprise, that of therapy.

Structural.   Our explanatory system is that of contextualized primary data. We do not look for underlying causes, but for a comprehension of the fullness of an event—its what/how/when (and when not). By "when," we refer to the context—to the temporal, physical, personal, and interpersonal aspects of the phenomenon, all understood as they are lived by the client and as they are perceived by the assessor. By "how," we refer to the shaped/shaping evolution of the event, to the process through which it comes into being. "What" refers to when and how, as seen through some particular behavior. This full description of the behavior is a description of its structure, which attempts to capture the holistic way in which biology, world, and experience are aspects of a unitary moment. In that moment the aspects imply each other. No one aspect is more essential or basic than any of the others. Notice that this account asks the standard question of a happening's necessary and sufficient conditions, but it has not had to ask the "why" question—which typically looks beneath human affairs to some other presumed level of cause.

Circumspect.   The human-science assessor is keenly aware that circumstances severely restrict the professionals' and clients' access to each other and to options. Not all clients can collaborate in a reflective, verbal way. Emergencies and heavy case loads often preclude thorough assessments. But this final guiding principle reminds us that all the others are just that—guiding principles to be followed as ideally but also as authentically as possible. "Authentically" here refers to a striving toward the possible while acknowledging the necessary (the givens, limits, requirements), not allowing either to be exaggerated. Human-science assessment is circumspect also in that assessors are mindful of the limits of one's personal, professional, theoretical, historical, and cultural perspectives. Moreover, to be circumspect is to respect the inherent ambiguity of human affairs. One ought to regard our sense-making as an overly static and precise imposition on complex, holistic, flowing, ever-changing phenomena. Even as we utilize our formulations, we ought to regard them as partial perspectives, always unfinished.

These guiding principles are both points of theory and suggestions for practice. They lead to individualized assessment—an understanding of a particular person's situation as he or she lives it and of personally viable options within it.

Questions and Responses

Question: Couldn't the assessor learn the practices and theory discussed in this book just by beginning to do assessments?

Response: It's my impression from teaching and from giving workshops and lectures that these notions and practices seem common-sensical only to persons who have not been trained in our earlier tradition. Often, when I belabor a point, I'm trying to show colleagues a comparison with some aspect of the system in which we were trained.

Question: Does it take years of experience to use tests effectively in this life-relevant way?

Response: Most graduate students, who don't have to unlearn old conceptions and practices, catch on very quickly. Chapters 6, 7, and 8 contain some reports written by first-semester M.A. students. These students still have to gain clinical knowledge and further skills, but as the reports indicate, the approach comes fairly easily to those who are interested.

Question: Isn't the Robbie Gordon report too long to be efficient?

Response: Most of my reports are shorter. In general, shorter reports are more effective. But notice that the Robbie Gordon report does more than describe the client: (1) It is an evaluation of the family as well as of the boy. (2) It is a report for school personnel as well as for the family, including the youngster. (3) It contains itemized suggestions for all three parties, including reasons and hints for carrying them out. (4) It tells the adult readers what the others have been told and what the suggestions were. Although lengthy, this report is efficient in its accomplishments.

Question: Doesn't use of first person in assessment reports make them seem chatty, informal, or nonprofessional?

Response: Use of first-person ("I" versus "the examiner") helps to demystify the report. It also helps readers to put themselves in the assessor's place and imagine themselves interacting with this particular client. The writer must be efficient and disciplined; one puts no more of oneself into the report than is necessary for describing the assessment situation and one's access to the client. Part of the professional's expertise is to render specialized knowledge in everyday terms. First person in the place of titles or of passive voice is part of that effort. Most readers, whether professionals or lay persons, respect these reports all the more because they understand and can make use of them.

Question: But what do mental health professionals think of these personalized, mundane reports?

Response: Most professionals are pleased with a down-to-earth, direct response to referral problems. But I have sometimes found it necessary to let certain colleagues in psychology and psychiatry know that the author of a report is fully credentialed and schooled in conventional techniques and research. For certain forensic cases, for example, I list "tests used" in a single column, double-spaced, down the middle of the first page. Occasionally I add a technical discussion (for example, MMPI profile, Rorschach ratios) that not only helps colleagues to understand the client, but also helps them to take my earlier descriptions seriously. Such ploys remind the professional that I have *chosen* to write descriptively although I am conversant with specialized conceptual systems.

Question: In the assessment of Robbie, why didn't you conduct an analysis of the WISC subtest scores?

Response: I did. I was particularly interested in any indications of specific learning disabilities. There were none. Additional findings of the subtest analysis I presented in terms of Robbie's directly observed comportment, which was more readily understandable to Robbie's parents and teachers. I do not report technical data unless there is a technical need for it. Such data are tools, not results. Results are useful understandings of the concrete ways people get into trouble and of the personally viable ways they might bypass such problems.

Question: What's the difference between therapy and the interventional aspects of individualized assessment?

Response: There are many similarities. An effective assessment is necessarily growthful because clients begin to experience themselves as able to assess and change their lives, and a constructive program is initiated. A major difference between psychotherapy and assessment is that the latter's interventions are in the interest of arranging for later intervention. Another difference is that interventional assessment is decidedly short-term, whereas therapy typically engages the client over a longer time, which allows for evolution of readiness and for working through issues in depth and breadth.

Question: Isn't the report on Robbie overly optimistic? Doesn't it minimize pathology?

Response: Robbie's progress in his new school has indicated that the report was realistic. The goal of an individualized assessment is to provide personally viable suggestions for the person and for his or her helpers. We have not finished our work when we stop with an analysis of problems. Stopping short leaves many assessments pathology-oriented. Writing in technological terms, instead of writing technologically informed descriptions of life events, also leaves readers feeling that the client's course is predetermined. Hence the frequent pessimism of assessments.

Question: Were you critical of the referrals as they were given? Do you object to asking diagnostic questions?

Response: The diagnostic terms and categories can be very meaningful, but we should remember that they are organizing devices rather than a state of reality against which we are supposed to match clients. Our primary data, life events, should be both our points of departure into reflection about diagnostics and our point of return from it.

Question: Does the human-science approach stress experience more than physical factors?

Response: In their present stage, the human-science approaches are directed primarily toward the experiential dimension previously neglected by scientific psychology. But our long-range goal is an integrated discipline in which we understand behavior as an expression of the person's situation—which is always simultaneously experiential and physical. Neither is more fundamental since both are aspects of a unitary phenomenon; both are essential to human events.

Question: Haven't educators already experimented with "life-events" approaches to assessment?

Response: Yes. Educators are working on "criterion-based" rather than "norm-referenced" tests, so that records can be kept of what in particular youngsters have learned, rather than where they stand in relation to other students. Employers have used job simulations to test applicants. In World War II, the Office of Strategic Services assessed candidates for military intelligence by observing them in stressful situations. Graduate schools in human services increasingly are adopting competencies criteria for certification, and these are frequently defined as field competency (rather than course work or tested achievement). For their referred clients, however, human-services professionals generally continue to look for explanations and answers in test scores. This is one of the reasons for this book; we require explicit alternatives to our habits of emphasizing test scores.

Question: Are test behaviors regarded as primary or secondary data?

Response: Since they are direct, prelabeled observations of life events, they are primary. The assessment session, unlike everyday life, is a specialized situation, but the client is indeed living through it. Secondary data are the test scores and the assessor's knowledge of theoretical constructs and research results.

Question: Aren't the practitioner's observations of a client sometimes actually secondary rather than primary?

Response: Yes, when the practitioner fails to put theories and categories aside for the moment to see what he or she can then be present to. A secondary observation might be, "This man is nervous"; a primary observation would be, "This man is glancing about rapidly while holding his body in a rigid posture, and I find myself wanting to calm him." Other secondary observations might have to do with "hostility," "schizophrenia," or "intelligence." We perceive in terms of meanings, and then have to check these meanings by asking what was there that others might see too. For instance, upon reflection I might decide that what I took for nervousness might better be described as eagerness. The meanings are our access to the client, but we must be circumspect about them.

Question: Since even "primary data" necessarily involve the perspective of the viewer, doesn't "primary" really refer to observations in which the assessor has tried to specify his or her personal access to publicly observable events?

Response: Right. I would only add that these primary observations are not entirely dependent on specific theories, categories, and explanatory interests.

Question: Does the emphasis on contextualizing suggest that each person is unique in every situation?

Response: No. We go about our lives in relatively stable, organized, enduring ways. I like to say that our patterns of experiaction are trans-situational, but not pan-situational. In other words, people are similar in similar circumstances but not the same in all circumstances.

Question: But how can observers be sure what a behavior means? Aren't test scores simpler to interpret?

Response: First, human-science assessors do not look for an independent true meaning. Instead we try to indicate the context in which particular understandings arose (and were revised), and we encourage the client and other readers to continue developing their own understandings beyond those in the report.

In regard to test scores, human-science assessors realize that despite the apparent clarity of scores, they do not reveal anything precise about a person's life or possibilities. The nature of human affairs is not as categorical and precise as mathematics. Properly used, test scores may be decidedly helpful and efficient, but they are only starting points for exploration of the complexity and ambiguity of a person's life. If the scores are to be informative about an individual, they must be explored in terms of observed and described comportment.

Question: Then are your "descriptions" as interpretive as the theoretical interpretations of other approaches?

Response: All descriptions are necessarily interpretive in that a viewer can see only from his or her own situation (including whatever part one's science and training play). Individualized description, however, presents events that can be seen by others. These events, along with the assessor's personal commentary, evoke the reader's similar life events and thereby a *sense* of what the client's situation is like. Individualized descriptions respect the ambiguity and complexity of daily events in their own interpersonal right. Thus, the most direct answer to your question is that this description remains in the realm of life as lived and reflected upon. It does not convert life events into a different order of reality, such as traits, dispositions, defense mechanisms, diagnoses, or personality types. The practical significance of this respect for ambiguity and complexity is its potential for reaching the client "where he or she lives," so to speak, and helping the client to discover new horizons visible from there. Communication among the client's family and other helpers is also facilitated. Most important, perhaps, the client understands which events people are concerned about and working on, and he or she can be an active participant in the planning and working. I strongly suspect that clinics would have fewer dropouts if intake interviews were individualized assessments.

Question: Will this book soon be obsolete because of the rapid advance of computerized assessment? Computers already individualize test administration in that they call up different subsets of questions depending on the testee's last answer. And computers already print out interpretations that take into account the particular person's age, education, gender, and so on.

Response: Microcomputers and word processors are a welcome boon for efficiency. However, the dangers of printouts being taken as personalized results, rather than as the probabilistic, impersonal data that they are, argue for greater training in individualized assessment theory and practice. Printouts are tools, not results. Assessment should be "computer-assisted," not "computerized."

Question: Do you see yourself within contemporary clinical practice? Or are you advocating a separate theory or movement?

Response: I definitely see myself within contemporary clinical psychology. But I want to be part of a corrective thrust. I'm hopeful that the term "human science" will drop out after a while, indicating that it has been absorbed into mainstream psychology. Similarly, I'm hopeful that "individual assessment" will come to mean "individualized assessment."

CHAPTER 3

Beginning the Individualized Assessment

STATEMENTS about a person's standing in comparison to various groups can facilitate many of the decisions for which assessment is requested. The decision maker may need to know, for example, which applicants scored highest on the entrance test, whether a defendant meets the state's criteria for competency to stand trial, if a youngster's IQ reaches the school district's minimum for gifted-student placement, or whether a surgery candidate's depression is situational or chronic. The following chapters, however, assume that the reader is already, or is becoming, familiar with procedures for conducting such decision-making assessments. These chapters present procedures for those occasions when it is preferable to address the individual as individual, not only to answer a referral question, but also to work with that person toward less restrictive, more productive, ways of going about life. The process of individualized assessment is, then, an assessment of process—an assessment of the person's ways of approaching, going through, influencing, and being influenced by situations.

This chapter provides a brief theoretical framework, which includes a survey of the functions of tests in individualized assessment. It surveys the training that is necessary for conducting assessments, and then describes the initial phase of the assessment process. A table of counterproductive inclinations, endemic among beginning assessors, helps readers to identify and modify such dispositions.

Theoretical Framework

We are what we do

We are what we do. Any moment of action moves our past toward our future, and in that way the action is a fuller and more dynamic portrait of ourselves than the tracks we have left behind. Testers traditionally have addressed tracks and finished products—Bender-Gestalt tracks, answer sheet marks, scores for intelligence test achievements. We have looked backward to see where clients have been and what they left behind. This backward view facilitates comparisons with other people; it is indeed more difficult to compare people who are moving, who are still en route. Also, records of what a person has done indeed indicate what might be done again, and in what directions and how far a person might go. But to understand *who* a person is, we must witness his or her biography in the making, rather than its finished accretion. We must be present to the individual's choice points, and to what they mean to that person's sense of life-to-date and of future possibilities. We must observe how the person moves among the options, thereby reshaping them.

The following is an illustration. A colleague remarked, "I heard that John Akbar resigned from the Board after the nominating committee declined to ask if he wished to run again for his office of Vice Chair. I never realized there was so much immaturity behind what I used to see as dedication." I had attended the meeting, and could only wish my colleague had been there to see John in the process of resigning. I had watched and approved as the Chair called John out of order when he tried to present a prepared list of his achievements while in office; I watched as he inquired evenly why standard procedures for asking nonattenders (not John) for their resignations had not been followed strictly; I watched as he no longer looked directly at the rest of us, but focused only on the Chair. I heard his voice quake when, after having labored with us on assorted public service projects for six years, he told the Chair that in the end we had proven to be racist: Only black nonattenders had been asked to resign; only he, a black, had ever in our history not been asked to stand again for office. He said angrily he would not continue to serve with us. I watched as he waited for another topic to engage our attention before he gathered up his folders, and quietly left the Board. As I helped to tidy up our room after the meeting, I discovered he had left his attaché case behind; he had not been completely in control of his departure after all. A sense of sadness and help-lessness told me that John's departure was in a sense a continuation of his dedication, and although in some sense it was "immature," it probably was very difficult for him also. I felt that, if need be, I would know how to discuss the incident meaningfully with John.

The point of the above account is that who we are is more available and evident in our ongoing action—in what we do—than in second-hand judgments of its outcome. Description of such action, although less succinct than end point or outcome data, tell us who a person is, and how we might enter the course of his or her life.

We know each other by where we are going

The action described above is, of course, not just behavior in a behav-ioristic sense. It is comportment—the way one carries oneself—or as von Eckartsberg (1971) has called it, "experiaction"—one's simultaneous affective/cognitive/actional engagement with the world. We understand other people in part through observing their circumstances and recollecting when we have been in similar situations; we assume that the experiaction too must be similar. We also realize where others are going when our present paths converge. Sometimes the other is known instead through opposition to one's own forward progress, as the Board came to see John Akbar differently through his interruption of the agenda. Where we are inclined to go from that point, both directly in relation to the other person, and in terms of picking up our prior course, also tells us who that person is—where/when/how she or he is going. My sadness, helplessness, and sense making at the end of the meeting said as much about John as about me.

The task of explaining my sense of John to my colleague was similar to the assessor's complex task. First, there was much more to the story than the verbal content of the Board's discussions. And of course both John and the rest of us were going multiple "places" all at once (for example, toward being responsible Board members, being good representatives of our professions, being capable of standing up for ourselves, and being calm under fire, as well as less noble "places" like not looking foolish, not appearing divisive to the community, and getting home in time to put the casserole in the oven). People always are avoiding some places, and moving on past others while they are on their way toward further goals. Another similarity to the assessment situation is that John's characteristics were not *in* him; they were *among* us. John was known only from the perspectives of Board members' assorted histories and ambitions. For example, some people mumbled about "rigid personalities that force your hand," while others spoke of his "intimidating character," and others of "circumstantial victimization." Some of us blamed ourselves; others did not. Finally, if we had been asked to develop a coherent characterization of John, we could have done so, but as in assessment, we would have recognized that there was no simple, single truth, and that we were part of the characterization.

Test comportment is a test of comportment

We know each other by where we are going. Where we are going becomes focal when we encounter choice points or obstacles. When tests are used in an individualized manner, the test items offer such opportunities and problems. The assessor, as observer, is aware of many ways in which the presented tasks could be encountered and coped with. The client initially is more aware of challenges to his or her customary or preferred ways of going about life. Tests present an opportunity to check, gauge, or prove oneself. For both participants, the items can serve as tests of the client's ways of being who he or she is trying to be. Tests provide a measure of the person.

We can discuss tests either from the perspective of psychometrics, or from the perspective of everyday life. We speak of passing a spelling test, or meeting the cut-off score for admission to a professional school. In daily discourse we may also speak of "a test of love," or "a test of faith," and we speak of contests as tests of prowess. Both perspectives refer to a basis for evaluation, a trial to demonstrate characteristics. Table 3.1 indicates that individualized assessment uses standardized tests in both the specialized (psychometric) and everyday senses. Each use of tests is consistent with the guiding principles in Chapter 2. That is, the approach to individualized assessment is structural, contextual, descriptive, interventional, and circumspect.

TABLE 3.1.   Functions of Tests in Individualized Assessment

A. Standardized administration and scoring (use of end products)

- Test scores indicate *general standing within, or similarity to,* some population. Examples: general achievement (IQ) compared to that of college students majoring in various fields; achievement in seventh grade science compared to national and school district norms; interest pattern compared with those of successful members of various vocations; Rorschach ratios compared with those of other ex-patients who have attempted suicide.
- These standings and similarities *assist clients and assessors in making decisions.* Examples: Am I likely to do well compared to my classmates if I major in architecture? Should I ask for a tutor in science? Should we release this patient to a supervised half-way house instead of to his home?
- Statistical standings and similarities also serve as a *starting place for exploration* of the ways in which the finding is both true and not true, and of what else should be explored if the person is to be understood.
- Standardized scores can be used as a *baseline for comparison with past or future scores.* For example, achievement scores and personality test scores provide a third-party view of progress for both client and professional. In the case of brain damage, comparative levels of performance on the WAIS–R (or a broader neuropsychological battery) may be the most efficacious way of assessing overall effects, and of whether these indicate deterioration or recovery.
- Standardized test profiles *may be regarded as the impressions of colleagues* who have examined the client with particular test items, from within their own theoretical perspectives, from their experience with particular client populations, and from their specialized concerns. An example would be an MMPI manual's description of persons who have 4–9 profiles. The assessor compares his or her impressions with those recorded by colleagues, taking into account the varying perspectives involved. The question is not whether their respective views are correct, but rather how altogether they broaden, amplify, or modify the assessor's understandings.
- *Clock-time for completion of a test may seem longer or shorter than experienced time,* thereby providing data about the assessor's involvement with the client, and hence about how other people too might perceive the client's performance. For example, when I find a person to be relatively uninteresting—easily predictable—I often experience that person as plodding along rather slowly. When the completion time is discovered to be actually faster than average, then I ask myself if I have reached premature closure and whether I am impatient to be finished. I ask myself whether the reasons are extrinsic (for example, having little time in which to complete the assessment), or intrinsic to the client and me and our differing purposes and values.
- Similarly, an *assessor may explore discrepancies between impressions of how well the person was doing and the actual scores the person earned.* For example, scaled scores on the WAIS–R that were lower than expected might lead to an understanding of how a client's confident, quick, articulate style falsely encourages his supervisors to expect similarly impressive conceptual achievements.
- *Finished productions,* like human figure drawings or Bender-Gestalt copies, *point back to process*—to a person on the way somewhere, from somewhere, in the meantime shaping and being shaped by the task. The assessor can use these finished productions to imagine different ways in which they might have come about. For example, what are the different ways in which a person might draw

TABLE 3.1.   *(continued)*

small but dark, reworked, designs? Perhaps being pulled-in but determined? Wanting to keep things within manageable proportion, relining to keep them in place? Despondently, heavily responding to the world's imposed demands?

B. Interventional use of test materials (assessment of process)

Development of understandings of the client's comportment:
- Test comportments are specialized instances of everyday comportment. Tests allow client and assessor to observe together how the client actually does whatever he or she does, thereby going beyond the client's initial report and the assessor's abstract conceptions.
- The situations presented by the tests, however, are less complex and more familiar to the assessor than are the client's problems in day-to-day life. Thus, the assessor can utilize prior knowledge both of the various ways people approach tests and of the different outcomes of these approaches.
- For the test-taker, the simpler, relatively removed (from daily life) character of tests makes it easier to focus and reflect on one's personal participation in events.
- The client's openness to reflecting about his or her comportment is facilitated by the unfolding of that comportment before both participants. That is, within the collaborative assessment context, there is a shared witnessing of something visible to both participants.
- The client's taken-for-granted, habitual ways of approaching and moving through situations become available for reflection and modification as they are recognized across tests, by both participants.
- The *client's moods, conflicts, dynamics also become available through the assessor's own experiaction* during the testing. For example, when I ask Ms. Mariani to turn the Bender paper back to its vertical position (rather than writing on it lengthwise), I find my back stiffening against what I experience as a glaring gaze. Now I am alerted to several possibilities: Was the glare a counterattack? Does Ms. Mariani feel vulnerable, that I am unfair, that her independence is at stake? Where might she be going that my request is to her a threat?
- Moreover, *as the client lives through a testing event* (for example, becoming anxious as the items become more difficult), *the event's affective/behavioral/ cognitive similarity to past events puts the client in direct touch with the past.* For example, 12-year-old Tony began the Bender-Gestalt by smoothing the paper, declaring, "This is going to be good," and carefully counting the dots on the first card. Then, as he went on to copy the next designs, he worked faster and faster, barely glancing at the cards. As he looked in puzzlement at how haphazard the last designs appeared, the assessor asked, "Does all of this feel like writing that English essay we talked about?" Response: [solemn nodding] "I feel good when I start, but then it seems like something's going to go wrong. I try to concentrate harder. But Ms. Myshna marks all over it that I didn't really try."
- Assessment events become *shared referents for discussions of similar events from the client's life.* Both participants know that they are attuned to the same phenomenon, and that it exceeds their verbal descriptions. The assessor can imagine similar instances, however, and can suggest these and ask the client for comment on how they compare to his or her situation.
- As assessor and client develop understandings of the person's ways of going about things, comportment with the next test can *surprise the assessor,*

TABLE 3.1. *(continued)*

appearing either as an apparent contradiction or as a compatible but different variation. These surprises disallow routinized comprehensions and premature, overly conceptual, closure. Understandings are revised throughout the assessment; even the concluding understandings are regarded as a progress report.

Occasions for trying out alternative comportment:
- The assessor may *disrupt the person's way of approaching a test item, thereby allowing that approach to become focal.* At the beginning of a WAIS–R subtest, for example, just as Mrs. Norman is about to repeat her disclaimer that she is not good at academic problems, the assessor anticipates and gently interjects (speaking for the client), "I don't think I'll do very well on these." The client recognizes at this point, and again as she experiences these words beginning to form during the rest of the test, that she has indeed prefaced her efforts in this way. Now she and the assessor talk about where else this has occurred, and what it accomplishes, both positively and negatively.
- This use of tests helps the person *to discover how he or she participates actively in shaping outcomes.* The focus is not on traits or capacities, but on process and options.
- As the client recognizes the effects of his or her shaping of events, it also *becomes apparent that it is not necessary to continue in this manner.* In Mrs. Norman's case, excusing her performance in advance had the unintended effect of bringing public attention to her educational level, and of distracting her from doing her best on the test items. Optional means of getting to where she wants to go now become salient.
- Coping with further test materials affords an opportunity for the client to *become aware of the landmarks that indicate he or she is moving toward trouble.* And hence the client could now look for an opportunity to pivot into an optional route. The landmarks are both externally visible in the terrain and recognizable through what it feels like to travel in that territory. For example, Mrs. Norman came to recognize that it was when she saw other people as "better educated," that she found herself explaining her nonacademic orientation. At the same time, she has found herself feeling small, pulling inward (even crossing her arms), glancing repeatedly at the face of the other person, and finding her throat tight as she tries to make her disclaimers sound casual.
- As the assessment continues, the test materials can become *occasions for trying out different approaches,* styles, routes, *until some are tailored as personally viable ones.* At first the person only self-consciously halts the old progression, smiling with the assessor in mutual recognition of the strength of the old way. Either of them may suggest an alternative, which is tried awkwardly at first, and then modified to fit smoothly into the client's other ways of moving through situations. Mrs. Norman was stymied at first, and just shook her head when she caught herself beginning to explain away her anticipated "uneducated, inadequate" answers. Then she tried modifying her protest to the simple statement, "It's been quite awhile since I dealt with questions like these." By the end of the WAIS–R, she had dropped all prefaces, and simply offered her best answer, with a questioning lilt indicating that she was aware that she might not be entirely correct.

TABLE 3.1. *(continued)*

- The assessor introduces further test materials, not just for pursuing new understandings, but *to allow the client to practice the revised approach.* Mrs. Norman simply nodded in acknowledgment when the Stanford-Binet intelligence test was introduced as an opportunity to practice; she continued to answer items directly, without self-deprecating prefaces. In other cases, use of further test materials may disclose limits of the client's adaptability.

- The assessment report's *suggestions are based on these instances of trying out alternative comportments.* The suggestions, thus, are workable: concrete, collaboratively tailored, personally viable.

- The assessor's *experiences of being pushed and pulled* in assorted ways by the client as they focus on how a task (test item) is getting done, *provide hints about what else the client is doing—where he or she is trying to go, who he or she is working to be.* These experiences can be explored directly with the client. When the assessor remarked that she kept wanting to reassure Mrs. Norman that she was doing fine, Mrs. Norman confirmed that she typically looks for signs of reassurance, approval, guidance. She had not been aware of her implicit requests for these signs.

- Conducting the assessment across a *variety of test materials allows both continued collaborative reformulation of participants' prior understandings, and emergence of new themes.* When asked to draw a person, Mrs. Norman drew a man standing with feet planted solidly. When asked to draw a person of the other gender, she drew a woman to the left of the man, smaller, tilting away, with her hand connected to his. As Mrs. Norman and the assessor shared their impressions of what this picture looked like, they agreed that the woman appeared both to be anchored by the man's stability (a variation of the "reassurance, guidance" theme) and yet also to be pulling against him. At this point Mrs. Norman exclaimed, "He [husband] won't let me lead; I always have to be in the shadows! I get so angry! But he does love me and takes good care of me; I don't know what I really feel." Discussion then pursued other instances of her feeling *both* of these inclinations and of her ambivalence about them.

- The above example also illustrates that *attending to where the person is going via the test materials provides instances* not only of simple patterns of comportment, but *of conflicted goals and the dynamic relations among them.* Unlike Mrs. Norman the client is not always ready, within the relatively short span of assessment hours, to explore apparent threats to preferred images. Nevertheless, a thematized concrete instance from the session may occasion later reflection, either with another professional or as the person continues to develop independently.

- Test materials can offer the client an *opportunity to discover something that the assessor has recognized much earlier.* Mr. Rothstein had persistently explained away his failures at work and in his social life as just "bad luck," "the way things are," and "things you can't do anything about." The assessor, after gently challenging Mr. Rothstein's fatalistic stance at earlier points in the session, but without getting through to him, asked that he make up stories for several TAT cards. After two predictably unhappy, pessimistic stories, the assessor enquired about what Mr. Rothstein thought could be some of the stories another person might tell. During this experiment, the client discovered that he was indeed the *author* of his "fate." With the assessor's guidance, he then tried out different scenarios, which were still his own but allowed a

TABLE 3.1.   *(continued)*

---

somewhat brighter, more flexible future. Now Mr. Rothstein could at least begin to construct somewhat brighter scenarios for his own life.

C. Communication of findings (individualized reports)

- Upon reading an assessment report, practitioners already familiar with the tests *find many of their questions answered by the descriptions of test comportment.*
- Description of comportment *helps readers to see the client in action,* to develop a sense of "who" the person is.
- *Test comportments* are simple instances of life events, and *serve as touchpoints with those other events for client, assessor, and readers.* All three parties can be assured that they know what kind of event each one is talking about. For example, during an assessment of a high school sophomore, it becomes evident that Dorothy's rushing through the Bender is similar to rushing through school assignments or making her bed.
- Description of *alternative comportment already tried out* with the test materials *provides examples that illustrate the report's suggestions.* Both the client and helpers can see how to vary the suggestions to meet their intent. Interventional efforts during the assessment to "make the Bender my own" can be applied at school and home by Dorothy and her helpers.
- *Instances of the client's trying out different approaches* to the test materials also *demonstrate to readers,* including the client, *that the client has already found ways to work toward change.* This progress encourages all parties to continue working together toward further progress.

Training and technical knowledge are essential

Within the above theoretical framework, the assessor must work from a base of professional and technical knowledge. First the assessor must be trained in the standardized administration of a broad range of tests in order to select test material that is most appropriate to diagnostic possibilities and to the client's problematic situations. If the assessor is not sufficiently experienced with a test to use it, the client can be referred to a professional who has that expertise. When I suspect brain damage that I have not picked up with my usual tests, for example, I consult a neuropsychologist, who can administer a Halsted-Reitan battery or the Luria Nebraska Test. That colleague, after hearing the client's history, may advise me to test for particular responses, to refer the client directly to a neurologist or neurosurgeon for a CAT scan, or to make an appointment for him or her to complete testing where I left off (parts of my battery are included in the Halsted-Reitan). My colleague has access to recent norms and knows their relation to developments in neuropsychological research.

Being trained in standardized administration of tests is important for several reasons. So that clients' productions and scores can be compared, either across time for one client or across clients, the administrations have to be the same. Familiarity with the kinds of responses people come up with in the "same" situation (the standardized testing) allows the assessor to note how the present client differs from others. Through standardized administration, one learns about the challenges and obstacles that are presented to the test taker by various tests, scales, and items. With that knowledge, the assessor can deviate from standardized procedures to select parts of tests for exploration of specific issues. Standardized procedures are a baseline from which the assessor should deviate only knowingly, for clear purposes. Thorough familiarity with scoring procedures and criteria is another important aspect of training with standardized material. One should learn to score while administering tests, both for efficiency and to make the scores available during the assessment session.

Training and experience with standardized administration allows the assessor to become familiar with his or her responsiveness to the different ways clients relate via the tests. For example, some of us find ourselves "pulling for" dependent, trusting persons, while others of us are impatient with them, and still others are inclined to run through the tests rather mechanically with these compliant people. Training encourages the assessor to recognize and constrain these inclinations, but also to use them. Recognition of one's inclinations helps the assessor in the ever-evolving process of learning about oneself and one's ways of influencing how other people appear in one's presence. The assessor's inclinations with a particular client also are primary assessment data, upon which one reflects in developing understandings of that client's goals, style, assumptions.

The following training methods help to sensitize assessors to how they do, should not, and could use materials. One should first experience all the tests from within the testee's perspective. That is, the tests should be administered to the would-be assessor. In this way, the assessor sees some of the dilemmas, restraints, and options confronting the assessee within a standardized administration. Through first-hand comparison, assessor-as-assessee also becomes aware of nontesting situations that are similar and dissimilar to these testing events. The impossibility of standardizing all of the test giver's stimulus qualities also becomes clearer from the other side of the table.

As another training method, one should be observed administering tests, by supervisors and by peers, and should also observe supervisors and peers using tests. Through comparative observation and discussion, assessors not only become aware of their style and its impact on the assessment process, but also see ways of modifying that style. As an extension of these training experiences, graduate students in my introductory assessment course are assigned in teams of two when they conduct assessments in mental health facilities. Besides offering one another support as they work together with the same client, they learn that there are many valid, fruitful perspectives. There is no one right thing to observe or say. They see that although they noticed different things, and pursued different topics with the client, the report (written by just one member of the team) presents the same person.

Testing and assessment experience with a broad range of clients is necessary before one can function professionally. "Range" includes categories of age, psychopathology, socioeconomic level, and subcultures. Familiarity with cognitive and interpersonal sequences of development, from childhood through old age, is essential, no matter in which age range one plans to specialize. Persons deemed "normal" by virtue of not carrying a label of abnormality constitute a vast range of their own. This experience with range is necessary if the assessor is to avoid the "textbook-template syndrome": in the absence of personal familiarity with a particular population, classifying a client into a textbook category simply because certain features seem to fit the text description. This mistake is akin to a layperson's trying to diagnose a skin rash by reading a medical book; until one has seen a spectrum of actual instances of the rash, misdiagnosis is highly probable. So is iatrogenic disease—"doctor-generated" problems appear where there were none before.

Interviewing skills are essential. Indeed, assessment often is characterized as an evaluative interview supplemented with behavioral observations. One must know how to listen to silences, to allow presentations to evolve rather than taking all statements literally, to be sensitive to posture, to pose inquiries in language familiar to the client, to be straightforward without being too "forward," to hold onto potentially threatening questions until they flow into the client's presented concerns. In addition, one should know how to conduct a standard mental status interview, designed to elicit psychopathological affect, speech, thought, or perception.

Another area of training is that of becoming familiar with environments, both those where clients are served and those where they live and work. Assessors should have visited the kinds of settings from which they are likely to receive referrals, such as schools, rehabilitation centers, psychiatric hospitals, detention centers. The idea is to develop an understanding of the concerns, constraints, and resources of each of these settings, so that referral answers and suggestions can be appropriately tailored. The assessor also should become used to leaving the office and going directly into clients' homes and neighborhoods. There the details of the client's world (things, people, activities, routines) enable the assessor to pose inquiries and suggestions in terms of actualities. On their homeground, clients find it easier to share their everyday existence, which they often assume is inappropriate for discussion in a professional's office. Assessors, however, have to learn the difference between social and professional presence in order to continue the latter when visiting in homes and work settings.

Technical knowledge of test-construction, validity studies, and norms is critical. For example, in comparing a youngster's Stanford-Binet IQ from a year ago with a current WISC–R IQ of 7 points lower, along with familiarity with statistical significance levels, one should be aware that the S–B contains more verbal material than does the WISC–R, and that the younger the testee, the less reliable scores are (that is, the less consistent the youngster is). The difference in IQs may not indicate a drop in level of performance after all. Another example is use of the MMPI manuals ("cookbooks") that provide computer-assisted descriptions of persons with various profiles. One should know that Gilberstadt and Duker (1965) descriptions were based on neuro-psychiatric patients admitted to a Veteran's Administration hospital in 1960, while the Marks, Seeman, and Haller (1974) descriptions were based on patients seen from 1960 to 1962 for short-term treatment on a voluntary basis at the psychiatry department of a university medical center. The assessor should take these contexts into account when reflecting on the cookbook descriptions of persons whose profiles match that of one's client.

One should develop a working knowledge of the works of several authors within a range of major personality and psychotherapy theories; for example, Anna Freud (1965) and Erik Erikson (1959, 1963, 1968) on psychoanalytically oriented understandings of development; Sullivan (1953) on a more interpersonal theory of development; Piaget (1950, 1951, 1958, 1967) on childhood cognitive development; Bandura (1965, 1971, 1974) and Sears, Maccoby, and Levin (1957) on learning-based models. By "working knowledge," I mean adequate familiarity with the spirit and details of a theory so that it brings genuine insight and appreciation of events. Working knowledge of several theories allows for a pluralistic approach—recognizing that theories are human efforts to make sense of things, that each carefully developed effort puts us more thoroughly in touch with a phenomenon, and that each effort will require modification. With this same attitude one ought to stay abreast of contemporary developments in personality theory, as well as in specialized research and theory in psychobiology, psychopathology, diagnostic systems, and therapeutic intervention. Knowledge of specialized therapeutic techniques heightens the assessor's sensitivity to personality functioning as well as to possible interventions.

An assessor must be familiar with theory and research on psychopathology and with the prevailing systems of classification. This allows the assessor to address other professionals' diagnostic questions and remain alert to particular features and biographical and prognostic patterns. By studying the historical development of our current diagnostic systems—for example, comparison of the *Diagnostic and Statistical Manual,* editions I, II, and III (American Psychiatric Association, 1952, 1968, 1980)—one gains respect for the difficulty of developing systems, and is reminded of their necessarily political and somewhat artificial nature. We should take diagnostic categories seriously but not literally.

Finally, an assessor's training includes the realm of ethical and professional standards. The written codes and guidelines of one's particular profession should be studied, kept at hand, and periodically reviewed. The most pertinent documents for psychologists include: The American Psychological Association's *Ethical Principles of Psychologists* (1981), *Standards for Educational and Psychological Tests* (1974), *Standards for Providers of Psychological Services* (1977), the *Specialty Guidelines for Delivery of Services* by clinical, counseling, school, and industrial/organizational psychologists (1981), and *Ethical Principles in the Conduct of Research with Human Participants* (1981). The *American Psychologist* annually publishes sample decisions of cases brought to the American Psychological Association's Committee on Scientific and Professional Ethics and Conduct (COSPEC). The *Ethical Standards* specify that one should be well informed about pertinent local, state, and federal laws and regulations. The assessor should not only "know the rules," but also think through the concerns behind each principle, such as the relation between the public reputation of one's profession and the usefulness of that profession to the public, and the balance between the welfare of a present client and that of future clients who might be affected by single-client advocacy. One ought also to heed contemporary social criticism of testing, classification, and evaluation, whether it appears in a professional journal, in the *New York Times,* or in a citizen protest to the local school board.

All of these "oughts" and "shoulds" are easier said than done, even though they are only a basic list that could readily be extended. Nevertheless, these are not prerequisites for beginning assessment; one usually obtains basic training in all these areas more or less at once. Practitioners continue to build on these foundations, and to modify them in the light of scientific and theoretical advancements. In the meantime, Appendixes A and B provide a general checklist for responsible assessment, and a sample checklist for using a standardized test (here, the WISC–R).

Getting the Assessment Under Way

The principles presented in this section probably pertain to all assessment situations in which the purpose goes beyond acquiring scores. These principles are particularly important as a prelude to individualized assessment, in which the client is an informed participant, working actively with the assessor throughout the session.

Consultation with referring persons

Upon receiving a referral, the assessor first explores the reason for assessment with the referring person. One does not simply accept the referral as stated and arrange an appointment with the client. Sometimes the process of clarifying the referral reveals that assessment is unnecessary or inappropriate. Example: A parent requests an intelligence testing of her child for admission to a "gifted student" program in the public school; it turns out that the child already meets alternative requirements without testing; those optional requirements are an A average, achievement scores two years beyond grade level, and the teacher's recommendation. Another example: A lawyer requests testing of his client in hopes of demonstrating incompetence to stand trial. The psychologist points out that the County Behavior Clinic probably has already conducted such an assessment, and that unless the data presented in that report seem contrary to the lawyer's knowledge of his client, a second assessment probably would not be in the client's interest, either financially or in terms of impact on the judge.

On other occasions the referral clarification, which typically takes place through a telephone conversation, leads the assessor to suggest a more appropriate assessor. That person, who might be a colleague in the same or another agency or someone in independent practice, would have special expertise with the presenting problem. I often pass on referrals to colleagues who specialize in childhood disorders, neurological impairment, or industrial accidents. Although my own work would be as effective as that of these colleagues in some cases, in others special expertise could make a difference. Another kind of cross-referral is to agencies that could conduct the assessment less expensively, such as a community mental health center, Easter Seal society, or children's and family service. Obviously, to function responsibly in this way, the assessor who originally receives these referrals must be familiar with the specialties of colleagues, with school and court procedures, and with community resources.

A major clarification of a referral should be "What is the problem, and for whom?" For example, a father requests that his 14-year-old son be evaluated to find out "what's wrong with him." Discussion quickly reveals that it is the family as a whole that has the problem; the assessor arranges a family conference rather than accepting the boy as the "identified patient." This example also illustrates the importance of considering who, beside the referred person, should be included in the assessment, and where the assessment should occur. In this case, it makes sense to assess the family as a whole in its own setting, the home.

Other ways of clarifying the referral issue include asking what decisions the referring person is confronting (for example, "Should I keep Ms. Petit in Personnel or move her to Purchasing?" "Should I use confrontational tactics in Mr. Gebel's therapy?" "Should we encourage Paul's parents to keep him in the special education class or go along with their desire to mainstream him?"). These concrete dilemmas say what is needed much more effectively than do abstractions like "Evaluate interpersonal versus accounting skills," "Test for integrity of ego functioning," "Assess severity of social/emotional disorder." Notice that the assessor should become familiar with the settings in each instance; in a sense, individualized assessments are also ecological assessments.

Another way of making the referral concrete is to ask about the incident(s) that served as the impetus for the referral. To further develop this understanding, the assessor also should ask about similar instances and about the circumstances in which they occurred. These questions are followed by asking about times when the problematic behavior has not occurred (the "when-nots"). This stage of the referral also includes inquiries into the referring person's understandings of incidents and the meaning of that person's terms (language), which often are quite different than the assessor originally assumed. A request to assess "self-destructive tendencies," for example, turned out to be about poor health habits (smoking, drinking, working under continuous stress), not about suicidal possibilities. In another case, "He comes home blotto every night" referred not to drunkenness but to dull, uninterested presence. Assessment conclusions and suggestions, to be helpful, must address these concrete understandings and situations.

Collection and review of background information

Because of the historical tendency of psychologists and educators to equate assessment with testing, testers too often have functioned as technicians, objectively administering and scoring their tests without regard for larger contexts.

Indeed, in the past, psychologists took pride in "blind analysis" of scores—interpreting from scores alone, without seeing the client. This exercise should be restricted to experimental and training contexts. The tester also was accustomed to providing technical information (test data) to someone else, usually a psychiatrist, who integrated such data with those provided by other ancillary specialists, such as social workers, teachers, nurses, and attendants.

Today, although still an expert in testing, the assessor is responsible for taking into account whatever information is necessary for properly completing the assessment. When the assessor is working independently with the client, then medical, school, court, employment, or other pertinent records should be obtained. Other professionals directly involved in the case should be consulted for information that might change the meaning of one's findings.

Some assessors prefer to look into background information only after the meeting with the client, so that they can observe freshly, without perceiving the client through the bias of records. In this case, the assessor has lost the chance to inquire into discrepancies between the client's story and the record, or to pursue hunches that arise from the records. I prefer to review records before meeting the client, and to share my knowledge and questions with the client. I check against "file bias" by first writing out alternative hypotheses that could account for the picture provided by records. I also ask myself what colleagues of various professions and persuasions would see in the records: "Well, Charlie would raise the question of borderline personality; Bill would point to the pervasiveness of self-deception; Arden would note the politics of diagnosis; Judy would want to know more about the family; Steve would want to know why lithium was administered briefly in 1979. Similarly, I ask myself of what relevance my recent reading might be, for example, on cognitive therapy of depression or on assessment of schizophrenic thinking. Toward the end of the assessment, I again ask myself what actual and fictive colleagues might have to say about my conclusions and how well my assessment data fit. These exercises go a long way beyond correcting for any bias arising from preliminary review of records.

Background data may be gathered also in the form of tests and inventories completed by the client and reviewed by the assessor prior to their assessment session. Clinics and assessment centers frequently send out such a battery as a matter of course. In a telephone discussion, I sometimes arrange with clients that they will receive and mail back to me some of the following: interest tests, a career aspiration chart, a stress checklist, medical and educational background forms, a family history chart, and an essay describing the referral issue. This procedure saves time for the assessment and thereby saves money for the client. Moreover, it encourages the client to think about the issues and his or her role in them prior to the session.

Preparations, seating, and referral clarification

One prepares for the assessment session by reviewing notes from the referral clarification and collection of background information. A mental or physical list is formulated, itemizing hunches and hypotheses, missing information, and issues to be pursued. Then one checks testing materials: sharpened #2 lead pencils with erasers, unlined paper, test forms, clipboard, stopwatch or wrist-watch with second hand, range of test material to select from as the assessment evolves. Especially if other testers use the same materials, kits and sets should be checked for completeness and order. All assessors should return material to its proper place and order. If the blocks are borrowed from a WAIS–R kit, they ought to be replaced immediately after use; TAT cards, Picture Arrange-ment cards, and the like, ought to be rearranged in numerical sequence or in standardized order of administration. Materials should be within reach and should not distract attention during the assessment. They should not be stacked in the open, where they may appear to be a formidable battery indeed, nor should they be hidden away as though they were secret weapons. One workable location for test materials is a chair next to the assessor.

I prefer to seat the client and myself six to ten feet apart, away from desks or tables, and at an angle of about 110 to 135 degrees. This arrangement allows each of us to see all of the other, and to regard one another without having either to "maintain eye contact" or to avert one's gaze after looking directly at the other's face too long. The arrangement also loosens the client's expectations of being interrogated and examined. Instead of presenting brief, factual, logical-sounding responses to direct questions, the client becomes engaged in reflecting while the assessor listens quietly; both allow understandings to evolve. If tests are introduced later, then we move to a work surface, but again I prefer to sit diagonally from the other person rather than squaring off face to face. Angled positions discourage both parties from falling into examiner–examinee or teacher–student roles. The danger of these roles is that both persons think in terms of right-wrong, reasonably short, already familiar answers, instead of being open to whatever occurs. Those roles also constitute the assessor as *the* expert, thereby dissuading the client from becoming an active participant in the assessment.

The assessor explains what he or she knows about the referral, and asks for the client's understanding of how it came about, and for any additional concerns on the client's part. Except for self-referred clients, most people begin with whatever assorted authorities have said ("My doctor said maybe I'm under stress." "Like you said the teacher wants to know if Sally should go in a special class.") The assessor asks for the concrete events and dilemmas, and for the "when-nots." This contextualizing of the referral introduces the client to the collaborative aspects of the assessment, thereby getting it started as a joint project. The assessor learns of the client's understandings, which frequently are at variance with those of other parties. The client learns quickly that perspec-tives vary and that his or her autobiographical expertise is as important to the assessment project as the assessor's expertise at interviewing, testing, and diagnosing.

Clarification of the referral is not, however, a once-and-for-all accomplish-ment. Upon meeting a stranger (the assessor), the client is not yet sure how much and in what ways to share. Moreover, early sharing typically is in the form of what the client knows explicitly. As a relationship develops, the client becomes aware of additional or deeper concerns. For both reasons, the assessor should check again with the client as the session moves along. Reclarification helps the assessor to understand not just the referral issue(s), but also the client's perception of the assessment session—which is the immediate context of the client's behavior with the assessor. Most often it is the assessor who suggests the possibility of concerns that go beyond original statements. Persons referred by mental health professionals, for example, often fear at some level that the assessor will discover them to be insane. As we get into the assessment and I think that we are both in touch with such a concern, I voice it. For example:

Client: [On the Rorschach] this is a butterfly. Sure it's a butterfly, see? What are these—feet? Oh, my goodness, it's a bat. Scary bat [glances at me, back distrustingly at the card]. A person can't always tell.

Myself: Sometimes you're not sure what you see. That must be as scary as the bat.

Client: Well, it can be. Do other people see the bat?

Myself: When people aren't sure what's there, sometimes they wonder if their mind is playing tricks. I imagine that probably happened too when you wondered if it was really you that sent that letter to Mr. Blackwell.

Client: [nods, looks surprised, interested]

Myself: With all that going on, I would guess it must have been scary coming here today, wondering if we would think you were crazy.

Client: What does "homicidal maniac" mean?

We then discussed what "homicidal maniac" meant to the client, how he thought it related to the initial referral ("Assess stress tolerance and dependency needs"), and what I thought at that point; I indicated that we would address these issues again in a little while. It is very important to establish just what the person means by various terms, such as "crazy," "homosexual," "retarded." Equally important is clarifying for the client what professionals do and do not mean by various terms.

Other previously unspeakable concerns that frequently are indirectly related to the referral, and directly related to how the client perceives the assessment situation, include a fearfulness of being found to be stupid or to be suicidal. Children sometimes think they are being examined as part of a procedure to turn them in for a better model. Even though the assessor in many cases may not regard these as serious possibilities, clients may. They often fear that long-hidden or denied frailties will now be found out, and that the assessor's finding them will somehow make them undeniably real.

Back to the beginning of the assessment session. During the initial unfolding of the client's understanding of the referral, the assessor ought to refrain from asking question after question. Clients respond to such questioning with brief answers and silence. To bypass this interrogation scenario, the assessor nods in response to the first answer and, leaning back in a receptive, unrushed posture, motions for elaboration. As clients discover that their own version of the situation is of interest, they find themselves elaborating, qualifying, filling in background, revising earlier statements. Herein an assessment precedent is set: it is all right to present apparently contradictory feelings, to describe without justifications, to puzzle aloud, to get to know oneself differently. In the effort to help the assessor understand their situations, clients thematize, sometimes for the first time, what it is like, how that situation looks to others, and how it differs from earlier times and from their desire or expectation. The collaborative, contextual, life-world orientation of individualized assessment is already under way.

The assessor reserves questions of fact ("How old were you at the time?" "Your brother lives at home too?" "Have you been under psychiatric care?") until clients have spun out their stories. This attitude encourages both parties to respect the importance of the client's perspective. Moreover, the answers often come up later in the narrative anyway, appearing in a form that indicates their significance to the individual. For example, I once held back from asking the age of a young man accused of attempted rape. As he told me the story of how his day had gone preceding his evening's attempt "to pick up" a street-walker, he spoke of his struggles to gain respect from the other men at work. During this presentation, he asserted, with fist striking the chair arm, "I'm more a man than a lot of them! I passed my GED by myself, and I'm married, and I have a son, and my wife's pregnant again, and I'm just 19! There are guys there 21 that haven't done so much." By not yet asking directly, I learned not only his age, but its significance to him.

I had not realized just how quiet I am during referral-clarification nor just how productive that quietness is until I audiotaped an assessment session to present to a graduate class. I knew that the client was not particularly articulate or introspective. But after listening to the first 20 minutes of the tape, my students suggested that he either had a prepared "con" story, or that he had been in therapy and had worked out his understandings there. Neither was the case. True, the man appeared to be talking on, with almost no inquiries from me; after the first couple minutes my voice was rarely heard. What was missing from the audiotape, but showed up in videotapes of later assessments, was my active listening—misunderstanding, confusion, impatience, and questions. My raised eyebrow, nodding, frowning, sitting forward, glancing away, squinting, or leaning back communicated my questions, confusion, impatience, interest, and so on. Following these taping experiences, I more deliberately postponed my questions. Assessors do not have to generate or exaggerate physical communication; it happens without effort when the assessor is genuinely attending to what it must be like to be in the client's situation.

It is largely through these quiet expressions of the assessor's understanding or nonunderstanding that the client comes to know who the assessor is. This familiarity does not have to do with the facts of personal life, but with a general sense about the differences between where the two of them have been and where they are going. Both parties will have to acknowledge these differences and take them into account as limits to contend with and as points of access to one another's ways of understanding. This process also builds the constructive working relationship usually called rapport. (See Chapter 9 for a discussion of this understanding of rapport, and its contrast to traditional notions about rapport's unilateral establishment.)

Later in the session, the assessor's questions may be asked more directly:

Assessor: Didn't you apply for a transfer?

Client: Yes, well, I don't know about your life in the university, but I don't think I've ever gotten anything I've asked for. Everything is politics. You just have to wait; it'll either happen or it won't.

Assessor: Oh, is that the same as what you said about it didn't matter what we find today?

An instance of questioning that occurred about 20 minutes into clarification of the referral illustrates a middle level of questioning. I told a woman who had relinquished custody of her first child that I found it hard to imagine myself voluntarily giving up my 2-year-old to its paternal grandparents and never seeing him again, as she had. As I elaborated that this was especially difficult for me to understand since it was now very important to her that she retain custody of the present children, she nodded. We fell silent for a moment, and then she pointed to a photo on a bulletin board near my chair, and said, "There's the difference." The photo was of my son securely perched in his proud father's lap. This resolution of my nonunderstanding led us into an important discussion of Mrs. Cronkite's feeling that she had never lived in a real home, that her husband resented the forced marriage, that she feels she does not know how to parent, how to show love. She gave up her son to loving grandparents to protect him from what she feared was her dangerous incompetence. (An assessment report on Mrs. Cronkite appears in Chapter 8.)

Comparison of the client's life with one's own, whether implicitly or explicitly, allows one's life to be a rich resource for comprehending how the other is both the same and different. Furthermore, a sense of common humanity gradually builds as the two persons struggle together, despite their differences, to understand the client's difficulties. Through this nonjudgmental, open, joint striving, the two people can regard phenomena unself-consciously, allowing them to emerge in a new light. They have established common ground through having traveled it together. (Chapter 9 discusses the relations among rapport, shared privacy, and intimate exploration.)

This traveling together, of course, encounters murky areas. For the assessor, there usually are some gaps in background, nagging but wordless concerns, distrust of conceptual clarity, and so on, that are not resolved in the preliminary stage. Some of these rough spots will turn out to be unimportant; others will be pursued when tests are used to clarify the issue; still others remain unclear.

An important aspect of referral clarification is the exploration of the "when-nots" of the client's problems; for example, under what circumstances is the person *not* anxious, incompetent, or whatever? Sometimes during this exploration, the client insists on the pervasiveness of some condition (for example, "I just can't do anything right. Everybody detests me for pretending to be competent."). Then the assessor takes time for the client to be convinced that the assessor does fully understand the profundity of that state. One may suggest occasions on which that feeling of incompetence must have happened.

Only then can the assessor move on to inquire into contrasting moments. One might say, "We've certainly seen your incompetent side and what a problem it is. Before we go on, though, tell me about times when you've noticed that being incompetent is *not* an issue. For starters, I imagine you pour a glass of water as well as anyone!" This process of openly recognizing the profundity of a client's state also applies to the exploration of the when-nots of nonproblematic comportment. For example, the assessor might say, "Well, it's certainly obvious that you've been a conscientious, devoted parent. But tell me about some of those nagging doubts that we all experience."

Typically, when this exploration has led to revisions of some earlier understandings, to mutual comprehensions, and to acknowledgement of remaining differences and puzzlements, a lull occurs. Both persons fall into quietude for a few moments. Then the assessor decides whether the referral issue already has been adequately resolved (a rare event!), whether to conclude the session by discussing and developing recommendations with the client, or whether to turn to tests for further exploration. For myself, this initial clarification process may involve anywhere from 15 minutes to an hour. During that time the client's "social history" (family background, education, medical history, and so on) has unfolded beyond whatever was provided by other workers and by any pre-session material provided by the client. Although it is imperative that the assessor be cognizant of this history, it is also important that "history taking" not be conducted as a search for causes to explain the later test findings. If the assessor is patient, much of the history will emerge in terms of its present importance—which is the most useful form of knowledge for assisting clients.

Taking notes

I do not take notes until I am sure that the client has already become a collaborative participant, and that I have allowed an initial, complex sense of the client to emerge. Facts and figures that emerge early can be recorded a little later in the session. If necessary, the client simply can be asked to repeat them. I do not record insights or themes the first time they arise. That is, it is important not to turn to paper too soon, prematurely "getting the client down." Neophyte assessors either are self-conscious about taking notes or are afraid not to write down everything. Conducting (and surviving) one or two assessments will be enough to convince the assessor that this initial delay is indeed worthwhile.

In advance, I have attached note paper, blank paper, and test forms to a clipboard, so that all are handy as needed. When it is time to take notes, I pick up my writing materials from my desk, and returning to my chair, I lay the clipboard on my lap. With my legs crossed, the clipboard paper is at an appropriate angle for writing. The writing is neither secretive nor distractingly within the client's sight. When I find that I am rushing my notes or not paying adequate attention to what the client is saying, I simply request, "Just a moment. I want to get these notes down before we go on." Far from being offended, the person usually is pleased that the earlier material is being taken seriously and that the emerging material is regarded as deserving full attention.

At some point the client is likely to peer over at the notes, especially during use of tests, when the assessor sits nearer. I explain that I am writing things down so I will not forget, and simultaneously I hand the clipboard to the person so the notes can be read. Because the notes mostly record what we have been talking about, they are not secret or too complex for the client. Most clients make a motion to decline, apparently embarrassed at being caught peeping. But I will not take the clipboard back until the notes have at least been glanced at. If I have to lay down my clipboard, I often leave it in full sight; at least I make no effort to remove it from the client's vision. These matter-of-fact transactions go a long way in building an atmosphere of mutual endeavor, where the person's life events—not esoteric tests and analyses—are the focus.

Sometimes clients ask me to explain the notes, because they are especially curious about the schematic organization that I employ. Then I pull my chair over adjacent to the client's and explain what I have been writing. I point out, for example, that I record quotations so I will have the person's own words; up here in the right-hand corner are some factual data I will need later for the report (age, address, spouse's name, and so on). Another cluster of notes has to do with a theme of "slowness" that the client and I have been exploring (notes on posture, reported incidents, my inclinations to hurry the client, a metaphor). The arrow from that cluster to another one is a reminder to look at the second cluster ("sureness") as another side of the slowness issue. In the top left-hand corner are issues I want to ask about when the timing is more appropriate. Whether or not I take clients on a tour of my notes, they often catch on to the spirit of the note taking and offer suggestions like, "Put down that those are the times when I'm late getting to work." Even when the upper left-hand corner jottings include notes like "hospitalizations?" or "right hemisphere impairment, temporal lobe?" most often the person can be told directly what observations led to these possibilities.

Of course, each assessor has a different way of taking notes. My cluster system developed on its own. Other people use preprinted forms with captions like, "Background," "Subject's View," "Habitual Comportment," "Problematic Comportment." The assessor records under the various headings as subjects arise during the course of the assessment. Reports can be developed readily from these notes, which organize the subject matter. However, I prefer to allow clusters of observations and questions to arise and develop without the constraints that forms impose; I do not want captions to prefigure my way of seeing the client. Moreover, when I use forms, I find that I begin working toward the report rather than allowing my notes to be a creative worksheet. In other words, overly systematic note taking can obstruct observing, dwelling, letting impressions change. For this same reason, one should not take notes as though one were a tape recorder. I record only when I know the significance of what I write, such as the relevance of those clusters, factual data needed for scoring or report writing, quotations that vividly illustrate the client's perspective, and issues to be explored later. I do *not* record whatever I happen to observe, in hopes of making sense of this information later. Sometimes, however, when the significance is not yet clear, jotting down a key word or making a quick line drawing of a motion can allow the assessor to let go of the preoccupation, knowing that one can return to it later. Checklists, to be scanned toward the end of a session, can assure the assessor that coverage will be thorough, thereby encouraging freedom during the evolution of the assessment.

Turning to tests

Often interviews, review of records, and field observations are sufficient for understanding a client's situation and for developing recommendations. One may turn to tests to add a "third party" perspective before summarizing conclusions. Similarly, tests may be used to help the client experience directly what the assessor has already surmised. Most often, however, one turns to tests when development of understandings and of a client's options would otherwise require observations across too many circumstances or over too much time.

In short, test materials are used either to measure comparative levels of accomplishment, or for client and assessor both to observe the ways the person goes about various tasks, and to find opportunities to try out alternative ways. Tests are used not to reveal underlying or causative traits, but to provide instances of the client's comportment. Tests are convenient, efficient substitutes for following the client around at home, work, play, or within other environments concerning which predictions must be made. Tests are simplified life situations.

One should never turn to tests routinely. Often direct observation of the client in the relevant environment obviates the necessity of testing. When testing is appropriate, specific reasons for using tests in any of the ways mentioned in Table 3.1 should have been formulated in advance. Otherwise one may use tests unnecessarily, wasting time, effort, and money. Without specific questions and anticipations, test comportment is less likely to surprise and inform. The varying character of the tasks and of the person's comportment may go unnoticed; scores may be attended to by default.

Turning to tests is accomplished matter-of-factly, with at most a remark such as, "Let's see if some of these tests give us something more to think about." No amount or kind of explanation is as effective as the client's direct experience of how the tests are to be used. Therefore, I prefer to begin testing with the Bender-Gestalt, which requires only 5 to 8 minutes before we begin collaborating on the result. Instructions are given in the standardized manner. I neither hide the nature of a test (for example, by covering print pertaining to "intelligence" or "aphasia"), nor do I discuss the nature of the test in advance. If the person asks, I give a brief, honest answer, such as, "Yes, this is an intelligence test. I'm hoping that we'll learn something about the way you handle different kinds of situations," or "This test might help us to see if those memory problems could be related to your car accident, to the possibility of neurological injury." I usually answer further inquiries with a statement to the effect that "we'll be talking about that in a few minutes when we're finished with this test."

Using the Bender as a first test allows me to attend focally to nonverbal, presumably nonintellectual comportment, and to begin formulating connections between the content we have been discussing and the client's ways (styles) of participating in those situations. I can observe as the person approaches the task, becomes bodily involved, and works his or her way through the entire project. With no responsibility except to turn the cards, I sit back and allow impressions to merge with recollections of how the person walked into the room, sat, and interacted with me. My observations during the Bender begin to modify and extend these initial senses and formulations. Use of further tests will continue this process. I also use this time to jot down notes from the prior discussion, often the first note taking of the session.

When the Bender is completed, I ask the client to sign and date it. In this way, the sheet is appropriately labeled for filing, I have checked the client's orientation for time, and I have observed the style of signing. Also, through signing the Bender, the client in a sense has owned the drawings. I wait a moment to see if the person will offer spontaneous comments about the drawing.

If I have no referral or discussion-relevant observations, I say so, but indicate with an example the sort of thing I was watching, and ask if the client has any remarks. For example: "At the moment, nothing particularly pertinent occurs to me. As you drew, I did recognize your way of being orderly—lightly lining off the paper so there would be space for each design—and asking me before we started how much time we would have. [Pause.] How about you—did you recognize anything familiar about the way you go about things?" Typically, the client smiles at the recognition, and especially at its occurrence on such a mundane, simple task. The collaborative comparison of testing events and other life events has begun. The client sees that the process of coping with the materials is as relevant as the products, and indeed that it was through that process that the copies turned out as they did.

The assessor may skip among tests, subtests, and items, choosing those most likely to approximate various everyday situations that confront the person. Always such departures from standardized sequence should be undertaken with specific objectives in mind. One must decide whether the objectives outweigh the importance of comparing the person against norms (via standardized administration). One must make a similar decision in regard to interrupting before the person has completed a test. Again, the purpose must be clear. Generally I wait until the end of the Bender, a Wechsler subtest, the entire Rorschach, a couple of Draw a Person drawings, or several TAT stories before intervening. This allows the client to live through a task, observing and sensing the similarity to other situations. If I jump in too early, before the person has developed this sense, then the ensuing discussions are likely to be abstract, defensive, underproductive. If I wait too long, such as until the end of the session, then a sense of what it was like to do the task may have disappeared for the client, and again the discussion may become abstract. Occasionally, as in the example of the "homicidal maniac" discussion during the Rorschach, waiting for a structured pause would risk losing a unique opportunity to explore a critical theme.

Although I tailor each session to the particular client and to the issues as they develop, I anticipate the following order of test materials: Bender-Gestalt, individual intelligence test, Rorschach, drawings, TAT. The Wechsler scales in particular allow us to compare a series of familiar school and work-related performances. Having continued the collaboration begun with the Bender, through the face-valid and nonmysterious intelligence scales, the client makes effective use of the Rorschach, observing and reflecting rather than merely responding. The assessor should be aware, however, that in this context, the Rorschach protocol, like those of one's therapy patients/clients, will be freer, less controlled, than those of normative groups.

At this point, I rarely am interested in administering drawings or the TAT for my own information; by now what I would see usually would be redundant. Sometimes nevertheless I continue with these tests because I know they will communicate meaningfully to other professionals. Most often, when I continue it is in order to help the client discover what I have already seen, and for us to work out alternative approaches and concrete suggestions. Both drawings and TAT stories are most likely to evoke interpersonal themes, which may not have been explicit earlier. Regardless of the primary function of the drawings, with adults I reserve them until a collaborative relation has been established and the client can make less defensive and less self-conscious use of the task. As for any multiple-choice paper and pencil tests, such as the MMPI or 16 P-F, which I have reviewed in advance of the assessment session, I generally bring any results that are either puzzling or elucidating into play when saliant issues arise during the session. If such tests are the principle take-off points for the discussion, then we deal with them more thoroughly. As appropriate, I use additional tests, such as the Wide Range Achievement Test, Trail-Making Test, or the Ishihari color plates. In addition I frequently set up role plays within the assessment session both for exploration and for development of alternatives.

Chapter 4 continues to describe the assessment process, and provides tables of excerpts illustrating the use of the tests. In the meantime, features differentiating the individualized—in comparison to normative—use of tests may be reiterated: (1) The tests are means of exploring the client's difficulties and options; scores are secondary to that pursuit. Only themes that are relevant to referral issues are explored; one does not review in the abstract all of the conclusions that might be drawn from each test. (2) Clients' ways of arriving at a finished product are as critical as are the levels and kinds of achievement. (3) The use of tests is genuinely collaborative throughout the session; the "results" are not merely shared by the assessor in the form of interpretations at the end of the session.

Being an Assessor

The assessor's task is to clarify who the client is in relation to the referring person's forthcoming decisions. Hence, assessment is of circumstances and options as well as of persons. The client is described as similar to and different from other persons, especially in his or her ways of participating in situations.

All of this must ultimately be expressed in terms of primary data—events that can be observed or shared with and discussed by all interested parties. Accomplishment of this complex assessment task requires a matter-of-fact task orientation, but one in which the client's active collaboration is essential. The assessor's expertise includes general knowledge of pathology, test usage, personality, and so on, and ways of helping clients to explore themselves and their options. The client's expertise is familiarity with his or her own life, as facts and events, and in terms of what he or she can afford to consider at this point in the way of insights and options. It is clients who know when understandings and suggested changes have been tailored adequately to fit their present lives.

At least at an initial level, the helping relationship is similar to that of other human-services professions. The dentist, for example, straightforwardly but politely asks you to open your mouth, and then goes right in with tools and expertise to assess what is wrong and what interventions are required. The dentist does not hesitate to tell you to open wider or bite down. Your dental problems are taken seriously, but are not regarded as overwhelming. There are no apologies about intruding, no embarrassment about equipment. As patients, we would be uncomfortable with an apologetic, hesitant dentist, and we would wonder about that dentist's competence. On the other hand, the competent dentist is as gentle as possible. We sense, without being subjected to declarations, that he or she is trying to make things painless. Moreover, if we are lucky, our dentist also attends to us as individuals, observing postures, glances, levels of secretion, and so on, and responds accordingly. For example, we may be told, "Oh, so that tooth is still sensitive. We'll wait another minute then." Although we appreciate a businesslike attitude, we would not respond well to a dentist who charged in without consideration for our apprehensions and personhood.

The above analogy applies to all human-services professions. It affirms the assessor's function as a special kind of expert. However, the assessor's expertise goes beyond technical knowledge, efficiency, consideration, and interpersonal skills. The assessor must also know how to attend to where the client is going—both intentionally and unwittingly, to how the client forms and limits his or her future en route, to what it must be like to be this person, and to possible pivot points at which the person could alter direction.

Table 3.2 identifies some pursuits on the assessor's part that impede such attention to the client's journey, to the client as becoming, to the client as process. The table lists an overlapping, interrelated series of counterproductive inclinations on the assessor's part. They are difficulties primarily endemic to beginning assessors. As one learns how both general and individualized assessment work, these inclinations are less likely to arise. In the meantime, they are listed here to aid the assessor in recognizing when one has fallen out of a disciplined, open stance. The groups of inclinations, although overlapping, can indicate which shift in attitude one has unintentionally made. Each group is followed by a statement of the ways in which the assessor's inclinations or actions are counterproductive to individualized assessment. Then reminders are provided of the alternative spirit and purposes of individualized assessment. Many of the "don'ts" are, of course, acceptable if they do not interfere either with the client's sense of personal responsibility or with mutual exploration of the client's life.

TABLE 3.2.   Counterproductive Assessor Comportments and Alternatives

Being sociable

This group of assessors' inclinations has to do with wanting to be friendly, to help the client be comfortable and feel good, to be polite, and to be seen as respecting social proprieties. In short, this is the "nice guy" syndrome. All of these inclinations indicate that the assessor: (1) is more concerned with being liked than with the task of conducting the assessment, (2) is afraid of accepting the power and responsibilities of an assessor, or (3) doubts that he or she can be useful as an assessor.

Don't:
- establish rapport by making clients feel comfortable—reassuring them that you'll take care of them and keep them safe while they're with you.
- chat with clients about what a small world it is—how you have so much in common.
- assure clients intermittently that they are doing well.
- offer gratuitous "uh-huhs" and "okays" to let clients know you are listening and approving.
- laugh along with clients' laughing dismissal of various problematic issues.
- flatter clients as a means of letting them know that you value what they value, and that you're on their side.
- reassure clients that, "that's normal," "that's perfectly understandable," "lots of people do that," "I've felt that way myself."
- introduce your own experiences as comparable to those of clients.
- finish clients' sentences for them, showing that you are listening, being empathic.
- address only the content of clients' narratives, to the exclusion of clients' experiaction and participation in the outcomes.
- revert to friendly advice-giving rather than continuing the work of the assessment.
- talk your way through assessment sessions, leaving no time to use tests.
- introduce each test with a reassuring explanation.
- apologize for using tests, or for a particular test's low face validity.
- belittle your status as an assessment expert ("I'm a therapist; I don't often give tests"; "I'm just an intern; I'm still trying to figure why they want me to give this thing").
- derogate your profession ("I know this sounds like something a shrink would say"; "I don't mean to psychoanalyze you, but . . . "; "I don't interpret tests the way a lot of psychologists do.").
- readily agree to stop testing when clients express frustration, boredom, or other displeasure.
- let clients interview you, as though that were only fair.
- share all of your own feelings and reactions during the encounter, so as not to be seen as secretive or elitist.

TABLE 3.2.   *(continued)*

Alternative approaches

The above comportments are counterproductive if they distract both parties from the task at hand. They may lead clients to believe the assessor lacks expertise, or that their problems are deemed unworthy of serious investigation. Worse, these comportments may imply to clients that they are judged too fragile to engage in genuine, straightforward evaluation, or that their problems are beyond the scope of mental health professionals. When you catch yourself wanting to behave in any of the above ways, it is advisable to withhold action, thus giving the clients a chance to fend for themselves and emerge in their own right. In short, take the person seriously, allow complexities and confusions to arise, withhold commentary when none is relevant, and wait to see what tests and your training will reveal.

Fortunately, this group of counterproductive inclinations usually fades away as the would-be assessor gains experience. With a little practice, one can get right down to business with a smooth but clear transition from the introductory social exchange to the work of the assessment. Likewise, discovery that one's assessments, as obvious or mundane as they may seem, have indeed been helpful to clients and to other professionals, goes a long way toward encouraging neophyte assessors to take their work seriously. It also helps to remember that although all assessments can be significantly helpful, none is perfectly so.

Being collusive or avoidant

These inclinations are additional ways in which assessors fall into sociability at the cost of failing to engage clients in their assessments.

Don't:
- avoid discussing seemingly negative aspects of the client's history, comportment, or situation.
- avoid topics that seem too personal.
- accept too quickly clients' early denials.
- accept the client's story as the only story without investigating other perspectives.
- accept clients' terminology at face value, in the manner of a commiserating bartender ("so they all hate you"; "your compulsive boss").
- totally accept the clients' presenting conceptions ("it's my inferiority complex"; "my depression acts up"; "it's just loneliness").
- avoid addressing observed patterns, in order not to be seen as accusatory or prying.
- avoid suggesting the advisability of treatment, on the ground that such suggestions are beyond the assessor's responsibility.

Alternative approaches

These comportments are counterproductive in that they sanction the client's self-deceptions and undercut an opportunity to help the client discover options. When you feel inclined in these directions, assume that you have been in an everyday judgmental, rather than clinical, attitude. That is, you have been thinking in terms of categories—things are either right or wrong, good or bad,

TABLE 3.2.   *(continued)*

rational or irrational. Your reticence to engage the client in open exploration was based on the additional assumption that you have encountered something negative about the person, and that it would not be "nice" to pursue the matter. The alternative is to remind yourself that the appropriate focus in assessments is the person's world as lived. Together you can explore how the client's perspectives and comportments both help and hinder the individual.

Being a technician

This group of counterproductive inclinations also has to do with assuming a fundamentally technical attitude toward the assessment—in this case regarding procedures as an end rather than a means, and thinking in terms of laboratory analysis and diagnosis. These inclinations indicate that the assessor (1) has not developed a theory of personality, especially not one that allows for nonmechanistic phenomena, (2) has reverted to taking action out of fear of becoming lost in the complexity and ambiguity of the other's life, or (3) has adopted a physicalistic framework—looking at quantification, outcome, categories, causality—in an effort to find simple, clear results.

Don't:

- race through test administrations, counting on the later scores to provide information instead of asking yourself or the client what is happening.
- focus only on clients' behavior and productions, to the exclusion of other observations, such as your own experiaction during the session.
- persist in administering all subtests of the WAIS–R, obtaining all three DAPs, and so on, without having in mind questions directly relevant to the referral issues.
- write down most of what you observe and what clients say, in the hope that somehow it will become significant later.
- conduct a unilateral interrogation, especially in the form of a series of prepared questions requiring only brief responses.
- talk in terms of nouns, labeling a problem domain instead of exploring process ("your anxiety seems to increase in social contexts"; "the problem seems to be lack of confidence").
- comment on or record comportments just because they occur ("You completed this task faster than most people"; "you haven't moved your hand off the chair arm since you sat down").
- address comportment at a derived level ("I see by your drawing that you identify with your own gender").
- address comportment as though it were a symptom ("The smallness of these figures is a sign of insecurity"; "I notice your eye twitches when you defend against my observations").
- discourse at a technical level ("You fall 0.8 standard deviation units below the criterion group's mean; "this is what we call 'field dependent' perception").
- pose questions in "Why?" form ("Why did you erase here and not over here?"; "Why did you file for divorce?"), rather than inquiring into circumstances ("What was going on that you decided to file for divorce?").
- accept clients' explanations and constructs as causal accounts ("So your inferiority complex interferes in nonacademic areas too?").
- focus on just the past or just the present (thereby building the impression that things inevitably are that way or were predetermined).

TABLE 3.2.   *(continued)*

- focus on level of performance to the exclusion of the approach through which it came about or of its significance ("You're doing quite well"; "Your spatial relations and arithmetic skills are well developed").
- stop assessing the first moment that everything seems to fit, instead of allowing ambiguity to arise again.
- force data to fit your categories ("That TAT story seems more dependent than independent; it's further evidence of your general dependency").
- present conclusions without offering clients the opportunity to complicate them through disagreement or modification.

Alternative approaches

The above actions are counterproductive because they look past clients to abstractions, unmindful of people's participation in what comes about. During such assessments clients experience themselves as determined by events; their sense of initiative and responsibility is undermined. They also may feel judged by external criteria, and hence will be unwilling to explore their situations and possible alternatives. When you find yourself in a technical attitude, recall that a major task of assessment is to be present to clients' ways of moving through their worlds, that those ways and worlds are not meant to fit neatly into boxes, and that clients are in a unique position to help us understand where they are. True, you must also reflect upon more than the client sees, and must draw referral-relevant conclusions. But the proper starting place is patience with yourself and with clients, letting phenomena emerge in their own complex right. You should ask not "which category of event is this?" nor "what made this happen?," but "how might this be described?" and "how did this come about?"

Being a rescuer

The following inclinations have to do with rushing in to rescue the client from the presumed pain or embarrassment involved in confronting limitations or adversity. Assessors are inclined to rescue a client when they (1) convert the assessor role into one of taking care of and fixing the client—the doctor syndrome, (2) are unsure of how to deal with the fullness of complex, distressing situations, or (3) do not appreciate patterns and levels of existence that differ from their own.

Don't:
- jump in with a plan of action ("Here's what you should do . . . ").
- discount the seriousness of an issue to clients ("Well, that's really nothing to worry about").
- be helpful *during the assessment process* in ways that are extraneous to that process ("Speaking of the stress of paying for car repairs, let me give you this address and phone number of a place that will give you a good deal").
- provide platitudes ("Well, of course everyone is anxious at some time or other"; "Life has its ups and downs").
- offer patent observations and advice ("As you get older, you'll appreciate your parents more"; "You should be more assertive").
- presume to resolve all issues ("We'll take care of that later; right now let's . . ."; "Well, I think we've got everything wrapped up").
- reassure clients that "everything's okay" ("I'm sure this will work out well for you").

TABLE 3.2.   *(continued)*

- help clients to earn higher scores, or to give "healthier" test responses.
- avoid administering tasks or asking questions that might be difficult for clients to answer.
- offer questions in multiple-choice form in order to save the client from floundering.
- reassure clients that they are not really different from other people ("I know just how you feel"; "Everybody has that difficulty sometime").
- sugar-coat presumably negative observations ("You're such an attractive person, I imagine that most people don't notice your stutter").
- cover over problematic areas through white-washed summaries ("Overall, I find you to be an intelligent, personable, conscientious person struggling in a generally mature way with your problems").

Alternative approaches

Rescuing or taking care of clients undermines the assessment process; clients' perspectives, limits, strengths, and personally viable options are not allowed to emerge. As with the sociable "assessment," here too clients may assume either that assessors have not seen what else is going on, or worse, that assessors (in all their professional wisdom) have judged them to be in need of rescue, flattery, reassurance, and so on. Ironically, assessors' rescuing efforts may thus imply to clients just the opposite of what was intended. Equally ironic, the rescuers in fact are in a negatively judgmental mode, disrespectful of clients' differences from themselves (for example, regarding a lower IQ or greater marital tension as signs of inferiority that *should* embarrass clients). A third irony is that since the would-be rescuer has not in fact assessed the client, efforts at helpfulness are not properly grounded. Such efforts are shallow. Moreover, they do not allow clients to discover how they co-author their lives, nor how they might themselves initiate changes in their authorship.

Fortunately, the doctor/rescuer syndrome typically fades as the assessor gains experience, learning that advice is cheap; that assessment is a worthy, productive enterprise at which one is indeed competent; and that to be significantly helpful, one must first assess clients' particular situations. In the interim, when you discover yourself rescuing/doctoring, it probably is best to suppress what you were about to do or say, instead allowing clients to speak and cope for themselves.

Being an opponent

This final set of counterproductive inclinations arises when assessors accept what seem to be clients' perceptions of them as opponents—persons on the opposite side, standing in the clients' way. In other words, these are defensive or competitive responses to (1) feeling distrusted (either personally or in terms of competence), or (2) not being taken seriously.

Don't:
- lecture to clients about your sincerity, expertise, or potential helpfulness ("I know you may not think so, but I really believe that these tests will clarify your situation immensely").
- attack clients' motivations or veracity.

TABLE 3.2.   *(continued)*

- argue with clients, either by attacking their position or by buttressing your position with more and more data.
- explain clients to themselves as a means of demonstrating expertise.
- thrust accusations or interpretations at clients as a means of "getting their attention"—of maneuvering them into taking the assessment seriously.
- blurt out the negative findings clients anticipated you would find, as a means of ending that tension.
- allow yourself to be intimidated out of pursuing certain issues or tests, for fear of confirming clients' view of assessors as intrusive, irrelevant, or whatever.
- silently administer test after test, thereby in effect "having the last word" without risking arguments with oppositional clients.

Alternative approaches

Assessors' accepting and playing out the role of opponent disallows clients to discover that the relationship could be otherwise. Moreover, while assessors are acting to protect themselves or to maneuver clients into cooperating, clients' situations are unavailable for understanding. The way out of this untenable posture is to postpone judgments about roles and competence, and to turn your attention to the clients' perspective. In other words, undercut the opposition by stepping over to the persons' situations, inviting them to help you understand what their lives are like, to put the situation in their own words. In this manner a collaborative relation begins; whatever differences in goals and perspective remain are matter-of-factly recognized as inherent to the situation, as issues about which you have agreed to disagree.

Questions and Responses

Question: Couldn't this approach to assessment just as well be an approach to psychotherapy?

Response: Yes. The approach is similarly relevant to interviewing in general and to intake interviews in particular. Specific purposes and practices do differ at critical points, though. If one sets out to be "therapeutic" during an assessment, chances are the assessment process will be compromised.

Question: Since uniformity of testing conditions is necessary for comparison of results, aren't your findings invalidated by your interventions during assessment?

Response: Comparison of *scores* does require standardized administration. When scores are required, they should be obtained by standardized means. Otherwise, the person's comportment and effectiveness can be described, including reference to the particular assessment context in which the comportment occurred.

Question: Don't interventions function as "leading questions"—don't they preform findings in ways that are avoided by standardized testing?

Response: Standardized testing is itself an intervention that preforms its findings. In testing, in research, and in life in general, our answers are limited by the form and content of the questions we ask. We should be mindful of the inherent limitations and possibilities afforded by both standardized and individualized intervention.

Question: On those occasions when you don't need a score, why do you use standardized tests at all, since you're likely to deviate from the standard administration anyway?

Response: The better-established tests provide representative samples of various challenges and allow me to explore how the person copes with them. Familiarity with these tests also allows me to notice more than I might with new materials. Finally, I do not deviate until I have a particular goal in mind. In the meantime, standardized procedures automatically provide observation situations, so that I do not have to invent my own. I am free to concentrate on the client.

Question: How can one be sure that the assessor's understandings are correct? Wouldn't some other assessor develop a different understanding?

Response: There is no single correct understanding. Indeed, each assessor would of course notice and thematize different aspects of the client's comportment. The criterion for validity is that the varying views and descriptions should not be discordant, but instead be complementary perspectives through which the client is recognized by various observers as the same person.

Question: Do you purposely avoid the term "unique" with reference to assessment of the individual?

Response: Yes, I typically do avoid it, since I've found that people tend to think that "unique" implies independence from general characteristics, as though a person were "a law unto himself." People are different, but not totally different.

Question: Would you say that you use standardized tests as projective techniques?

Response: Yes, I typically do avoid it, since I've found that people tend to think that "unique" implies independence from general characteristics, as though a person were "a law unto himself." People are different, but not totally different.

Question: Why do you not mention special education tests like the ITPA [Illinois Test of Psycholinguistic Abilities], or picture vocabulary tests, or social skill inventories? Aren't they important, and can't they be individualized?

Response: Yes, the individualized approach is applicable to most assessment contexts, including, for example, teacher-constructed mastery tests and management appraisal. I mention only some of the best known psychological tests in this text. The principles and practices apply to most assessment contexts and instruments.

Question: In regard to exploring the client's concerns about being "crazy," what do you do when the person is, for example, schizophrenic?

Response: We discuss how that professional label is often used to describe just the set of problems that the client already knows she or he has. Clients almost always know that they hear voices that others can't hear, that they speak illogically, and so on. DSM III's fairly straightforward description of essential symptoms lends itself to being shared with clients—who usually are relieved that the text does not assume that labeled persons are also evil, uncontrollable, and so forth, and that the set of problems is itself understandable.

Question: Isn't it appropriate sometimes to challenge clients' motivations?

Response: Yes, when the challenge is not an attack, but rather is questioning intended to broaden or deepen both persons' understandings. In contrast, when a challenge is intended or interpreted as an attempt to disprove a client's contention, it fosters an oppositional rather than an exploratory attitude. In short, it is the purpose and manner of the challenge that matter.

Question: What's wrong with reassuring clients that everything will work out?

Response: First, if the reassurance is offered before client and assessor have thoroughly explored the issues, then the reassurance is empty and perhaps will even prove to be false. Second, in the face of such premature comforting, the client either wonders whether the assessor has any idea about the complexity and depth of the issues, or takes the comforting as an invitation to allow the assessor to take care of everything. The latter reaction is the third danger of premature reassurance: It undercuts clients' responsibility for their lives when, in fact, how "things work out" usually depends significantly on the client.

It is appropriate, however, to answer an inquiry about an imminent assessment in a manner such as this: "Yes, I'm sure that if we work together, in one way or another the assessment will be helpful." At the end of an assessment, circumspect assurance may be appropriate, such as: "Yes, I agree that if you do [such and such], then things have a better chance of turning out [thus and so].

Question: What is wrong with reassuring clients that they are not terribly different from other people? Isn't it true that sometimes such reassurance partially relieves people of the pressure they're burdened with?

Response: Again, it's a question of context, timing, and purpose. If such a statement is part of an exploration of the client's co-authoring of his or her life, both past and future, it may indeed be constructive. The danger to be avoided is that of minimizing the problem or the client's part in shaping it.

Question: Don't the alternatives to counterproductive inclinations manipulate clients as badly as do the technological attitudes?

Response: Such changes are indeed intended to solicit a particular kind of participation on the client's part. The critical differences from technological manipulation are that here active, accountable *participation* is sought and the assessor respects the client's perspective and choices.

CHAPTER 4

Assessing Process

THE word "process" is derived from the Latin *procedere,* meaning to advance, to progress, to move onward. Individualized assessment directly addresses progressing. From the point of view of a human-science psychology, tests are simplified and specialized versions of challenges that also face clients elsewhere. They are challenges to clients' progress—to their continuing the courses of their lives. Clients cope with the challenge, whether defensively, offensively, or routinely, as they cope with similar events in similar situations.

For certain other forms of evaluation, it is sufficient and appropriate to address only the milestones that have been passed, the achievements left behind. Sometimes such data are used to predict what other milestones and achievements might be reached in the future. Some evaluations regard test profiles as products of various cognitive styles or psychodynamics, and thereby attend to process, albeit indirectly. Assessors can, of course, look to test scores and patterns for clues to process, which then can be pursued directly with clients.

Witnessing and Exploring Process

Whether studied in clients' environments or in an assessor's office, the process through which a person approaches, goes through, influences, and is changed by situations, is most accessible when the person is directly observed coping with challenges and then discusses what it was like, and how it was similar to and different from other situations. Clients, however, may offer explanations for what has happened rather than describing events directly and holistically. A major part of the assessor's task is to encourage the client to present events phenomenally—as they were lived at the time. A person progresses, after all, through a simultaneously affective/cognitive/actional engagement with the world.

To begin to explore process, the assessor first must be present to it. In particular, one does not ask "why," but instead asks, *who* is this person? Where is she or he going? What is her or his world like? Within that world, which things are seen as obstacles and which as invitations? What assumptions are made? What futures are possible from such positions? Process may seem to be internal to the client, but his or her travels are inextricably engaged with the worlds we share—the physical world, the world of past common experience, and the world in which our respective projects touch, clash, or cooperate. We know each other by what we do and where we go. Process becomes visible as style through first-hand encounters with the client's pathways, sequences, strategies.

To enhance sensitivity to process, the assessor should make conscientious use of her or his own biography and experience while with the client. In particular, it is appropriate to pay attention to one's associations, so long as they are not a continuation of an unrelated personal preoccupation. Even though the associations are the assessor's, they occur in the client's company and provide one avenue for understanding that person.

Explicit anticipations of where the client will go next allow the assessor to be surprised, to direct well-grounded requests for clarification to the client, and to reformulate. Throughout, the purpose is to continue reformulating, reunderstanding, until the referral can be answered in terms of this individual's life and until recommendations can be tailored. There is no need to search for absolute categories or explanations. It may be appropriate to judge, for example, whether one person is brain-damaged or whether another person fits the Borderline Personality Disorder designation. But to the extent that the assessment is to be individualized, greater priority is given to how the person lives her or his life—what the person's world looks like, and how the person perpetuates problems and perhaps could modify them.

An assessment is not intended to be a total portrait; the assessor does not look for themes or categories that would explain a person completely. The assessor remains open to complexity and to the diverse meanings that co-exist. Early confusion should be allowed to continue until the assessor discovers that a certain sense of things has begun to evolve. Actually, the assessor's presence, or attention, moves through many vicissitudes: openness to impressions, reflection, calculation, recollection, back to openness, and so on. The point is that unless the assessor becomes an access to the lived world of the client, calculations and deductions cannot lead to an individualized assessment.

During the assessment, meanings may occur to the assessor before their source is identified. For example, one may experience a client as evasive even though she or he is providing immediate, enthusiastic, elaborated answers to inquiries. The assessor should trust the impression long enough to search for its source and appraise its significance. In one case, the assessor recognized that the "evasiveness" of his client was his own impatience with the client's lengthy answers, which were tangential to the *assessor's* unspoken concerns. It was he who had not yet come to the point.

Another assessor experienced a client as haughty. He located that impression, after a while, in her turning away and tilting her head upward when he expressed concern for her. Then he noticed that the client's knuckles were white as she clutched the books in her lap. He realized that although she appeared to be haughty, she was also feeling tense and uncertain. He could now share both impressions with the client, pointing to their sources in what was visible and in his own differing reactions. This is another important reason for locating the source of impressions: The client can then "see" what others see, and can discuss what the observed event was like from the actor's perspective.

At other times, the assessor notices details that seem somehow meaningful even though the specific meaning is not clear. A lapel stickpin worn at an odd angle may be noticed early, only to gestalt much later with other "off center" ways that the client establishes independence. During discussions and in the report, a concrete example such as the stickpin can serve to collect or to recollect other instances of referral-relevant themes.

Ambiguity should be regarded as possibly inherent to phenomena rather than necessarily a deficient or confused form of knowing. This approach helps the assessor to accept both sides of apparently contradictory observations. The haughty woman was *both* disdainful of the assessor's solicitude *and* anxious about what they might discover. Apparent contradictions are in fact the dynamics of a person's moving toward goals.

While observing two graduate students making a class presentation, I noted that Pat directed Kevin and that she waited for Kevin's agreement. Upon reflection I saw that her *way* of taking charge considered others' perspectives and desires; but this solicitude occurred in a context of being the leader. That Pat is experienced by most acquaintances as both pleasantly serious and quietly dynamic has to do with the tension of her living toward both goals (directing and waiting) concomitantly.

There are many ways to be present to process. In general, one should remain open, not interpret too readily, not reach closure prematurely, not explain away what one has witnessed. To keep myself attuned to process, rather than becoming sidetracked in a search for explanations, I ask, "How could this event have come into being?" I ponder the evolution of a completed Bender (the task that asks the client to copy freehand nine geometric patterns) much as one ponders footprints along a beach. One might guess the owner's height, weight, and gender fairly accurately. But where was this person going? Perhaps just for a walk; the prints follow the tide's edge as though the goal were to follow the tideline rather than to reach some particular destination. Yes, the prints are relatively flat—unlike those where the hurried walker's heels have struck the wet sand sharply. Perhaps the walker was on a nature stroll. But look at all these intriguing shells that the stroller left unturned and the huge horseshoe crab he did not investigate. How could a nature lover ignore these things? Perhaps they are familiar; maybe he was just walking home along an habitual route. Perhaps he ignored these marvels because he was preoccupied—I wonder about what? Here, the tracks veer to avoid walking through a child's small, crumbling moat. Although preoccupied, the stroller noticed it and cared. . . . This form of presence to process enriches perception and helps one to address meaningful questions to the client.

Other queries that I pose to myself and later address to the client include: Where does this experiaction bring the client? How and when does it work for him or her? When not? What is the short-term outcome? Long-term? Is the person winding up at places that were not intended? Where else is the person going? And coming away from? And avoiding? Because people often are not focally aware of all these facets of their travels, the assessor must be all the more alert to those moments when the client is in touch with a pertinent aspect of his or her movement. Those moments are entry points for joint exploration.

In general, the assessor accepts a client's account *as the client's account,* and then suggests additions and modifications as they become apparent. Even these revisions are revised as the session goes on. When the client resists a line of inquiry, the assessor has failed to begin that inquiry within areas of the client's world that he or she experiences as familiar and traversable. Common ground was not adequately established. Sometimes, however, clients for their own reasons or because of severe disability do not allow the assessor access to more than end-product data. In all cases, as long as one's impressions can be documented with primary data, they should be retained and reported, even if the client does not agree, or does not understand. The client is an expert about what he or she remembers, and about what he or she is now concerned about and believes; but the assessor's differing impressions may be just as valid in a broader sense. Both views are important for understanding and planning, and both should be reported.

Table 4.1 illustrates the collaborative exploration of process. Many of the excerpts forerun activities illustrated in Table 4.2, on developing viable options. In actuality the activities of exploration and option-development are not so distinct. Both sets of excerpts illustrate the functions of tests that were outlined in Table 3.1 and the guiding principles of individualized assessment presented in Chapter 2 (description, context, collaboration, intervention, structure, circumspection).

TABLE 4.1.   Witnessing and Exploring Process: Excerpts

The client is a 28-year-old program monitor, a woman, self-referred for career guidance.

Assessor: Sandy, what was your turning the paper horizontally about? [The client's Bender drawing paper is placed vertically, but was repositioned twice by the assessor after Sandy moved it.]

Client: I don't know. It just seemed better that way.

Assessor: Most people just leave it the way it's placed. You moved it to suit your preference. Is that like anything you've done at work that Mr. O'Pake might have seen as "going off on your own [part of the referral issue]"?

Client: No. It's just that the cards run this way [horizontal], so I thought the drawings would fit better if my paper were running the same way.

Assessor: Oh! So perhaps what Mr. O'Pake and I have seen as persistent individuality may be instead your effort to be even more conscientious than other monitors have been? [Sandy then describes how her work has been demonstrably more thorough and more timely than that of all others in her office, but superiors in her present and prior jobs have criticized her for unorthodox, sometimes defiant, sometimes lackadaisical work habits.] Well, you know we already talked about how surprised I was when your copies of the designs turned out to be so precise. As I was watching you, taking your time but not erasing or otherwise appearing to me to be concerned about accuracy—you were chatting with me most of the time—I expected the copies to be haphazard. At the end I still had that feeling, even though each design had turned out just fine. I think I'm beginning to see what Mr. O'Pake may be responding to.

Client: [Long pause] Well, that's it in a nutshell. I guess I've just got to find ways of letting my supervisors see that I am in fact doing exactly the job they want done. I'd hate to do it, but maybe I should ask them to check my work en route so they can see *it* instead of *me*. At least that would be easier than changing careers!

TABLE 4.1.   *(continued)*

The client is a 19-year-old college junior, male, referred to the Guidance Center by a business law professor for trouble in attending classes regularly.

Assessor: You seem to enjoy the challenge of these test items. I have trouble imagining you being bored with Dr. Pressinger's course?

Client: That's why he said I should see somebody. When I'm in class, I enjoy it and I participate. And like I said, I write the papers. On other days I get up early, but on business law days I often just sleep in. I know I ought to, but . . .

Assessor: Ought to? Who says people should go to early classes? [Client: You just should.] What happens to people who go to their early classes?

Client: [Laughingly] They get good grades, get elected to offices, and grow up to be responsible executives.

Assessor: And who wants you to grow up to be an executive?

Client: I do. Well, I mean it's expected, and I do have the skills and the opportunity. . . .

Assessor: Who's doing this expecting? [Discussion continues, as the client discovers that he feels as though he has been pushed into his father's career line. An appointment is made for career advisement assessment, through which the client could make some informed choices, including possibly his present business major.]

The client is a 41-year-old marketing manager in a corporation-sponsored manager-development assessment.

Assessor: Many people who score as high as you did on these two scales have been described as stubborn. [Personality Research Form, high dominance and endurance scales].

Client: Well, it's sure right about that! My wife would tell you that!

Assessor: Yes? What would she say?

Client: Well, that I'm not satisfied until something is finished, till it's done right. [Assessor: Like?] Like putting up the dry wall for our driveway; took me all summer a couple years back, but ours is the only one that didn't buckle during these severe winters we've had recently.

Assessor: Your approach certainly paid off. But what do people call your being stubborn when they don't like it?

Client: What do you mean?

Assessor: What do your kids, or your subordinates at work, say about your being persistent?

Client: Oh, I see what you mean. I'd say the boy and my daughter don't much notice unless I'm after them to do something right. Then they say I'm picky. [Assessor: And at work?] Perfectionistic. [Long pause] I guess we're onto something. This seems to relate to what we were saying before—about my having trouble delegating authority. Like you said, it's not a question of my knowing how to analyze a problem and break it out into assignments. I just don't like to let go until I know it is done right. Lord, I just remembered [smiling]: my house painter told me he was going to increase his charges if I didn't get out from underfoot!

Assessor: Okay. Tell me some times when you *do* get out from underfoot.

Client: Do you mean like at home? [Assessor: Okay—whenever.] Well, it would never occur to me to interfere with my wife's cooking. And of course I don't insert myself into the sales manager's side of things. If anything goes wrong there, everyone knows it's got nothing to do with me.

TABLE 4.1.   *(continued)*

Assessor: Is that similar to when you were copying the designs [Bender-Gestalt]? You said you hadn't been "assiduously careful" since you didn't see what they had to do with your intelligence or your management competence? [Client nods.] Then so far it seems that being persistent and proud of a job done right has been an asset except in those situations when you're afraid that someone else's work will reflect badly on you? Is that a key to when you haven't "let go"?

Client: I guess that's fair to say, although I'd never thought of it that way before.

Assessor: As we go along, let's keep an eye out for what else might be involved.

The client is an 18-year-old college freshman, woman, self-referred for academic problems.

Assessor: I noticed just now [on the Bender-Gestalt] that you started out very carefully—checking the card several times, making small drawings. Then toward the end you only glanced at the cards, and the drawings became bigger and somehow more casual. Do you recognize that as something you've done before?

Client: I've never done this before [the Bender].

Assessor: I meant have you done other things in the same way? For example, if you're cooking with a recipe, do you start out double-checking the instructions, and then toward the end just trust your inclinations?

Client: [Laughs] That's exactly what I do! Unless it's a recipe I've done several times. Then I just review it once.

Assessor: What was it like while you were doing the drawings? How did it become different when you began to draw them on your own? Somehow you looked both more confident and more impatient at this juncture [pointing to the Bender-Gestalt reproductions].

Client: I wouldn't say "confident." I just decided it was pretty silly to take something so simple so seriously.

Assessor: Okay. Is that what has happened on your English term papers? Maybe your instructor was partly right—perhaps you didn't follow the instructions carefully, especially if you've already done other papers. And I'll bet since you *did* study the instructions very carefully at first, you assumed you remembered them.

Client: Oh my!

The client is a 60-year-old male stroke (CVA) victim, a lawyer, assessed for recovery of function.

Assessor: This graph [WAIS–R profile] shows how well you did on each of the sections. Here's Vocabulary and here's the section with the items about the mailbox and getting out of the forest. You earned about the same score on each of them, and I think it's probably at your prestroke level. Does that square with your experience? You didn't feel as though you were at a disadvantage on these, did you?

Client: No. Do they [scores] compare favorably with other lawyers'? [Assessor: Yes] Except the one with copying of the figures [Digit Symbol]?

Assessor: Yes, you're right, your score on it is way below where it probably used to be. This one [pointing to profile] has fallen significantly too; could you take a guess at which one it is [Digit Span]?

Client: The one with the blocks?

TABLE 4.1.   *(continued)*

Assessor: Here's Block Design. That's in the middle range of your scores. I really don't know whether it was much higher before or not. But you felt disadvantaged while working with the blocks?

Client: Toward the end I was feeling nervous—my insides knotted up.

Assessor: Okay. And how about when you repeated numbers to me?

Client: I managed to forget that. Yeah, that really scared me. Where's that one [on the profile sheet]?

Assessor: Here. Now let me ask you: How did your insides do on this [holds up Trail-Making B test sheet]?

Client: I figure I did all right. I just was careful to slow down. But I don't like that; it feels like I'm a kid in school just learning his letters and numbers.

Assessor: Again, you're right on target. You made very few mistakes, but you took as much time as a schoolboy to do it. Let me tell you what I think is involved on all these tasks where you had trouble. They all look pretty simple at first, but they're things you don't do every day, things that require you to figure out and then remember the principle. Especially when you realize that in earlier years you could have done these tasks more or less automatically, you become "scared" and tighten up.

Client: Yes, but that's preferable to faking answers—or throwing things [which he reported he had done].

Assessor: Indeed. And as we agreed before, you seem to acknowledge these new limitations and cope with them honestly when you are with somebody who knows about the stroke. We can make this recommendation to your wife and partners: Whenever you're confronted by something that's a little new for you, family or staff should be around. Another recommendation is that when you go back to work, you've got to limit yourself to things you know how to do by heart, things that don't require you to think on your feet. I imagine title searches and wills wouldn't give you trouble . . . ?

Client: But what about numbers? These tests all had numbers.

Assessor: I don't think it's numbers as such that throw you. See—here's where you scored on Arithmetic; that's not at all bad. And your wife tells me that you're back to balancing the checkbook, and that you come within pennies of estimating the grocery checkout total.

Client: That's true. You know, I vacillate between extremes: One minute I'm afraid I can't do anything, that I've no business thinking about going back to the office. The next minute I'm furious about being restricted to jobs any punk law clerk could handle.

Assessor: And sometimes you worry that you're getting worse, that your brain is deteriorating? [Client looks up, surprised, and nods slowly.] The only danger of that is if you had another stroke. You've probably recovered about as much as you're going to from the damage you have, though. [Long silence] You *will* have to restrict your assignments. For example, you shouldn't argue trial cases in court anymore; you'd probably miss some of the abstract points or unfamiliar lines of argument, like you did on this Concept Formation Test. [Extended discussion of other tasks at work and at home that he could or should not undertake, followed by a discussion of his embarrassment at returning to what he felt was "clerk status."] You've already come a long way in coping realistically with your stroke. Frankly, I admire your courage and honesty. But as you said, there will be a lot of ups and downs as you develop ways of accommodating at work. You'll make some mistakes, but a good way to minimize them is to respect those signs that you're moving into dangerous zones. What are the signs?

TABLE 4.1.   *(continued)*

Client: Knotted insides! And feeling impatient and wanting to dismiss obstacles. Or feeling like a schoolboy—that precedes impatience.

Assessor: Yes, it's important to catch yourself there, before you became impatient. And what were our suggestions in that regard?

Client: Here, I made notes on that too. (1) If there's time, just slow down as I did on "follow-the-dots" [Trail Making]; (2) if not, or if I'm not sure I'm getting it right, go to someone for consultation.

Assessor: Right. Of course, these steps are new for you, so you'll have to go slowly with them too! Seriously, it will take considerable practice. But since we'll work this out with your family, partners, and staff, they'll understand what's going on. Let's ask your wife in now, to explain our progress and then continue our discussion. All right?

The client is a 24-year-old man, arrested for car theft, referred by his lawyer.

Assessor: You mentioned that your parole officer accuses you of not planning ahead? [Client nods.] And that other people have said that too, but you disagree? [Client nods.] Well, I don't know yet whether I agree with them, but I'll bet we've got an example right here [Bender-Gestalt] of what they're talking about. You did all of these [pointing to early designs] accurately and efficiently, but look how these later ones had to be squeezed in on their sides. Could that be an example of not planning ahead? What I mean is, you could have figured out the space ahead of time, especially since I mentioned how many designs there would be.

Client: I don't waste time planning for easy things. I just know what to do without thinking. Corsky [parole officer] says that's impulse; I say it's intuition. If you don't have it, don't knock it. Besides you said yourself it [Bender copy] was pretty good.

Assessor: Yes, it is. So I guess going by intuition worked pretty well this time. Tell me some other times it worked well.

Client: Like what?

Assessor: Well, I don't know. I need for you to tell me. But I would imagine that another example would be getting ready to come here today. Some guys would lie awake planning what to say. I'll bet you thought about it a little, and then figured you'd know what to do when you got here. [Client nods approvingly.] Okay; so can you think of other times when somebody else might have to do a lot of figuring, but you don't have to?

Client: Sure, all right. I did some boxing at Haywood, and everybody said I was a natural. [Assessor writes that down and nods.] Or if I'm going out drinking, the way to do that is you must flow with the tide. Have a good time. This one time I wound up on the other side of town in this executive's penthouse. To this day I don't know how I got there, but I helped myself to breakfast.

Assessor: Tell me about times you've wound up someplace by surprise, but it didn't work out so well. [Client looks startled. "You mean . . . "] Yes, go ahead.

Client: [Avoiding assessor's gaze] Well, I guess that's like how I wound up getting arrested. I mean we was all in the car, and I was driving, but I didn't mean to steal it.

Assessor: Right. So generally, going by intuition works quite well for you. But it doesn't work all the time. When it doesn't work is when people say you didn't plan?

TABLE 4.1.   *(continued)*

Client: [Slowly] Yeah, I guess. But see, I plan by taking things as they come, one day at a time. [Picking up speed] See, I knew this fellow . . .

Assessor: Hey, hold on. I want you to tell me about times you *have* planned—perhaps planning what to take on a trip, or calculating how many months you have left on parole.

Client: Well, yeah. What the _____ does Corsky know. I probably have planned more than he ever knew how! [Assessor: Give me some specific instances.] Once I took this shop course, and the instructor really knew his stuff. I made this wood-based lamp, and gave it to my mother. [Assessor: And that required a lot of planning?] Oh, yeah, lots. You have to use a template and measure and check. And choose a die and figure what you had to get done before the shop closed.

Assessor: Okay, so the point is that you can plan, and in fact often do so quite well. But you don't plan "when to plan": You get in trouble when a situation calls for planning, but you keep going on intuition.

Client: When you put it that way, it's true.

Assessor: Okay, as we go on here, let's keep one eye out for signs that might tell you when to shift from intuition to "planning to plan." Mr. Corsky probably could be more helpful to you if he knew those signs too.

The client is a 35-year-old self-referred graduate student in a Humanities Department, who wants to know if he is "officially paranoid" or whether his university's faculty and administration are in collusion against him.

Assessor: You know, I think I know how that woman security officer [at his university] felt when you were explaining your complaint. *You* knew that what you were saying made sense, but until the very end, she didn't. Just now [during copying of the Bender-Gestalt] I couldn't imagine that this design [twelve three-dot parallel slanted columns] was going to come out right. I've never seen anyone do it that way. [Client smiles.] Most people draw an entire row or column at one time. You were all over the place—a dot here and one there. I was amazed when it all came together. I think she and I were both confused [client nods, smiling broadly], and I think you thoroughly enjoyed and abetted our confusion. At this point I find this intriguing, but I'd guess that in her shoes I'd have felt used. No wonder she began avoiding you, and being short with you on those other visits. What do you think—are we onto something?

Client: Yes, that is an astute and accurate assessment. People have to learn to appreciate the internal beauty of the universe. Instead, the sheep . . .

Assessor: Yes, well, I see that you regard me as one of your sheep.

Client: A likely proposition, but one that remains to be proven.

Assessor: Well, if you have repeatedly told your advisor, chair, and dean, in one way and another, that they are all sheep, you thereby make it impossible for them to want to spend their time with you. I suspect that you make us into sheep by nipping at our heels, and lurking behind trees waiting for us to be caught off guard. [Client nods, smiles derisively.] Let's see what else we can learn together. [Rorschach, including inquiry, is completed.] What struck me most here is that even though you appeared to be relaxed and fairly low key, in fact you were very actively searching through each card, looking for connections, building up a story that would take everything into account. Many people just say what this part or this one looks like [pointing to areas on card] and let the rest alone if it doesn't

TABLE 4.1. *(continued)*

seem at first glance to fit in. I have a better appreciation now of why you have
insisted on receiving the full year's syllabus, and why you don't want anyone to
interfere with any one step on your worksheets.

Client: That's correct. They don't see that there's an entire system involved. So you
tell me who's schizo.

Assessor: Let's talk about that. It's clear to me that you do not match the official
category that we call schizophrenic. You don't experience hallucinations, or see or
understand things in bizarre ways. You're not crazy. But there are some categories
that you do match and these categories do include the word *paranoid.* Not crazy,
but paranoid. What does that word mean to you?

Client: If it doesn't mean crazy, what does it mean? It's a label for not having to deal
with people who are different.

Assessor: As always, you do have a point there. But there is also some worth to this
label; it refers to being suspicious, competitive, angry in a certain pattern, one
in which a person tries to read other people's motives at the cost of letting
them be.

Client: I let others be! What else can I do as a "mere" student?

Assessor: Let's look at this card [Rorschach] again. You put together an image that
was complex, didn't leave anything out, and so on. It was quite amazing, very
unusual. And you enjoyed doing that and impressing me. That's the "good news";
the "bad news" is that while doing all that, you missed what most people notice,
namely that this whole thing [holds card up and out at a distance] strikes most
people as a bat. Or here, this part strikes many persons as a woman.

Client: [After a moment of silence] I'm not most people! I don't give a rat's ass what
they see! It's got nothing to do with me.

Assessor: They're all sheep? Look, your creative side is admirable, but your way of
being creative puts others in a one-down position. You've been doing it to me ever
since we started. Even though I'm trying to be objective, and even though I don't
know what actually happened on your campus, I find it very easy to sympathize
with the faculty and administrators. [Client starts to protest.] No, let me answer
the questions you brought to me. (1) You're not schizophrenic; (2) but if you took
the university to court [client's reason for consulting the assessor], the lawyers,
judge, jury would all see your complaints as paranoid—they would see from the
way you would treat them that you probably did the same thing with university
representatives. That is, that you did not look at their side, that you ignored
usual protocol, that you made it difficult for them to be sympathetic to your
complaints, that you looked everywhere for evidence of their inferiority and their
disregard for yourself. Whatever validity there is to your complaints, and I'm sure
there must be some, the judicial system would probably find in favor of the
university. You would be your own worst enemy in court. [There ensued an hour's
discussion, in which the assessor stood by the above conclusion, but pursued what
she felt were the client's worries about undergoing some kind of breakdown in the
future, and his deep (albeit vehemently denied) longings for approval, support,
and love. The assessor spoke of ways the client might moderate (not give up) his
aggressive stance, just to take some pressure off himself. She also said that she felt
he deserved an opportunity to explore his concerns with a therapist—somebody
who would hear him out, who could be sympathetic without taking sides, and
who could offer a place of refuge. About a month later, the client entered therapy
with another psychologist, although he attended erratically. He backed off his
threatened law suit against his university, and settled into a more or less workable

TABLE 4.1.   *(continued)*

relation with his professors. Of course he maintained his basic defensively competitive stance. He refused to pay for the assessment he had contracted.]

The client is a 22-year-old male, accused of attempted rape, referred by his attorney.

Client: [During Rorschach.] Jesus, you must be making something of all these insides I'm seeing. [Assessor: I am a little surprised; what do you think is going on?] Maybe you think I'm falling apart. [Long pause] Maybe you think I think women are just anatomy.

Assessor: There's probably something to both of those points, but not quite that severe. Back here [Card VI] you mentioned "muscles tautened" [sic]. Tell me what about the card helps give that appearance?

Client: The way they are. See, they're knotted and straining. This darkness shows how they're stirated [sic]. This is a larger section but it looks smaller because it's behind this section.

Assessor: I don't think you're breaking down, but I do think that you're doing a lot of struggling—trying to keep things in perspective but feeling caught, maybe held immobile, when you'd like to just do something. [Client nods incredulously but vigorously.] Okay, tell me—just let your thoughts go wherever they want to—of a time, any time, when *your* muscles were like that.

Client: Okay, but I don't know if this makes sense. [Assessor nods and shrugs.] I think of when my father chased my mom around the kitchen table with a butcher knife. He cut her too. She went to the hospital. [Assessor: And you were where?] In the corner. God, was I scared. I wanted to save my mother, but I was too little. My father and I, we respect each other now; but we keep our distance. He didn't come to my wedding. [Assessor: That must have hurt, and made you mad too.] Naw. Well, yeah, it did.

Assessor: I know it was different too, but were you feeling "knotted" the day you picked up that woman?

Client: Yeah, at least all afternoon. [Client tells that he was tired that day, had been teased in front of the secretarial staff, and had collected his pay check only to spend it all at a local bar on pinball machines and buying drinks for his "buddies," who left him there after his money ran out. Further discussion reveals that in his own way the client recognizes the dynamics of his having struck the woman who refused to go with him that night, but that he does not know what he could have done instead.]

Assessor: Tom, let me tell you what I'm going to say to Mr. Letterman [lawyer] in my report. I'm going to say that in fact it is possible you could threaten or hurt a woman again in similar circumstances, you know—if your manliness and competence are severely challenged as they were that day: being fired, the men laughing at you, the woman calling you a "kid." [Client nods, looking to the floor.] But I can also say that you don't want it to happen again and that there is an unusually good chance that, if you see a psychotherapist regularly to explore other ways of handling challenges, you won't show up in the judge's court again. I'll also write to Mr. Letterman about the vocational options we have discussed.

The client is a 24-year-old male arrested for reckless driving and resisting arrest, referred by his attorney.

TABLE 4.1.   *(continued)*

Assessor: [After Rorschach] You know, I can see just from how you sit back, keeping your distance [assessor gestures between herself and client] as you go through these tests that most people must see you as laid back. Is that true? [Client: Yeah.] But I can also imagine that there are a lot of situations when you also feel vaguely restless, kind of tense, like you wish you were going somewhere, but you don't know where.

Client: [Wide-eyed, but slumps further back into his chair] Where did you get that?

Assessor: Well, like this card [Card VI]. It's hard for many people to see that this skin could be stretched out and pulling against the nails while it's drying, unless they know what it's like to be stretched that way.

Client: I don't let nobody push me around.

Assessor: I understand. But sometimes there's no person there, and you still feel that way, right? [Client: I guess.] Maybe, since you're already feeling held down, you're sort of ready to strike back if somebody crowds you.

Client: Yeah, I guess. But that's the way it has to be.

Assessor: Not if you had a sense that you were getting somewhere, that you were on the way somewhere.

Client: I *am* going places. I *am* somebody.

Assessor: Uh-huh, [gently] you're somebody who's going to jail. You're somebody who smarts off with police officers instead of keeping cool.

Client: That's what you have to do. I'd rather do that than get pushed around.

Assessor: We have to stop in a few minutes, but we'll finish tomorrow. I want to leave a thought with you today. I think that in a vague, kind of haunting way, you long to be more of a somebody than you already are, that you long to be on your way, and that you wish people would help you instead of getting in your way. [Client: Nah, that's shrink stuff.] We'll have to agree to disagree about this. I really don't know how to be clearer about what I'm talking about. But I do know that whenever you're feeling "nailed down," you're aware that life could be different for you, that it would be nice if everybody could be more gentle with everyone, and you could take care of yourself without having to fight back. [Client sighs and sits quietly for a full minute, then leaves without a word. The next day he showed up early for his appointment.]

The client is a 31-year-old technician, being screened for employment at a nuclear facility.

Assessor: Considering the reason we're doing this evaluation, I don't think I should use the word "explode" in my report. [Both smile.] What's another term for that feeling you've had when different supervisors have given you conflicting instructions?

Client: It [the explosive feeling] only happened when it went on for a long time and when there wasn't anybody, except my wife, I could talk to about it.

Assessor: Yes, but it's happened twice, you say? [Client nods.] Anyway, how shall we describe the feeling?

Client: Torn apart. Like if I'm not going to wind up in shreds, I'd better quit the job or keep on drinking. I did each once.

Assessor: Okay. That's the language we'll use. I'm going to tell the New York office that you do meet their criteria for clearance under special supervision; that they should advise your company's personnel section of what you consider to be

TABLE 4.1.   *(continued)*

stressful work conditions, and that you would appreciate an early opportunity to discuss with your superiors your concerns in this regard. The idea is that you'd like to have an advance, agreed-upon strategy for handling any such conflicts.

Client: I wish I had done that on the second job. [Discussion follows of the ways the client could cope with disagreements.]

The client is a 6-year-old girl, referred for "gifted student" evaluation.

Assessor: I'm going to tell you two things you said, and you tell me what's different about them: (1) "I don't know. There's some. Is it five pennies?" and (2) "It's when there's snow. It's a season." [Client's tone is imitated.] What's different about you in those two answers?

Client: I was smart about winter. [Assessor: And what about the number of pennies in a nickel?] I was ignorant about pennies.

Assessor: Ignorant? Who says "ignorant"? [Client, giggling: Eddie, he's my brother. He's in fifth grade.] But you knew the right answer; five is correct. What's ignorant about that?

Client: I didn't know if I was sure. I didn't know ahead of time if it was right. [Assessor: If I hadn't kept at you, do you think you would have guessed by yourself?] Nope, I mighta made a mistake.

Assessor: Here's a new test [Stanford Binet]. This time the rules are that you're supposed to guess, even if you might be wrong. Okay? [Assessor continues with the S-B, documenting that client in fact has been earning misleadingly low scores because of her fear of looking ignorant.] Marie, you know what? I think you were "smart" when you guessed. I'm going to suggest to your mother and father that they tell Eddie that sometimes it's "ignorant" not to guess. What do you think about that?

Client: Eddie says you're not allowed to guess at school or kids'll make fun of you.

Assessor: Maybe they do sometimes, especially if you're being silly. Let's practice some more guessing, and see if you can tell when it's silly and when it's not.

The above clients were not unusually responsive or reflective. The transcription does, however, make the tempo seem faster than it was. At the time, there were many pauses within and between sentences and between interchanges. For the sake of economy, these excerpts do not show the gradual evolution of the dialogue. In addition, the false starts, unintelligible mumblings, and "ums" and "ahs" have been deleted. The excerpts do not show the long periods of working and observing, during which the participants do not converse.

The assessor does not mention everything that seems interesting; interjections are carefully selected and timed, are calculated to reach clients at their present state of awareness, and are all referral-relevant. (The brief identifications of clients preceding the excerpts are not the clarified referrals, but are meant only to provide the reader with a brief orientation.)

The assessor's Rorschach remarks were not mere intuitions, but were based also on empirical research, most often that reported by Exner (1974, 1978).

This research is particularly useful in that it reports the relations of test patterns to actual life events, such as going through a divorce or waiting for the results of a gross anatomy examination. The remarks addressed to clients are not based only on a single, just-observed comportment. Rather, prior observations of similar comportment have suggested that it would be productive to share these related impressions with the client.

One does not simply "dream up" daily life parallels to clients' test comportment as one goes along. Comportment has been observed directly from the moment the client knocked on the office door. The person's knocking, greeting, and way of walking into the room and taking a chair are all life events. Comparing these to test comportment helps the assessor to look for parallels with preassessment events.

These direct observations also provide a link for my graduate student assessors with two of their training exercises. First, each time a student encounters a distinctive production (DAP or Bender, for example) with a volunteer "client," the student later reproduces that drawing several times. The student tries different approaches and notes his or her own posture, breathing, attention, and so forth, as for instance, one draws tiny, light figures in the lower corner of the page, and later draws large, bold, one-per-page figures. This exercise attunes one to what it may be like to be the client in those moments. The light lines, for example, may be tenuous, delicate, or evasive; all are (nonexclusive) possibilities. The second exercise is to notice how people go about everyday tasks, such as short-order cooking, waiting tables, mowing a lawn, driving, carrying on a conversation, conducting a media interview, and so on. Assessment attunement develops as one has imagined how the cook, waitress, mower, driver, whatever, would approach a DAP, Bender, or Rorschach.

I have developed a stock of common tactics people employ in carrying out school and household tasks and in entering new social situations. After observing a copy Bender evolve, I might remark that "I'm reminded of a friend who cleans house by starting with windows, discovers a cobweb in the casing, begins dusting all corners, discovers fingerprints around a light switch, goes to the closet for a sponge, and is surprised to find the windows only half done." I would then indicate the step-by-step parallel with the Bender's evolution. This client might respond, "No, no. I always stick to one thing at a time till it's finished. But I do go back to wipe up streaks in the midst of washing another pane. My husband says I'm deceptively unmethodical for being such a meticulous person." It does not matter if my comparison is not accurate, so long as the client can use it as a starting point for providing actual instances similar to the Bender performance.

Finally, reading excerpts such as those in Table 4.1 often dissolves assessors' reservations about sharing written reports with clients. What makes a difference is the way the assessment was conducted. Its findings were not just judgmental, but rather took into account the person's own view of the situation. The person's approaches were not viewed as good or bad in themselves, but as working for the client in some circumstances and for some purposes, and against him or her in others. The assessor's focus on actual events—primary data—

allowed the client to be an active, genuinely informed participant. The written report reviews this collaborative assessment; it does not surprise, offend, or mystify the client. The assessor need not fear the clients' response to reading the report.

Developing Options

Table 4.1 has illustrated how an assessor can help clients to see that existing patterns may not be necessary patterns, that clients can author their lives differently. However, these discoveries are rarely sufficient to initiate change. A person must find himself or herself already functioning in a different way before that possibility is fully experienced as personally viable. Therefore trying out alternatives during the assessment is intended to serve three related functions: (1) to explore just what is personally viable—what fits the person's sense of who he or she has been and where he or she wants to go from there; (2) to help the client recognize landmarks—signs that one is moving toward trouble—and to locate pivot points where the client could shift to an optional route to reach the destination; and (3) to practice taking that optional route, so that it feels familiar and reliable and can be taken again on other journeys.

Efforts to develop options continue the assessment of who the person is. The client may discover further aspects of his or her circumstances that should be taken into account. For example, a secretary noted that she could indeed ask her supervisor to clarify instructions, but now she realizes that she could not ask in front of the other secretaries. Moreover, a client may encounter additional motivations that the old comportment served. While practicing drawing Bender designs with lighter strokes and less concern for perfection, another client remarked: "You know it is frightening to feel the heaviness of having to do it just exactly 'their' way; but up here [lightly skimming over the paper instead of darkly tracing] I realized that I'm free to take 'their' demands lightly, and go my own way. But I don't know what my way is." TAT stories later elaborated on the ways the client had resented the burden of others' demands and yet had diligently answered them rather than risk failure on her own. It is in these practicings of alternative approaches that self-deceptions, incompatible goals, and other previously nonfocal concerns—in short, unconscious motivations—become concretely available for collaborative exploration. These pursuits usually occur after the assessment is well under way. Earlier phases of assessment typically emphasize discovering and describing *what* the client does. Previously unexamined assumptions and habitual, taken-for-granted comportment become apparent well before conflicted, dynamic comportment is evident.

Trying out alternatives early in the assessment serves to explore which of these options are already available for the client. I find it helpful to ask myself the "when/when-not?" question as I notice the person taking some particular approach. To protect myself from assuming that what I am witnessing is the only approach this person takes, I consider the client's present circumstance and how different circumstances might promote different comportment. This reflection leads me to intervene with suggestions that help to clarify where different alternatives should be developed. Although more practicing occurs toward the end of the assessment, it typically arises in earlier form as a "trying out."

I have purposefully used the term "different comportment," rather than "new comportment." For an optional route to be personally viable, it must be a variation of present approaches; it must branch off from where the client is now, and it must accommodate familiar action. Using the client's terms, such as "lightly," "heaviness," and "doing it their way" in the example above, can help the client to recognize what is familiar in a different approach. While inquiring into the "geography" of a client's journey—where he or she is going, away from what, among what, and so forth—I also ask "for whom?" Sometimes clients know explicitly; other times the answer remains vague. It may be helpful to ask, "Who would be proud to see you do this?" Or who would be surprised, jealous, or angry?

The excerpts in Table 4.2 illustrate the development of personally viable options.

TABLE 4.2.   Developing Options: Excerpts

The client is a 32-year-old woman, referred for assessment of "chronic depression."

Assessor: Some people just automatically turn these cards over, but you waited for me to do it . . .

Client: Oh, I didn't know I was supposed to turn them. You didn't tell me to, did you?

Assessor: No. Either way is fine. But I was reminded of how you waited outside my door instead of knocking. What would you say was the same?

Client: I don't see anything wrong about waiting. I was taught to be polite.

Assessor: I see. And what would be the opposite of polite?

Client: Pushy. Getting what you want at someone else's expense.

Assessor: I wonder if being polite isn't sometimes at *your* expense? You must have felt a little apprehensive waiting in the hall, wondering if I was going to remember.

Client: No. [Assessor: What then?] Impatient. No offense, but frankly I heard you laughing on the phone, and it was on my time.

Assessor: I'll bet you were impatient that I was writing instead of turning the cards.

Client: Well, yes. But you're the psychologist.

Assessor: I'd like to try an experiment. Let's start over. [Assessor lays out the Bender cards and new paper.] But this time, turn the cards yourself if you feel like it. [Assessor repeats original instructions.]

Client: [After turning four cards] Are you going to tell me what this experiment is about?

Assessor: Sure. And by the way, your inquiry just now strikes me as quite appropriate, not the least bit impolite. I was wondering if turning the cards felt all right.

Client: Well, yes. You said I could.

Assessor: So it's not just a question of being polite, but also of waiting for permission. [Client looks startled and nods.] And waiting can be frustrating, especially when other people are not being considerate of your deference.

Client: My what?

TABLE 4.2.   *(continued)*

Assessor: Deference—putting the other person's initiative or plans ahead of yours. I can imagine that sometimes you could become quietly teed-off? [Client makes a dismissing gesture with her hands, but nods.] Being polite while you're wondering if you're being taken advantage of can be awfully wearing. [Testing and discussion continue.]

Client: This [Block Design] was harder than the others. [Assessor: What seemed harder?] You didn't say whether you were counting errors or just timing me or what. I didn't know what to concentrate my effort on. I felt like quitting, but you're not supposed to.

Assessor: And being caught in that bind, you were also a little angry. You did hang in, but you were glaring at me from time to time. [Client nods hesitantly.] You know, in a different situation I might have tried to avoid you so I wouldn't risk having you mad at me.

Client: But I was the one on the spot. You were in charge.

Assessor: Granted, I'm in charge, but let's do another experiment to see how you can avoid being "on the spot." Maybe ask for clarification so you don't have to wonder, or choose what *you* think is most important. [After re-administering the Block Design subtest twice, up through the fifth design, the assessor pointed out that both she and the client felt more comfortable. Through the remaining subtests, the client practiced asking for clarification.]

Client: [At the beginning of Rorschach inquiry] You didn't tell me I was supposed to explain everything the first time!

Assessor: You weren't. Going back through the cards this way is standard procedure. What's interesting is that you assumed I was criticizing you. And in turn I felt just now that you were criticizing me for putting you in an awkward place. I'm beginning to see how both you and Marianne [neighbor] are right. I'll bet she *does* avoid you, leaving you politely waiting again, but that probably happens after she has sensed your unspoken criticism.

Client: Maybe so [silence]. But I don't see what you expect me to do. [Both laugh in recognition of a familiar theme.] Okay, as you've been telling me, I guess the question is what I expect and what I could initiate. But that is not easy to do, you know. [At the end of the session assessor and client summarize the ways the client can recognize when she is setting herself up to become resentful. They role-play successful interchanges with the neighbor. They agree that behaviorally oriented counseling might help her to avoid the trap of becoming resentful in nondirective therapy, and help her to take more responsibility for her own action.]

The client is a 16-year-old high school junior, female, referred for declining grades.

Client: This is horrid [DAP]. I can't draw. This didn't come out right at all.

Assessor: Okay. If your *were* an artist what would it look like?

Client: Like an artist's drawing! [Assessor smiles, gestures for client to continue.] You know, no erasures, confident lines, perfect rendition of an elegant woman.

Assessor: Uh-huh [both laugh]. So here we are again, with you comparing yourself to perfection! That sure is a rough thing to be doing to yourself so often.

Client: Yeah, and the worst part is that I don't know when I'm doing it.

Assessor: There's hope! You knew you'd done it this time! But I'd like to pursue something else here. If you could draw well, this drawing would have been of an elegant woman? [Client blushes, nods hesitantly.] Let's draw it with words. What about the arms—what effect were you after?

TABLE 4.2. *(continued)*

Client: This arm should be gesturing emphatically but gracefully. This one should fall easily to her side. [Client illustrates, although remaining seated.]

Assessor: Yes! Look at you! You're doing it. Granted, you're not standing, and it was just a quick gesture, but it was certainly more "elegant" than this woman [DAP]. Kind of symbolic, isn't it? Instead of trying out, practicing, being elegant, you and she [DAP] hide your hands behind your back? [Client and assessor chuckle.] Like a lot of young women, you're not sure whether or not to hide the fact that your breasts have developed? [Assessor points to erasures of lines indicating sizes of breasts. Client nods; after further discussion, assessor asks client to draw her elegant woman, even though it won't be perfect.]

The client is a 21-year-old female graduate student who volunteered for a practice assessment during class.

Assessor: So you have often behaved as though things were against you, as was the case in your TAT stories? [Student: I certainly have. This even came up in my peer counseling session last week.] All right. Do you have some concrete instances you wouldn't mind sharing with us?

Student: Well, I barely could believe that I had actually graduated from college, and friends had to convince me that I should apply to a master's program. Now people are telling me I should apply to the doctoral program. I just never thought that I could be that sort of person.

Assessor: Wait a minute. That sounds more like "level of aspiration" than what we were talking about before. [Student: What do you mean?] I'm not sure yet. Tell us some more instances. [Student goes on with further instances until finally she rejects the "against me" theme and renames it "aiming low." Discussion also pursues the student's readiness to agree with others' opinions.] Do you remember this card [TAT #10]? Well, you told a story of two older persons quietly dancing together. Did you know that some describe the man as sneering down at the woman?

Student: Oh my! I didn't see that before. That surely could be.

Assessor: There you go again! [Student laughs and asks a classmate to recount a similar experience they have had together.] Okay, when does this "taking the other's stance" work out well for you? For example, I can see that your classmates feel you understand them and are gentle with them; and they in turn respect you. [Classmates offer other variations along these lines, plus instances of when she had given up her own point of view prematurely.]

Client: Let me summarize the "landmarks" of when I'm moving into "aiming low" or "giving priority to the other's stance." It's when I'm in unfamiliar territory and regard others as experts. I find myself pulling back, both figuratively and literally—like wanting to hide. And from there I find myself glancing into the faces of others, looking for cues.

Assessor: On this card [TAT 3BM], you described a young woman catnapping before finishing cutting out her pattern. Sounds pretty evasive to me! How about this gun here? [The object on the card is ambiguous.]

Student: Each to her own! [We all laugh in celebration.] No, seriously, I can see the gun—or maybe it could be a hypodermic in today's times. It surely could be a gun; maybe she's shot somebody or is thinking of killing herself. Yes, I can certainly see your point. But I think that for myself, I'll stick to my story. [More congratulations from the class.] Wow! This stuff is powerful. I mean I've

TABLE 4.2.   *(continued)*

known about those themes, but not in this way. I can do something with it now!
Of course, there's a lot more to it, that I'd rather not share in a group. But now
I'm beginning to see more clearly how "aspiration" and "aiming low" goes way
back into my family's dynamics.

The client is a 9-year-old boy referred for academic problems.

Assessor: Hey Timmy, what are you doing? [During Block Design of WISC–R]
Client: I made a wall [matter-of-factly].
Assessor: Did you make it so this design [pointing to card] is on your side?
Client: Uh-huh [starts to break them apart, to get ready for next design].
Assessor: Hold on! [Assessor gets up, walks to client's corner of the table.] From
    my side, I can't see whether you did what I asked. My word! You did indeed.
    [Assessor returns to her seat.] Tim, I'm beginning to see how Ms. Cunningham
    would say you don't pay attention, even though you say you do. Pretend I'm Ms.
    Cunningham, and I told you to make this design with these blocks. Okay? And so
    Tim says, "There, I did what she said." But come over here to Ms. Cunningham's
    side of the desk. Now look at the wall from her side! See, from her desk, it doesn't
    look like you did the design at all.
Client: Oh! [Assessor: What do you think Tim could do so Ms. Cunningham could
    see that he pays attention?] Turn it around this way after I'm finished?
Assessor: Now that's a good idea. Let's try it. [Assessor administers the next card.
    Client makes a wall, and then turns it for assessor to see.] Yes, now I can tell that
    you did it right. Tim, could this be what happened when I was in your room this
    morning? The art teacher—what is his name? [Client: Mr. Simms.] Mr. Simms got
    a little impatient with you when he told everyone to clean off their desks. You said
    you did and he said you didn't. If you were Mr. Simms, looking across the room
    at your desk, what would you see?
Client: Pieces of construction paper. But I was saving that for recess; it wasn't
    garbage. I didn't spill any paste or anything, and I put the scissors in my desk.
Assessor: Is there anything you could have done so Mr. Simms could *see* that you
    followed his directions?
Client: I guess put the paper in my pocket.
Assessor: Sounds good to me. I think you already know what to do from now on so
    the grown-ups can *see* that you're following directions.
Client: Can we do some more [blocks]?
Assessor: Sure. [Later] If I told your mom about the wall and about the construction
    paper, would she know some other times like that at home? [Client gave
    examples. A conference was held with Tim, two teachers, and both parents, so all
    could hear about the examples, what Tim planned to do in the future, and how he
    would like the adults to help him.]

The clients are a married couple, in their late 20s, who had referred their 6-year-old
son for an assessment of "shyness." The following session was held at the family's
kitchen table after the psychologist had met with the boy.

Husband: [Card I, Rorschach] Obviously this is a folk festival ethnic dance. Two men
    with capes swirling, a woman with arms raised in the middle. Yes, definitely.
    Ukranian, I'd say. That's it.

TABLE 4.2. *(continued)*

Wife: [Pausing, while walking past with coffee pot, to look over husband's shoulder] Oh, now I can see that. The woman is wearing a filmy dress. She's probably on her tiptoes.

Husband: [Card II] This one is more complex. These red parts should be integrated. It's a circus. These are dancing bears; this is an elephant's upturned barrel—the kind they balance on. This red is bunting—the overall impression of center ring.

Wife: [Chair pulled up beside her husband's] Oh my. The bears could be playing patty cake, couldn't they?

Assessor: [Presenting Card III] Miriam, pull your chair over here [to side of table diagonally from husband]. This time, you tell us first, what could this be?

Wife: Oh, well, I . . . I don't know what Dave would say. [Assessor: Go ahead.] Could it be more than one thing? [Assessor: Sure, there are lots of possibilities.] Would it be all right for these to be two native dancers?

Assessor: Why in the world not? Miriam, what's the worst possible thing you can imagine could happen if neither Dave nor I agreed with you?

Wife: I'd feel dumb. I'd be lost. Well, he'd help me, but I'd be afraid I was wasting time. Besides, he's always right, he really is. [Assessor asks if what just happened were familiar—that Dave organized a response, and then Miriam accepted it and filled in. They immediately provided such examples as Dave's buying their new house without Miriam's having seen it (although they had agreed in advance which criteria it should meet), and her then selecting wallpaper, rugs, and furnishings. The same pattern was identified in regard to raising their son, Ricky. They agreed that although Miriam and Dave generally found the pattern comfortable, Ricky's holding back until given directions and permissions was not working well for him.]

Assessor: I suspect that if Ricky saw you [Miriam] being more flexible—initiating plans yourself, and sometimes offering your opinions first, he would begin to do so too.

Wife: You know, I never thought of this before, but sometimes I see him [Ricky] holding back, and my heart just aches. I know what it's like.

Assessor: Holding back has been painful for you too, at times.

Husband: Honey, I sensed that too, even when you say it's okay.

Assessor: [Ricky peers around the kitchen doorway.] Hi, Ricky. You're just in time. Come sit here on your side of the table. Here's what we're going to do. Do you remember these pictures [TAT]? I'll show all of you a picture, and each of you will think to yourself what could be happening in the picture. Then we'll take turns being the first to tell what we thought. [All four tell a story to each card, taking turns being the first. Assessor points out that nobody was wrong, that there were many possible stories, and that Dad feels okay about all this.] All right, let's see some other times when Ricky and Mom could "go first." Mom, tell Dad some ideas for this year's vacation—just some random thoughts about what would be nice. [Laughter and apologies are followed by suggestions. Ricky is then asked to pretend the assessor is his teacher, and to make a request for which morning song the class should sing. Other practicings follow. Assessor acknowledges that the family's pattern works very well in many circumstances, but suggests that they all continue the exercise for a week, and then decide whether they would like further guidance from a family counselor who would conduct similar sessions with them.]

The client is a 9-year-old retarded boy, referred by his EMR teacher for reevaluation of his intellectual level.

TABLE 4.2.   *(continued)*

Assessor: Milton, let's practice that. Tell me how the boy makes a happy ending [TAT card 1BM].

Client: His name is Sammy—Sammy rides my bus. This is one of those things you play [violin]. Sammy doesn't know how to play it. [Assessor: What can he do to make a happy ending?] He does what his teacher says to, and once upon a time he makes a song come out. [Assessor: Good. That's a happy ending. What will Sammy do to make a happy ending if Brooks teases him?] Brooks says, "That's gross! That's baby noise." Sammy says, "Go away. My teacher says I play it good."

Assessor: Okay! [Handing Milton his human figure drawing of himself] What can Milton do to make a happy ending?

Client: Milton tells the lady at MacDonald's that he wants a big french fries. She tells him it's not enough money. [Assessor: That's not happy! What will Milton do?] He'll cry.

Assessor: Milton, what would happen if Milton said, "What do I have enough money for?" and the lady said, "A small french fries," and Milton said, "Okay, I want a small french fries," and then he told his mother that he didn't cry and that he did everything by himself?

Client: Milton's mother would go back to her job and Milton would have to live by himself. All alone with Walpole—that's our cat. [Further practicing of "making good endings" confirms Milton's fearfulness that being competent may result in his being abandoned or overwhelmed by increased demands for independent accomplishment.]

Assessor: Let's talk to Mr. Remy [teacher]. I'll bet he would understand if you told him when you were afraid of "too much." [Milton brings Mr. Remy back from the classroom. Assessor retells Milton's stories and explains his fears. They role-play Milton telling Mr. Remy that he wants to finish just one page, so the work won't become "too much"; that is, escalate too quickly. Mr. Remy reassures Milton that nobody will move him to Mr. Bono's class without discussing the move with Milton, that he will visit the class first, and that after transferring he may come back to see Mr. Remy. Similar discussions were later held with Milton and his parents.]

The client is a 55-year-old housewife, self-referred for job guidance.

Assessor: [As client begins to tell a story for TAT card #9GF] Hold it! You're about to tell me that this woman up here looking from behind the tree is thinking that the woman down below running on the beach is going to get somewhere first, that she got a head start!

Client: [Taken aback at first] No, you got there first! I'm not going to give you the satisfaction of telling you how accurate you were! [Both laugh.]

Assessor: That's a nice twist—my getting there first. I'll bet you could imagine all kinds of other stories here. Try a few. Yes, go ahead.

Client: Well, this one [behind tree] could be plotting how to stop the other one. [Assessor: Sure! What else?] Or she could maybe be thinking how to follow her footsteps, so to speak, to get to the same place. [Assessor: Right. I wonder if you could tell me what's happening for this woman who's running?] She probably doesn't even know someone's watching. She's probably just trying to get somewhere on time. You know, I just realized, she looks worried, but determined [laughs]. Pretty tricky! I see what you've just done! But it's true: Whatever I do, whether it's keeping up with volunteer work from home or getting a salaried job, I'll still be worried and determined. So I might as well be getting paid!

TABLE 4.2.   *(continued)*

Assessor: Okay, so try that out with this picture. Tell me the story here [#17BM].
Client: [Long pause] He's on the way up this rope in some sort of Olympic
competition. He's decided it's not so much whether he wins or loses medals, but
that under the circumstances he does his best. And how about this: and that he
enjoys it!
Assessor: Quite a difference from the story on Card 1! By the way, when you told that
first one, were you aware that there were different potential stories?
Client: Intellectually. But none of them occurred to me.
Assessor: I'd say that you came to me already prepared to try out some different
perspectives.
Client: I guess so, in a way. But I didn't realize how much it was me holding myself
back. I guess I'd be willing to try that job interview role-play now. But you promise
to help me with cues?

The client is a 24-year-old woman bank teller, referred by her counselor for differential
diagnosis between neurotic depression and borderline personality disorder.

Assessor: [Client has been protesting that she wants to be more independent but that
people won't let her be so.] Look how lightly you've done all your pencil work; it's
barely visible! [Assessor holds her penciled notes up by way of comparison.] Here,
how about retracing these [Digit Symbol from WAIS–R], making them darker?
Press harder, keep going. What's it like to press harder?
Client: It feels good. And nothing's getting messed up.
Assessor: Let's do these again [Presents Bender cards and fresh paper.] Okay. But
putting pressure into what you do doesn't have to be laborious. Go faster; you've
been here before! Okay, and how shall you sign your name? Ah-ha! Well, I imagine
that you could practice putting more pressure into other things you do too. It's like
putting yourself more firmly into whatever you do. Let's try that out another way.
Let's move over here to these chairs, and pretend I'm Dr. Caligny [counselor]
telling you that I want you to see a psychologist, and you tell me just what you
think about that. [Role-plays ensue.]

The client is a 23-year-old heroin addict, assessed at a methodone treatment center as
part of intake procedures.

Assessor: So this turned out to be worth your while after all?
Client: See, I talked to this shrink at the lockup, and that was nowhere. And my
girlfriend, she's had four different therapists, no offense, but they were nothing.
Thought they knew it all, and they didn't know nothing.
Assessor: You've met Tom Walker? [counselor; client nods.] Well, after you and I
have read and made any changes in my written report of what we learned today,
we'll ask Tom to join us. He'll have a copy of the report. We'll tell him what
changes we've made, and he'll ask us questions to be sure he understands. Then the
two of you will continue where we've left off. You can work out different goals as
you go along—as we did—and role-play, and he'll tell you what impressions you're
making. I don't think he'll use tests, but otherwise counseling can be very much like
what we did today.
Client: That Walker fellow seems okay. . . . See, I thought therapy was getting
lectured at. And I get to keep a copy of my own of the suggestions, the same ones
he'll have?

The last excerpt in Table 4.2 illustrates how the assessor may encourage a client to enter counseling or therapy with positive expectations. The client's success during the assessment is compared with therapy activities to show the client that therapy would be an extension of what he or she is already familiar with (if that would in fact be the case). The absence of any tests in the excerpt is a reminder that assessment does not necessarily involve continuous use of tests. Interviewing, counseling, and therapeutic techniques also are prevalent, but Tables 4.1 and 4.2 focused on testing examples because the other individualized techniques are well known.

The options developed in these excerpts are only those that clients are ready for at the time of the assessment. Often further restructuration will require protracted professional assistance. The assessment report's suggestions may include recommendations for treatment, further evaluation, and environmental changes, in addition to the tried-out options. In addition, many of the assessor's shared observations slowly germinate as the person later goes about his or her life, proving to be helpful at some later point.

The assessor makes use of technical and diagnostic knowledge even when it is not presented as such to the client. These secondary data are the assessor's tools for exploring primary data—how the client approaches the assessment tasks and similar daily life situations. Informed observation of these primary events is the most productive information to share.

It is not always necessary to obtain a completed assessee production, such as the "other gender" drawing in the "elegant woman" DAP excerpt in Table 4.2. Just getting started on a task often puts the person in touch with his or her inclinations, resistances, concerns. These responses and their pivot points into options are then available for joint exploration. In an individualized assessment, such exploration, rather than completed "productions," is the point of using test materials.

Finally, in those instances where individualized assessment is appropriate; that is, where testing is not merely for establishing comparative levels of achievement or category of best fit; assessment certainly is broader than administration of tests. Individualized assessment is also a testing of optimal environments, interventions, and ways clients can help themselves.

Concluding the Session

The assessment session draws to a close when individualized responses to referral requests have been formulated and, where appropriate, concrete suggestions have been developed for the client as well as for helping professionals. By this time, what has been learned coheres—it appears as various aspects of a whole. No tortuous reasoning is required to hold findings together, and there are no major gaps in understanding. There remains much that the assessor has not shared, and much that has not been explored, but these aspects were not essential for responding to the referral or to developing tailored suggestions.

On the average, I spend about four hours with the client during which I make use of, for example, a Bender-Gestalt, partial Wechsler, complete

Rorschach, and a couple TAT cards. When graduate students are given time constraints, they too can complete the assessment within four hours. Without imposed restraints, however, neophyte assessors typically find themselves talking and counseling rather than assessing, thereby adding hours to the assessment. I prefer to break the assessment into two sessions when possible, allowing the client and myself time and distance to mull what we have experienced together. Ideally, at a third session we review the written report. As the client reads through the entire account, some aspects of it inevitably come across somewhat differently than they had during our previous discussions. Discussion of the report now continues the assessment. The client literally leaves his or her mark on the written account by completing the commentary section and signing it.

Regardless of the number of sessions and whether time and travel contingencies allow for a joint review of the written report, before the client leaves the formal assessment session, I review what will be in the report, first to myself and then with the client. I often hand the person pen and paper and suggest that while I review my notes, he or she may want to jot down any ideas that we have left out or questions that I might try to answer. This suggestion is much more effective than asking "Do you have any questions?"—to which clients respond too quickly with "No, I guess not."

During my private review I ask myself if I adequately pursued alternative hypotheses, obtained all the factual information I will need for the background sections, and recorded concrete examples to illustrate my impressions and conclusions. Some assessors prefer to prepare a standard checklist, which they quickly review at this point. Many find that when they conduct assessments regularly, they no longer use the checklist, but that in the meantime it has allowed their interviews to be constructively open-ended.

My review with the client then begins with requests for missing information. Next I ask for the client's summary of what we have learned and of the suggestions we developed. In this way I can see what has been most important from the client's perspective, and we can clarify any misunderstandings. Then I orally fill out the clients' rendition with the remaining themes and suggestions that will be in the report. None of this comes as a surprise, because we have discussed these themes during the session. Elaborations and additional, related suggestions often arise at this point, however. I frequently ask for additional past instances of assessment findings, and sometimes ask for an instance that may be less private or value-laden for the report.

Finally, we review future steps, such as holding a family conference, referring the client for medical evaluation, or arranging for a meeting with a psychotherapist. Although I am careful to leave room for the client to take initiative and to voice reservations, I also try to clear the way by providing lists of resources and phone numbers, and sometimes by placing calls myself. The client signs a release form, specifying who may receive the written report. When the form is not part of the report (which the client has just read), the form also states that the client may have access to the report. I give the client a business card and indicate that if questions occur later or if any problems with the report arise, I can be reached by phone. I also mention that I telephone a sample of my clients months or even years later to see if the assessment has been as helpful as we intended. I ask for permission to call if this assessment turns out to be in the random sample.

The "doorway phenomenon" is one of my criteria for a successful assessment. As the client pauses before leaving, he or she frequently remarks with pleased bemusement, something like, "You know, you didn't tell me anything I didn't already know." This statement is followed by qualifications like, "But I hadn't thought about it this way before. And now I know how to begin to do something about it."

Questions and Responses

Question: Do clients really cope with the rather unique situation of being assessed in the same way they handle other situations?

Response: A major reason for engaging the client collaboratively is to explore which other situations are and are not like the assessment session. We are not looking for precise equivalents, however. The session is a point of entry and a point of departure into past experience to explore a range of similar situations. In any case, the assessment will not be the only situation in which the client behaves in these ways. It is, after all, the client who comports himself or herself through the assessment; that comportment is not due just to situation specificity.

Question: Isn't there a significant drawback to collaboration? Don't clients sometimes agree with assessors' formulations just from being overwhelmed by the apparent power of tests and the assessor's expertise?

Response: That particular danger is obviated by asking clients to give examples of what they have just endorsed. Often the example leads the assessor to reformulate. The formulations also are tested when clients try out the suggested alternative approach. Nothing affirms or counters propositions as forcefully as behavior. Incidentally, these same exercises result in continual revisions of assessors' adapted theories of personality and dysfunction.

Question: But doesn't collaboration backfire with persons who want to con the assessor into believing them? Don't criminals and malingerers, for example, make up examples and distort their behavior for the assessor's benefit?

Response: Those manipulations certainly do occur, but they occur in recognizable patterns that become familiar to assessors. Assessors solicit clients' "stories," which are critical for understanding their positions. But assessors also actively explore what clients do not say, to clarify whether that omission is conscious defense, dissimulation, unconscious defense, or simply nonsalience from the clients' perspective. In any case, collaboration never requires giving up the assessor's expertise.

Question: The excerpts seem too penetrating to have come from single-session assessments. Does an assessor require extensive training in therapy to conduct effective interventional assessments?

Response: If you watched three hours of individualized assessment, you would see perhaps one-half to one hour of these culminative excerpts. There are many blind alleys, reformulatings, and quiet administrations. Beyond that, I can say that psychotherapy experience—from both sides—although not necessary, certainly helps. Likewise extensive experience with individualized assessment enriches one's therapeutic presence and activities. It is also true, however, that first semester M.A. students in my introductory assessment classes continue to teach me through their own quick recognitions of the similarities between assessment and nonspecialized events.

Question: How do you distinguish between assessment, and therapy or counselling sessions?

Response: Collaborative interventions serve three purposes: (1) to assess when the person comports himself or herself in the observed and in alternative ways; (2) to assess which options might be personally viable, so that workable suggestions can be made; and (3) to afford the client opportunities to be an active participant in developing understandings and suggestions. In short, assessment interventions are primarily for the purpose of assessment, not for therapy.

Question: Why do you score tests on those occasions when you already know that individualized assessment is called for?

Response: There is nothing anti-individual about scores themselves. After all, we are all members of groups, and scores do indicate some of our assorted standings. Individualized assessment goes beyond such statements to explore just how a person lives his or her membership and standing. Of course, individualized assessment also addresses issues that have nothing to do with standing as such. Nevertheless, even qualitative observations are always implicitly comparative; we inevitably understand individuals in comparison with other persons we have encountered. We ought not be too quick to turn away from traditional measures in efforts to individualize.

Question: Why not complete a standardized battery and then intervene and collaborate?

Response: In fact, a variation of that form is typical. A Bender-Gestalt, several Wechsler subtests, a Rorschach, several TAT cards, and so on, may each be completed in standardized form. Intervention within one of these segments occurs only if it appears that the opportunity would otherwise be irretrievable. If an entire battery is completed prior to discussion, however, the client's sense of what it was like to be engaged with a particular test is lost. Discussion becomes academic, abstract. Opportunities for the client to try out alternative comportments are lost.

Question: But don't the interventions that occur within testing distort what clients do on later tests?

Response: There is no "true" response to be distorted. But yes, intervention does affect how clients approach remaining tasks. So, of course, assessors must specify that context in reports and note it on test forms. The purpose of individualized assessment is not to determine how clients perform during standardized administrations, but to explore when they perform in what ways, and how they might be assisted to go about their lives in still more fruitful ways.

Question: Am I correct in assuming that you purposely disregard the past in your emphasis on the present?

Response: Yes and no. Emphasis is on the present because this is where the past is now operative and where influence into the future must occur. Inevitably there is discussion of the past within the assessment context, but focusing on the past in its own right during an assessment usually ends in intellectualized understandings. Focus on the present is based on pragmatics. It simply is more productive in short-term assessment to deal with what pertains now. Ideal understanding of the present, of course, would include knowledge of how it evolved. In practice, exploration of that evolution is better pursued in psychotherapy.

Question: Is client-insight or cognitive understanding necessary for change?

Response: It is always helpful, but often practicing a change renders it more readily available than conceptual understanding alone. For some severely restricted persons, the change that occurs through practice is the only understanding possible.

Question: If you worked with more severely troubled people, would you get less confirmation from them?

Response: Yes, of course. I chose these excerpts as examples of successful collaboration. Not all efforts work, especially not immediately. The more severely restricted the client is, the less he or she can productively reflect and discuss. Part of the assessment task is to determine to what extent the client can reflect, discuss, and alter course. The great majority of assessees can participate in the ways illustrated in this chapter.

Question: Most of the time I didn't see the relevance of the excerpts to the person's diagnosis. Did I miss something?

Response: No, you're quite right. The assessment report would make clear how examples from the session(s) did, and did not, exemplify a diagnosis or other answer to a referral question. In the tables, I included diagnostic or referral information just to tell the reader something about this background.

Question: Are your "alternatives" and "options" what behavior therapists refer to as modified "target behaviors"?

Response: There is definite similarity. However, individualizing goes beyond identification of "environmental contingencies." First, and already attended to by cognitively oriented behavior modifiers, *the client* learns to identify what I call "landmarks." These landmarks are not limited to externally visible signs, but also include the client's bodily and affective recognition of familiar terrain. Second, *explicit use* is made of personally viable "pivot points" within the person's ongoing comportment. The person can continue progress by smoothly pivoting on familiar ground into a different action. Even while moving in the new direction to reach a prior goal, the person retains his or her own rhythm, stride, and so on. In short, the intervention is into individually assessed *process*.

Question: Couldn't I provide the rationale for all the excerpted interventions and collaborations through cognitive social learning theory?

Response: Yes, I think that any of the major theories of personality could be used as a general framework for these practices. One should, however, bear in mind that theories are ways of organizing and developing knowledge. They are meant to be modified to suit data; data ought not to be forced into the theory. Because any one theory tends to focus on certain kinds of data to the relative exclusion of others, it is essential that assessors work out their own expansions or combinations of theory. Having an explicit way of comprehending personality, motivation, and dysfunction, both in general and for specific populations, also allows one to modify those understandings in light of further experience.

Question: Couldn't the word style *be used instead of the somewhat unusual words* comportment *or* approach?

Response: Yes. In fact, I often refer to a person's style of moving through environments. I try not to overuse the term, however, because it can be seen as a trait—something static—instead of evoking a sense of co-authoring, or proactive as well as reactive movement, of dynamic process.

Question: Doesn't individualized assessment take too much time?

Response: No, not if individualized assessment and planning are what is needed. In that case, the time spent is cost-effective. When one person has conducted a thorough assessment, fewer total staff hours are expended in developing a growth or treatment plan. Moreover, clients are less likely to drop out of programs, because they have participated in developing the plan and see its viability for themselves. Different cases, of course, require different degrees of individualizing. In short, individualized time and effort are expended to the extent required "to do the job right."

PART TWO

REPORT WRITING AND
SAMPLE REPORTS

Part two presents the concrete guidelines that maintain the principles of individualized assessment through the important process of individualizing the report. Children and adults are considered separately. Three chapters of individualized reports serve several functions: Besides presenting a range of report formats and styles, these chapters illustrate the assessment process itself. The reader will recognize the similarity of approach that is present through many variations and will see that there is no "one right way" to do assessing and reporting.

The division of reports among the three chapters was somewhat arbitrary in that several of the reports could have appeared in either of two chapters. No single report embodies the entire range of individualized guidelines and practices. The reader will identify the styles, rationales, techniques, and phrases that are most congenial with his or her own work, and may borrow and elaborate upon these.

Chapter 5 provides a practical overview of the process of writing an individualized report. One table indicates the information that should be included, and another suggests alternative subheads. Other tables illustrate problematic writing and suggest improvements. The final table is a checklist for reviewing the first draft of a report. Much of the chapter is applicable to writing any assessment report, not only those reports that should be individualized.

Most of the reports in Chapter 6 were written by first-year M.A. students in an assessment course, and hence they indicate assignments that a beginning assessor could undertake. Many of these reports include the client's written commentary. Chapter 7's reports on children and adolescents were written by graduate students, professional colleagues, and myself. Most of Chapter 8's clinical and diagnostic reports are my own, so I have taken greater liberty in pointing out shortcomings as well as positive features. The chapters cover a range of client ages and assessment settings.

In order to illustrate the assessment process, I selected many reports that are long, even for individualized assessments. Each of the three chapters of sample reports also includes one or more examples of brief decision-making or adjunctive assessment reports, however, as reminders that even though in most cases individualized principles and practices are appropriate to some degree, fully individualized assessments are not always necessary.

Each report is introduced and discussed in terms of its particular exemplification of individualized assessment. Readers will see that these assessment procedures and reports could be revised, and those observations will assist them in developing their own ways of individualizing assessments. Like previous chapters, each of these ends with a section of responses to the kinds of questions that are frequently raised by both students and colleagues.

In general, these four chapters on individualizing reports illustrate a variety of ways in which (1) the referral is contextualized in terms of life events; (2) the client, assessor, and involved others collaborate in exploring the client's situation and his or her participation in it; (3) understandings are in terms of the world as lived rather than in terms of independent causes; (4) the referral questions are answered concretely; (5) suggestions are tailored to the person's ways of approaching and moving through situations; and (6) through representational description, the client appears vividly as a particular individual, and as one who can take at least partial responsibility for his or her life.

CHAPTER 5

Writing Individualized Reports

BEFORE beginning the writing process, the assessor should consider what purpose the report will serve. What *are* reports for? Although at first this question may seem too elementary to pose, keeping the answers in mind will go a long way toward encouraging effective, helpful reports. The general purposes of any assessment report are: (1) to report the expert's findings (conclusions accompanied by illustrations) back to the referring party; (2) when requested, to communicate suggestions based on the findings; and (3) to provide a record for professionals who may be working with the client in later years. We too frequently write our reports with only present concerns in mind. We should remember that the person who is in trouble now, or who is trying to get ahead now, may very well be in a similar situation in future years. At that time it is likely that the workers presently involved in the case will have forgotten many of the circumstances and concerns surrounding the assessment, if indeed these workers are still available. The client's file, containing the assessment report, may be the sole informant.

Additional purposes of an individualized report are: (1) To present findings in terms of events in the client's daily life, so that (a) a broad range of helpers can work directly with these specific behaviors and situations; (b) the client and helpers can have the same concrete referents in mind as they work together; and (c) professionals with different theoretical orientations can formulate their own versions of the conclusions; (2) to provide points of access into the client's particular ways of going about his or her life, so that interventions are viable modifications of what the client is already up to; and (3) to provide the client the same document being used by his or her helpers, thereby facilitating understanding of what these people are trying to do, while also encouraging the client to participate actively in this process.

Finally, it helps to remember that *reports are for the readers,* not for the author. Reports are for communicating key findings, along with illustrative support, to readers. The report is *not* a repository of everything the assessor did and noticed; or a place for the assessor to wander around and finally discover the outcome; or a laboratory report of esoteric, scientific indicators; or an arena for the assessor to demonstrate personal clinical prowess, superiority of insights, technological wizardry, and so on; or a place to test the elasticity and comprehensiveness of the assessor's theory; or the occasion to demonstrate the author's literary potential. To repeat, reports *are for readers.*

Preparation for Writing Individualized Reports

An experienced assessor generally continues the assessment session long enough to answer to referral questions and develop individualized suggestions. One goes as far as possible in this direction, even if awaiting other data such as previous records or neurological findings, or if one did not manage to score all of the tests. Before going on to other responsibilities, the assessor jots down any changes to be made in standard format (report organization), key themes, and any issues that still require thought. Most assessors also asterisk, color-code with felt-tip pen, or otherwise highlight their notes so later they can quickly find specific themes. In short, when the assessment ends, the assessor already knows in general what the report will say. One does *not* sit down with a collection of scores to figure out what conclusions they lead to.

Ideally, report writing does not begin until the next day, when one's sense of the client has gestalted more cohesively, and the interesting but unessential impressions and facts have dropped away. During this interim, scenes from the assessment session appear to me as I go about other business. My thoughts follow these scenes into imagined variations, and then I ask myself which of them fits my sense of *this* client. On other occasions, especially while driving, I find myself recalling similar clients, a research report, somebody's theory. I've learned to let all this occur and run its course, somehow readying me for report writing.

The next step is to return to one's desk, test materials, notes, and the referral. Problematic cases may require searches through norms, consultation with colleagues, and perhaps scheduling of further assessment sessions. When one is sure that conclusions are not premature, that alternative understandings have been duly considered, then preparation for writing begins. At this point the assessor decides whether the referral calls for brief normative or categorical findings for the sake of decision making, or whether a more fully individualized description of the client is appropriate. Then one writes and reviews the tentative outline to be sure that material and data are at hand to present a consistent, tightly woven, referral-relevant account.

The report should *not* record all that the assessor saw and learned, nor even all that he or she went through to arrive at the ultimate conclusions. The assessor asks, "What do I know now that it is important for others to know in order to make their decisions and to work with *this* person?" The reader will find it easier to remember these findings if they are organized within no more than three major themes, preferably with subheads, such as, "Findings of Brain Damage, Prior Personality, Current Situation" or "Threatening Situations, Safe Situations, Learning to Become Safe."

Then one looks back for examples to illustrate and document for the reader what the assessor has learned. The examples should be ones that bring the client to life, making concretely visible what you the assessor came to know. Testing instances should be indexed to other life events, with both chosen for their potential for reverberating with readers' lives. Thus, universal events (for example, missing a bus) should be included along with events that are relatively uncommon (such as being committed to a mental hospital). Sometimes examples are chosen to speak to particular readers' concerns or theories. For instance, some readers find it easier to understand or plan for a client if they know about his or her recreational pursuits or current relations with parents. Examples are chosen to illustrate not only a present point, but also ones to be explored more explicitly later in the report. Early examples should foreshadow later ones. Finally, examples are selected to illustrate experiactional pivot points—those moments in the client's participation in problems where a constructive shift will be suggested. Note that one does not build a case test by test, but theme by theme. With this preparation, the report may then take the reader through a more or less chronological account of how various understandings evolved.

True, it is often difficult to meet these criteria for selection of examples. But if the assessment session was individualized and collaborative, the client has aided in the search for differentiating instances. Usually the difficulty is in sifting through a wealth of instances to find a few that "say it all." The most effective example is one that speaks beyond its immediate context in the report to exemplify later themes too. When this occurs, each statement does not require its own example. Examples will be more powerful, more profoundly effective, if they are used as organizing devices for the entire report. A few carefully chosen and presented images are more memorable than a series of lesser examples.

As the assessor seeks words to express what he or she knows, new meanings emerge. The selection of examples, and commentary on them, should encourage the reader, too, to respect the ambiguity of human affairs—their richness, multiple potential for meaning, their way of exceeding our systematizing of knowledge.

The last step prior to writing is to review the outline and notes to see if the report will cohere in its explicit answer to referral issues.

Once all my materials are before me, the above preparation takes about 20 to 30 minutes. A report of four single-spaced pages requires 20 to 40 minutes to dictate, then 10 to 15 minutes to correct and modify the rough-draft typescript. My dictated reports require less time and are more clearly expressed than my hand-drafted reports. While dictating, I attend to central themes instead of becoming bogged down with phrasing, rereading, inserting more examples, wondering if I should reorganize the format, and so on, because I know I can amend the typist's copy later. When I look at this typed version, after some time has elapsed, I usually discover that salient points have come across more clearly than I expected. After copy editing and one or two clarifications, the report is ready for final typing. Some authors can dictate to themselves, so to speak, typing their own rough draft as they go.

Unfortunately, the same report may require three, or even four, hours to write in longhand. And even though I check the report before having it typed, I still have to copyedit the typed version. Assessors who have to write reports by hand often have difficulty finding enough uninterrupted time to devote to writing; hence the report is delayed. Delayed reporting is delayed service, which leads to poor morale all around, including the assessor's. Moreover, after about four days, especially when I am seeing many clients, the vividness of the session dissipates, and I have difficulty illustrating my conclusions. Delay, however, is less likely when the author already knows at the end of the assessment session(s) what the report will say. Efficient reporting is a significant payoff for the effort put into the assessment process.

Format: What Goes Where

The format suggested in Table 5.1 follows traditional guidelines but includes a few modifications consonant with individualized assessment. After the assessor has decided what major ideas readers will need, sections with appropriate subheads can be tailored for each client's report. The subheads serve as an outline (map or agenda) for the reader. The data under each heading should represent life events as clarified by formal assessment procedures. Test behaviors are simply life events in a specialized context. The report should not be a running record of the assessor's activities and working notes. It should tell readers explicitly only what is relevant to the referral.

Table 5.1 provides a schematic overview of the way reports can be organized. The material in brackets is not titled. The second and third columns show some alternative headings for similar sections of a report. One may select items from different columns to suit one's tastes. Many other section titles are possible, of course, and sections may be combined within a broader category. Frequently, some sections are omitted as not relevant to a particular case; if a heading is not useful, don't use it.

Table 5.2 annotates the headings of Table 5.1. The captions and annotations provide a general standard by which to tailor one's reports, and a check for full coverage. To emphasize the importance of tailoring, I want to mention that no two of my private practice reports follow exactly the same outline or sequence. Sometimes I bypass a section on Introductory Description, for example, placing the client's attitude toward the assessment in the Opportunities for Assessment section, and arranging for physical description to emerge early in the text. Occasionally a didactic section may be appropriate. In a child custody case, for example, I once included a section of "Research on the Single Parent." A more radical variation is that of organizing the report by Suggestions, with assessment-based rationale and illustrations under each suggestion. This format is most likely to succeed when the primary reader is the client or the persons already working directly with him or her, such as teachers or therapists.

There are two criteria for tailoring a report's format: (1) suiting it to the client, and (2) suiting it to the readers. Many nonpsychologists anticipate, from experience, that these reports will be highly technological. Therefore, it is helpful to select headings indicating that the content is explicitly relevant to the readers. For example, the title of a psychological report could be "Assessment of Readiness for Discharge." Suggestions could be subheaded for different readers: "Suggestions for Therapeutic Activities Workers," "Suggestions for Nursing Staff," "Suggestions for Treatment Team." In a typed report, headings should be underlined so they will stand out for the reader.

TABLE 5.1.   The Organization of a Report

Areas of a report	Alternative headings	
[Letterhead]		
[Title of the report]		
[Client's name]		
Identifying Information	Actuarial Data	
Referral	Presenting Issues	Purpose of Assessment
Prior Records	Background	Case Review
Assessment Procedures	Opportunities for Assessment	Assessment Resources
Physical Description	Introductory Description	First Impressions
Mr. Doe's Understanding of the Referral Issue	Interview	Background Provided by Mr. Doe
Findings (with subheads)	The Assessment (with subheads)	Mr. Doe as Seen through the Tests (with subheads)
Additional Factors	Constraints on Intervention	Environmental Contingencies
CONCLUSIONS	Summary	General Outcome
Suggestions	Recommendations	Implications
[Assessor's signature and title]		
[Supervisor's signature and title]		
Mr. Doe's Commentary		
[Mr. Doe's signature]		
Release Permission [and client's signature]		
Technical Appendix		

TABLE 5.2.   The Sections of a Report, Annotated

Letterhead

The letterhead printed on the practitioner's or agency's stationery names the person or agency, indicates its functions (such as "Clinical Child Psychologist" or "A United Way Agency for Youth in Transition"), and gives the address and phone number. If this information does not appear on a letterhead, it should be typed under the signature of the writer.

Kind of Assessment (title of the report)

This information is generally centered at the top of the page. Examples are: Psychological Assessment, Neuropsychological Report, Educational Evaluation, Vocational Assessment, Intake Summary.

TABLE 5.2. *(continued)*

Client's Name
    The client's name usually appears next, also centered. I prefer to type the name entirely in capital letters.

Identifying Information
    This section often has no title of its own; instead it is composed of a series of underlined subheads for actuarial facts, often arranged in two columns. Minimal information would be client's address, age, dates of assessment sessions, and date of the report. Additional information essential in various settings could include grade, parents' names, school's name, social security number, educational background, current employment, date of hospitalization, medical diagnosis, medication at time of assessment. Identifying Information helps the reader to become oriented to the client at a demographic level. It also helps record keepers and reviewers to locate context information. The author should be aware that such information creates expectations; thus, information should be recorded knowingly and responsibly. For a 19-year-old male who had been arrested for harassing a young woman, I recorded that he held a steady job, was the father of a two-year-old, and that his wife was pregnant. Presumably, this orienting information distinguished the client from less responsible individuals facing similar charges. Wittingly or unwittingly, the author can set up negative expectations by noting information that seems to be diagnostic by itself: for example, Admission Diagnosis or Prior Admissions. Data presented under Identifying Information is never merely factual; the author's selections already foreshadow later impressions.

Referral (or in the case of a self-referral, "Presenting Problem")
    The referral as it was initially presented is repeated here, along with names and affiliations of the persons who made the referral. Referral clarifications are reported: What were the concrete precipitating events? What decisions must be made? What do the referring parties hope to gain from the assessment? What is already known about the occasions when the focal problem does and does not arise? The assessor usually has to confer with the referring persons to obtain these clarifications.
    The referral also introduces any issues that the author has discovered to be important during the assessment, such as the possibility of previously unsuspected brain damage, suicidal preoccupation, or (on the positive side) career motivation. The Referral section should anticipate the themes that will run through the remaining sections. In other words, the Referral presents the report's story lines.

Prior Records (or "Background," or "Case Review")
    This section should be limited to information that fills out the more succinct Referral. It is the background against which the assessor undertook the assessment; it is *not* the client's full life background in the sense of a social or developmental history. The location of such records should be indicated (for example, "transcript available from the DA's office," or "Medical Records has the summaries from prior hospitalizations"). This section usually summarizes prior evaluation and treatment records as they pertain to the Referral question. The reader is told at least implicitly in what direction patterns of information seem to point. Occasionally the author will say outright that there is no available information on this particular issue. This section is needed only when a complex review would clutter the Referral section (where this information often appears, as part of the contextualization of the referral). Again, the author should be careful not to build an artificially cut-and-dried case through the manner of packaging the prior records.

TABLE 5.2.   *(continued)*

Occasionally, new referral-relevant background information will be provided by the client during the assessment process. Examples are qualifications for veterans' benefits, past psychotic episodes, or head trauma. This new information should be presented as such in this section.

Assessment Procedures (or "Opportunities for Assessment," or "Assessment Resources")
In the days of test-oriented assessment, this section was labeled simply "Tests" or "Tests Administered." Among other sources of impressions, tests *are* listed here, with complete, properly capitalized names, followed by the initials by which the name of the test is abbreviated in the report. If more than one form or edition is in use, the particular form or edition should be indicated. I list the tests in the order in which they were used, and when only part of a test was administered, I indicate in parentheses which portions were used, such as TAT card numbers, or WAIS–R subtests.
Prior to this column of tests, I indicate in either sentence or column form where the assessment took place. Any field observations of interviews that were part of the assessment process are described or listed along with the tests. If not specified earlier, any documents the assessor read are named here. Usually at the end, I mention "collaborative discussion" with the client if indeed we did successfully share impressions during the course of the assessment. In short, this section indicates the occasions through which the assessor came to know the client. Tests historically have a significant basis for psychology's and education's claims to status as scientific professions, but today assessment reports place test performance among other comportments that the assessor takes into account in reaching an understanding of the client. Indeed, it is now acceptable for a psychologist to omit use of tests when they would be redundant in an assessment.

Physical Description of Mr. Doe (or "Ms. Doe," "John," or "Joan"; or "Introductory Description," or "First Impressions")
This description reports the assessor's initial (as well as any later contrasting) impressions of the client and the client's initial and later attitudes toward being in the assessment situation. It also introduces the reader to the client, in a more direct (no longer just actuarial) manner. Thus, the heading may include the client's name. This is the section that appears in some authors' reports as Behavioral Observations. Here, however, the description is intended not just to indicate general appearance, mental health status, and attitude, but also to foreshadow the client's ways of *participating* in situations—that is, his or her ways of getting into trouble, out of trouble, and into successes.
Vivid images of *ongoing action* help the reader envision this person as the report describes various comportments during observations, testing, and discussion. The images are a foundation and reference point for the remainder of the report. These descriptions should be chosen as representative of the person the assessor came to know, so that the reader will nod in recognition as the client is presented in the remaining text. For adequate imagery, include physical details, such as height, hair style, clothing, postures. However, these must be accompanied by an explicit "so-what"—a statement that the details cohered into a particular, specified impression for the assessor.
Criteria for selection of incidents include illustration of how the client contributes to others' impressions, the assessor's contribution to who the client came to be for him or her, and, of course, relevance to the referral issues. If possible, the introductory samples should illustrate briefly not only any inconsistencies among the client's comportments, but also those moments in which the shifts occurred.

TABLE 5.2.   *(continued)*

Mr. Doe's Understanding of the Referral Issue (or "Interview," or "Background Provided by Mr. Doe")

This section is not necessarily a social history, but can be a brief review of the client's understanding of the referral issues and of the specific events that led to the referral. The person's understanding of problems and options belongs here. Where a fuller account of the person's past is necessary (because it is not available elsewhere and hence has not been summarized in Background, or because the client's understanding of that background differs from expectations, then a prior section might be titled "Social History as Given by Mr. Doe," or "Social History as Given by John's Parents." When—as is most often the case—this social history emerged not only during an interview but throughout the session, then the author should say something to that effect in the first sentence of the section.

The reader should be told of any shifts in the client's attitudes toward the referral issues or toward his or her history that occur during the course of the assessment. The reader should also sense which material was explicit for and organized by the client, and which was thematized by the assessor.

Findings (or "The Assessment," or "Mr. Doe as Seen through the Tests")

This is the main body of the report, in which the assessor conveys what this client's life is like as it pertains to the referral issues. Here the assessor presents the events that led to the Conclusions and now illustrates how the Conclusions hold true for this client. Generally, the author will devise subheads after the material has taken on a gestalt of its own. These subheads often are themes developed and named with the client during the assessment. In such cases, quotation marks help to identify the client's own words. Some sample subheads follow:

- Findings in Support of a Special Education Placement; Findings in Support of Mainstreaming
- Areas of Executive Strength; Areas of Relative Weakness; Strengths and Weaknesses Dependent on Context
- John at School; John at Home; John at Play
- "Being Brave"; "Being Safe"; "Being Scared"
- Evidence of Left Hemisphere Dysfunction; Mr. Doe's Ineffective Ways of Coping with His Loss; Mr. Doe's Successful Ways of Coping with His Loss
- The Big Shot; Playing Cool; Being Lonely

Even in settings where the assessor works predominantly with homogeneous referrals and has developed some standard formats, for the findings one nevertheless should provide individualized subheads to help the reader understand each particular client.

In those cases where the major themes are not complex; that is, where the reader will not lose sight of them, the text may be organized in terms of what emerged (relevant to the referral) test by test. This format allows the client's approaches to be seen as they varied across tasks. Test-related findings and illustrations may be presented in the order in which they occurred, thereby providing a sense of context; the reader can see at which points the client collaborated and how these points led to later suggestions. The danger of this organization, of course, is that the author may become test-oriented rather than client-oriented (test outcomes may be reported "just because they're there" rather than because they throw referral-relevant light on this individual; or test productions may be seen as signs of underlying forces causing similar behavior).

I am generally opposed to segmenting a person into the all-too-common categories such as Intellectual Functioning, Social Relations, and Emotional Components, which usually refer to IQ, TAT, and Rorschach, respectively. These categories are rarely

TABLE 5.2.   *(continued)*

conducive to fresh and holistic thinking about an actual person.

Whatever the headings, the text should describe the client's particular ways of participating in his or her difficulties, the short- and long-term outcomes for self and others, and the person's presently viable options. The contexts in which the described style does and does not work for the client should be included, along with situations in which the client does *not* get into difficulty (the when-nots of problematic comportment). When possible, counterparts drawn from daily life should be integrated with these more specialized observations of tests or interview experiaction. Ideally, the text will report the landmarks and physiognomies of the client's world as he or she moves toward trouble, and then identify the pivot points toward alternate, already viable, routes that were discovered together in the session.

Where tests are mentioned, it often helps to underline their names so readers can locate that material. The kinds of tasks involved on each test should be apparent to nonassessor readers. Note that findings are *not* test scores; findings are understandings of life events, including test comportment. Scores are tools used in the development of those understandings.

Additional Factors (or "Constraints on Intervention," or "Environmental Contingencies")

Here one can place information that should be taken into account in carrying out Suggestions, but which either did not fit into prior story lines or might have prejudiced readers if presented in Background. Factors would include placement deadlines, race, medical history, mental health systems policies, client preferences, family resistance. Most often, however, such information can be incorporated directly into Suggestions.

CONCLUSIONS (or "General Outcome," or "Summary")

This section answers the referral issues point by point (diagnosis, placement decision, and so on). In a brief report, the Conclusions appear at this point in the report, just before Suggestions. In lengthy reports, I prefer to place Conclusions right after Referral or Procedures, so the reader is assured that in fact the text of the report does address the points at issue. In this case, I type the heading in capital letters (and when I have access to a typewriter with two typing elements, I choose a darker or bolder one for the entire section), so that it will be readily located, despite its unusual placement. The reader is spared having to read or skim an entire report to get to these answers. The reader who wishes to understand the client as an individual, buoyed by these direct answers, goes on to read the rest of the report. Now the point of the text is clear to the reader, who already knows where it is leading. The reader remembers the concrete clarifications of the Conclusions. Rarely do readers who have read an early Conclusions section experience the rest of the report as too lengthy. Regardless of where it appears, if one literally has written the Conclusions section before the text, then the text is more streamlined, more to the point. This practice serves as a report-writing discipline for the author, as a check for coverage, relevance, and efficiency, as well as an efficient communications technique for the reader's sake.

Suggestions (or "Implications," or "Recommendations")

Even if the report has been written concisely (efficiently, following referral-relevant themes, with no nonessential material), a Conclusions or Summary section is usually helpful immediately preceding Suggestions. If this section appeared at the beginning of the report, the author may wish to insert a sentence referring back to it.

Suggestions should be numbered, with referral-specific items listed first. Suggestions to different parties may be grouped together under subheads (for example, Suggestions

TABLE 5.2.   *(continued)*

for Vocational Counselor, Suggestions for Instructors, Suggestions for John Doe). The last may use second-person form of address, for instance, "John you might want to . . . " The general purpose of each suggestion should be stated along with specifics about who, when, and how. Nothing should be introduced here without prior grounding in the report. Some of the suggestions should repeat the everyday landmarks that indicate the client is traveling into trouble; the suggested alternative courses should be those already identified as personally viable. When possible, reference should be made to trying out similar interventions within the session(s). For the client these references are reminders of the actual session and of *how* he or she managed to *succeed* with an alternative approach. For other readers, references to the interventions help to illustrate how suggestions might be carried out or revised. Indeed, most suggestions should come across as anticlimactic, as almost self-evident, or as summaries of what has been explored with the client. In addition, the assessor should indicate which suggestions, if any, were developed after discussion with the client.

Assessors who work with homogeneous populations such as learning-disabled youngsters, school-phobic children, or stroke victims may print handout sheets of detailed instructions for the client and the caretakers. The assessment report's suggestions can then mention ways to tailor the sheet to the specific client.

Assessor's signature and title

Under the author's signature should be the typed name and degree (M.Ed., Ph.D., or Psy.D.) and the author's position (Clinical Psychologist, Educational Specialist). If the letterhead does not provide precise information about the assessment facility, this too should appear under the assessor's name (for example, agency, address, phone number).

Supervisor's signature and title

If the assessor requires supervision, the supervisor's name, degree, and title should be provided.

Mr. Doe's commentary and signature

After reading the report, the client or guardian may be encouraged to write on it directly, indicating general impressions, corrections, or clarifications, and any new reflections or decisions.

Occasionally, especially with counseling assessment reports, the assessor and client will together edit a draft of the report, and then both will sign the report as co-authors.

Release Permission

This section consists of the following sentence, the list of persons or agencies, and the client's signature:

Persons/agencies listed below have my permission to read or receive copies of this report:

[Client's signature]

Technical Appendix

If it seems likely that other professionals may want to know more about scores, they can be summarized here in schematic form. Profile sheets, TAT stories, Rorschach structural summaries, and the like, also may be attached. If standardized administration was changed to allow for collaborative procedures, those procedures should be noted directly on these records (as well as within the body of the report).

Conventions and Principles

Even though reports are individualized, some practical conventions are followed so as not to distract the reader with unexpected deviations. The initials for tests are all capitalized without periods, for example, WAIS-R (*not* Wais-R or W.A.I.S.-R.), TAT, DAP. Initials are used only after the full name of the test has been spelled out. Capital letters should be used for the first letters of score ranges and subtests, thereby indicating formal categories rather than descriptive terms; for example, "IQ was in the High Average range," or "Client was Average in Arithmetic." The term *test* is generally reserved for fully standardized, objectively scored and normed instruments; the term *technique* is used when less standardized procedures are followed, for example, when the Bender-Gestalt or House-Tree-Person drawings are used without scoring. It is helpful to the reading professional if within-text references to tests and techniques are underlined, so those sections can be located readily; for example, "It was on the Digit Span subtest that Betty realized how anxious she had become." In consonance with contemporary publishing standards, many words that used to be hyphenated are now streamlined, for instance, subtest, pretest, (not subtest, pre-test).

Follow general principles of effective communication. Do not put anything in the report that is not referral-relevant or useful to readers. Address the social/political/practical contingencies with which readers have to deal (Appelbaum, 1970). When you think something is important, but you are not sure why, include it with an explicit statement to that effect; for example, "Perhaps at some later time, it might be useful to know that John had originally planned on a sales career," or "I don't know whether it is relevant to current treatment planning, but perhaps John's fervent antisemitism should be mentioned here." Tell the reader outright what point you're trying to make; clarify any possible misunderstanding. Examples: "What I want to highlight with this array of activities is that . . . "; "I did not wish, however, to leave the impression that . . . "; "placement was fastidious, but not obsessively so."

Admit what you do not know rather than allowing readers to assume that you've taken it into account: "The above conclusions assume a nonsignificant medical history; however, we haven't yet received the 407 records"; "He said nothing about his father's death; however, because it had slipped my mind, I did not pursue the matter."

Say what you mean in concrete terms rather than dressing up the text in professionalese. In Mann's (1971) words, "dare to be ordinary." For instance, say not that "the patient tends to overcompensate," but that "Mr. Zamprelli made a point of using big words and assuring me that being the person with the least formal education in his family has not made a difference to him." Alternatively, you could qualify technical terms so both professional and nonprofessional readers will know just what you mean. "I see Mr. Zamprelli's often unnecessary use of big words as overcompensation for what he privately experiences as an educational deficiency." One should be familiar with both jargon and technical terms so as not to use them inadvertently just to be descriptive. Frequently misused terms are *impulsive, acts out, denies, projects, depressed.*

Write with precision, neither overstating, overqualifying, or fudging. Examples of overstating: "always," "constantly," "Mrs. Johnson denigrates her accomplishments" (Totally? Always? All of them?). An example of overqualifying: "It seems to me that perhaps . . ." Fudging, in report-writing, is the use of qualifying terms that seem to be descriptive but in fact are not discriminative. Examples are: "John tends to . . ." (actually does it or just feels inclined?), "He sometimes . . ." (When? How often?), "She has a great deal of confidence." (How much is a great deal?), "It would seem that . . ." (Would under what circumstances? To whom does it seem? Is it so or not?).

Specify the source of information. Don't say, "Mr. Zamprelli is a sixth grade dropout"; say, "Mr. Zamprelli describes himself as a sixth grade dropout." Specify the sources of assessment conclusions, whether they are observed behavior, interview data, test comportment, comparison of scores with norms, or all of these. When referring to normative standing, specify the comparison group; for example, "Nancy is still shy around strangers, which is not unusual for youngsters her age." "Compared with other hospitalized persons diagnosed as psychotically depressed, Mr. Zamprelli's suicide indicator scores are in the bottom decile; but when compared with the general population of men his age . . ."

Help the reader to know the general character of the tests you refer to. For example: "When asked to copy sample geometric designs freehand (Bender-Gestalt), Mr. Zamprelli . . . " Specify the assessment and life contexts in which reported comportment has occurred (their "whens" and "when-nots"). Life context should include pertinent information on daily environment, social relations, stresses, options, and constraints.

Remember that the null hypothesis can be disproven, but not proven; write to help readers understand that. Examples: "If Mr. Bergstrom has undergone neurological changes, they have not affected his performance on any of the tests we used." "Although our tests cannot rule out the possibility of brain damage, we found no evidence of impairment."

Advocate for the client, but not against others. You serve the client's interests by rendering his or her particular situation understandable and accessible to intervention, but you should be careful not to take the client's side against presumed antagonists. Good guy/bad guy presentations are invariably inaccurate and usually are a disservice to both parties. The following is an example of a statement that either purposely or inadvertently puts the parents in a bad light: "Kurt figures that because his parents don't trust him, he may as well do the forbidden things that they'll blame him for anyway." The assessor could write instead: "Kurt explained that he allows himself to break rules because he believes his parents would blame him even if he were not guilty. At this point I don't know how the parents view the 'rule breaking.' "

Relevant negative features, however, should be presented forthrightly rather than hedged. If they are presented within context, including the client's perspective, they will not be judgmental nor come as a surprise to the client.

For example, rather than hedging by speaking of "Mr. Johnson's mild speech difficulty," one might refer directly to "the stuttering that Mr. Johnson says occurs whenever he is self-conscious."

In addition to the Appelbaum (1970) and Mann (1971) references on report writing, see Tallent (1958, 1983) on individualizing of reports. Sattler (1982) includes a consonant discussion of report writing in his book on *Assessment of Children's Intelligence and Special Abilities*. Seagull (1979) has written a constructive overview of "Writing the Report of the Psychological Assessment of a Child." Tallent (1976, 1983) is the author of a comprehensive textbook on report writing. Hollis and Dunn (1979) have published a practical paperback on writing reports.

General Writing Principles

The author of an individualized assessment report must be an accomplished assessor of an individual's particular ways of exemplifying and exceeding general patterns. He or she must be mindful of report requirements even during the assessment, and develop effective, flexible report formats and special report-writing techniques, including ways of portraying the client in action. But successful communication also depends on mastery of general writing principles.

Authors would do well to review a standard textbook or handbook on grammar and rhetoric, such as Walsh and Walsh (1972). The American Psychological Association's *Publication Manual* (1983) and the National Education Association's *Style Manual* (1966) also provide schematic reviews of punctuation, grammar, and style.

The greatest deterrents to effective communication are: (1) *long-winded sentences* (where the reader loses the subject and verb among too many dependent clauses), (2) *other awkward constructions* (where word placement derails the reader), (3) *imprecise wording* (where the language is too colloquial, general, or abstract), and (4) *superfluous verbiage* (unnecessary words that distract the reader from the central communication). Frequently occurring examples of the last two types of deterrents, taken from assessment reports, are found in Table 5.3. Readable, painless, even humorous exposition on all four topics can be found in Newman (1975), Ross–Larson (1982), Strunk and White (1972), and Zinsser (1976; see especially Chapters 2 and 3 on Simplicity and Clutter). General writing principles, however, are not merely rules to apply in getting thought onto paper. In each report, as I struggle to write effectively for the reader, I discover that my own understanding has been imprecise. In the effort toward clear expression, thought also becomes clearer for the author.

In short, *nonobfuscation* and beyond that just plain *clarity* and *efficiency* in writing are essential if the assessment processs is to culminate in the client's best interest. Efficient writing gives the reader more than clear understandings; it also assures the reader that the assessor is competent, unpretentious, and considerate of readers' time and intelligence. As a result, the content will be taken more seriously.

Table 5.3 presents general writing problems that I most frequently note on trainees' reports. Supervisors can add some of their own peeves, and assessors can add errors they are already working on, to build a more comprehensive or more personal checklist. The suggested revisions for the excerpts were those that seemed reasonable within the particular reports; still others might be appropriate.

TABLE 5.3.   General Writing: Excerpts, Revisions, and Principles

Excerpt	Problem or principle	Revision
In questioning her, she said . . .	The dangling participles (*questioning, asking, speaking,* and *explaining*) do not pertain to the subject of the sentence.	In response to questions, she said . . .
In asking him about this, he replied . . .		Replying to my inquiries, he said . . .
In speaking about her parents, I had the impression . . .		Listening to her speak about her parents, I had the impression . . .
After briefly explaining, we went on . . .		After I briefly explained, we went on . . .
At this point in time	All points are in time; *point* is superfluous.	at this time at present today
John's acceptance represents a chance . . .	This is an inaccurate expression; simpler terms are more accurate.	John's acceptance presents a chance . . . John's acceptance is a chance . . .
It is interesting that the parents . . .	If the material is interesting, it will be so without pronouncements.	The parents . . .
I should note that this applicant . . .	The preface is unnecessary and draws attention away from the subject matter.	This applicant . . . Note that this applicant . . .
It is worth mentioning that Mr. Peters . . .	If something is worth mentioning, it should not require justification.	Mr. Peters . . .
. . . not to mention the home situation	These are contradictory expressions.	. . . including the home situation.
. . . needless to say,		[delete]
her self-dignity . . .	For some readers, "self" is a theoretical construct; for all readers, *self* in these examples is superfluous.	her dignity
his self-confidence . . .		his confidence that he could . . .
She would not allow herself this self-disclosure.		. . . allow herself this disclosure
She spoke in an easy, self-assured manner.		. . . in an easy, assured manner.

TABLE 5.3.   *(continued)*

Excerpt	Problem or principle	Revision
Ms. Hardy expressed that . . .	Was the expression explicit or implicit?	Ms. Hardy said . . . Ms. Hardy implied through a gesture that . . .
Ray showed a marked embarrassment.	Was the showing an intended exhibition?	Ray seemed markedly embarassed.
The patient made eye-contact.	Was this an intentional accomplishment?	Mr. Wecht looked directly at me as he answered.
This student demonstrated a high IQ.	Again, did the student intend to put on a demonstration?	This student scored in the upper decile on the intelligence test.
The physician verbalized that . . .	This use is inappropriate; verbal vs. other expression is not an issue here.	The physician said . . .
The patient presented as a hysteric.	This medical phrase is out of place in a nonmedical report. (Did the patient intend to come across as an hysteric, or did he/she strike the author as being an hysteric?)	The patient struck me as being an hysteric.
She felt really at home only when . . .	*Really* implies both intensity and purity; the intended meaning should be expressed more precisely.	. . . fully at home when . . . . . . comfortably at home when . . .
Max really wanted to go.		Max wanted . . . Max definitely wanted . . . Max had been planning the trip all week.
She is not really retarded.		. . . not so seriously retarded that . . . She feigned retardation. She is not retarded.
On these occasions ask yourself if this is what you really want.		. . . if there is something else you want instead.
I suspect that this was not how he really felt.		. . . that he also felt scared.
Marlene really puts a lot of pressure on her pencil.		Marlene printed with dark, heavy lines.
. . . nothing to be really concerned about.		. . . probably will not happen. . . . is not noticeable to others.

TABLE 5.3. *(continued)*

Excerpt	Problem or principle	Revision
The patient's real motives . . .	Real implies most true or ultimate; this is usually *not* an accurate description. Again, precise expression is preferred.	. . . additional motives . . . unspoken motives . . . strongest motives
Mr. Johnson should be encouraged to express his real self.		. . . encouraged to try out fuller ways of relating to others. . . . encouraged to act independently
The Rorschach was a real test of the patient's tolerance for ambiguity.		. . . was a test of . . .
This patient needs to be put on suicide observation status.	"Need" implies one of four meanings: (a) biological welfare; (b) felt drivenness; (c) desire; (d) in-order-to. The precise meaning should be stated so that it is not fused with the others.	For the sake of this patient's safety, he should be put on . . .
She needs to see that she can do well.		If she comes to see that she can do well, then she will enroll. In order to enroll, she must first see that she can do well.
Mrs. Smythe feels a need to perform well.		Mrs. Smythe feels she must perform well. Mrs. Smythe wants to perform well.
She lacks motivation.	These absolute characterizations are inaccurate through overstatement and non-contextualization	She has not been interested in . . .
The lack of social opportunities . . .		The scarcity of formal social opportunities . . .
She lacks the aggressiveness needed . . .		She has not approached prospective clients assertively.
. . . dealt with constant interruptions from her son . . .		. . . continued interruptions . . . . . . repeated interruptions . . .
He is always aware of . . .		He is frequently . . . . . . usually . . . . . . repeatedly . . . Whenever he sees her, he is aware of . . .
. . . and constantly learned from his mistakes.		. . . and continued to learn from his mistakes.

TABLE 5.3.   *(continued)*

Excerpt	Problem or principle	Revision
She hides a great deal of herself.	Uninformative quantification can be deleted as extraneous; specify what is meant. (Just how much is *extremely, very, a lot, an amount, a number*?)	She has hidden her serious concerns.
Andrew approached this task with considerable self-confidence.		. . . clearly approached this task confidently.
She seemed very nervous and uncomfortable.		. . . seemed nervous and uncomfortable.
. . . especially if he is concerned a lot about how he appears to others.		. . . concerned about how . . .
. . . unsettling amount of confusion.		. . . unsettling confusion.
The youngster was very cooperative.		The youngster cooperated throughout the session.
A certain amount of decorum might be preserved . . .		He might preserve decorum . . .
For an 11-year-old, he is extremely tall.		He is eight inches taller than the average 11-year-old boy.
There are a number of reasons for . . .		Among the reasons for . . . are . . .
. . . would often tap the pencil.	Superfluous words clog communication. As Zinsser (1976) says, they should be "pruned."	. . . often tapped the pencil
She would become flustered when . . .		She became flustered when . . .
The instance that stands out in my mind . . .		The instance that stands out . . . [delete "in my mind"]
The theme that is present involves Michael's emergence . . .		The theme is Michael's emergence . . .
. . . in each test involving any arithmetic skill, . . .		in each test involving arithmetic, . . .
The fact of prior hospitalizations points to . . .		Prior hospitalizations point to . . .
Two issues seemed to arise: . . .		Two issues arose: . . .

TABLE 5.3.   *(continued)*

Excerpt	Problem or principle	Revision
Because of this feeling of empathy, . . .		Because of this empathy, . . .
My thoughts on this matter are that perhaps . . .		Perhaps . . .
For a period of time, until . . .		Until . . .
The expression of enthusiasm in Lisa's voice . . .		Lisa's enthusiastic conversation . . .
She had a good deal of difficulty in relating honestly with me.		It was difficult for her to be honest with me.
She expressed the fact that in a way she is not very happy.		She said she is not altogether happy.
Mr. Rooker manifests strength in his seeking out the support he desires.		There is strength in Mr. Rooker's seeking support.
The style that Donna displayed . . .		Donna's style . . .
The WAIS–R scores are revelatory of . . .		The WAIS–R scores illustrate . . .
The application of the paradigm of competition to her relationships with male peers . . .		Competing with her male peers, . . .
An example of this was apparent when he spoke of a possible misunderstanding . . .		An example was a possible misunderstanding . . .
She had been "going out" with . . .	The reason for quotation marks is unclear. Were these the client's words? Is the author trying to indicate awareness of the term's colloquial status? Or does the author mean the client was only going through the motions?	. . . going out . . .
Her "anxiety attacks" have occurred . . .		She suddenly has become anxious when . . .
		What she refers to as "anxiety attacks" . . .
		These so-called anxiety attacks . . .
Mr. Jameson's "unconscious" reasons . . .		Mr. Jameson referred to these reasons as "unconscious."
		. . . unconscious reasons . . .

TABLE 5.3. *(continued)*

Excerpt	Problem or principle	Revision
		. . . the reasons, of which Mr. Jameson was unaware at the time, . . .
Mr. Petarsky was anxious to get started. This time she seemed depressed. She was hyperactive during the first part of the session.	*Anxious, depressed,* and *hyperactive* are technical terms implying pathology. Other descriptive terms should be used if these diagnostic meanings are not intended.	. . . was eager to get started. . . . was quiet, downcast. I had difficulty keeping Adria seated and focused on the tasks at hand.
He does not feel natural around the opposite sex. This is natural, of course.	*Natural* can imply healthy, statistically normal, at ease, or mundane (vs. supernatural). Say what you mean.	He does not feel comfortable around women. This is an adaptive response. . . . not unusual. . . . understandable, given the circumstances.
sub-test pre-school post-graduate	Current editorial policy deletes nonessential hyphens.	subtest preschool postgraduate
firstly, secondly,	The adverb is incorrect when *first* and *second* do not modify the verb.	first, second,
towards empathetic	The briefer form is more efficient.	toward empathic
irregardless	There is no such word.	regardless
first of all,	The enumeration probably will not be of "all." The briefer form is more efficient.	first,
While he was eager to find out his scores, he was afraid to ask.	*While* means "during."	Although he . . .
Pam was clearly effected by the presence of the stop watch.	*Affect* means "to influence"; *effect* means "to bring about."	. . . affected . . .
Samuel has lead his class in arithmetic	*Lead* is a present-tense verb or a noun (the metal).	. . . led . . .

Writing to Individualize

Languaging either perpetuates habitual thought or creates new visions. Compare the following excerpt with an alternative statement and consider their relative impacts:

Excerpt: "This lack of aggression carries over to her nonconfrontation with the ex-boyfriend."

Alternative: "Similarly, she has not confronted her ex-boyfriend."

The first sentence encourages thinking in terms of anonymous forces, and leaves the client and reader feeling pessimistic about the feasibility of intervention. (How does one fill a "lack"? How does one build "aggression"?) In contrast, the second wording encourages attunement to the client's responsibility for "what has happened." If there is a meaningful pattern, it is one that the client could address and alter. One wants to know more about this boyfriend and about the missed opportunity for confrontation; indeed, one wonders what is meant by "confrontation." Rather than explaining away, the wording invites exploration. Notice that regardless of the intention of the excerpt's author, the objectivistic wording has had a finalistic effect.

The purpose of individualized assessment is to comprehend the client's situation as one in which client and helpers work together for efficient, constructive change. The following techniques are steps toward individualized report writing.

Say what you mean specifically. Some statements are flashing red lights that warn one to stop, reread, reflect, and perhaps reword before going on in one's writing or proofreading: overstatements, totalizations, empty quantifications, professionalese, other jargon, extraneous words and clauses, and constructs.

Constructs are hypothetical notions, traditionally attributed with varying degrees of reality status and explanatory prestige, but which I personally regard as organizing devices for helping us hold on to similar yet different events. We may, for example, refer to assorted effective approaches as being "intelligent" and then abstract still further to speak of "intelligence." A construct is useful as a form of shorthand but dangerous when the term is used as a name for something that exists by itself, and to which we attribute causal force—for example, when we "explain" classroom effectiveness in terms of intelligence scores. Circular reasoning results from the improper use of words like *ability, need,* or *intelligence.*

Saying what one means, both in speech and in writing, requires one to anchor abstractions in concrete examples. Ask yourself how you would explain what you mean to a 12-year-old. If you can't figure out how to do that, then you do not yet know what you mean—what your technical formulations come down to in terms of your client's life.

Convert nouns and adjectives to verbs and adverbs. Constructs are danger signs, especially when a noun is preceded by a possessive verb (for example, "Sam *has* an inferiority complex," "Sue *has* a high IQ.") and when that noun serves to answer questions (Now we see why Sam hasn't asked for a promotion, and that Sue could succeed in math if it weren't for her anxiety). Adjectives that in effect say "such-and-such type of behavior occurred" might as well be nouns. For example, "Sue was nervous during the testing" may be saying "she belongs to the category 'nervous persons.' " That category then functions as a construct.

After stopping at the dangerous noun or classificatory adjective, ask yourself what you have *seen* the client *do* that has been collapsed into the noun. Then describe that doing; verbify, adverbify! Describe the comportment directly; for example, "During the interview Sue smoked a dozen cigarettes, fidgeted with a medallion, and shifted posture every few minutes," or "She answered my questions, all the while nervous*ly* smoking, fidgeting, or shifting in her chair." Verbs and adverbs help the reader to picture the client in action—acting as well as reacting, determining his or her future as well as being determined by circumstances. This vision leaves room for crediting the client with greater responsibility, for looking toward possibility rather than causation, and for exploring interventional entry points into the client's ways of doing things. Verbal and adverbial description evokes background and context for the action. The phrase "angry person" leads us to think mostly conceptually; the wording "angrily pounded the table" leads us to think situationally. In the latter case, questions are more likely to arise and readers are more inclined to pursue reflections. (I wonder if I might have seen the pounding as frustrated rather than angry.)

After describing concrete actions, the assessor may *then* introduce a noun or adjective as a gathering device. For example, "these hostile attitudes" or "such aggressive stands . . ." The reader already knows what is meant in this case by these terms. It is even more helpful to use any terms the client has introduced during exploration of the comportment; for instance, "Mr. Kernick experiences these outbursts as 'announcements of frustration' " or "Other instances of what Arnold refers to as his 'craziness' are . . ."

Use past tense. Present tense generalizes ("John *is* a reflective person" or "John reflect*s* before acting"). Use of past tense ("John reflect*ed* before beginning to draw, just as he had paus*ed* before answering my questions") helps readers to think in terms of concrete events that occurred in particular contexts. Past tense suggests that although the future will not be unrelated, that future is still open. Past tense disrupts inclinations to think in terms of closed categories, reductions, totalizations, and so on. The phrasing, "Mr. Towsend *is* hostile" says he is that kind of person, and hence may behave in that way anywhere at any time. In contrast, "Mr. Towsend complain*ed* to supervisors in an angry, hostile manner" invites the reader to wonder what was going on, under what circumstances Mr. Towsend complains in this manner, when he does not, and how he might be assisted to cope more effectively with problematic situations in the future.

Own your perspective and conclusions. Beware of the anonymity of the assessor ("After establishing rapport, the examiner . . . ," "The tests say that . . . ," "Profile analysis reveals a paranoid personality").

The assessor was part of the assessment situation. It was in the context of his or her presence, interests, and concerns that the client appeared in particular ways. The fact of that context, and something of its nature, should show up in the report. Use of first person (*I* and *we*) encourages readers to picture actual people working on tasks together, in contrast to a vague sense of a type of person undergoing an evaluation. Use of the assessor's reactions ("Several times I drifted off in thought while Tommy laboriously finished his drawings") suggests both how other adults in similar situations might respond to the client and that persons different in particular ways from this assessor might relate differently with him.

Describing the test, as well as your observation of the client working with it, also helps the reader to compare that situation with other tasks that the client faces. "After I had scrambled the colored cubes (Block Design subtest), Ms. Boynton lined them up according to color before looking at the pattern she was to duplicate. She persisted in this approach although my obvious use of a stopwatch indicated that she was losing time. She later confirmed that her parents used to refer to this sort of behavior as 'stubborn.' "

Present the client as a participant. Stop signs: reporting only test productions ("The precision of the designs was above age expectancy," "Her scores were in the average range for her group"); referring to the client only as a member of a class ("This 32-year-old Caucasian female . . . ," "The patient . . . ," "The prisoner . . .").

Referring to the client by name, and without irrelevant reference to classes of membership ("this black unemployment welfare recipient") helps to interest the reader in the person's life. However, if the client is to come across as an individual who can take responsibility for his or her past and future, then that person's active participation in the assessment should be described. In particular, the person's participation, whether knowing or unwitting, in the outcomes should be represented. Techniques mentioned earlier are helpful here too: use of *we,* quoting the client's own words, and description of actual comportment. Another technique is inclusion of examples offered by the client ("Mr. Brunswick agreed that looking for concepts to integrate everything he saw on the Rorschach card was similar to his approach to other threatening events. An example he gave was collecting evidence that his wife was having an affair."). Disagreement, as well as concurrence, with the assessor's perceptions illustrates the client's collaborative participation in the session(s). Mention of disagreements also illustrates the perspectival nature of impressions. For example, "Mr. Brunswick did not agree with my observation that what we named as his 'search for connections' may result in strained logic; rather, he suspected that my own and most other peoples' capacity for logic is 'sadly conventional' "; "It was while working on the Digit Symbol subtest (timed copying of a code) that Janet recognized what I had earlier referred to as 'leaving a distinctive impression'; each circle ended as a curlicue."

Make exceptions advisedly. In an individualized report, exceptions to the above advice should be made only with full awareness of the possible impact of the questionable element. Constructs and anonymous references are sometimes permissible in a paragraph that has otherwise addressed process, context, and perspective. Avoid rewording that results in clumsy sentences and detracts from the main thought. Make these reasonable exceptions; but never use them as the easy way out of thinking your way through the issues.

Table 5.4 provides some further examples of writing to individualize. The excerpts can sensitize authors to problematic wording of two major sorts: (1) writing in terms of constructs rather than comportment, and (2) writing in terms of generalities rather than specifics. The alternative wordings illustrate some workable options; they are meant to be suggestive rather than exclusive.

TABLE 5.4.   Writing to Individualize: Excerpts and Alternatives

Excerpt	Alternative wording
A. From Constructs to Comportment	
Uncertainty about the future creates an unsettling confusion, resulting in an insecurity about his ability to organize that future.	He has been confused and insecure in the face of his uncertain future.
Mr. McCullough has a sense of humor.	Mr. McCullough told his story in a humorous manner.
His expressive difficulty causes a sense of insecurity and inhibits his desire to participate fully in class discussions.	In class discussions he has expressed his ideas tentatively and incompletely.
She is unable to express her anger.	She has found it difficult to let others know she is angry when . . . She has not yet experimented with ways of being openly angry.
Anxiety was evident in the patient's foot tapping and response urgency.	Mr. Smith answered questions before I finished asking them, all the while tapping his foot against the desk. He was less anxious later when . . .
The situation is complicated by her lack of confidence in her ability to handle such matters.	The situation is complicated by her anticipation that she will be awkward in dealing with managers.
Mark has a tendency to move ahead rapidly.	Mark moved ahead rapidly. Mark preferred to move ahead rapidly. In such circumstances, Mark has moved ahead rapidly.
He went into the interview confident of his ability.	He went into the interview confidently. He went into the interview knowing that he could answer the questions.

TABLE 5.4.   *(continued)*

Excerpt	Alternative wording
As she began to doubt her drawing ability . . .	As she began to doubt that she could draw . . .
An example of Kathy's ability to overcome her initial doubt . . .	An example of Kathy's overcoming her initial doubt . . .
Jan experiences great pressure because of an inability to refuse friends' demands on her time.	Jan has felt pressured by unfinished work after she gives in to friends' demands on her time.
	Jan has given in to pressure to spend time with her friends.
Mr. Neil is afraid of his capacity to hurt others.	Mr. Neil fears he may hurt someone.
He has feelings of hesitancy.	He described himself as hesitant . . .
	He has often begun new tasks in a hesitant manner . . .
	He hesitated before beginning to . . .
Michelle evidenced signs of uncertainty.	Michelle seemed uncertain . . .
	Michelle's tone was uncertain . . .
	Michelle did not seem to know . . .
The inability to make contact in some of the Bender-Gestalt figures can indicate schizophrenic dissociation.	Mr. MacIntyre's drawing the figures so they no longer touched may have been an instance of schizophrenically disordered perceiving or desiring to keep things at a distance.
He drew stick figures on the DAP. This evasiveness is characteristic of repressors.	Mr. Johns drew stick figures rather than full persons, just as he had earlier avoided a full discussion with me about his family situation. This way of not dealing with problems head-on is what his prior records refer to as repression.
The urgency in Kevin's gestures expresses his need to gratify his impulses.	Kevin's quick, forceful gestures were another instance of what I saw as his rushing to be rid of obstacles.
Dr. Harper had thought that his career would provide enough action and involvement for his needs.	Dr. Harper had thought his career would provide the action and involvement he enjoys.
Due to her extroversion, . . .	In an extroverted manner, she . . .

TABLE 5.4.   *(continued)*

Excerpt	Alternative wording
This anticipation causes a stammering . . .	This anticipation is followed by stammering.
This withdrawal indicates a fear of . . .	This fearful withdrawal occurred in the face of . . .
Her anxiety causes her to rush and blocks her ability to separate the task into parts.	When she rushed anxiously just to get through the task, she did separate the task into workable units.
Being group-dependent causes assignments to pile up.	Going along with others has resulted in assignments piling up.
Hoping to find out why she gets so frustrated, . . .	Hoping to discover how she has become so frustrated, . . .
We explored what he wants and why he wants it.	We explored what he wants and how he came to want it.

B. From Generalization to Specificity

Debbie is too hard on herself.	Debbie agreed that she has often been too hard on herself.
Rushing is a theme in Mr. Petrack's life.	"Rushing" became a theme for us . . . Mr. Petrack said "rushing" has been thematic . . .
She approaches employees as though . . .	Up to now she has approached employees as though . . .
He gives rapid responses . . .	On this task he gave rapid responses . . .
This 14-year-old girl of Bright Normal intellectual potential . . .	[Delete altogether; say instead whatever is relevant about her being 14 and Bright Normal.]
Projectives demonstrate that . . .	On the projectives, one could see . . . On the projectives, we began to explore . . . John's way of responding to the projectives was . . .
The Rorschach too revealed underlying depression.	On the Rorschach David was again slow to give responses, and these were unimaginative, simple ones except for those involving darkness and heaviness. So here too I saw him as depressed.

TABLE 5.4.   *(continued)*

Excerpt	Alternative wording
The low Afr indicates that she withdraws from emotionally ladened stimuli.	Instead of reporting still more perceptions on the last cards, which are colorful and complex, Mrs. Goldbloom offered fewer responses than she had to the earlier cards (Afr = .54).
	Scores from the inkblot technique (e.g., Afr = .54, L = 1.2) are consistent with Mr. Goldbloom's reports that his wife has preferred to "keep things simple" and has expected him to handle unforeseen complications with the relatives, "rebellions" from the children, and obstreperous service persons.
But the low F% reflects poor reality testing.	Only about 60% of the perceptions he reported while examining the Rorschach cards have been frequently mentioned by other subjects. Here, too, his perspective was idiosyncratic. Nevertheless, I could see what he reported, and when I prompted him, he found the things that most people see.
	Just as he is in disagreement with his union about management's intentions, he noted small details of the cards and saw in them meanings that do not initially occur to most people.
The tests indicate that . . .	From the tests I conclude that . . .
This is a despondent man, desperately trying to maintain denial.	Although he adamantly insisted that "everything's just fine," he nevertheless at other moments struck me as despondent.
Mae's dependency manipulates others into helping her.	I found myself wanting to help Mae discover the right answers as she openly deprecated her own efforts ("That's probably a second grade word").
After rapport was established, the WAIS–R was administered.	After we discussed the referral, I presented Mr. Petrack with the WAIS–R subtests.
She does not have executive potential.	I do not believe she is ready for an executive position.
	I believe that at present she would not satisfy the company as an executive.

TABLE 5.4.   *(continued)*

Excerpt	*Alternative wording*
	Her scores on the Ajax selection tests were all well below those of executives who were rated satisfactory.
The joviality is a cover for fear of failure.	Mrs. Janette clearly enjoyed being jovial, but she seemed also to be working at it, perhaps as a way of avoiding . . .
Underneath the dependency is hostility.	Even as she looked to me for support, I felt she resented being in that position.
She is actually an insecure person.	She is a competent manager, but she also has repeatedly doubted whether she could become a good wife and mother.
The DAP is evidence that he sees women as towering over him.	The DAP led us to explore Tom's feeling "insignificant" around certain women.
	The DAP reminded me of Tom's early admission of "inferiority" in relation to women in positions of authority.
	The DAP self-drawing in comparison to the drawing of a female can serve as an emblem of Tom's present situation.
Behavioral observations: The subject arrived on time but was somewhat unkempt. He was dressed in denim slacks and sport shirt. He was distracted, almost flighty, but cooperative. He was motivated to do well, and persevered.	Dino showed up only two or three minutes late. He was short of breath from hurrying, and explained that he had had trouble finding a parking place and had parked illegally. His hair was windblown and his winter coat open, which added to my initial impression of haste and flusteredness. He waited hesitantly for permission to leave to repark his car. This initial scene turned out to be like other occasions when Dino finds himself flustered and off to a "poor start" at the beginning of projects. However, as he gets further into . . .
Mrs. Thornton was nervous throughout the assessment, but she was also determined to do her best.	When I arrived, Mrs. Thornton was rapidly pacing the corridor. She put out her cigarette but soon lit another one. My first impression, that she was nervous but determined, held up throughout our session.

Checklist for Reviewing a Report Draft

The checklist for reviewing rough drafts consists of my suggestions and criticisms in response to students', trainees', colleagues', and my own reports, along with ideas borrowed from other authors. I long ago borrowed the "so what?" term from Appelbaum (1970), "Barnum effect" from Meehl (1956), and "Aunt Fanny" from Tallent (1958). The checklist includes items discussed earlier in this chapter and adds some additional self-evident principles. General writing principles and report-writing standards are intermixed with individualized assessment criteria. The list presents positive features followed by negative ones.

The checklist is too lengthy to review for every report one writes. I suggest instead that you read it over once and mark or copy your own weak areas. To this reduced list you may add your particular Achilles' heels as well as items that are important in your particular professional setting. A child guidance clinic checklist might include "pre-, peri-, and postnatal development"; a justice system clinic might include "name of probation or parole officer"; in some settings "insurance company and policy number" are important. Some recipient agencies require explicit statements of DSM category, number of years behind grade level, and so on. In short, assessors should tailor the checklist for their own situation.

In addition to maintaining a continuously revised checklist for their own reports, trainees may wish to critique some of the reports in this book against Table 5.5. No report meets all these criteria. However, just as I have learned about report writing by responding to students' efforts, so others may learn by identifying weaknesses in the reports in this book. This exercise is most productive when used to develop concrete, constructive alternatives, rather than just to identify weak points as such.

Not every item in the checklist can or should be applied in all cases. The items are guidelines to be approximated as much as purposes and practical considerations allow. It is their overall impact and utility that count. For each criterion not met, however, one ought to ask, "if not, why not?" For instance, perhaps it is not possible to make a report understandable to a severely retarded person. Still, the reader should find in the report the language and activities through which the assessor and client worked together, so that the reader can help the client to understand how remedial activities are related to the assessment experience. Often the answer to the "why not?" query will be that the report is part of a decision-making process for which individualized understandings and recommendations are not necessary. Although such omissions may be legitimate in view of time and money constraints, a service provider may wish to make use of the report prepared by the decision maker. At that point, the reader requires details about the particular client's life and experiaction. Often the author must strike a balance between writing for present classification concerns and for possible future service concerns. That balance is, inevitably, a difficult one to strike; the easy dismissal of individualizing efforts is usually a cop-out.

At other times the reasons for *not* meeting the checklist criteria will be mundane deficiencies—the assessor's having forgotten to inquire into certain areas, a child's bathroom call having invalidated a subtest, inadequate time having been scheduled for testing, or the assessor's not being familiar with a scoring system that one of the readers prefers. If the missing information is important, one should simply acknowledge the omission outright. The explicitness of the acknowledgment not only helps the reader to make sense of the report, but also encourages the assessor to correct these deficiencies in future work.

TABLE 5.5.   Checklist for Reviewing the Draft of a Report

Positive features

____ Is relevant identifying information (full name, address, age at time of testing) provided?

____ Are the dates of testing and reporting given?

____ Is identifying information limited to directly relevant data? (It need not include number of siblings or race, for example, unless these are important to know at the outset.)

____ Is the referral contextualized? Which actual events or behaviors were of concern, to whom, for what reasons?

____ In future years, will readers understand this report? What were the concerns and circumstances? Under whose auspices was the assessment undertaken? Where are additional records located?

____ Does the referral include precipitating events (for the decision at this point to seek assistance)?

____ Does the referral specify any additional issues that the assessor found it advisable to explore?

____ Does the referral set the stage for what will be discussed in the conclusions and suggestions?

____ Does a background section indicate which factors the assessor has taken into account (for example, family situation, medical aspects, developmental history)?

____ Is background information accompanied by its source—"according to whom"?

____ Does a titled section (such as Sources, Procedures, or Opportunities for Assessment) indicate all background and sources of Conclusions and Suggestions (tests used, documents reviewed, observations in the classroom or on the ward, joint discussion with the client, assessment within the client's home, conversation with the principal)?

____ Does the report's organization help the reader to find particular information without undue searching?

____ Do the headings effectively indicate the nature of each section's contents?

____ Does the report take into account the concerns, sensitivities, and educational background of probable readers?

____ Are adequate data provided for use by other professionals? Do professionals have enough information to judge the author's conclusions? Do they have adequate technical data against which to compare future performance (scores, prior diagnoses, and so on)? Would they want to know how the client performed on some other test?

TABLE 5.5.   *(continued)*

Positive features

_____ If an appropriate range of tests and other sources of data have not been provided, has this omission been acknowledged or otherwise accounted for?

_____ Are appropriate qualifications provided in regard to the limitations of various tests (reliability, validity, age factors, generalizability)?

_____ Are scores translated for the lay reader?

_____ Is the reader given a sense of what each test involves, of what the client is asked to do?

_____ Can a lay reader skim past any technical material and still understand the report?

_____ Does the report's text specify what each test contributed to the assessment outcome?

_____ Does the report provide an integrated picture of the client? Are personality, emotions, developmental stage, skills, achievements, and so on, presented holistically?

_____ Does the reader sense what the client's situation is like for the client?

_____ Is the source of all attributive statements clear? Does the assessor ground characterizations of the client in direct observation, in his or her own reactions, in research on test patterns, or in a particular theory? Are shifts from one of these grounds to another made clear?

_____ Is the client's viewpoint indicated? Does the report include his or her understanding of the reasons for assessment, personal goals and concerns, perspective on reported past events and on the assessor's conclusions and suggestions?

_____ Can the reader readily distinguish between assessor's and client's viewpoints?

_____ Can the reader visualize the client in action? From the report, could an actor or artist vividly portray the client's appearance and style?

_____ Can the reader picture the client in several of his or her environments? Can the reader anticipate the client's comportment in several different situations?

_____ Is the client's participation in outcomes clear? Does the report indicate how the client helps to bring about accomplishments, mishaps, and other "things that happen"?

_____ Have concrete examples illustrated variations of how this client gets into and through situations?

_____ Does the reader see both the short-term and long-term outcomes of the client's approaches to situations?

_____ Can both the reader and the client identify pivot points within the client's experiaction?

_____ Is the assessor's own participation in the sessions apparent? Can the reader imagine how the client might be different with another assessor?

_____ Can the client comprehend the written report?

_____ Is it clear that the client participated actively in the assessment? Is there an explicit statement in an Opportunities for Assessment section, examples within the text of the report, or a Client's Commentary section at the end of the report?

_____ Do the individual suggestions stand out (for example, by numbering)?

_____ Is the purpose of each suggestion clear? Will readers know what outcome to anticipate?

TABLE 5.5. *(continued)*

Positive features

_____ Do the suggestions form an interrelated pattern? Does the reader see the client's problems and options holistically?

_____ Have the Suggestions taken local resources into account (or taken their lack into account)?

_____ Are the Suggestions tailored to the client—to his or her experiaction, style, goals, situation, and to alternative approaches tried out during the assessment?

_____ Will the reader (including the client) recognize the bases and feasibility of the Suggestions? Are they explicitly tied to specific events that happened and that were discussed during the assessment? Are connections with the client's daily life clear?

_____. Are all the Suggestions grounded in earlier parts of the report?

_____ Do the Conclusions and Suggestions address the Referral issues directly? Is there a tight story line running from the Referral, Background, and text, through the conclusions and suggestions?

_____ Are lines of argument and inference clear, and are assumptions specified?

_____ Is the author's use of a diagnostic label clear? Will readers know which of the client's actual experiactions it refers to?

_____ Can the reader tell that the assessor has considered different understandings of the client—"alternate hypotheses"?

_____ Is the draft organized and corrected in a manner that will allow the typist (oneself or someone else) to type without confusion?

_____ Will the general appearance of the final report be of professional quality (letterhead, margins, page numbers, clean copy)?

_____ Is the report well written in terms of grammar, sentence structure, and paragraph organization?

_____ Are the assessor's degree and title provided? (For example, "John Smith, M.Ed., Educational Specialist," "Andrea Jones, Ph.D., Clinical Psychologist," or "James Brown, Graduate Student in School Psychology, State University Guidance Clinic.")

_____ Is the supervising assessor properly identified?

_____ Have headings and space been provided for the client's comments and signature?

_____ Will a confidentiality statement be stamped or typed onto the report?

_____ Will a client's right-of-access statement appear on the report?

_____ Will the bottom of the report, under Client Commentary, include a signed statement indicating whom the client has designated as permissible readers and receivers?

_____ Has a Technical Appendix been attached if needed by other professionals (for example WISC–R scaled scores, MMPI profile sheet, Rorschach structural summary, Bender-Gestalt time, TAT stories)?

Negative features

_____ Does anyone come across as the "bad guy"? Are any of the clients involved others scapegoated via absence of their perspectives?

_____ Are there other signs of partisanship? Has the assessor prematurely sided with one party? Is the report a prejudiced advocacy statement for the client, or for a program or a theory?

TABLE 5.5.   *(continued)*

Negative features

____ Aside from technical jargon, is there any unexplained jargon?

____ Might a reader be confused by terms that have multiple technical meanings, or technical as well as everyday meanings? ("John's vocabulary and information were depressed," "John projected a healthy image," "John has superior intelligence," "He denies hostility.")

____ Is "so what?" an issue anywhere? Does the reader wonder what the point is of any statement?

____ Are there any extraneous (unnecessary) clauses or sentences?

____ Does awkward sentence structure derail or distract the reader? Are phrases or clauses out of place? Are sentences too lengthy to keep the main point in focus?

____ Are there any unclear passages? Are reasons for inclusion unclear? Are the referents for *this, it,* and *that* vague?

____ Does the absence of concrete examples and use of abstract statements leave the reader unsure of the assessor's accuracy or unsure of the statement's meaning in relation to this client?

____ Is any information repeated unnecessarily?

____ Does the report ramble rather than coming directly to the point?

____ Are there jarring juxtapositions of information—unrelated adjacent content? ("John wore jeans, sneakers, and a soccer shirt. He attends Walt Whitman Junior High," and "John's WRAT scores average one grade below expectancy and his Rorschach reflects liability.")

____ Does an unconventional format confuse the reader (for example, absence of subheads or typical subheads out of anticipated order)?

____ Does specialized idiom, slang, or literary reference offend, bemuse, or confuse the reader? (Examples: "being-in-the-world," *angst, karma,* "as Vonnegut would say")

____ Does the Identifying Information, Background, or Referral section cast the client as a "type"—black unwed mother, juvenile delinquent, depressed homemaker?

____ Are there any empty (uninformative) quantifications, such as "great deal," "extremely," "a number of," and so on?

____ Are there any Barnum presentations—descriptions that presumably were developed from testing, but which in fact are true of nearly everyone? Barnum statements often serve (invalidly) to lend credence to subsequent, less trivial, characterizations.

____ Are there any gratuitous truisms ("Aunt Fanny" statements, such as "This patient is sometimes anxious")? Such statements are true of one's Aunt Fanny and everyone else too.

____ Does use of the present tense inadvertently imply pervasiveness or inevitability? ("John takes the easy way out," "This patient resents authority," "The applicant is not motivated to succeed.")

____ Is the report pathology-oriented at the expense of positive features?

____ Does the report underplay relevant pathology, weaknesses, dangers?

____ Is the report's tone otherwise unduly optimistic or pessimistic?

____ Are there any invalid reductions (circular reasonings) from events to specious causes (which are merely general ways of speaking of those events)? (Examples: explaining low achievement as due to low underlying intelligence, explaining fist fights as due to hostility.)

TABLE 5.5.   *(continued)*

Negative features

_____ Is achievement on a particular test or subtest presented as though it were an evaluation of a more general competence? (Example: from Wechsler Scales: "John's strength is in comprehension; he is relatively weak in coding and information.")

_____ Does anything not previously presented appear in the Summary?

_____ Is there personally sensitive information that could be replaced by equally relevant but less personal material?

_____ Does the report contain any data whose relevance is not clear or that appear to bring the conclusions into question?

_____ Does the assessor appear to be hiding behind anonymous roles? (Examples: "the examiner," "tests were administered," "the tests indicate," "it appears that.") Who is the person who is doing the examining, administering, interpreting, concluding?

_____ Are test data regarded as more real or more valid than other observations?

_____ Similarly, does the report focus on test scores or interpretations at the expense of addressing behaviors or situations?

_____ On the other hand, are test data disregarded in favor of observations or theory?

_____ Is there a theoretical bias (not just an orientation) at the cost of a fuller picture?

_____ Does this client come across as very much like previous clients this assessor has described? Is the individuality of the client subordinated to the assessor's preconceptions? Might the assessor just as well fill in the client's name on a preprinted report?

_____ Does the report tell you more than any reader wants to know, at the expense of clear focus and integration?

The Nonevolution of the Literature on Report Writing

This chapter is *commonsensical*, but the individualized practices that it advocates are not yet *commonplace*. The old criticisms of psychological reports are still being raised. For at least the last 40 years, articles, chapters, and books have exhorted authors of psychological reports to write in more useful ways. Each critic has repeated some of the familiar do's and don'ts, and then posed a new line of argument to impress authors with the importance of writing useful reports. During the 1950s and 1960s, journals published empirical studies on the (in)effectiveness of psychological reports as rated by various professional groups. Even in the studies with more or less encouraging results, the researchers concluded their articles with those old exhortations. See Tallent (1976) for a review of the "pitfalls" of report writing that have been identified over the years, and for a summary of the report-rating research.

Of course, there have been some changes in the report literature over the last 40 years. During the 1960s, authors began referring to "clients" rather than to "patients." During the 1970s, articles began to include advice about writing for paraprofessional readers, and about being mindful of clients' subculture and socioeconomic backgrounds. More emphasis was placed on knowledge of the mental health system (regulations, resources, politics) and on environment (social, physical, and as the source of reinforcement contingencies). Greater emphasis has been placed on behavior and less on psychodynamics. Indeed, there is now a speciality of "behavioral assessment." Nevertheless, the major exhortations are still necessary: *Don't* use jargon, don't write in technological terms, don't dehumanize the assessee, don't emphasize scores at the expense of describing the person, don't write in generalizations, don't hide behind tests, don't write from only within one theoretical framework. *Do* indicate the relevance of findings, do qualify general statements, do indicate context of reported behavior, do make concrete suggestions.

Why do we continue to find it so difficult to follow these oft-repeated pleas for making our reports useful to readers? In part, of course, difficulties result from the assessor's position as problem solver. That position encourages an analytic, categorizing attitude, a search for causes, and the application of known (general) principles to the identified problem. But in greater part, the difficulties have to do with the historical, now sometimes only implicit, model that we assessors have emulated: that of the applied physical scientist. In our care to obtain and report findings with proper objectivity, we often have functioned as lab technicians, duly administering standard tests and reporting scores, leaving it to others to determine relevance to actual lives, or merely tacking on clinical insights, interpretations, and suggestions. Either way, we have been restrained by an allegiance to objective tests. Hence we hear the repetitious plea for relevance to clients' lives.

Psychology and the related disciplines have developed well beyond scientism's reductive, technological attitude. If the assessor is not to lapse back into functioning as a lab technician, however, he or she cannot just tack individualization onto earlier test-oriented training. Individualized assessment requires explicit grounding in a nonscientistic approach, such as that of human-science psychology.

To cope with our clients as individuals, we assessors should be clear about the legitimacy of (circumspectly) moving on from our psychometric, psychodynamic, and behavioristic heritages. We should develop explicit understandings of such issues as the relationship of perspective to data and constructs, the relationship of biology and experience, the character of changing comportment, and the ways in which people are at once both free and determined.

I believe that the understandings and examples offered in this book will encourage us to individualize our assessment practices more consistently.

Questions and Responses

Question: Under what circumstances would you write a report that is not individualized?

Response: It is not necessary to individualize a report written primarily for a decision maker rather than for a person who will be working directly with the client. The decision maker has contracted with the assessor in order to learn how the person compares with other people in certain regards. At this point the decision maker is not concerned with the individuality of the person. Examples are determination of eligibility for programs, such as for the "gifted program" in public schools or for a management training program in a restaurant chain; or on the other hand, screening for problems, such as for preschool learning disability or for emotional problems among applicants for police work. Full reports are not called for when the assessment is adjunctive to someone else's work with the client. Examples are a therapist's request for evaluation of suicide potential, or of a possible thought disorder. Even here, however, I state the answer in terms of how it is true of this particular individual.

Question: Does your critique of the lab technician model imply that assessors should not follow the scientific tradition?
Response: There is more than one tradition of science. Assessors should be scientific, but not in the manner of classical physics. A more appropriate model is one that addresses orderliness within human affairs and is critical of mere subjectivity, but also respects the open-endedness of human existence.

Question: It is my impression that the same psychologist who thoroughly individualizes her or his psychotherapy is likely to fall into nomothetic psychological report writing. How do you account for that?
Response: I've often encountered this occurrence. We tend to think more categorically and more causally when we are confronted with short-term tasks, such as assessments, especially when we are expected to use customary tools. In the case of assessment, those tools are tests intended to classify people. However, our actual assessment sessions are more humane, open, and collaborative than the reports indicate. The short-term task of communicating in writing also lends itself to categorical, explanatory accounts. It is my impression that written psychotherapy summaries, regardless of the nature of the sessions, typically are as reductive as our least individualized assessment reports.

Question: If we are serious about tailoring reports for both helpers and clients, shouldn't we write separate versions of the report for each reader?
Response: No. The findings, for both professional and lay reader, are life-context understandings of comportment. Moreover, because there is no single correct understanding, and no one way of presenting the understanding, it is all the more important that readers see the same document and share a common referent. Technical material desired by professionals is available in the appendix of the report. Any additional technical material in the text does not disturb lay readers, in that everyday instances are indexed to specialized events, and the significance of the latter for the client is included in the report.

Question: But what happens if the client isn't ready to read certain things about him- or herself? I sometimes write a separate note to a child, but it is just a note, not a different version of the report.
Response: Collaboration during the assessment process should have brought the views of client and assessor as close as possible at the time. The

assessor's understandings come as no surprise to the client upon reading the report. Any significant differences in viewpoint are specified as such.

A single-version report also allows readers to see by the client's commentary just how far or in what sense that person has understood the assessor's views. Too often authors and readers erroneously assume that if an assessment has been collaborative and is reported in nonjudgmental, nontechnical terms, the client understands it in the same way professionals do. On the other hand, the prospect of the client's commentary encourages the author to write in ways that the client is indeed ready to see. Occasionally that commentary on the single-version report shows readers that the client was readier than anticipated, or alternatively, that the assessor may have been off base.

Question: Do you include IQs in the text of the report?

Response: Usually not, because they are a tool rather than a result of the assessment. Percentile standing and bandwidth reporting, however, often provide helpful comparison with vocational and educational standing. An exception occurs when readers, especially the client or the parents of a youngster, already have knowledge of a nonvalid score. Then the new number is one's most convincing argument against the old one. However, because numbers have such totalizing power, I do not routinely include the technical appendix, which would include IQs, with the client's copy of the report.

Question: Is special literary skill necessary for writing individualized reports?

Response: No. But technological writing is *not* adequate for the task. Authors do have to struggle at times to find ways of going beyond mechanistic formulations to capture a multiplicity of perspectives. It is especially difficult to see, and then to communicate, a sense of process—of the ways a person perpetuates, changes, and is changed by situations.

Question: Doesn't inclusion of the assessor's viewpoints and reactions distract from focusing on the client?

Response: Not if it is done properly; there definitely should be only one subject of the report. Gratuitous references to the assessor are inappropriate. The assessor's presence should serve only as a reminder of the multiperspectival nature of knowledge, and to specify the context in which this client appeared in certain ways. Deleting that context simplifies the report, but at the risk of flattening the client into a simple, presumably univocal, perspective.

Question: Do people read these longish reports? Don't they prefer brief explanations to descriptive understandings?

Response: Decision makers want brief, direct answers, so they can classify, select, reject, place, and so on. That information is presented concisely in the Conclusions. Persons who work directly with the client, however, do read the entire report. If it is tightly written, they appreciate the detail. They recognize the client, see the touchpoints with their own efforts, and understand how to modify those efforts and how to continue the assessing and intervening process.

To ensure that one's reports are indeed helpful, and that they become more so, in addition to soliciting immediate feedback on reports, the author should mark his or her calendar for follow-ups at regular intervals. Three- or six-month telephone checks with clients' helpers let one know what suggestions did and did not turn out to be helpful over the longer range, and in what respects predictions were and were not on target. Follow-up simultaneously contributes to one's diagnostic development, identifies obstacles in the delivery system, and encourages referral sources to ask for exactly what they want of the assessor. Learning to write useful reports is an ever-continuing process.

CHAPTER 6

Counseling Reports: Adults

My introductory assessment course, for which most of these reports were written, begins with training in standardized administration of individual intelligence tests (Wechslers and Stanford-Binet), the Bender-Gestalt, human figure drawings (DAP), and the Thematic Apperception Test. Then each graduate student completes two individualized assessments with undergraduate volunteers before going to a field placement with a partner. The assessors are encouraged to break an assessment into two sessions, so that the client's variations in comportment become more evident. For the field assignments, each partner takes primary responsibility for writing the report for one of the two assessments that they conduct together. The clients, whether volunteers or field-referred persons, meet with the assessor a third time to read the report and write their commentaries on its last page.

In accordance with the principles of individualized assessment, the graduate students view comportment as primary data and tests as occasions to observe comportment in different situations. Assessors are told to re-present comportment rather than claiming "the tests say." Tests and subtests are chosen for their similarity to referral-relevant situations. When standardized completion of a test would interfere with collaborative exploration of themes, the standardized procedures are forsaken. Nevertheless, the assessors are encouraged to use a range of test materials to allow themselves both to recognize similarities across variations and to be surprised by deviations from their expectations.

Among their early re-presentations the assessors include verbal pictures of the client in action. These images help the reader to picture experiaction that is presented later in the report. Images also help to settle readers' preconceptions, thereby allowing the particular person to emerge with greater individuality. Ideally, the visual image should portray the person in action, thereby intimating how that person shapes his or her environment even while being molded by it. Interventions and the modifications that were developed during the assessment are mentioned again in the Suggestions so that the client and other readers recall how he or she already has varied an habitual style into a personally viable alternative. Continuation and further development of this accomplishment are thus encouraged.

Most test data are reported as observed events (as primary data rather than as derived scores). Moreover, rather than automatically reviewing performance on every test, the graduate student assessors first decide what the major outcome of the sessions was, and then choose illustrative instances to share with readers. References to the assessors are in first person (*I* and *we* rather than "the examiner"), and Suggestions are often addressed directly to the client ("John, you may want to . . . "). In this way readers become present to the assessee as a particular person, and to the interpersonal context in which he or she emerged as this particular person. The assessee recalls the actual session(s), now also picturing the events from the assessor's perspective.

All but the last two reports in this chapter were written by first-year M.A. students. The reports were selected to illustrate a range of assessment settings, clients, and styles of reporting. However, one representative setting is missing from this sample, namely the client's home.

I have classified these reports as "counseling" rather than as "clinical" in that most of them were written for the client as either sole reader or as one of the primary readers. Diagnosis of psychopathology was not at issue, and even though most of the assessees were in treatment facilities, the referrals did not deal with choice of treatment. Emphasis was instead on offering understanding and guidance to the client and to the client's employer or helpers. This guidance focused on everyday difficulties and opportunities. However, familiar clinical patterns inevitably emerge through careful re-presentational description even though the graduate student assessors were not yet trained in psychopathology and diagnostic classification.

The reports were written carefully both out of pride in a developing skill and in order to meet grading requirements. The students spent four to ten hours on each report. I reviewed and corrected the reports before they were presented to the client and to the facility staff. Mental health workers sometimes protest that in the midst of multiple assignments, responsibilities, and time constraints, they usually have to write their reports in a single draft. But any draft is of higher quality if one has gone through a training period in which great care was taken to communicate as relevantly, effectively, vividly, and efficiently as possible. That accomplishment improves later work, however hurried.

The most frequent difficulty graduate students encounter in writing individualized reports is not having to write so much, but rather deciding what to leave out. A danger of individualized assessment is the desire to share one's full sense of this person that one has just come to know so well. Another danger for the beginner is the temptation to record all the steps through which one came to an insight. Instead, the report writer must consider how to communicate the client's individuality and fullness strictly in terms of the referral and selected instances of what the reader should know in order to understand the grounds of the Conclusions and Suggestions.

To protect the identity of clients in the reports that follow, clients' names and names of the human-services facilities and of their staff members were invented. Clients' pseudonym signatures, imitating the style of the original signature, accompany reproductions of client commentary on four of the reports. The actual names of the graduate student assessor were retained, but supervisors' names have been deleted.

Each of the following reports is accompanied by a brief introduction and a comments section, to highlight various features of individualized reporting.

These reports are only a sample of the many variations that are possible. The last two reports serve as reminders that reports of individualized assessments need not be comprehensive in order to answer the referral request, and that one must decide case by case whether and to what degree reports should be individualized.

Assessment of an Undergraduate Volunteer: Marie Grabowski

This report was the graduate student's second assessment with undergraduate volunteers. Because this volunteer was not particularly communicative, the assessor did not have the opportunity to try out a full range of individualized assessment practices. Nevertheless, he recognized that Marie's way of being reticent was not merely a defense against becoming involved, but was also her way of participating. In fact, that manner of participating became the focus of their work together. Thus the report illustrates both some of the difficulties that confront the beginning assessor, and some positive ways of responding to them.

In this case, the assessor avoided the trap of accepting "shyness" as a trait. Instead he explored Marie's shy manner by inquiring into its everyday occurrence. He asked about instances when she had been shy and when she had not been shy ("when-nots"). He explored the contexts in which a shy manner worked for Marie, and those in which it resulted in discomfort. Even though Marie was difficult to engage in a collaborative assessment, the assessor remained nonjudgmental. In particular, rather than focusing on her refusals as such, he tried to imagine what it might be like to be in her shoes, and he described *how* she *did* participate in the assessment activities. He made use of his feelings during the assessment to acknowledge and reflect on his part in creating a situation in which Marie was uncomfortable. He shared some of these feelings with her as part of the assessment findings. Finally, he avoided the temptation to recount Marie's behavior test by test. Instead, test comportment was given its proper place as an access to Marie's everyday ways of dealing with tasks and with people.

The assessor was a student from the University of Leiden (in the Netherlands), enrolled as a special student in our graduate program in order to learn more about our human-science approach to psychology.

Psychological Assessment of Marie Grabowski

March 8, 19 ____

Identifying Information

Marie is 18, a freshman at Duquesne University and lives with her parents in Pittsburgh.

Focal Issue

In Marie's psychology course an announcement was made that students could volunteer for practice assessments by graduate students. Marie signed up. But when I called, the long silences on the other end of the line told me that she was uncertain about the project. When we met, I realized that the idea that she should present an issue for exploration had not come across. "I thought there would be some experiments," she said. When I explained again and asked what she would like to concentrate upon, Marie said: "I am shy." Looking back I believe that my ambiguous presentation of the assessment process, followed by my becoming overly directive, contributed to our finding it difficult to work on her issue in a more thorough fashion.

Opportunities for Assessment

We met twice for an hour and a half each time in the Duquesne Psychology Center (March 2 and 6). We worked with the Bender-Gestalt, several subtests of the WAIS, and the Draw-A-Person. The tests presented opportunities for us to observe Marie's more general styles. At times we related what happened with the test material to other aspects of her life.

Introductory Description

I found Marie to be a very attractive girl. That is what first stood out for me. Her figure is slender and elegant, her hair was carefully arranged, and when her brown eyes searched me—which was not often, they were surprisingly twinkling and expressive. I say "surprisingly" because Marie was usually silent, moved slowly, and although she sat upright her head often hung down, her lips firmly closed. Her appearance was still that of a girl, but I could easily imagine her becoming a lady of style.

This first impression of an attractive girl then became overshadowed by her long silences and the uncomfortableness with which she spoke to me. I too felt uncomfortable with these silences. They were not those of a person whose thoughts are elsewhere. She was clearly present, and I believe that at these times she notices nearly everything going on around her and has her own opinions about it all. However, I found it extremely difficult to tell from her conduct what she was thinking. Sometimes I felt that I had to pull words out of her. Especially when we spoke of more personal matters, the silences and pullings gave a certain strain to our dealings with one another. For instance, I asked Marie if she could give me a concrete example of a situation in which she had not been so quiet. Her face lost all movement; she sat upright and stared away from me at the window. As she took a full minute before she spoke, I found myself thinking, "it looks as though you are waiting for a bus." As I looked more closely, though, I could see that she was working on something. Her upper lip moved intriguingly slowly a tiny, tiny bit. Seldom have I noticed such slow, longlasting movements in a face. Under the table her right leg swang back and forth in a contrast that made me curious about what was going on. It seemed to me that she was directing her energies into remaining self-contained.

This picture changed when we worked on the performance-oriented parts of the assessment. While she was doing the Block Designs, Marie was quiet in a charming way. She made me feel more quiet. She looked confident and composed as she completed the designs with few mistakes and at her own pace (125 seconds for #s 9 and 10). To my surprise she said after this subtest: "These blocks drive you crazy." At least to me this had remained invisible. Not being able to tell from her face what was going on and even making wrong guesses made me uneasy. Maybe other people in such situations also feel uneasy with Marie.

The picture shifted again when the focus was not on her nor on her performance, but when she asked me some questions. She had noticed my foreign accent and was interested in where I came from and what I did here. We talked for a while in a different atmosphere. Marie more often looked into my eyes, turned her body away from the table and more toward me. I remember her voice as gaining speed and liveliness.

Marie's Viewpoint

Marie came to the assessment sessions knowing that she can be shy and that she doesn't let people know her easily. However, there are many situations in which Marie does not feel shy. For example, she feels much more at ease in her job as a ticket-taker at a theatre. She is not shy when she is talking with her mother. In general she does not feel greatly distressed about being shy. Rather she sees herself as a serious person with opinions about the things that go on around her. She takes being shy as a fact and as something she has more or less accepted. Early in our meeting she said, "I have nothing more to say about my being shy than that I am shy."

However, as our sessions went on, it became clearer to both of us that Marie's shy manner has occasioned difficulties as well as successes for her. She gave me an example of feeling totally embarrassed in class when the teacher pressured her to tell more when she did not know any more to say. She said she not only felt the teacher's eyes on her but also the eyes of all her classmates, who didn't know her except by this incident. She felt judged.

Marie's Participation in Her Difficulties

It was when I asked Marie about herself that she seemed stuck and awkward, which made me feel the same way. Sometimes I felt left out, as when she seemed to be staring at a blank wall. Other times I felt pushed away and devalued, as when she said of the person drawings, "I can't see that there is something of me in there," and "These drawings are not about me; I have nothing to say." I then pulled harder to get her to say something, becoming more direct in my questions. She was then turned off, and became suspicious and more distanced. She became even less inclined to talk about herself. I wondered if this was like what had happened to her and the teacher in the embarrassing class situation.

Nevertheless we did talk. Eventually Marie told me about other situations in which being shy had been uncomfortable. At first she spoke only of facts and as if we were speaking about someone else. It was also as though she were saying "This is just the way things are; there's no use trying to change them." I realized then that when one is shy, one is faced with a difficult dilemma: it would be nice sometimes to break out of being shy, but being shy it is hard for one to speak about it let alone to try out new forms of behaving. And other peoples' pushing only makes it more difficult to break out of the circle.

Marie and I agreed that she thinks a lot about the things she hears and sees. Toward the end of our sessions, she again remarked that "Tests can't show much; they can be destructive." At that point we began to see a relationship between her holding so many opinions about other people and her feeling so uneasy about the possibility of being judged. Marie didn't tell me exactly what was becoming clear to her, but from her nodding head and her "mmm-mmh" sound I could tell that she had seen something of importance for herself and that she wanted to do something about it. Unlike most of our time together, I felt that in this moment Marie let me see herself considering the desirability and feasibility of change.

Marie's Participation in Her Successes
The above description gives a rather stiff picture of Marie. But that stiffness was present primarily when we focused directly on her, especially when I asked specific questions about her. In other situations, Marie's self-contained manner struck me as positive composure and grace. For example, on the Picture Arrangement subtest, her style was one of quietly thinking and then deliberately doing. She took average time—not too slow, not too fast—and made no mistakes. I was reminded again of a lady of elegant style.

On the Digit Span subtest, Marie matter-of-factly repeated the digits, with no signs of self-consciousness, or of being otherwise distracted. She did unusually well (8 digits forward, 7 backward). Here, as in those courses that do not require class participation, her quiet, distanced style was appropriate and effective. She was comfortable and confident.

Although our talking about Marie's life did not proceed smoothly, our relationship did grow. As I learned to share some of my feelings. Marie seemed more open and responsive. When I mentioned feeling left out and sometimes kept out when she held her head and eyes down, she acknowledged that she had heard that from other people. Then from time to time she tried to look more openly into my eyes. I could imagine that she undertakes similar accommodations at work and at home, and that she is appreciated for them. I imagine also that she is appreciated for giving others lots of space. Finally, when Marie is not worried about being judged, others no doubt are responsive to her liveliness and warmth—of which I saw only fleeting moments.

Summary
In the assessment situation with me, Marie was a girl who didn't let me get to know easily who she is or what she thinks. She is quickly embarrassed and suspicious when people want to get to know her in this potentially judgmental way. Working with her was like looking into many grey clouds on a winter day, but every now and then the sun broke through changing everything into a vivid, bright vision.

In our short time together I did not get to know Marie well. But I think that through our sessions she has seen more clearly some of the ways she is shy. She has seen the strengths, but also how her silence can sometimes affect others so that they contribute to a mutual discomfort. I felt uncomfortable during the times when it was impossible for me to tell from Marie's face what her mood was. Often I felt there was something she was about to say but didn't. When she looked directly at me, her face changed, and I felt an invitation to talk.

Suggestions for Marie
1. Your eyes are beautifully expressive, and I think it is a pity you hide them so often. Perhaps sometimes when you are hiding your eyes you could remember that in our sessions looking up into the other person's face was not so difficult after all, and that the situation looked better, not so dangerous, then.

2. Also, the next time you feel uncomfortable when you are holding yourself back, you might remember that your closed mouth and unexpressive

face may be putting the other person too into an awkward, uncomfortable position—as happened with me. If you wished, you could then break the circle through a brief conversation like those we had.

3. Many of your quiet ways are effective and also pleasant to behold. Perhaps it would help to remember that "being shy" is neither good nor bad in itself, nor is it something that just is. As we saw when you practiced looking into my face, you can guide your ways of being yourself so they work best for you.

Reynout van der Poel

Marie's Commentary

To me, this assessment was very interesting, and I believe that it may help me very much in understanding the way I see myself as compared to the way others really see me.

The summary of myself and the remarks about my behavior were very identifiable and explicit. I agree with them for the most part, and this will make me understand that sometimes I do not always make people feel comfortable in the way in which I am silent, and possibly this may further motivate me to overcome my problem.

Marie Grabowski

March 9, 19___

Comments

The introductory description of Marie is notably effective. The contrasting profiles presented there not only foreshadow the report's themes, they also disrupt inclinations (including Marie's) to think of the focal issue as a trans-situational trait. Instead, readers are introduced to a sense of dynamics. They also sense that Marie could develop in many directions. In order to present this introductory description, the assessor had to look for such variations during the assessment sessions. Usually it is not until the end of the sessions that the assessor knows how these profiles cohere as different aspects of the same person. Only then can one choose which incidents best reflect what the client and assessor have learned. The most effective illustrations are those that described the person in motion—moving through specified situations. Readers are thereby assisted in imagining pivot points into and out of positions in which clients find themselves.

Because Marie was self-referred for the assessment, she was the primary reader of the report. If someone else such as an employer or counselor were the primary reader, additional kinds of information probably would be required. This information might include clarification of Marie's reasons for signing up for the assessment, and a background section on her social and academic life.

In this report, I would like to have seen more sentences on what "I am shy" means to Marie—what she likes about it, when she experiences herself as shy, and when she thinks others experience her as shy. Nevertheless, as Marie's Commentary indicates, recognizing oneself in the simple descriptions of the assessment activities is a powerful experience. The client does not require background sections. In fact, for the client, such sections often distract from and hence diffuse recognition of oneself in the behavioral portrait.

Marie's Commentary also helps us to understand how it was that no interventions were undertaken during the assessment sessions. Even while reading the report, she was coping with still-evolving realizations that others may perceive her differently than she had thought, and that her shy ways influence others' actions toward her. Although she had cognitively understood the suggestions, she is not yet ready to try them, just as she was not ready to participate in developing them with the assessor. Marie may make use of them later. In the meantime, her comments tell the assessor and any other readers that although the assessment was both collaborative and accurate in its particular way, the assessor's report is still ahead of Marie's understandings.

Finally, this report illustrates the importance of allowing readers to see who the assessor was—how he responded to Marie, what he felt and did. Through his various reactions one can imagine how other people too might respond to Marie in similar situations. Moreover, one can readily imagine that Marie's portrait would have varied with either a more directive, task-oriented tester or with a Rogerian, empathy-oriented counselor. An assessment report is always a portrait from a perspective; if that perspective is clear to readers, the report becomes multiperspectival. Readers realize that the client may be understood in different ways, and in fact is different with different people.

Assessment of an Undergraduate Volunteer: Lea James

The following report is from another assessment by a master's student. Again, the primary reader is the undergraduate volunteer. Unlike professionals who might read such a report, the subject of this kind of assessment does not find the report too lengthy. Instead, the detail helps the person to recall the assessment and surrounding events. In my courses, the graduate students learn first to describe in detail, and then to present the same material more concisely. Later, the time constraints of most work settings encourage the students to re-present events from the assessment more selectively and hence more efficiently. In the meantime, a report of this length, clearly organized and well written, is helpful to the undergraduate volunteer. The report also provides a good description of what individualized assessment sessions are like, and illustrates the helpfulness of taking mundane problems seriously.

Lea's presenting problem certainly is not unusual, and the report's suggestions are the commonsensical sort that the graduate student could have offered without going through an assessment. However, the assessor knew that common sense was no more sufficient for Lea than for the rest of us when we attempt to change our habits. The graduate student accepted the problem as presented and waited for examples of it to arise during the assessment sessions before suggesting options. Practicing and tailoring some of these options and discussing their similarity to the assessee's life situations rendered the options personally viable. Assessment procedures are not the only route to that end, of course, but they certainly can be efficacious.

Finally, this report illustrates how a working relationship evolved over three assessment sessions (two mandated by course requirements, and one that was due to Lea's and the assessor's scheduling according to the only time slots that were mutually available). In addition, when I asked the graduate student if she would revise the report for use in this chapter, she included an addendum about a fourth meeting. The addendum is representative of what one might write in a clinic, and it attests to the "progress report" character of any individualized assessment write-up.

Date of report: April 24, 19 ____
Sessions: April 16, 20, 22.

Psychological Assessment
LEA JAMES

Lea James is a freshman at Duquesne University. She turned eighteen on the last day of this assessment. She plans to major in Political Science and is considering Journalism for her minor. Lea volunteered for this assessment through her Introductory Psychology class.

Presenting Problem

Lea originally volunteered because she was curious about what it would be like to take psychological tests. She was interested to see how she would do on the intelligence test and what new things she could learn about herself. When Lea and I conversed on the phone to arrange our meeting, I suggested that she think about a personal issue or problem that she might wish to explore during the assessment.

Lea proposed as a focal issue that she had too many things to do and not enough time to do them all. She explained that she wanted to do everything at once and usually ended up scheduling too many things in too short a span of time. It has been important for Lea to devote time to her school work, her sports activities, her family, friends, and her boyfriend whom she has been seeing for a year and a half. However, between moving at a fast pace to keep up with all these activities, and feeling cramped by the pressures of time, Lea has been jumpy and tense during much of her day and it has been difficult for her to unwind and relax. She mentioned, for example, that the night before our first meeting she couldn't get to sleep, her thoughts raced, and she mulled over plans a mile a minute. Lea wanted to do "something" during the assessment that related to the stress she was feeling, even though she didn't have a clear idea about what that "something" would or should be.

Assessment Procedures

Lea and I met three times at the Duquesne University Psychology Center, spending a total of five hours for the assessment.

We began the assessment with a brief conversation, then moved on to the following tests:

Bender-Gestalt (Bender)
Wechsler Intelligence Scale for Adults (WAIS)
Draw-A-Person (DAP)
Thematic Apperception Test (TAT) (Cards #1, 2, 3GF, 8GF, 12F, 16, and 17BM)

As we moved through the testing process, Lea and I dialogued our impressions and observations about her style of approaching the assessment situation and how this related to other events in her life. This report presents our findings.

Appearance and Comportment

Lea arrived early for the assessment. She sat waiting for me in the hall of the Psychology Center, leaning back comfortably, with one arm draped over the side of her chair, and her legs crossed and extended straight out in front of her. Her other arm was perched back and resting on the arm of her chair as she twirled strands of her light brown hair in circles around her fingers. She was casually dressed in beige corduroy pants and an off-white, colorfully patterned sweater. She smiled in a bright, friendly manner as we introduced ourselves.

Lea is almost of average height and she has a petite, trim figure. Her big blue eyes looked alert and attentive and her glossy, shoulder-length hair was neatly kept. Her youthful appearance added to her air of healthy, athletic, well-being.

As we began the assessment, Lea sat looking relaxed yet ready to begin. She began each task throughout the assessment readily and self-assuredly, as if confident that she would do well. But when she reached a difficult part in a test, she often paused, knitted her brow, and pursed her lips, as if she were concerned about getting an answer wrong or not performing well on a drawing. When Lea was engaged in the drawing or performance tasks, she sat leaning forward over the test materials, working quietly, quickly, and diligently. She looked thoroughly engrossed in her task. When we talked or when she answered verbal questions, she sat back in her chair looking calm and reflective, yet she delivered her answers quickly and decisively. I had the impression that Lea tried to do her best on each test.

Although Lea was responsive to my questions and easily engaged in conversations about herself, she usually remained quiet until I spoke to her. She seemed to require my overtures before she would talk about herself.

Background Provided by Lea
During our talks, Lea acknowledged that she was confident that she could do well in school and she said that her classwork has not been a problem. She mentioned that her parents expect more from her academically than any of the other children because she has, as she put it, "the most brains in the family." She added that even though her parents expect her to do well in school, they don't push or force their expectations upon her. Her boyfriend also expects her to do well, and encourages her to try harder in her studies so that she can go to a better school such as Carnegie-Mellon University, where he will be studying next year.

The Assessment
Squeezing Things In
Just as Lea tries to do too many things in too short a time, she drew the Bender in a similar manner. She worked as quickly as she could and she drew her figures as compactly as she could. When I pointed out that her drawings were close together, she remarked that she usually wrote and drew things that way. When she takes notes or writes letters, she squeezes her writing in closely together. She said, "I feel that I need to conserve space."

When we talked about her having drawn her Bender figures rapidly, she repeated that she usually tried to do things quickly. She also added that when she goes out with friends and she doesn't have much time to be with them, she becomes "worked up" and tries to do as many things with them as possible. Lea ends up moving from one fast-paced activity to another, giving herself little time to slow down.

In contrast to her many fast-paced activities, Lea likes to write essays and poetry. Writing poetry relaxes her because she has to slow down to think carefully. As she slows down she becomes totally absorbed with what she is doing. Writing poetry is one activity that Lea doesn't rush herself with. She gives herself all the time that she needs to work on a poem, so that she can get it just the way that she wants it.

Trying Hard to Do Well All the Time
Lea's feeling pressured and stressed around scheduling so many activities in too short a time is compounded by her simultaneously trying to do the best job she can with the things she does. When Lea drew the Bender drawings she tried to draw them as neatly and as accurately as possible. When I asked her about this she replied, "I figured I can't go wrong if I do them just right!" When Lea got to the fifth Bender card, a dot drawing, she laughed and made a grimace. She described her feelings as: "Oh no, do I have to get these dots exactly right . . . . . oh forget it, it would take years to get them perfect."

Lea tries to do her best on her school projects. When she cooks she follows the recipe to the tee so that she won't make any mistakes, and she tries to do her chores just right. She becomes frustrated when she can't do a good job on a task. In social situations she puts similar pressure on herself when she is with friends or with her boyfriend because she feels that it is up to her that they share a lot of fun. She becomes upset if she and her friends don't have a good time when they are together. She feels that she has disappointed them and let them down.

I suggested to Lea that she do the Bender over again, only this time dropping her own expectations that she had to do the Bender perfectly and as quickly as possible. Even though she still drew the Bender rapidly the second time around, she looked more relaxed and became playful with the task. She followed the movements of her pencil around with her head as she drew, in a sort of dance, mimicking with these motions the contours of the lines and curves that she put down on the paper. She accompanied her movements with little whistling sounds and laughter as she drew.

When Lea finished the Bender, she looked at me and said, "It was funner that time." She was surprised that she had been almost as accurate on the second Bender as she had been on the first. Seeing this reminded her of her poetry writing. She explained that sometimes when she finally stopped trying so hard on a poem and just let herself go with it, her writing came out as well, if not better, than if she were trying to make it perfect.

Wanting to Please Others

When Lea and I met for the third meeting of the assessment, I asked her if she had any questions or concerns to voice before we moved back into the testing. She made two comments. First, she said that she hoped that I would get all the "stuff" that I needed for my report. Second, she wondered what I thought about how she had done on the test battery. These remarks hit at the heart of an important issue for Lea, and we stayed with this theme for the rest of the session.

Many of the things Lea does, she does in order to keep other people happy. She becomes concerned about what other people think of her. She wants people to like her and to think that she does a good job with things. She mentioned that her boyfriend reminds her, "You can't please everyone."

Lea explained that she often sacrifices what she wants to do in order to go along with what other people want her to do. Lea becomes tense and pressured when too many people place demands on her at the same time. She feels guilty when she says "no" to someone, particularly if that someone is special to her, such as her boyfriend and family members. She also becomes scared that people will be dissatisfied with her if she does something she wants to do just for herself.

Lea realizes the bind she puts herself in when she doesn't say "no" to others' wishes when they are too much for her. She knows this puts her under pressure but she has not felt ready to change.

Lea described a situation that arose over the weekend when she had gone home. Sunday afternoon her mother wanted her to stay home and help her with things around the house, her boyfriend wanted her to go for a walk in the park with him, and at the same time she knew that she had to get some schoolwork done. Lea tried frantically to figure out how she could do all these things in the short time that she had and she ended up becoming very tense and edgy. Somehow she managed to squeeze them all in.

When I gave Lea the blank TAT card (#16), at the end of the session, she described a scene in which a boxer is getting pummeled in the ring. He is losing the fight. He knows that there are better ways to make a living, but he also knows that he is not ready to give up the ring. He'll just keep going back for more beatings.

Her story reminded her of herself in two ways. It reminded her of her present life because she feels defeated when she can't say "no" to people.

However, she does not feel that she can change this pattern yet so that she can "get out of the ring." Her boxer story also invoked some feelings of concern she has about her future. Lea set a goal for herself a long time ago to pursue and to establish a career for herself that she will enjoy. Now she becomes scared sometimes that she'll end up settling for a job that she doesn't enjoy or find creative. The tension that she becomes caught up in on a day-to-day basis, when she foregoes her own wants in order to satisfy others, accentuates her fears that she may compromise herself and not be able to reach her career goal.

When Lea had finished her TAT story, she paused for a moment and said, "Ya know, I feel lousy when I comply with others and sacrifice myself. I don't want to feel lousy and depressed anymore and I have to think of how I can change that." Lea and I then talked about what she would have to do to be able to say "no" to others. She would first have to say "yes" to herself. We talked about how when she feels herself becoming tense and edgy in a pressuring situation, she could stop and reason out what her priorities are. Lea said she would have to make sure that she just wasn't being selfish, that she wasn't hurting anyone else and, most importantly, that her decision would work out for others as well as for herself.

I asked Lea to think back to the tense situation that had arisen the weekend before and to imagine herself saying no to someone's requests in order to take pressure off herself. Lea thought carefully for a moment and said that she would tell her boyfriend, Mike, "I have a lot of things that must be done today. I don't have time to take a walk with you but I do have time to see you while I'm doing chores and packing."

Just Being Herself

When Lea drew herself in the DAP drawings, she enjoyed the picture she drew. She explained that she drew her "carefree and easygoing self in her old bummy jeans." This is the way she likes to be the best, "just being myself, being relaxed, and not caring what other people think of me."

Summary

Lea's presenting problem, that of feeling tense and under pressure with having too many things to do and not enough time to do them in, remained our focus throughout the assessment. The assessment process provided an opportunity to explore and discuss many of the personal elements that combine to create this problem for Lea.

Lea's manner of drawing the Bender is indicative of the way she goes about doing many of her daily activities. She often tries to do the best job she can, giving herelf a minimum amount of time for each of her many tightly scheduled activities. Stress builds up for Lea as she races from one activity to another in this way.

Just as Lea wanted to help me with my assessment project, so she often wants to please other people. She tries to live up to the high expectations that she feels other people have of her. She gets herself in a jam when she tries to do too many things for, and with, too many people. She has had a difficult time saying "no" to others when they request her time, even when she knows she is overtaxing herself by complying with their wishes.

Suggestions

Lea, here are the suggestions we developed in the assessment:

1. We talked about how just as you chose to draw the Bender as quickly as possible, you often just automatically undertake projects that lead to your becoming "worked up." Try to pay attention to this pattern when you recognize yourself moving into it, and ask yourself if this is the best or only way to undertake your activities.

2. You know from your experience writing poetry and drawing the second Bender that you can still do a good job with things even when you're not pushing yourself to do them perfectly. Remember also that you remain more relaxed and enjoy your undertakings more fully when you do them as you did the second Bender.

3. We talked about the uncomfortable binds you put yourself in when you don't say "no" to others' requests when they are too much for you. We discussed a "how to say no" process, which you then practiced in our session. Implementing this process within pressuring situations will offer you a way of avoiding being overburdened.

4. As your DAP drawing of yourself reflected, you enjoy yourself when you have times to relax and not care what other people think of you. Keep this in mind, and try to give yourself time during the day to let yourself go like that. It may give you a chance to unwind and just let yourself feel good about yourself for a while.

> Catherine Burke
>
> Graduate Student
> Department of Psychology
> Duquesne University

Lea's Commentary and Signature

Excellent review-assessment suggestions very helpful. Very glad I did the assessment, or rather participated in the assessment. Thanks for the help.

_____ Lea James
Signature

Lea wrote the following comment in the text with regard to the issue of saying "no."

"I'm beginning to start to change now, doing more of the things that I want, but not being pushy. It should work out for the better with any relationship."

Addendum (6-12-_____)

Lea and I met to talk about the changes that she had been making in the month and a half since the meeting at which she reviewed the assessment report. During our discussion, she said with surprise, "You know, I really didn't think that I would get much out of the assessment when I volunteered, but it has really made a big difference for me." Lea enthusiastically explained that now she can slow down and relax from time to time, and that she no longer feels as though she is under constant pressure. Specifically, she now pays more attention to when she needs time to do her own work and to pursue her own interests. Lea also remarked that telling other people, such as her mother and boyfriend, that she doesn't have time to do things with or for them has presented her with a new problem: they sometimes become angry with her.

CB

Comments

Again, we see in this report that the primary data of individualized assessment are life events, and how testing activities make those events concretely and holistically available to assessor and client. Even though Lea probably had told herself earlier the same things that appear in this report, change became personally viable for her as she lived through familiar happenings in the company of the assessor. Not only did Lea and the assessor thematize what they saw, they also broke through habitual totalizing self-characterizations to identify past when-nots and contexts. Lea came to recognize when she was moving into hurrying and accommodating. The test materials also afforded Lea and the assessor opportunities to try out alternative comportments (as with the relaxed Bender). Later those experiences served as vivid reminders, holistic images of the newly available ways to move through previously problematic situations. To promote that function of the assessment interventions, the assessor was careful to mention them concretely in relation to each suggestion. These reminders are not just cognitive; Lea recalls experientially and bodily how she had already accomplished the suggestion.

As is most often the case, we recognize Lea in her Commentary. In particular we see her pleasing the assessor even while taking her own stance, and we see her jotting down her remarks in a hurried but efficient manner. Sometimes the client's Commentary elaborates or adds to the report, either because a point seemed to require greater attention than it was given in the report, or because only upon reading the report did the point occur to the client.

Never have I read a Commentary that disavowed the assessor's account of the sessions, but I have seen some that led me to wonder whether the assessor had missed or at least not represented an important aspect of the client. Examples are a bold scrawl from a person described primarily in terms of cooperativeness and accommodation, serious spelling errors by a person whose academic credentials had gone unquestioned by the assessor, and snide remarks from a person who had come across as domineering in the assessment but not as unkindly so. Whatever the client's Commentary, it is an extension of the report, inviting the reader to continue evolving his or her understanding of the client.

The assessor's Addendum is another reminder that assessments are not psychological x-rays of permanent, basic personality. Since clients are always evolving, any report is partially outdated even as it is written. In the Addendum, we see the progress Lea has been making, in large part as a function of the assessment. We also see another truism that beginners sometimes forget: Progress usually involves new problems (for Lea, others' unhappiness with her recentering).

Community Mental Health Center Referral: Linda Mariani

This is the first of the four assessments in this chapter that were conducted in clinical settings by masters students toward the end of the semester. Because the individualized report is longer than most reports the center's staff were accustomed to, the authors chose to place a summary (General Outcome of the Assessment) immediately after the Presenting Problem section to assure readers that the report responds to the referral. In addition, the Outcome section serves as a preparatory overview for readers, and as a reminder for Linda of what she achieved through the assessment.

The introductory description of Linda is particularly effective. Through its vivid images the reader can picture Linda while reading the remainder of the report. The images were carefully selected to represent (re-present) Linda's contrasting ways of being, and to presage the report's description of how those ways had worked both against and for her. The primary author's responses to Linda's various comportments show Linda and other readers how she helps to shape other people's attitudes toward her. These accomplishments of the introductory description were possible only through concrete instances of Linda in action. Another effective aspect of this report's introductory description is its nonjudgmental frankness. Linda's comments at the end of the report indicate that she recognized herself and felt accepted.

Individualized Assessment of Mrs. Linda Mariani

Date of Report: Nov. 19, 19 ____

Mrs. Linda Mariani is 44 years old and is currently attending community college. She lives with her husband, Frank, their only child, Leslie (age 22), and her mother in a southern suburb of Pittsburgh.

Presenting Problem
Linda has been in individual psychotherapy at the Community Mental Health Center in Haverford, with Ms. Janice Davis, for the past month and a half. Ms. Davis recently invited her to participate in an assessment so that they both might gain a better understanding of her problems and options. In our first meeting with Linda, she stated that she "wanted to know why (she) wasn't more self-confident" at school, particularly when she is being observed by classmates or teachers. Linda's purpose for going to school is to learn secretarial skills that will help her get a job. As she encountered problems at

school, she became discouraged and has questioned whether she will succeed in the outside world of work. She attributes many of her problems at school to the way she becomes anxious: "The hands will shake, the voice will break, and the heart will pound."

General Outcome of the Assessment

During the assessment, Linda became increasingly involved in looking at the situations in which she is uncomfortable and testing out new ways to approach these situations. Her initial approach to the assessment seemed to shift rapidly from expecting to be told about herself to actively exploring with us the problems she has had. Linda seemed to enjoy the venture as she realized it would be cooperative, commenting that she was looking forward to our report and to writing her comments about whatever might strike her as "off the wall." This process of sharing her concerns with others seemed to be, in itself, an important outcome of the assessment. It was a vivid example for her of how, when she spoke honestly and was vulnerable to others, she did not feel weak or anxious, but at ease.

In our work with the assessment materials, we identified several styles of approaching tasks that seemed to hinder Linda in the assessment as well as in everyday situations [see "Linda Mariani's Participation in Her Difficulties"]. As Linda related these ways of working to the times she has felt anxious, she explored with us some alternate approaches. She discovered that she has felt more at ease in what had been anxious situations when she has communicated with others about her feelings and decisions instead of cutting herself off. The most memorable incident of the assessment occurred when Linda role-played a discussion with her husband in which she told him, for the first time, how much she needed and loved him. This was one way that Linda began to experiment with what she called "opening the doors of communication" with her family, her classmates, and her teacher. By doing so, Linda may gain support and guidance as she becomes re-oriented toward what she wants personally and in her marriage [see the last pages for suggestions to the client]. The remainder of this report reviews the process of the assessment.

Opportunities for Assessment

The assessment was conducted over three sessions by Andrea Jones assisted by Kareen Malone, graduate students of the Department of Psychology at Duquesne University. The sessions took place at the Haverford Community Mental Health Center on Nov. 6 (2 hrs.), Nov. 10 (2 1/2 hrs.) and Nov. 14 (1 1/2 hrs.). Test materials used during these sessions were: the Bender-Gestalt, the WAIS (Information, Arithmetic, Similarities, Vocabulary, and Block Design subtests), the DAP, and TAT cards #'s 17BM, 16F, 2, and 10.

Introductory Description of Linda Mariani

Linda is a short-statured woman of 44 whose tight, greying curls neatly surrounded an open and expertly powdered face. During the assessment she wore colorful, fashionably loose blouses which made her figure, although slightly heavy, seem attractive. Her dressy earrings complemented the quality of her make-up. She seemed to take great care in her appearance, even as she dressed "casually."

At our first meeting, I invited Linda to take a seat with us at the empty circle of chairs. While commenting that she didn't want to sit in the overstuffed chair, she headed right toward it and then slowly sat down, as if testing it out. When I urged her to take a different chair, she wavered a bit and then seemed relieved to comply. Somehow, in seeing her hesitate as if she wanted to move but couldn't, I had felt called on to help her get what she wanted. It turned out later that Linda rarely allows others to see her hesitation and wants.

Linda perched herself on the wooden swivel chair, her knees held close together and her large purse stationed on her lap. Despite the apparent immobility of Linda's lower body, she seemed poised and ready to leave at any moment.

Scarcely ten minutes into the interview, Linda's voice assumed what seemed later to be an habitual loudness, and her hands moved emphatically with her speech. As she spoke, Linda gazed directly into Kareen's eyes; the strong lines of her face made her delivery seem more forceful. Kareen seemed to become mesmerized. Linda's well-articulated and lengthy descriptions of her current and past problems dominated the first session. Kareen and I both hesitated to interrupt.

During the following sessions and as we moved into using the materials, Linda's posture and speech seemed more relaxed and varied. Her purse was placed on the floor and her lower body no longer seemed static as she shifted in her seat. As the assessment progressed, she moved her gaze more frequently from Kareen to me and back. Reciprocally, the two of us became more active in talking with her and were surprised at how easily we interrupted her when her stories became long.

Linda Mariani's Viewpoint

Over the past several years, Linda began to establish and realize some of her own personal goals, beyond those of caring for her family. She has been a member of Weight Watchers and has lost 70 pounds. Over the past winter, Linda decided that she wanted to get out of the house and find a job as a secretary. She feels that she has received little recognition for the work she has done in the home and would like to pursue a job that would "give [her] a feeling of self-worth." In addition, it is important to her that she feels she can stand independently of her husband's support. In order to achieve this goal, Linda studied for and received her GED this past Spring and began courses at Community College.

Linda's attempt to master shorthand and typing has been a constant struggle for her. She has felt ready to cry when she makes mistakes; her hands have felt frozen at the typewriter during speed tests; she has been afraid of her voice breaking when she speaks up in class or talks with the teacher about her problems.

Despite her past successes, these new difficulties have provoked Linda to question whether she <u>will</u> move away from being "only" a housekeeper toward being an "independent" person who holds a paying job. As Linda told us at the beginning of the second session, she entered the assessment with the fear that she would be told that "there are things that I think I am capable of doing that I am not capable of." Linda has stated emphatically, however, that she "won't go back to being a dowdy, fat, little housewife." She seemed determined to do whatever it took to remove any roadblocks from her path. She seemed to consider both therapy and the assessment as ways she could learn to handle her problems more effectively.

Linda Mariani's Participation in Her Difficulties

One theme that ran through the assessment was how Linda "jumped in" to situations and decisions, without checking out what she was doing until later. Her approach to many new situations has been to plunge ahead without looking like she needed any assistance and without turning to others for support. The problems and the opportunities created by this approach were examined within the context of the assessment itself and were related to Linda's life situation (see also "Linda M's Successes and Options"). We discovered ways in which Linda has cut herself off from other people and from her own potential success through this "jumping in" style.

Linda's responses to the questions and tasks of the assessment came with unusual speed. During the WAIS, her eyes became glued on Kareen; her forehead wrinkled and her hands twisted around a pencil as she fired her answers back. Eager to do it right, Linda jumped into the B-G and the Vocabulary subtest, missing key aspects of Kareen's initial instructions. When questioned, Linda stated that by jumping into the B-G task she prevented herself from thinking about it and thus did not become anxious about her performance. In both instances, however, she had to stop in the middle of the task to request information before proceeding.

Linda has faced similar situations in her typing class and at her new part-time job. On two specific occasions, as Linda plunged on with a task at hand, she neglected to listen to the typing teacher's lecture on punctuation marks and to the store owner's explanation of how to make a bank deposit. By concentrating on what was immediately present to her, she avoided worrying about how she might handle these new complications. This approach backfired when she discovered later that these explanations were necessary for doing her job.

On the Vocabulary subtest, Linda's jumping in to answer right away had led Kareen to assume that she understood how the test was set up, and thus Kareen didn't continue to point out the words on the Vocabulary sheet. After four vocabulary words had gone by, Kareen and I were surprised to learn that Linda was confused about the purpose of the Vocabulary sheet.

Linda described other situations in which she put herself out, alone on a limb, by appearing to be in control of a situation while she was really unsure of herself and wanted help. After spending seven weeks struggling to learn shorthand, Linda was told by her teacher that she didn't understand how Linda could be having problems because she seemed so "optimistic." Linda realized that because she had acted as if she didn't have any problems, the teacher probably didn't realize how desperate she was for help. It seemed that the way Linda jumped quickly and enthusiastically into situations that were new and difficult for her made it less likely that she would be offered the consideration and help of those around her.

Linda's experiences of being anxious, "the voice breaking, the heart pounding" and "feeling not able to do it," seemed to occur in situations in which she was afraid of being pitied and seen as emotionally "weak." We talked about this when Linda described how she felt anxious and her hands were clammy as she waited for the second session to begin. She said she was worried that she would "kill her dream" of becoming a self-supporting person. At school, Linda felt anxious when she imagined her teacher would think her "a poor, dumb meathead" if she were honest about her difficulties. Linda felt anxious when she wanted help or support from others but imagined that if she were honest about her problems, she would get put down. By not checking with her teacher, her husband or her friends to see how accepting they might be of her, Linda set herself up for becoming more afraid and anxious.

Linda Mariani's Successes and Options

The same "jumping in" style discussed earlier may also be an asset to Linda in that it is the way she gives herself a critical push towards making a change. For example, being willing to jump into new situations could be considered a strength when it meant that Linda left the well-known world of her housewife duties to do other things of which she has dreamed.

I was impressed also by the determined way in which Linda has pursued her newly formed goals, even after she first experienced failure. On the WAIS, her willingness to stick with something until she had it right was shown in her work with the Block Designs. On several of the most difficult designs, Linda almost completed the design and then realized she wasn't getting it right. Frequently checking with the model, she worked steadily until her figure was correct. Similarly, Linda has realized that her present career "design" may need to be revised. She plans to check out her alternatives more carefully, by attending a career planning seminar.

In addition to Linda's determined way of "jumping in," I also saw a more reflective side of Linda when she listened to our comments and shared with us her thoughts and feelings. She seems also to have established this give and take in her therapy. Linda spoke to us of how she had begun to use this style in her everyday world by beginning to talk with her classmates about what they think and feel about the class. As she does this, she is finding out that she is not as alone as she thought.

During the assessment Linda practiced saying things she had wanted to say to certain people but had not thought it possible that she ever would. She addressed her typing teacher by whom she has often felt intimidated. Linda hestiated at first to directly address her. She then seemed to gain resolve, however, and looking straight into my eyes (I was the typing teacher) she told me how hard shorthand had been for her and the real reason that she had dropped it. Unlike how Linda had characterized herself, she did not seem weak to me. After the role-play was over, Linda said she realized that she had the option of "opening up" to the teacher about her problems, with the possibility of getting help.

Finally, as we were working with the TAT cards during the last session, Linda came back to speak about the relationship she has with her husband. She described the image of the loving couple on card #10 as something she would like for her own marriage. When I asked her to direct her comments to the man on the card as if he were Frank, she began to speak in earnest. She held the card firmly, but gently; her voice came slowly and often with tears. She said: "I would like to say to him that you don't realize just how much I love you or how much I need you . . . . I never told him I needed him because I never gave that impression. And damn it I do need him." With tears in her eyes, Linda's voice sounded the strongest and the surest that I had yet heard. She seemed vulnerable but not weak, aware of her past history with her husband, and determined to work for a change.

Suggestions

Linda, as we talked about some of your relationships with other people, you explored ways you might make yourself more comfortable while making yourself better known to the other person (how you feel, what you think, what you want). Here are some suggestions you may want to try out.

1. You've already talked to us about the success that you had in talking with your typing classmates and discovering that you did share things in common. When you go to the career seminar you may want to try a similar tactic. Since you'll all be new to each other you may have to be a little imaginative to come up with a way to get a conversation started. One surefire method is to ask people how they heard about the seminar and what they hoped to find out, or to accomplish by coming. Teachers are also usually approachable in such situations. You may want to talk to a couple of them about your vocational interests and see what kind of response you get.

2. You spoke of how you felt at ease with Kareen and me because you were being honest with us. My guess is that when you are feeling anxious, in some way it is not "O.K." for you to be honest. Sharing yourself honestly may mean: letting your teacher know that you are having problems, sharing with others your feelings about going back to school, or telling your husband that you do need him. My suggestion is that when you feel anxious, you stop to reflect and ask yourself how am I not letting myself be honest. Upon reflection you may discover, as you did in the assessment, that some of the things you thought too risky to say became more possible for you. Allowing yourself to communicate more openly seems to be one way you have of putting yourself more at ease.

3. Both Kareen and I were deeply touched by your conversation with your husband. From all that you said it seems that neither one of you is good at giving recognition and expressing love towards the other, despite the fact that the feelings are there. If you are interested in opening up this relationship, you might try following through on your "role-play" and express your feelings directly to Frank. You might find that you are able to touch Frank and that he will respond by being more caring himself. As you did in the role-play, I suggest that you try to work from the strengths of the relationship, from the enduring nature of your love for each other. An added benefit may be that you will find that by allowing yourself to be vulnerable, you may regain a sense of where you stand that seemed to be missing in the way you drew yourself on the Draw-A-Person. In addition, as you work with Frank, you may find it useful to jointly seek guidance from a marital counselor sometime in the future.

Andrea Jones
Kareen Malone

Graduate Students
Psychology Department
Duquesne University

Linda Mariani's Comments

The report isn't quite what I expected. I thought because of the tests I had taken, they, Karen and Andrea were going to judge me more on my mental ability. This is why I once stated that I wasn't sure I wanted to read this report. I must admit I agree with the report. I was also surprised at the way they completely analyzed the way that I sat, dressed ect. I feel stronger for reading this. I'm feeling right now that maybe I'm not quite so bad after all. There were positive action that I od took that I wasn't really aware of. Again I can only say I feel stronger for reading this.

Linda Mariani
Signature

I expected the worse and got the best.

Comments

This report was particularly helpful in showing the client and other readers that a person's ways of approaching things is neither good nor bad in itself. Rather, they facilitate or impede progress depending upon the situation. Linda discovered during the assessment that she could pause and choose among her ways of being, to adapt them to her goals. This discovery was not merely a cognitive revelation, but one that was demonstrated through experienced success.

The authors took care to show that the events that occurred during the asssessment sessions were instances of the kinds of events occurring in Linda's life outside of the assesssment. The assessors did not fall into the trap of trying to explain any of Linda's behavior in terms of traits or other constructs. In particular they did not explain her difficulties in terms of "anxiety" and "defenses." Instead, they show us Linda's discomfort ("anxiety") and her ways of participating in her difficulties ("defenses"). Readers understand Linda's comportment in its own right. Psychodynamics are directly evident in Linda's struggles to be two kinds of person at the same time; for example, needy in relation to her husband even while being a competent, independent person.

The sense of Linda as an individual was enhanced through use of quotations. She tells us her concerns in her own words. In doing so, she shows us not only her conception of what's going on, but also that she is more articulate than we might have anticipated from her formal education. The authors help us to avoid other false expectations by omitting a detailed history. We come to know Linda through her present comportment.

Correctional Facility Screening: Max Manarino

Hurvitztown Correctional Facility is a minimum security prison, housing primarily young men serving short sentences for first convictions. The professional staff uses the reports by our master's students, along with their own interviews and review of group test profiles (such as the MMPI), to screen for psychiatric problems like addiction, suicidality, and psychosis, as well as for difficulties that a resident might have in cooperating with a minimum security program. In addition, the staff looks for individuals who might benefit from counseling programs. The two master's students assigned to assess Max Manarino were instructed to address the referral, but to leave placement recommendations and diagnosis to the staff.

In this report the assessors "tell it like it is"; through their straightforward description, the nature of the young man's criminality is clear, and the referral issues are answered directly. The authors accomplished this through representation of what they saw and what the offender explained to them about his own views. Although the prognosis and difficulties of working with him are made obvious, one also sees where the fellow is coming from—what it is like from where he is. Taking sides for or against him was not necessary. Nor did the assessors find it necessary to resort to theories of criminality, test data as signs of traits, abstract psychodynamic formulations, or to other professional jargon. The graduate students were not experienced with offender patterns and program options, but because the correctional facility staff was, the students' individualized assessment skills provided a powerful and useful portrait.

There is no client Commentary section in this report because the prisoner was transferred to another facility before a follow-up session could be scheduled.

Psychological Assessment
Max Manarino

Age: 21   Date of assessment:
Home address: Hamburg, Pa.   2/21/____
Present offense: Simple assault   Date of Report:
Sentence: 5-23 months   2/30/____

Referral Issue

As a resident of the Hurvitztown Correctional Facility, Max is required to participate in a routine psychological assessment. Mr. Kensington, the Facility psychologist, directed us (the two graduate student assessors from Duquesne University) to complete the Facility's interview form with Max, and to assess any "patterns of criminal behavior." Specifically, he was interested in a description of the situations in which Max did, and is most likely to, get into trouble with the law. Related standard concerns were whether Max might encounter troubles residing at the Facility, and whether he should be transferred to a higher security setting.

Assessment Resources

The assessment took place in the HCF testing room. The assessment is based on the following:
- HCF interview form
- Bender-Gestalt
- Wechsler Adult Intelligence Test (WAIS)
- Thematic Apperception Test (TAT)
- Discussions with the resident of the assessors' impressions

Personal Impressions of Max

When Max entered the testing room, my partner and I rose to greet him and to shake his hand. He nodded to us and sat down in a chair across from me, slouching in his seat and folding his arms over his chest. He had dark, wavy hair, a moustache, and looked to be of average height and weight. He was not unattractive in appearance, but an uninterested, sullen look on his face made him seem unapproachable. I hesitated before explaining to him why my partner and I were there and what we were going to do in the assessment.

His uninterested, sullen, and unapproachable look bespoke the attitude he had toward the assessment. He was not interested in taking the tests nor in our interventions and observations. He asked, "What does any of this have to do with me being in jail?" He was specifically interested in knowing what this assessment had to do with his getting out of "jail." This attitude foreshadowed for me one of his ways of getting into trouble. It later turned out that he has gotten into trouble during those times when he has not been interested in what other people thought about him. In particular, he was not interested in considering the consequences of his actions toward them. When he struck six police officers, he did not care what they thought and he did not consider the consequences of striking them.

He was interested in getting out of jail, however, and in telling his version of his offense. When he talked about the latter, he did not look sullen or unapproachable. He spoke both sadly and angrily, and I felt invited to listen to him. I told him that he did seem interested in talking about himself and in being listened to while he told his version of the offense. When he spoke in this interested and concerned way, I felt invited to listen to him. When he spoke with an uninterested, "I don't care what you think" attitude, I did not feel like listening to him. Instead I felt angry with him. We talked about how this same "I don't care what you think" attitude could have worked against him when he was being interrogated by the police, and about how it might provoke someone to "club" him. (He claimed the police clubbed him during the interrogation.)

Max's Understanding of His Problem

Although Max has been in and out of five different juvenile institutions for running away from home, his present incarceration is for his first criminal offense. Max said of the latter that after he had been picked up by the police for drunken driving, at the police station he was interrogated about a hit-and-run accident. In addition to wanting Max to take a breath-analyzer test, the police wanted him to sign an affidavit testifying that he was the hit-and-run driver.

According to Max, when he refused to comply with these orders, six police officers started "clubbing" him. He said he suffered a broken nose, face lacerations, and a concussion as a result of this clubbing. He, in turn, assaulted the six police officers. Max spoke indignantly about this. "I will not tolerate anyone putting their hands on me." He claimed that he had assaulted the police officers only in self-defense and that he did not deserve to be sentenced for this.

Max said that he imagined no other possible ways of handling his confrontation with the police. Complying with their order to take the breath-analyzer test and to sign the affidavit were not options. He thought that if he had complied with these police orders, he would have been confessing to a crime he did not commit, to hit-and-run driving. He also did not consider sitting with the police, which he saw as tantamount to letting himself get clubbed. He saw assaulting the police officers as the only possible way of dealing with them.

Max suggested that behaving assaultively toward others was sometimes the only way to cope with people who, he thought, were abusing him or taking advantage of him. He said that his father, too, used to abuse him physically. Sometimes his father beat him so badly that his mother tried to cover his bruises with makeup when she sent him to school. He said that when he got "big enough," he "beat [his] father's ass." Now his father does not abuse him anymore. He thought that this was an instance of how his assaultive behavior worked for him. Although Max's assaultive behavior toward the police resulted in his going to prison, he thought that, here too, it worked for him. It was his way to stave off getting his head "smashed in."

Max said that he would not tolerate getting badgered by other people, that he would retaliate, even if it meant going to jail. Max said that he can imagine himself getting picked up for drunken driving again; he can imagine the police giving him a "hard time"; he can imagine assaulting them and being sent to jail a second time. He laughed when he told me this and said that he would not be at all surprised if this very thing happened to him. He said that he can even imagine getting into trouble at the Correctional Facility and being sent to a different institution for not complying with some of the "petty rules and regulations" there.

When Max talked about all this, he spoke as if he thinks things just happen to him, as if he is the helpless victim who has to defend himself against a hostile world that tries to force him to comply with rules and regulations, and that punishes or abuses him when he does not comply.

Later, Max agreed that his drunken driving, his resisting and assaulting police officers, his "I don't care what you think" attitude, all had something to do with his getting into trouble. But he was not interested in discussing or exploring how this might be so, or in changing his attitude and behavior. He seemed to want other people to change, the police to not harrass him for drunken driving, and the staff at HCF to stop making him go through "bull shit" things like this assessment.

Max as Seen through Testing

Since Max did not think that this assessment had anything directly to do with his getting out of incarceration, he did not want to take the tests. During the Information subtest (WAIS), Max fidgeted in his seat, sighed, and answered agitatedly. Among his responses to the questions was the retort, "I don't know and couldn't care less."

During the Block Design subtest, Max seemed absorbed in making the blocks match the design, and he made no agitated comments. I recalled his having told me earlier that he likes to work with his hands, that he hopes to get a construction job when he leaves the institution, and that he is a "master carpenter." When he finished all the designs I said to him, "You seemed to enjoy working with those blocks. When you work with blocks and when you do your carpentry or construction work, you literally have things in your own hands. You are the one manipulating things and you have them in control. This makes me think that when you get into trouble, you might feel that you are in a situation that is out of your hands or out of your control, like when you were interrogated by the police. When you were interrogated by me, when I asked you questions from the test, you did not like that either. But you did not mind working with the blocks."

He agreed that this was true. He said he does not like to feel helpless or to feel that other people are deciding things for him. He felt helpless when he was interrogated by the police, and he did the only thing he could imagine doing in order to not remain helpless and in their hands—he assaulted them.

I told him that by getting picked up for drunken driving, he had already put himself into the hands of the police, and that this was something he could have avoided by not driving under the influence of alcohol. In response he shrugged his shoulders, as if to suggest again that he was not interested in hearing or seeing how his behavior and attitude had something to do with getting into trouble and ending up in the hands of people who are in a position to decide things for him.

When we worked with the TAT cards, Max said, "This fantasy stuff is bull shit." He did not want to make up stories for these cards and said a couple of times, "I don't see nothin'." He said that he could not imagine what the characters in the picture were thinking, feeling, or doing, that he did not care, that it did not interest him.

Since one of Max's complaints about the cards was that they were just pieces of paper and that he, therefore, could not make up stories about them, we (Max, my partner, and I) agreed to try to imagine stories about each other. We agreed to imagine what each other was feeling at that moment and to imagine different ways one might act on those feelings. This exercise was intended to be a way of showing Max that there are different ways one can act on his feelings. And it seemed like a way that Max could also try imagining different ways of acting on his own feelings; to see that feeling frustrated, abused, or restricted does not mean that one has to act assaultively.

When it was Max's turn to make up a story, he said, "How can I imagine what you are thinking or feeling?" He repeated that he was not interested in trying to imagine this. My partner and I reminded him again that this "I don't care what you think" attitude was one of the ways he participated in his own difficulties. Although it may not cause him problems in certain situations (for example, he might not need to care about what a clerk in a store thinks about him), this attitude did cause him trouble when he was dealing with people, such as the police, who are in a position to make some decisions that affect Max's life.

Summary

During the interview, Max suggested that he resists complying with rules and regulations that he does not want to comply with, like when he resisted taking the breath-analyzer test. When Max feels that he is being forced to comply with rules and regulations he does not want to comply with, and when he feels that he is being pushed around, he is likely to do things that get him into trouble with the law. By his account, after six police officers tried "clubbing" him into taking a breath-analyzer test and into signing an affidavit for a hit-and-run accident, he assaulted them.

Max said he hoped he would not become "fed up" with some of the rules and regulations at the Hurvitztown Facilities. If he did become "fed up" with them, he imagined he would get into some kind of trouble which would warrant his being sent to a different institution.

Max felt that he had been sentenced unjustly on the assault charge; after all, he said he had been defending himself against badgering police officers. If, when released, he gets into a similar situation with police, he said he would defend himself again, even if it meant going back to jail. He also said that he would not be surprised if he did get into a similar situation since he likes to drink and suspects that he might get picked up again for drunken driving.

Suggestions

1. It might be helpful for Max to see how his attitude and behavior toward people, in particular those in authority, do have consequences for him. Group therapy seems to be one way for Max to get supportive and instructive feedback from people concerning the consequences of his behaviors and attitude toward them.

2. Max said that he likes to do work with his hands and that he likes to keep busy. If there is a way for Max to get involved in some type of construction work or carpentry while he is a resident at the Hurvitztown Facility, this might give him a chance to feel that he is managing part of his life there, and thereby to feel not so helpless. Max suggested that when he feels helpless, as he did with the police, he often behaves assaultively.

Priscilla J. Friday
Kerry A. Finegan

Graduate Students
Duquesne University

Comments

People often remark that individualized assessment is all well and good with cooperative, reflective clients, but that it will not work with unmotivated persons. In this assessment of Max we see that even though he was decidedly uncooperative and unreflective, the report nevertheless presents a clear portrait. His resistance to intervention (imagining stories) illustrated the difficulties that would confront helpers. For example, readers understand, without being told explicitly, that although suggestion 1 is worth undertaking, suggestion 2 is more viable. Even though Max was not interested in how the tests might help him, and even though readers can anticipate the report's conclusions through the introductory sections on "Personal Impressions" and "Max's Understanding," the described use of test materials allows Max to emerge as a particular individual, not just another character disorder. Seeing Max dealing with the tests and the assessors helps readers to picture him in other situations too, especially since some explicit similarities are presented (for example, between carpentry and Block Design).

In addition, the assessors' own reactions to Max (experiencing him as unapproachable, being angry with him, and later feeling invited to listen) help readers to imagine what it would be like to interact with him. Max's account of his family history helps us to understand him without either hypothesizing causes or excusing his actions. Inclusion of whens and when-nots (such as the shifts in comportment that elicited the assessor's different reactions) illustrates strengths and points of access as well as problem areas. The straightforward, first-person description of actual events allows the correctional facility staff to share the report with Max, and to discuss the implications for his stay at Hurvitztown.

The authors were careful to specify when they were reporting Max's view rather than established facts. For example, they pointed out without taking sides that it was Max's contention that he was "clubbed." The phrase "according to" was useful in this regard.

At the time of the referral, the staff was not interested in levels of achievement on the intelligence test. Inclusion of scores might have detracted from the main focus by sidetracking attention to questions of intellectual "potential." However, because the scores might be useful at a later point, perhaps for educational or vocational guidance, they were calculated and included with the other testing records in Max's file.

Motivation for Methadone Detoxification: Benjamin Dowd

The Westover Drug Treatment Program works with heroin addicts by maintaining them on methadone, a synthetic opiate that can be reduced gradually without causing withdrawal symptoms. In the meantime, each person participates in both group therapy and individual counseling, and goes to school, to work, or both. Graduate students from our master's assessment class, as one of their field assignments, work in pairs with an addict to address a counselor's referral concerns. These experienced counselors do not expect answers from the assessment. Rather, they have found that the assessors' description provides another perspective, one that gives both counselor and addict a fresh look at the addict's progress. Moreover, the collaborative aspect of these assessments reinforces the program's emphasis on taking responsibility for directing one's life.

The addicts often are surprised to see the overlap between the assessment report, which they helped to shape, and the themes that their counselors have developed with them earlier. The addicts then give these themes more credence, especially when they discover that their counselors too acknowledge the overlap and the validity of the addict's situation as seen through the report. The events of the assessment session, such as interventions that occurred with Block Designs, become concrete points of reference to which addict and counselor together can compare ongoing events. Similarly, the counselor can assist the addict in carrying out and modifying the report's concrete suggestions, especially because both persons recall from the assessment session, and from its report, those points within the addict's comportment which he or she could recognize as the signs of forthcoming difficulty and then pivot into a more productive course.

Individual Assessment
BENJAMIN DOWD

Dates of sessions: 11-14-____, 11-17-____
Date of report: 11-24-____

Identifying Information

Ben is a twenty-seven-year-old white male who is currently enrolled in the Westover Drug Treatment Program. He lives with his parents on the west side of Pittsburgh. He is the third of four children and the second of two sons in a working-class family. He has been employed steadily for the last four years in a laundry, where he works the night shift. Ben came to the Program two years ago addicted to heroin, and has been on methadone maintenance since then. Ben's counselor, Marianne Phillipe, told him of the opportunity to participate in an assessment with two graduate students, and he agreed to take part in it.

Presenting Issues

The focal issue presented by Marianne Phillipe was whether Ben was committed to the Program. She said that although he sometimes was enthusiastic and energetic about his eventual detoxification from methadone, at other times he seemed to be either resistive or at least unmotivated. She also requested an evaluation of Ben's intellectual functioning. Although he has a tenth-grade education, sometimes he has seemed unable to follow directions and to express himself articulately.

Assessment Procedures

Two sessions were held at the Westover Drug Treatment Program Center on 11/14/_____ and 11/17/_____. They included the initial discussion of the referral issue, Bender-Gestalt, Wechsler Adult Intelligence Scale (WAIS), Draw-A-Person (DAP), and Thematic Apperception Test (TAT). Also included was collaborative discussion with Ben of our observations and impressions.

Introductory Description of Ben

Ben is of average height and weight, with dark brown wavy hair, dark beard, and wide-open, brown eyes. He appeared at both interviews dressed neatly in clean blue jeans, a long-sleeved polo shirt, and tan loafers. Ben has a robust build and looks several years younger than his 27 years. His expression was often one of benign, friendly openness.

Ben moved very quickly. He walked through the halls of the center with such purpose and speed that we sometimes lost track of him. He often jumped around in his seat, gesturing rapidly with his hands while speaking. His speech was detailed as well as rapid, which gave the impression of efficient and willing cooperation. Ben seriously applied himself to each of the tests, which evoked a supportive, cooperative response from us.

Background Provided by Ben

Ben said that he began using heroin ten years ago just after his steady girlfriend had broken off their relationship. He was down about it and the heroin made him feel good by removing the pain. As Ben stated it, he felt good in that he didn't feel anything. Since then, Ben has had a number of girlfriends. He described his present girlfriend as much more volatile than himself. He stated that although he becomes "emotional," or upset sometimes, she blows up more often and less predictably. At these times he leaves her, only to return eventually and go through the same pattern. It was our impression that Ben does not feel that he can influence her and the relationship, except to abstain from contact when involved in a dispute. When discussing what he would most like to have happen in the relationship, Ben said he wished his girlfriend would be more even tempered and steady in her treatment of him.

Ben related to us that he had been involved in the methadone Program now for two years, and that he would be going through detoxification in the not-too-distant future. He both eagerly awaits and dreads this occasion. Although the methadone Program serves as an anchor for him and "keeps [him] off the streets," Ben is also weary of the control that both it and his drug addiction have over his freedom. Although Ben greatly fears premature expulsion from the Program for misconduct, and also dreads the physical suffering accompanying withdrawal, he looks forward to the time when he is free of his drugs for himself, rather than at the demand of others. He pointed with pride to the fact that he was still physically in good shape, and would still be able to enjoy good health when he triumphed over his addiction.
enjoy good health when he triumphed over his addiction.

During the sessions, Ben spoke freely of some of his disappointments with the Program. When we suggested that he take up his problems with a staff member, Ben refused, stating he didn't believe it would do any good, and in fact might be the cause of his being rejected from the Program. In this way Ben's relationship with the Program staff resembles his relationship with his girlfriend: He does not imagine that his action could influence others and he simply waits to find out what is expected of him.

Ben's Participation in the Testing

Ben's friendly but noncommital attitude led us to suspect that his WAIS scores would be lower than they were (high Average). Specially, in the first minutes of both the Bender-Gestalt and the WAIS, he responded to many of our requests with statements such as, "I don't know," and "I guess." After answering the question or drawing the figure, he added such questions as, "How's that?" and "Is that what you wanted?" But after a few minutes of questioning, Ben's face became stern and he answered the next few questions saying, "I don't know, and I don't care," and "I could be making up these questions for you!" We later returned to this subtest and asked what had been happening to him. Ben reported that one of the questions reminded him of a speech by a politician he recently saw on television. He then went on to describe the content of the speech and exactly what about the politician's stand was distasteful to him. It was at this point that our liking for and expectations of Ben increased, as we realized that he did have ideas of his own, and was able to express his opinion clearly.

Although Ben worked hard and applied himself with great intensity to the test material, he might have accomplished more had his focus been more on the tasks than on the motives of the assessors. He waivered between asking many questions before beginning, and jumping right in with an initial answer which he then elaborated until he reached what he considered an adequate answer, or until he could think of nothing further. On the WAIS performance subtests, he moved so quickly into the problem-solving, that it was difficult to believe that he was thinking at all. When we asked about his jumping in so quickly, Ben explained that he saw that he was being timed and assumed that we wanted him to work as quickly as possible. On the Bender-Gestalt, Ben vacillated between heavy and light pencil pressure, speed and precision, and unsystematic and planned placement of his figures on the paper. We surmised that the ambiguity of the situation contributed to Ben's uneven performance, and we invited him to focus more on the test, and less on the assessors. Ben's performance then improved when we asked him to return to the Block Design subtest and assemble a design without regard to time or others' expectations. Although he had already unsuccessfully attempted the design, this time his face looked more relaxed, and he assembled the design well within the time limit and in a smooth, flowing manner.

Conclusions/Summary

Ben is eager to become detoxified. His noncommitment is his fearfulness about undergoing the process of detoxification, especially since he is uncertain about how consistently supportive his environment will be. His friendly appeal to others for support, followed by anger at being dependent, preclude Ben's maintaining a course and expressing himself directly. He often jumps in only to pull back. In the testing situation, even with this approach, he scored in the high Average range on the WAIS.

During our sessions, Ben grappled with his way of being overly agreeable and noncommital at the expense of the expression of his own ideas. He explored the ways in which this attitude could be influencing the way people viewed him, and might contribute to his girlfriend's sometimes angry way of responding to him.

Ben's responses to us and to the test situation were instances of his looking to others for his own sense of self. A counseling situation in which Ben is encouraged to express his feelings without fear of reprisals, while giving him feedback on his impact on others, could be of benefit to him. It might also be helpful to focus concretely on Ben's future plans and to share with him the details of the detoxification process, in order to diminish some of his anxiety around these issues.

Suggestions for Ben

1. Continue to experiment with making statements rather than asking questions when speaking with friends, family, and the staff at the Program Center. That way people can respond to <u>you</u> rather than who they <u>think</u> you are, just as we began to respond to you more as a person when you shared your opinions with us.

2. Instead of responding immediately with the phrase "I don't know," try omitting that phrase and letting whatever you do know come out in its place. That way you won't feel as helpless or as angry.

3. Try to focus more on the task than on what others may be expecting of you, as you did with the Block Designs. When you were not concerned about hurrying, you completed it in less time and with greater ease. When you feel yourself hurrying, stop for a moment and ask yourself if it is really necessary, or if you are just reponding to what you believe is expected of you.

Suggestions for Counselor

1. During the assessment Ben mentioned his confusion around the level of his methadone dose, how gradual his detoxification would be, and the conditions around his withdrawal, such as where it would take place. If it is within the regulations of the agency, a discussion of these issues might help alleviate some of Ben's fears. However, he should be encouraged to ask these questions.

2. We identified some ways that Ben depends on others for his sense of direction and of work. It might be helpful in counseling to encourage Ben to further explore this pattern and to experiment with expressing himself in an active way.

Dawn Stember DelMonte
Patricia Pepe

Graduate Students
Department of Psychology
Duquesne University

Ben's Comments

This assesment of me seems to have capture much of the way I am. Specially the part about my friendliness with anyone. Also the way I can openly agree with people even if my point of view may very although then no one wants to believe it about me. It wasn't hard for them to see how jumpy and nervous I act. I think there isn't really much more I could comment on. Them seem to have captured me the way I am.

Signed: Benjamin Dowd

<u>Technical Appendix</u>

The following are Benjamin Dowd's scores on the Wechsler Adult Intelligence Scale, administered to him on 11/14/80 and 11/17/80, by Dawn Stember DelMonte, Graduate Student in Psychology, Duquesne University.

Subtest	Raw Score	Scaled Score
Information	13	9
Comprehension	18	10
Arithmetic	11	10
Similarities	19	13
Digit Span	12	11
Vocabulary	40	10
		Verbal Score: 63
Digit Symbol	54	10
Picture Completion	14	10
Block Design	34	10
Picture Arrangement	27	11
Object Assembly	42	16
		Performance Score: 57

Verbal Score: 63; IQ: 102

Performance Score: 57; IQ: 110

Full Scale Score: 120; Full Scale IQ: 106

Comments

Much more occurred during the sessions with Benjamin Dowd than could be reported; the report merely illustrates the grounds for its conclusions, representing what the assessors believe will be a helpful range of examples. The assessors did not attempt any grand insights or final resolution. Nevertheless, the simple description of Ben's ambivalent relation to the detoxification program, and indeed to people in general, helped to remind the counselor that the question was not whether Ben was motivated, but rather what he was motivated both toward and against. Seeing Ben vacillate in his approach to the assessment materials resolved the counselor's questions about possible intellectual deficits. She now saw that Ben's difficulties had to do not with intellect as such but with his habitual ways of dealing with situations.

The Suggestions are not intended as cure-alls, nor are they the only possible suggestions from the assessment session. They do provide a bridge between habitual behavior (for example, saying "I don't know") and newly tried alternatives (saying what he does know). Explicit grounding in assessment events facilitates Ben's sense of what it was like to try the alternatives, and thereby makes those alternatives more readily available in the future. Placement of the WAIS scores in an appendix rather than in the body of the report helped readers to focus on how Ben gets himself into and out of situations; the measured outcomes did not distract readers from the process through which they came about. Nevertheless, the Technical Appendix makes the scores available to professionals who may be concerned about current level of achievement.

Ben's commentary and signature illustrate another instance of the report's themes. For example, we see that Ben's friendly overture is made at the cost of his taking a reflective, personal stand. His hurried omissions, misspellings, and cross-outs show that here too he jumped in and rushed through the task, adding points until he felt he had written enough. But even though Ben says this portrait is accurate, we wonder to what degree he has understood its implications. Thus, in this case the client's commentary has served not only to continue the client's engagement in the assessment process, but also to remind us that agreement with a reasonable sounding report does not necessarily imply full integration of, or intentions to act on, the findings. That observation is an important closing reminder for people who are working with the client.

Psychiatric Unit Referral: Donna Murdock

The hospital psychiatric staff had examined Donna Murdock, ruled out learning disability, and made a diagnosis of schizoid personality disorder. The unit psychologist, who was familiar with the individualized assessments that our M.A. students conduct, hoped the patient would profit from interaction with the students—who would take her seriously and explore with her some small, viable ways of becoming more engaged with people. He also hoped that the assessment report would serve as a bridge to the Community Mental Health Center staff, who were to follow Donna on an outpatient basis. Because the report was to be read by Donna, as well as by hospital and center staff, all three would see how she had habitually isolated herself and also the concrete alternatives that she had begun to try.

The report shows us how Donna's usual approaches to situations have left her isolated and other people feeling that she is rather strange. Therein we see the ideography of what our diagnostic system calls "schizoid personality." We also see that to work with Donna as a particular individual, one can enter her world—where, diagnosis notwithstanding, she is responsive to interpersonal overtures and is courageous as well as fearful. Her commonality with us all becomes as clear as her schizoid differences. Although we do not anticipate radical transformations of the latter, we do see that significant, albeit slow, changes in Donna's comportment and in her understanding of what happens to her are possible. Hospital and center staff see better how to meet her where she is, and how to continue to collaborate with her to expand her world.

This report illustrates innovative variations of standard format, calculated to enhance Donna's sense of herself as an active participant—someone who can more purposively shape her life just as she helped to shape the sessions and the report. Among the innovations are tailored headings (including the report's title) and metaphors that encourage both Donna and other readers to appreciate her individuality.

April 12, 19 ____

A Glimpse into Donna Murdock's Style of Relating to People

Donna, age 20, has been diagnosed at Regis Hospital (Psychiatric Unit) as a schizoid personality with obsessive-compulsive tendencies. This was her first experience under psychiatric care. She was asked by her psychologist, Dr. Robert Ligget, if she would volunteer to help us conduct a psychological assessment, which is part of our graduate student training at Duquesne University. She consented, but did not know what to expect. She was unsure whether she was helping us or we were to help her. We agreed that each of us would benefit from the experience.

Dr. Ligget suggested that we try to capture a good stylistic description of Donna. He commented on Donna's "lack of sociability" and that this might be a valuable area to explore with her.

Our Meetings

Our initial meeting was conducted on a gray, snowy, Saturday morning (April 6th; 10:30 A.M.) in one of the meeting rooms on the Psychiatric floor where Donna was staying at Regis Hospital. Our session was interrupted for a floor meeting and lunch, and was resumed at 12:30 the same afternoon in Dr. Ligget's office. We dispersed shortly after 3:00 P.M.

Our second day of meetings was held on Monday, April 8th from 4:50-6:30 P.M. It too was a dreary, rainy day.

Our Activities

We began with the Bender-Gestalt (Donna was asked to copy nine geometric designs freehand), which was later supplemented by the instruction to imaginatively draw design #5 the way Donna wanted it to look rather than the way it looked on the card.

In the first afternoon session we conducted some of the performance sections of the WAIS (a test of school-related skills).

Both activities generated insightful discussion and the opportunity for role-playing, all of which helped the three of us to understand the social and task-oriented aspects of Donna's life.

Our Understandings

As we worked together, we developed two metaphors, one characterizing Donna's social presence and one for her task-oriented presence.

"Oil and Water": Donna's Social Presence. By this metaphor we want to convey a sense of insolubility of the two: society, at the social level, being the oil, and Donna being a drop of water. Picture, if you will, a slick of oil with enough surface tension so that it arches above the plane upon which it rests. Thus, if a drop of water were placed upon it, the water would bead and tumble to the periphery and remain there. This metaphor was concretely embodied in Donna's drawing of several of the Bender-Gestalt designs, Figures #A, #4, and #8 being the most representative. Donna told us that she liked Figure #A more than most of the others because it was "closed" and "complete." After drawing #4 she was dissatisfied with the curve not touching where it was supposed to. Mike asked if she would like to redraw it, which she did, this time succeeding at the "point of connection"—a point which she saw as focal for this design.

Design #8 was Donna's "favorite," though none of them really appealed to her. She liked its completeness. Each of the figures she liked touch but do not intersect. In her imaginative rendition of #5 she "closed" the design but did not venture into the circle.

In telling us how her drawings were like her social situation, Donna mentioned that if she were to enter a room of people she would go sit next to someone though she might not talk to him. She would not sit in the center of the room or by herself. When Mike left one of our meetings Donna explained that she felt "unprotected" in his absence; she decided she would be more secure and comfortable if she could sit in a chair next to the wall.

Similarly, Donna's social interaction on her wing at Regis is characterized by the peripheral: she mentioned that she "can handle" a conversation if it remains "social," but she becomes uncomfortable or "panicky" if it gets personal. She has preferred to stay on the periphery.

This discussion reminded Donna of her attitude toward climbing the hospital's "status ladder" by which she would gradually succeed in being discharged. Other patients on the floor had encouraged her to apply for a "monitor" position. She was reluctant but complied, and received the position. It seemed to Mike and me that this sliding along against others' demands was similar to her consent to enter the present assessment situation: she was "afraid" of not knowing what the assessment was about, and she expressed an extreme distaste for "being used," but she consented. When we asked why she did, she said it was because Dr. Ligget said it would help Mike and me out. She was also participating in another psychological study in which they used electrodes affixed to her head with electrode paste. As she brushed a few flakes away, she explained that the paste "looks like dandruff, but really isn't."

I never sensed that Donna asserted a standard of her own. She was not concerned with being meticulous or fastidious. For example, she completed the Bender-Gestalt in six minutes—one minute faster than the average, and made no erasures. She dressed neatly but without individualizing her appearance. She was clean and apologized for drooling one time (which, she explained, "the medication causes"), but her makeup had not been carefully applied. The electrode paste bothered her, but her hair was uncombed both days we were there.

How did Donna see her insolubility with society? Often "I feel separated from things—as if things are going on around me, but I'm not really a part"— she is with others but is not participating in their lives. She also complains that her "reflexes feel slower" than her thoughts. As she commented on the WAIS Digit Symbol, "there feels like a block between my hand and my mind." Part of this she attributed to her medication, but she stated that this was not the sole reason.

Moving on from the "oil and water" metaphor, we also came to see Donna as living out a saying that has passed through her family for at least three generations: "Take care of the edges and the center will take care of itself." She butters her bread around the edges and leaves the center unbuttered; she attends to the "details," that is, the small and less important aspects of her room when she cleans it, before proceeding to the larger and more important; in school she worked at the "little stuff," that is, small assignments and instructions, before attempting the larger assignments. Yet this slows her down and often causes her to get behind in her work, which leads us to another related perspective of her style—her task-oriented life.

"Body-Surfer": Donna's Presence to Tasks. Whereas the metaphor of the "oil and water" pointed to Donna's sometimes being inert, insoluble and self-contained, the metaphor of the body-surfer points to instability and inundation. These two metaphors may help Donna to see herself when she is approaching situations in either of these ways, and perhaps then choose to shift her course.

The sea of accomplishment has various faces for Donna—when the waves are small she can build up enough momentum of understanding and experience that she can catch them and ride them successfully to shore. But as the sea becomes rough, she seems unable to build up enough momentum to catch a breaker; it passes her by and she tries with all of her strength to catch it but cannot; her attempt to catch what has already passed puts her out of position to catch that which is yet to come. She feels overwhelmed.

This process was most vividly encountered on the WAIS Digit Span. The three, four, and five number series were easy to remember. The longer series became harder. Donna said that on these she got "panicky" because she could not remember one of the numbers after I said it. So she tried to recover it after it had passed, and in concentrating on this did not attend to the remaining numbers. She lost in both directions—the future and the past.

In school, because she had to reread the instructions so many times before she grasped them, she had expended much of her time and energy before she got to the assignment per se.

At present, she really would like to be able to finish her political science degree in college—she had hoped to go into law or foreign service—but she sees those hopes passing her by too. I sensed genuine excitement in her voice when she began to speak of finishing school, followed by a sense of hopelessness (her face and tone of voice dropped) at the realization that this might not be possible.

In her job as a sales clerk there was "no room for error." As she made mistakes people began "pushing"—"I feel it's too much pushing. People think I'm retarded—they say, 'Do you understand??!' " "I'd seem to miss something and got fired." The pushing and the degradation are a "pipeline" wave—everything breaks at once, and Donna needs to pull out and dive for the stability of the bottom lest she be dashed against the shore. But the momentum of the pushing prevents her from successfully extricating herself from the danger.

We switched roles for a moment and let Donna administer the Object Assembly of the WAIS to me—here I was the body-surfer and she the wave. She seemed to enjoy it, responding with a hearty "Sure" when asked if she wanted to give me a test. Mike showed her what the procedure was and she carried on quite successfully on her own from there. She was not nervous giving the test as she often was when taking it, especially while being timed. Afterward she voiced doubts as to her "supervisory" ability. Both Mike and I said that we thought she handled the situation as well as we did on our first attempts. It might be valuable to explore the possibilities of similarly responsible but low pressure work situations for Donna after she leaves Regis.

In short, one might say that Donna would make her greatest progress if she could find a friend or instructor to accompany her through the waves. She expressed her like for being with someone else who could help her when she runs out of ideas or words to say—someone who would help her meet her responsibilities even while understanding her anxiety. With or without help she must build up her own momentum by increasing her repertoire of successful experience.

Collaborative Proposals

We three concluded that efforts with Donna's social relations would lead to more successes in her work. We also agreed that it would be good if Donna were to establish a close friend on the hospital floor as well as one in her outside world. Heretofore she had not been successful at the former due to the large turnover of patients every week or two. However, her outside world also has few friends. Mike suggested that the area of basic "social gestures" would be a good direction to pursue.

At the onset of our meeting Donna had gazed almost continually into space, seldom if ever establishing eye contact with either Mike or me. Slowly, through the progress of our first meeting, Donna began to look at us and eventually smiled appropriately now and then. We both commented how good it made us feel to have her look and smile at us. Donna, in response to our question, admitted that she guessed she really did not look at others—she would "observe" them, but not really acknowledge them through eye contact. Her habit of "observing" kept her in "contact" with others but did not plunge her into the middle of the social arena. Her "observing" helped her maintain her peripheral, insoluble stance.

When confronted with the fact that she could and initially did look at us on her own initiative she was somewhat surprised and happy that she could do something she previously thought impossible. When conscious of "looking" at the other she was uneasy and turned away. We suggested that to look into another's eyes was a form of speaking—of acknowledging the other's worth and importance to the looker. She saw the social gesture as a viable possibility, and we encouraged her to try it that weekend.

Donna returned Monday with a disappointing report—she had tried our mutually acceptable suggestion for a short time but then felt it was "kinda crazy." We entered another role-playing situation in which I became Donna the "observer" and she became Doug the "looker." We carried on a conversation for three or four minutes in which she looked into my face but I stared into space or "right through her." She immediately got the idea, stating that she would not like someone who did that. She guessed that practicing "looking" was difficult but not so "crazy" after all. She got the message, but it remains to be seen whether or not she will be self-aware enough to catch herself when she begins to stare. She commented that often she does not even know when she is staring.

We hope that, beginning with this rudimentary gesture, Donna may convert her repellant, "observational" "oil and water" separateness into a more mutual "looking." To broaden her openness to others we jointly derived the following suggestions:

1. I will practice establishing my eye contact with others. (We joked that if you could look intermittently at Mike and me for all of these hours you surely could look at anyone else for a few minutes!)
2. Doug and Mike see my smile as a really wonderful way of making them and others feel good. I'll have to try "speaking" by smiling.
3. I can initiate conversation—don't always have to wait for others to come to me. I can begin to work my way away from the "edge" and toward the "middle" by:
   a. Talking with other patients.
   b. Talking to the staff about one of the patient's problems.
   c. Talking to the staff about something that's bothering me.
   d. Talking to the staff about their interests and concerns.

   Spend a few minutes planning what I will say beforehand so I won't feel nervous or panicky once I get into the situation.

Upon parting I mentioned that I had to hurry and write this report for Dr. Ligget since he was not sure how much longer Donna would need to stay. At this, Donna's face brightened and she blurted out a happy, expectant

"Really?—How soon?" I told her I was not sure but that he wanted the report within a week. Her spirits seemed revived, and she indicated that she would try to work on what we had discussed.

Doug Trook
Mike Myszka

Graduate Students
Psychology Department
Duquesne University

Donna's Amendments

The first part of the report was quite honest in appraisals of me, although there was one minor error that is the example of buttered bread I butter only the edges and then in fact I cover it all. Other than this it was quite accurate a detail.

There was only one point at which there was error made in the second part and that referred to my job as salesclerk incorrectly in the engineering firm job I held

Also on the area of job pressure, I prefer work with some pressure but not a lot.

Signature *Donna Murdock*

Comments

The assessment and report promoted Donna's sense of agency—her power to shape her life. This goal was accomplished through involving Donna as an active, collaborative participant during the sessions, through intervening in her habitual patterns to try alternatives, through addressing the report's suggestions directly to Donna, and through asking her to write her comments and signature on the report. In addition, the assessors chose to sign the report as "Doug" and "Mike" rather than as Douglas and Michael, in order to underscore the person-to-person character of the sessions. They purposely described the dreary weather of the assessment days, and the hours and places of the meetings, to remind Donna of the time they had shared. This emphasis on mutuality served as a reminder of Donna's engagement in the assessment, and hence of her possibilities for future interpersonal involvement. In short, the report mitigates inclinations on the part of both Donna and staff to regard the assessment as something that a schizoid patient passively underwent.

Although the Regis staff was fully aware of the circumstances that led to Donna's admission, as well as of the basis for her diagnosis, I wish the report had briefly reviewed these points. Such a review would help Donna see the relation of past events to the assessment and to her future, and would be helpful to later readers, such as those at the CMHC, who probably would not have access to the full Regis files. Reports should always be written for the long-range future as well as for immediate purposes. I wish also that the report had provided more physical description, so that we could visualize Donna more vividly. Inclusion of her height, specific clothing, and representative postures would fill out our images of Donna brushing off flakes, glancing up at the assessors, and so on. Vivid imagery in reports helps to correct readers' stereotypes and to bring a series of reported incidents into coherence.

The metaphors did bring coherence and individuality to what otherwise might have been presented as a series of symptoms. Metaphors are particularly useful for integrating material for easier comprehension and recollection, while not explaining away the material as theoretical constructs often do. However, authors have to take care not to force a metaphor to cover more events than it should, nor to ignore events that do not fit the metaphors. To be useful, metaphors should be based on common experience that is understood by most readers.

The report authors do not believe that their understandings, interventions, and suggestions are sufficient for bringing about changes in Donna's social orientation. Rather, their aim was to describe that orientation and assess the viability of some starting places for Donna and her helpers. Donna's comments attest to the importance of others working with her to practice, vary, and further develop the suggestions. Even though the changes must be incremental, however, they are likely to make a difference in how Donna lives her life. In this case the changes will occur in response to interventions that are directed into the way she approaches and experiences situations.

A staff member who read the report said that through the assessors' description of Donna's impact on them and of their relationship with her, she (the staff member) had realized how to transform her unilateral intervention attempts into collaborative ones. She also said she could now see that what I have called the "when-nots" of problematic comportment are ideal locations for expanding effective actions (like looking at the assessors). These interventions are similar to contemporary behavior modification techniques; but I believe the latter can be used most effectively within a framework that consistently takes into account clients' perspectives, experience, and ways of co-authoring their course.

Probation Consultation: Jack Risso

The following report was written under a contract between Duquesne University's Psychology Department and a nearby probation office. In this case a faculty member, rather than a graduate student, conducted the assessment.

After discussing the referral, the probation officer and psychologist agreed that a "diagnostic work-up" was not in order since it probably would not add substantively to the existing records nor to the probation officer's knowledge of offenders. Instead, the psychologist agreed to accept the referral as described below.

Subject: Jack Risso
Probation No. 73283
Age: 20

Date of Sessions: 8/25/___, 9/1/___
Date of Report: 9/7/___

PSYCHOLOGICAL ASSESSMENT

JACK RISSO was referred to me by his probation officer, George Provost, who has found it difficult to be of service while both of them are somewhat mystified and frightened by the form of Jack's "nervousness": jolting speech and peculiar muscular spasms. I hope that in rendering these features more understandable, the following description will provide relatively safe ground from which Jack's probation officer can develop a constructive program with him. Moreover, it is my hope that comprehending his "nervousness" in the familiar context of his own life will enable Jack to participate more actively in directing his future.

I spent an afternoon with Jack in which we pondered his spasms. Mainly we considered these movements through their traces in his amateur art work. Initially, however, Jack ventured some comments as to their etiology recalling that in parochial school he felt his activities restricted, his movements compressed so that he wanted to scream. It was as if in the pall of the place, his springiness was recoiled to a point that it was ready to burst. He told me that when people were hard on him he felt similarly compacted and to get relief from their denseness (sometimes he thought they were really dumb) he would pierce it with a cry. Here we talked about the intransigence of his parents in the face of Jack's street life style and I wondered why he found their indifference to his arguments so compelling. He thought maybe it was because he wasn't sure of himself.

Indeed, Jack said that for the most part the dumbness that constrained him was his own. When he painted, his hands on occasion held back their expression, and it was as if he had to break through them to realize a particular movement. Indeed, sometimes he would puncture his hand with a pencil to facilitate its release. More often he runs or hikes a rugged terrain in order to work his body over.

In the faces Jack paints, spirals turn in on themselves, grow tight until in this crush they erupt into features. We talked long about his work. Here I was impressed that when he uncoiled his pent-up movements they were more than spasms, more than jerks; he could make things out of them. Jack found this hard to accept. He was afraid of his springiness. Then I advised him, and Jack agreed, that the more he resisted his springiness and the harder he came down on himself, the more his movements would be like a jolt and a spasm when he finally expressed them. He had to find ways to accept himself more in order not to be so tight all the time.

I saw Jack again after a space of a few weeks at which time he read the above impressions and told me that what I had said was very much how he felt. After exploratory discussion, we concurred that art school or some form of dance therapy, even ballet school, might encourage Jack to direct himself toward positive expressions. He was tentatively willing to try himself out with George Provost, his probation officer.

Jay Greenfield
Psychologist

Comments

Readers typically respond to this report with either strong praise or dissatisfaction. Some readers complain that the report is not really psychological, that there are no tests and no diagnostic impressions, that nothing has been explained. For those of us who are positively impressed with the report, however, these are pluses. The report *is* psychological in that Jack Risso's previously frightening comportment is now understandable to himself and to the probation officer. Context, feelings, and alternatives are clear. Client and officer are now free to work together. Both have seen that Jack can participate in making sense of his "springiness," and that it is not a foreign force but an aspect of himself, one that he can shape toward a constructive transformation.

The nature of the springiness has been outlined. Although much more could be filled in, brevity renders the portrait more powerful. My own inclination would have been to include more background data and physical description. The probation officer knows all of that, however, and any future readers will encounter the report amidst that other information in Jack's file. Moreover, inclusion of further information probably would have diluted the powerful description of Jack's situation. Rather than *understanding* Jack's tension, readers would try to *explain* it to themselves in terms of social history, test performance, or diagnostic category.

The author clearly answered the referral question and yet did not yield to temptations to include additional findings or to "wrap up" the case in more inclusive abstract terms. The probation officer declared the report and his consultation with the psychologist to be among the most directly relevant and helpful of all those he had experienced in his career.

On the other hand, many officers request IQs, diagnoses, and causal explanations. One such person, upon being shown this report, complained that art school or dance therapy would not cure Risso. That reader could not see that the report was not intended to explain or "cure," but to develop understandings and entry points for further work by both client and officer. To be genuinely helpful, the assessor must become familiar with the referring person's framework and expectations, taking them into account while also presenting individualized perspectives of the client. In the present instance initial discussion of the referral with the probation officer assured the psychologist of the appropriateness of this form of report.

Employee Appraisal Interview: William Nathan

It is not always necessary or appropriate to use tests, conduct a comprehensive assessment, or fully individualize an assessment.

In the following case I served as a field psychologist for a national personnel consulting firm headquartered out of state. Such firms assist businesses with their hiring, placement, and promotion decisions. Among other services they may also offer seminars or workshops on, for example, salesmanship for management skills. A consulting firm had a contract with a retail chain for which William Nathan had been working as manager of one of its smaller stores. The company wanted the consulting firm to add their impressions from an overall testing profile to help them plan for Mr. Nathan's development with the company and in particular to decide whether to promote him to district manager (supervisor of several store managers).

The consulting firm sent me a seven-hour test, which was to be timed and supervised. The battery included tests of interests, personality, knowledge, and cognitive skills. I was to return the battery, unexamined, to the consulting firm, where the tests would be scored and compared with appropriate norms. I was to utilize a folder that listed identifying information on the cover, and included a full-page observational rating form (the person's punctuality, grooming, initiative in asking questions, and so on). On a sheet calling for strengths for the position, weaknesses for the position, and summary/suggestions, I was to record my impressions from a 30- to 45-minute interview. My contribution thus was not a full assessment, but rather firsthand observations, impressions, or concerns that should be considered by the psychologists who were to review Mr. Nathan's test profile. I composed the following notes at the typewriter immediately after the interview, using the provided form.

Interview Notes

A forty-minute interview with Mr. Nathan resulted in the following impressions, with which he is in agreement.

Strengths for the Position
- Eager to get ahead, aggressive, competitive—hates to lose, takes initiative.
- Bright—looks for the "big picture," then handles details rapidly.
- Task-oriented—more interested in getting the job done right than in being liked.

Weaknesses for the Position
- May make premature decisions; he describes himself as being "a fidgety person," as not "standing still," as being full of "nervous energy." He acknowledges having thrown himself into projects over his head.
  On the other hand, he learns very quickly from his early blunders.

- He is inclined to be impatient with what he regards as incompetence. Similarly, he can be a bit condescending to persons he perceives as low in rank or expertise (example: the difference in his comportment with me over the phone when he took me for a secretary, and his conduct with me in person).

  However, he does feel that he has been learning to be consistent with subordinates, and that his task-orientation serves to keep him fair in his dealings with them. His respect for the competence of superiors also bodes well for learning from them.

Summary/Suggestions
- The above possible weaknesses are clearly open to revision. Although Mr. Nathan hates to admit mistakes, he does learn quickly. His strengths clearly outweigh his liabilities.
- It would seem wise to follow what Mr. Nathan describes as company policy, that is, transfer him to a larger volume store before promoting him to a higher level of management.
- It might be helpful to encourage Mr. Nathan to ask questions of his district manager rather than pretending to be knowledgeable. Although he can usually figure out the answers by himself, he may well avoid some mistakes by questioning first.
- Mr. Nathan could benefit, perhaps more than he would like to admit, from management-level workshops on human-relations skills. (Note: I am not waving a red flag here; this is a growth suggestion as much as a suggestion for correcting a possible problem area.)

Comments

The above remarks about Mr. Nathan *are* an assessment in that they answer the questions addressed to me by the consulting firm, and they are the result of evaluative activity and reflection on my part. But these interview notes are closer to what I have called a "decision-making appraisal" than to a fully individualized assessment undertaken to understand and work with a person. Other examples of assessment situations that fall between decision-making and fuller, descriptive demands are letters of recommendation, initial intake appraisals, and interviews for admission to graduate school. In each case, the author reports from a relatively limited perspective, and leaves any further exploration to others. Many people mistakenly assume that this book's approach demands that every assessment be a fully individualized effort—descriptive, interventional, and so on. This just is not so. The assessor must decide what is appropriate in each case.

Because the consulting firm hoped to offer developmental as well as decision-making suggestions to Mr. Nathan's company, I felt that my brief remarks should follow individualized assessment precepts: Mr. Nathan was involved collaboratively; we developed some when/when-not examples together; I included some of his language and a concrete instance of our interaction; and the suggestions were tailored to Mr. Nathan's situation with his company.

I should acknowledge, however, that I spent about 30 minutes of non-contracted and hence nonreimbursed effort greeting and offering coffee to Mr.

Nathan, and administering the timed tests myself (rather than having the receptionist do these things), glancing over the "Educational and Employment History" form, inserting my own form that asked Mr. Nathan to write paragraphs on "The worst and the best impressions people sometimes have of you," and typing more than the required observations. These activities allowed me to observe Mr. Nathan's ways of going about the day's work. Given my prior knowledge of what store management at various levels involves, I could imagine similarities between what I saw in my office and what others might see in Mr. Nathan's comportment as a manager. We discussed and expanded these comparisons.

Individualized assessment requires extra time and effort. In private practice one cannot earn a living by giving time away. In agencies, time given to one client is time withheld from another. In Mr. Nathan's case, when I first spoke with him on the phone to schedule a meeting, I sensed that I would probably expend extra time. Such choices are not always worthwhile, but this one resulted in a brief note from the consulting firm's vice-president, saying that the "detailed and clearly followed [understood]" remarks were of critical assistance in making sense of Mr. Nathan's test profiles, and that he and his staff appreciated the professionalism involved in my undertaking the extra effort.

Questions and Responses

Question: Were the graduate students' reports based on relatively simple cases, or were they written by your best students—perhaps students returning to school after work experience?

Response: The reports are representative both of the settings in which our students do field assessments, and of the clients they encounter there. Those clients appear much more complex, of course, prior to the exploration and sense-making of the assessment. The reports in this chapter are probably among the top third in terms of sensitivity, economy, and clarity. Students differ in their attunements and clinical skills, but for the most part persons who have worked in the mental health field find such experience to be an initial drawback. They have to learn to bypass their psychodynamic, or test- and category-oriented training in order to see and describe comportment directly. Once they have developed their approaches to individualized assessment, however, their earlier training becomes a definite plus.

Most students are remarkably astute if they are instructed to be concrete, to address the referral concerns, and to deal with actual life events throughout the assessment. Their greatest difficulties are avoiding the pitfalls of Table 3.2 (Counterproductive Assessor Comportments), taming their desires to include everything they learned during the assessment, and heeding such principles of clear writing as those in Table 5.3. I did ask the students to edit these reports for publication.

Question: Have your students studied psychopathology?

Response: No, not yet. The master's students are enrolled in theoretical courses on human-science foundations, content courses such as developmental psychology, and practica on therapeutic and group psychology. Their apparent diagnostic or psychodynamic sophistication has more to do with their not being confounded by diagnostic systems, scores, and test lore. They are asked to see first whatever patterns are directly and personally visible in clients' comportment, guided only by referral questions and a general human-science assessment approach—contextual, structural, collaborative, interventional, descriptive. At this stage, the students often do not realize that they have described classic patterns of psychopathology. Later, as they learn psychodynamic theories, diagnostic systems, and research findings, they allow this knowledge to guide their exploration and reflection, but they distinguish between firsthand knowledge about an individual, and knowledge of general patterns that may or may not be helpful in understanding that particular person.

Question: Wouldn't it be helpful to attach at least a page summarizing such data for professionals who might make use of IQs, the TAT stories, and so on?

Response: Yes, even if such data may not be useful at the moment, professionals may find them relevant in the future. Therefore all test productions and profile sheets are given to the agency for whom the assessment was done. Sometimes such addenda are attached to the report, and sometimes they are filed with the agency's testing records. Or a summary may be attached, such as the Technical Appendix to Benajmin Dowd's report. If the TAT stories "tell the client's story" particularly vividly, they are attached directly to the report. Reports submitted to me as part of assessment course requirements are accompanied by all materials so that my teaching assistant and I can review them to raise points with the graduate student assessor.

Question: Isn't it overly familiar or, on the other hand, condescending, to refer to clients by their first names?

Response: My background leads me to be more comfortable with the formality and respect of last names. But sometimes, when use of titles and surnames seems artificial, contrived, or manipulative, use of first names may be appropriate. The undergraduate volunteer assessees have told us that they find the use of first names with our graduate students to be natural and more personal. The assessment experience thereby is more direct and more relevant for them. However, it seems to me that except when a child or adolescent is being assessed, or when there are several decades separating the ages of the assessor and the client, any use of first names ought to be reciprocal—that is, by the assessee as well as by the assessor.

In the case of Max, he and the graduate students were close in age; they had been introduced with emphasis on first names, and the young counseling staff of the facility worked on a first-name basis with residents. Later, when one of those counselors reviewed the report directly with Max, the use of his first name rendered the report immediate and personal and therefore more useful.

Question: Does the age or gender of the assessors make a difference in the assessment?

Response: Very possibly. In the case of Max, the assessors were women and were not part of the power structure of the correctional facility. The report made these facts apparent so that readers could weigh them along with other data. Although the report may show us only one profile of Max—that of him with the two young, female graduate students—there is no evidence that that profile would be significantly different with other assessors. Occasionally such evidence does arise, for example, when a resident's major interest is convincing the students to advocate for him with the staff. Such circumstances are made explicit in the report, and are taken into account by the assessors. Every psychological report necessarily presents whatever profile was available and attended to during the assessment sessions.

Question: Is the report on Jack Risso, the man on probation, a complete psychological report?

Response: No, it would be advisable to title a report like this a psychological consultation. That title might help readers to anticipate a brief advisement rather than a full evaluation. Such consultations are clearly appropriate if recent evaluations are already on file, which was the case in this instance. The consultation was of greater help to the probation officer than further testing would have been.

Question: The Technical Appendix on Ben Dowd's report came after his commentary and signature. Does that mean that the client does not read the appendix?

Response: Yes. Ben read in the report that his score was in the "high Average" range, and the assessors discussed with him what that meant statistically and personally. Such discussion provides a more accurate picture than does a number. I would rather that Ben focus on the understandings and suggestions that arise through test performance, observation, discussion, and so on. When test scores are not at issue, I prefer to write the report without them and attach the appendix for future use by professionals after the client has read the report. However, this is not an absolute rule. There are exceptional occasions when people require numbers to make decisions about themselves, or when they cannot believe their standing until they see their scores. The point is that scores should not dictate our action; we should decide in each instance what the function(s) of scores should be, and for whom.

Question: Did Ben Dowd read the "Suggestions for Counselor"?

Response: Ben and his counselor read both sections of Suggestions. In that way, each knew how the report might lead to specific efforts on the other's part. Thus their collaborative relation was enhanced even though they understood that each had separate responsibilities.

Question: Do you disregard clients' developmental and social histories?

Response: Despite the absence of separate social history sections in these reports, the assessor must know how to take background events into account, whether they are cultural, environmental, developmental, educational, vocational, social, or medical. If this information is not provided by other team members, such as social workers, teachers, or nurses, then the assessor must know how to obtain it.

Although assessment should not be narrowly construed as tied to tests, the use of tests with interviews *is* the unique contribution of assessors to the human services. Therefore I have purposely limited the focus of this introductory book and of my initial assessment courses to first-hand assessment.

Pursuit of a person's history too readily leads the assessor, as well as report readers, into viewing that person's present life as a product of history. When we *explain* in terms of the past, we thereby attenuate interest in *understanding* the complexities and ambiguities of the person's present life. We also thereby undervalue the person's potential for redirecting his or her own life. The reports in this book demonstrate to readers that regardless of the various contexts that should be taken into account, clients can and should be understood and described in terms of their present lives. It is within that realm that helpers intervene and clients actively cooperate. Hence even in my clinical reports, I usually restrict background information to what I found to be directly relevant to the referral, and I usually place that information in the Referral section or in the Client's Perspective. When directly relevant information emerges that is not appropriate for either of those sections, or when it is relevant for future planning rather than for understanding the person, I may place it in an Additional Factors section or in the Suggestions section.

Question: What did you mean when you said "assessment should not be narrowly construed as tied to tests"? Doesn't formal assessment depend upon testing?

Response: The term "formal assessment" has often been used to refer to the traditional inclusion of tests (for example, Korchin, 1976). However, the same scientific, theoretical, and clinical training that grounds assessment via tests can also ground assessment without tests. Remember, a major function of tests is to provide an efficient range of situations in which to observe a person's performance. Direct observation, interaction, and intervention in relevant settings often are more helpful than activities in the somewhat removed testing situation. Similarly, consulting with the client's involved others may provide sufficient instances of comportment to enable the assessor to be of service. In other words, the primary data of individualized assessment are comportment; many sources of derived or secondary data, including tests, assist in exploring and understanding that comportment. Although psychologists, counselors, and educators are specialists in the use of tests, they become mere technicians if their expertise is restricted to use of their equipment. The consultation report on Jack Risso and the interview notes on William Nathan are examples of assessments that did not require tests for their particular purposes.

Question: Isn't it disruptive to break an assessment into multiple sessions?
Response: No, not for individualized, collaborative assessment. Each session is a mini-assessment: understandings emerge, and some possible actions are

discussed. At the next session, the client reports further reflections on these issues and the outcome of any experiments. The assessor too comes to the second session with a new openness, a readiness to refine and extend the earlier understandings. Yes, this process does require more time than simple administration of tests followed by unilateral feedback. But the purpose of individualized assessment is well served by the multiple sessions, which are experienced by both participants not as disjunctive, but as progressive efforts to develop understandings of how the client shapes his or her world, and to explore personally viable alternative ways. When the client leaves the last meeting ready to continue these efforts, then the multiple-session format has been coherent rather than disjunctive. It is cost- and time-effective in the long run.

Question: Is it essential for individualized assessment to occur through multiple sessions?

Response: No, multiple meetings definitely are not essential. I include a multiple session requirement in my first assessment course to ensure that the graduate students have time to reflect in a more leisurely manner and an opportunity to experience how different a person is in changed circumstances. Returning to work with a now familiar assessor, rather than a stranger, is indeed a different circumstance for the client.

Question: What did you mean when you said that the report should present the client "holistically"?

Response: The illustrations, language, and style of writing should evoke a sense of the *person.* The reader should not have to add up partitive analyses of the client's "intellectual functioning," "emotional make-up," "response tendencies," "defense system," and so on. Although thinking of the client in terms of such notions can be helpful, the ultimate goal for individualized assessment is to describe that person, who was on her or his way to various places, encountering both assorted obstacles and smooth roads, before the assessor analyzed and abstracted that progress into separate realms.

CHAPTER 7

Psychological Reports of Children and Youths

AMONG the psychological reports that I encounter in my clinical work, the ones that are most individualized are about children. This chapter draws examples from a wide range of ages (5 to 16 years) and settings (home, clinic, camp, detention center, school). The fact that there are many more reports on male than on female youngsters reflects the actual distribution of referrals in most agencies serving children and adolescents. There is a greater diversity of report-writing styles in this chapter than in the others. Somehow, trying to do justice to children inspires creativity.

Half of the reports in this chapter were authored by professionals, and half were written by graduate students during their field placements for their M.A. assessment course at Duquesne University. The authors have protected assessees' privacy by changing their names and those of involved persons, facilities, and geographical locations. The actual names of the reports' authors are retained.

Ellipses (. . . .) indicate where material has been deleted for the sake of economy. None of these reports include written commentary by the youngsters. Only rarely have we asked children below age ten to write commentary, because involvement with that activity usually distracts them from the meanings of the assessment. Our reports on older youngsters, however, often do include their comments and signatures. Even without that particular form of collaboration, all of the assessments and reports in this chapter were individualized. Brief camp reports and an Individualized Education Plan (IEP) were included as reminders that even when assessment records are not meant to be full-scale or thoroughly individualized, they can nevertheless address the referral issue in ways that evoke a sense of who the youngster is as an individual. The other reports illustrate more thoroughly how to go beyond considering end products (such as test scores, finished drawings). They show us ways to attend to and to describe the processes through which the end products evolved. The reports point to the mutuality of the comportments of the youngster and of his or her adults. The co-creation of events by youngsters and their adults is represented through individualized assessment report-writing practices: concrete, descriptive re-presentations of comportment, context, intervention, and collaboration. These are followed where appropriate by suggestions tailored to the youngster and to the referral resources.

Kindergarten Referral: Melvin Schreider, the Iron Bunny (5 Years)

The "Iron Bunny" report was written by graduate students in my department's M.A. assessment course. It was written toward the end of the semester, as one of the two field assessments assigned to each team. The field setting was an experimental, private preschool, where graduate students from several local programs received training.

Although the authors spent more than six hours with Melvin Schreider, they judiciously selected just a few examples to illustrate their findings. The report is all the more powerful for its brevity. The "iron bunny" metaphor effectively uses the assessors' personal experience of Melvin to integrate two apparently opposite comportments that had been observed previously. Because the report evolves around the two apparently opposite comportments, the metaphor also serves to remind readers of the content of the report. To enhance that function of the metaphor, the authors placed "Iron Bunny" in the report's title. The report sticks to its story line; the connection between testing events and classroom behavior is made explicit, and the Alternatives (suggestions) follow directly from the report.

Psychological Assessment: MELVIN SCHREIDER

Melvin, the Iron Bunny

Age: 5 years, 3 months   Dates of assessment: 12-2, 4, 9, 13, 19____
Grade: Kindergarten   Date of report: 12-15, 19____

Referral

Ms. Judy Sontag, director of the West Side New School, believes Melvin to be seriously distressed, and wondered if our observations might help her staff to minimize the difficulties he now experiences (and that are likely to increase in public school). Specifically, the staff has been concerned about (1) Melvin's "aggression" toward other children, and (2) his "withdrawal," which is accompanied by "a funny look on his face." One of his teachers further explained to us that Melvin hates the children, throws things, and when there is surrounding commotion he goes off by himself.

Opportunities for Assessment

We met with Melvin four times over a two-week period for a total of 6 1/2 hours. We first observed him in his classroom playing with other children, and later played with him ourselves. During our second and third meetings with him he did the Bender-Gestalt, the Draw-A-Person, and parts of the Wechsler Primary and Preschool Scale of Intelligence (WPPSI). In our fourth meeting we participated in a play therapy session with Melvin and Ms. Sandy Harst, a child development intern.

First Impressions

What we noticed first about Melvin was his dirty physical appearance. His hair was uncombed, his hands and face unwashed, his clothes torn, and his body smelled of stale urine. Then Melvin, although only five years old, began to remind us of a little steelworker. His square face, solid chin, and prominent forehead reminded us of the features of a man, not a boy. Similarly, his broad shoulders and a large torso reminded us of a little football player. In our first meeting with him he put on a helmet, took out a football and started throwing it to us or running with it like a halfback.

Melvin also definitely struck us as warm, friendly, and gentle, and he moved with caution when we first began playing football with him. His play with us was discontinuous; he sometimes stood in the corner waiting for us to ask him to join the game. He then quickly joined in, running around with the football and enjoying physical contact. He seemed to like the individual attention from us and smiled appreciatively. When a few other children entered the game and it became noisy, Melvin suddenly ran over to a small space next to the rabbit cage and crawled into it. Melvin's face seemed sad, his mouth was twisted, and his eyes frowned in a faraway gaze; this was the "funny look" that his teacher had told us about.

Melvin as Seen through the Assessment Materials

When we first played with him, we thought that Melvin was not particularly intelligent. He did not talk much and when he did he used baby talk. He was also clumsy, uncoordinated. In trying to catch the football, he did move his arms toward the ball but waited for it to land wherever his hands already were. However, as we began going through the assessment materials with him, we discovered a bright little boy. Here Melvin was attentive to his surroundings. On the Picture Completion subtest of the WPPSI, which requires the identification of the missing part of an everyday situation or object, Melvin got 22 out of 23 questions correct. He carefully scanned the picture, concentrating on it until he found the missing part. Melvin was also quick to learn a manual task. On the Animal House subtest, where the child has to match colored pegs with animal pictures, Melvin finished the task in three minutes, well within the five-minute time limit. He started the task before we actually finished the instructions and he did not make one error. Later, Melvin took out the board and pegs by himself, saying that he wanted to play with them again. He then, from memory, correctly matched the colored pegs with the animals.

There were some things that Melvin could not do initially but it was not because he lacked understanding of the task. For example, when we asked him to draw certain geometrical figures (Bender-Gestalt, Figures 1, 3, 6) Melvin took the pencil and tried, but as soon as he made a mistake he stopped drawing and said "can't do that," sometimes slapping the paper or throwing the pencil. When he made one mistake, he quickly gave up. On Figure 6, Melvin started drawing and then threw his pencil down, giving up. When we pointed out to him that he had completed half the figure, and encouraged him to continue, Melvin finished the drawing, pleased and surprised. A similar sequence occurred on the maze subtest of the WPPSI: on the more difficult mazes, Melvin began and after making one mistake jumped away, saying, "I don't want to do it." One of us encouraged him to continue by helping Melvin guide the pencil. Melvin welcomed the help, and continued, even on the most difficult mazes. On the Vocabulary subtest, Melvin refused to talk, despite our encouragement. His face took on that "funny look" again, and he looked as frightened as a scared rabbit, holding his hands to his face, squinting his eyes, and shaking slightly.

Similarities between the Assessment and Classroom Situations

In watching Melvin's behavior in the classroom with other children, we saw many similarities with his behavior on the assessment materials. In both situations, when Melvin did not know what to do to get what he wanted, he behaved in an ineffective manner. Most often these were occasions when other persons could have helped him if he had known how to turn to or otherwise engage them. In the assessment situation he threw down the pencil or hit the paper and in the classroom situation he hit other children or threw some toys. When the situation got out of hand for Melvin, he stopped talking altogether and went away by himself. In the classroom situation this meant going off in a corner, and in the assessment situation this meant avoiding any participation with us on the assessment task at hand, although he remained in his seat. At these points Melvin took on his funny look and said nothing more.

In both situations, Melvin apparently wanted to participate actively. He was friendly with us, willing to participate patiently in most of our tasks. Likewise, he sought the company of other children and enthusiastically joined in playing with them. At one point we even saw him walk up to a girl and ask her if she was his friend. At times, Melvin could play effectively with the other children. For example, he cooperatively joined in a game of Twister with us and two little girls in his class. In other words, although Melvin sometimes acts inappropriately with other people, he typically wants contact with others and when given support definitely is an open, friendly boy.

Summary

We have tried to illustrate that Melvin's difficulty is not one of "aggression." Rather, it is that at present when he becomes lost he either hops away into seclusion like a frightened bunny, or he tries to hold his ground by throwing things or hitting children. His steelworker appearance and physical strength probably result in children and adults alike perceiving this inappropriate form of assertiveness as "hostility" or "aggression." Surely both children and adults must be tempted to avoid Melvin not only during these misdirected physical assertions, but also in the face of his apparent unpredictability. And then there's his dirty appearance and the odor of stale urine. Melvin unknowingly contributes to an environment in which others turn away from him.

Alternatives

1. Perhaps Melvin could remain more consistently and constructively engaged with persons and activities if adults would intervene to help him remain involved. A crucial point in his movement is the moment when he meets the first obstacle, when he makes the first mistake. At that point he often gives up. When Melvin has been helped over the mistake, he usually has continued. This is a matter of saying to him, "Come on, Melvin, you can do it," and showing him how he can correct his mistake. In our interactions, Melvin consistently responded well to individualized encouragement.

2. When put into a situation with a lot of people or commotion, Melvin often has either hit somebody or hopped away. Noisy situations seem to have been aversive and confusing to him. We suggest that, when possible, his group activities be limited to a small number of people. In line with this, when Melvin is involved in a group task, it might help to pair him with a quiet, easygoing child who could help Melvin over his obstacles. Such cumulative experiences may gradually allow him to experience classroom commotion as less threatening.

3. We think it is advisable for Melvin to be referred for a preschool developmental readiness screening. It is possible that some of his perplexity may be due to perceptual difficulties, although admittedly what we observed could equally well be attributable to underdeveloped coordination. The latter could be either constitutional or the outcome of insufficient supervised play at home. Examples of what we noticed are: when playing with dominoes, Melvin held them close to his face in order to count the dots; he also had difficulty catching the football—it seemed as if he did not see where it began its trajectory.

4. Similarly, supportive physical play with Melvin seems in order not only to provide constructive intervention when he becomes lost, but also to provide for the development of motor coordination. An additional example here is that Melvin holds his pencil too far up and hence cannot control it effectively. Although this individualized encouragement and gentle supervised play is of course not always possible for already overloaded teachers or for parents with their complex concerns, the more often it can occur, the better off Melvin will be.

5. After Melvin's parents have studied this report and perhaps devised additional suggestions with the West Side New School staff, this report and the additions could be provided to Melvin's first grade teacher. That teacher will be a critical person in aiding Melvin toward an integration of his assertiveness and sensitivity. At any rate, we feel that this report might help to alert her to whichever aspect of Melvin is not immediately apparent in the public school classroom, whether the steelworker or the bunny.

Marc H. Kaplan
Mary Ablan

Graduate Students, Psychology
Duquesne University

Comments

The straightforward, concise presentation of Melvin helps us to see the seriousness of his situation. Concomitantly, Melvin's responses to the assessors' supportive interventions, as well as their observations of adaptive comportment, alert us to a nonpathological side. We see possibilities of relating to Melvin's strengths and of helping him to develop. The graduate students' achievement in this dual presentation is especially remarkable in that they were requested by the West Side faculty to not "scare off" the parents by explicitly mentioning their fear of parental criminal neglect or abuse. West Side teachers were working with the parents, encouraging them to seek guidance for themselves and further care for Melvin. In the event that the school's efforts failed, however, assessors and faculty alike wanted this report to be strong enough to help provide "just cause" for intervention by Child Welfare authorities. The report optimizes chances that upon reading it, the parents would recognize the importance of their responsibility to Melvin and yet not be thrown into rigid defensiveness.

An effective report enables helpers to recognize the person they already know—that is, to see the similarity between their own observations and the report's description. The assessors were successful in this regard partly because of their extended observations in the classroom. Assessment description, however, also transforms readers' earlier perceptions and conceptions of the client into a fuller vision, one that integrates apparent discrepancies, such as the "hostility" and "withdrawal" that had been noted by Melvin's teachers. No underlying causes were posited to account for these behaviors; neither feature was explained in terms of the other. Rather, the way each comportment developed was specified. Readers see the circumstances within which Melvin changes from little man of steel to frightened bunny and back again; readers also recognize that both profiles are the same Melvin. Adults thus see how they participate in Melvin's transformations, and how they might do so more mindfully in the future.

Finally, this report is noteworthy for two other ways of reaching staff and parents. First, both parties were engaged through specific references to them throughout the report. Second, because the assessment took place in Pittsburgh, the metaphor was chosen to speak to Pittsburghers: we are the home of the Steelers football team, named after our men of iron, the steelworkers. The bunny image was a particularly effective contrast because of the staff's and parents' familiarity with the classroom's bunny hutch being Melvin's place of refuge.

Family Service Agency Referral:
Family Assessment—The Jabby Jungle
(Bobby Harrell, 6 Years)

A field placement supervisor in a family service agency asked two M.A. students to assess both a counseling client and her son. The mother, Barbara Harrell, had reported difficulties in coping with her six-year-old son, Bobby. He appeared to be doing well at school in terms of grades and conduct, but he was difficult to control at home. He frequently made excuses to stay home on days his mother would be there. She wondered if other children were teasing Bobby or if teachers expected him to perform beyond his age because he was tall and husky. At home he was often demanding and sometimes threw temper tantrums. Barbara wondered if he had a blood sugar problem and gave him peanut butter or candy when he became irritable. She had not, however, consulted a physician.

The assessment team asked for permission to visit the Harrell home on a Saturday morning. There they encountered Bobby's younger brother and sister and Marlan Harrell, Barbara's husband, who had just returned after living alone for a year. After joining the family's informal breakfast routine and then talking with the parents, the team administered a Bender-Gestalt and Wechsler Intelligence Scale for Children with Bobby, asked him for some drawings, and played tic-tac-toe with him. They returned three days later to talk with Barbara. On that visit they made use of the Bender-Gestalt and the Comprehension and

Block Design subtests of the Wechsler Adult Intelligence Scale to explore her ways of coping with challenges. With parental permission, the team then observed Bobby in his classroom, and discussed the contrast to their home observations with Bobby's teacher and the school counselor.

The team then returned to the Harrell home with a report describing the family interactions, the separate assessment activities with Bobby and with Barbara, the school observations, and their initial suggestions. Barbara and Marlan modified and expanded the suggestions, which encouraged Barbara to be more consistent and explicit in her dealings with Bobby. The assessors then wrote a separate report for Bobby in the form of a fable. The fable was intended to help Bobby understand what the assessors had seen, and how his mother was going to try to be more consistently responsive to his needs for structure and guidance.

The excerpts below present the report's findings, illustrate the assessors' approach to a family, and describe their exploration of two contexts in which a youngster appears to be quite different. The fable turned out to be a remarkably effective means of communicating with all parties. Marlan is not in the fable, just as he is often not in the home. The report indicates that he and Barbara married just out of high school, but his sales job has kept him away from home most of the time. Barbara at first focused her life on Bobby, but then began working as a clerk two days a week, doing outside housework on call, and working on women's social action projects. Marlan, a large-boned, husky man, wore wire-rimmed glasses and spoke softly. His astute but unobtrusive remarks showed that he was genuinely concerned about Bobby. The Harrells were uncertain about their future together.

Barbara was described as 27 years old, tall, slender, attractive, with waist-length brown hair. The following excerpts further describe her.

> Generally, through the Bender-Gestalt, Block Design subtest, and the DAP, Barbara assumed what appeared to be a casual posture and attitude, resting her head in one hand and performing the tasks with the other hand. Her drawings were completed quickly, lightly, and without detail . . .
>
> What at first appeared to us as patience with her children when they were demanding or whiney often later appeared to us as avoiding confrontation with them by giving in (for example, by letting them fill up on cookies and cheese twists before dinner). It also seemed that she didn't let them know what was expected of them in a consistent manner (specification of mealtimes, bedtimes, homework times, and so on). This is partly a result of her work schedule. Barbara admitted that she felt she was both lazy and an avoider. She believed it would be a 24-hour vigil to keep her kids under control—she's too tired after a day's work and just wants peace, which she attains by not taking a firm stand with her children concerning their behavior.
>
> During the Block Design subtest, Barbara mentioned that she likes "good precise directions." She said she strongly sensed the absence of lines on the stimulus card, which would have indicated the boundaries of the blocks. Barbara likes boundaries, because they indicate to her straightforward direc-

tion. (Would this be an easier way for her to make decisions—step by step?) She sometimes becomes lost in general directions (and likewise "gives in" with her children). She told us about an older woman at work who criticizes in general statements. Barbara would rather she would criticize directly. "I don't know where I stand with her." We asked Barbara if she considered herself straightforward with her children. She paused, and answered, "My fault is plain laziness—I don't take the time." She also referred to "getting up on two feet when you'd like to sit down." . . .

Is she perhaps confusing being straightforward with being pushy? Concerning her problem with Bobby's behavior at home, Barbara feels, "*I* don't like to be pushed, therefore, I don't want to be *pushy* . . . *I* don't like to be nagged, therefore, I don't like to *nag.*" Barbara also appreciates straightforwardness and would like to be straightforward in her expectations of Bobby's behavior. But on the other hand, she does not want to nag or push. Herein lies an inconsistency. How is Bobby to know what his boundaries and rules are at home when (1) they are often not made clear or are not even spoken, and (2) Barbara does not consistently stand behind her expectations (allows herself to be pushed, is permissive when tired, and screams when her "fuse burns up")?

Barbara often seemed to evade our questions regarding her role in the referral; at one point she began unloading the dishwasher. Other times we felt strongly pulled by her to discuss only generalities. We felt confused because several times Barbara requested concrete suggestions on how to handle Bobby, yet eluded attempts to delve into areas that we felt might be underlying the problem. Barbara was warm toward us in expressing her concern, opening her home to us, preparing meals and snacks for us. But at the same time, she was cool toward us in that it was often difficult for us to locate where she was in relation to us from moment to moment.

The report describes Bobby as resembling his father in appearance: tall for his age, large-boned, husky, brown-haired. In contrast, though, he was energetic and quick to smile. He bounced into the kitchen, demanded breakfast, and was unafraid to ask questions throughout the assessment. During the testing he often set up his own boundaries, finding ways to do tasks a step at a time. He enjoyed "winning," and took pride in mastery, in terms of both accuracy and completeness of answers. However,

> without boundaries and discrete steps, and with only a broad time limit, Bobby felt hurried and often seemed agitated. He seemed lost in space when he wasn't given clues or directions as to how to pace himself.
>
> During the assessment sessions, when Bobby floundered with a task for the above reasons, we both felt pulled to help him ("Hey, *wait*, there's something the matter"). Other times his strength in diversionary tactics made us feel subtly manipulated, and we were angered to find ourselves in this circumstance. He often controlled the test situation, and only firmness and persistence on our part brought us all back to the assessment.

The vulnerable six-year-old who skips school to stay home and to keep his mommy home also was represented in the report. Several times during the WISC Bobby's answers made reference to a television *Lassie* movie, in which a little boy fell over a cliff and was trapped in a canyon all by himself. Bobby had cried during the movie even though the boy was eventually rescued. When the assessors asked Bobby if he thought he was somehow like the little boy, he squirmed in his chair, and acknowledged, "Yeah."

When Bobby was observed in the classroom, he was involved and cooperative in class activities. He was sometimes slow to leave earlier projects to begin a new assignment, but responded quickly to reminders. He was in the top reading section. His teacher and counselor said they had never seen a tantrum. His size had not been problematic so far as they knew. They had wondered about his occasional failures to return to school after having lunch at home, but had seen no connection with happenings at school. The teacher was described in the report as "handling her classroom in a firm but gentle manner, explaining her expectations of the children carefully and clearly, and consistently enforcing them."

Bobby's Report

This is a story we created for Bobby, as his copy of our report. We attempted to simplify somewhat the situation as we see it, while still retaining essential relationships, movements, and suggestions.

Portraying Bobby as a bright-eyed baby elephant, we sought to emphasize his strength, size, ineffectiveness in coping with situations beyond his control, and his wanting consistent, dependable patterns in his life. Portraying Barbara as the little bird perching on the baby elephant's back, we tried to evoke the lightness (ineffectiveness) of her presence in providing stable, dependable guidelines. In her birdlikeness, Barbara is at times "fluttery and flighty"—hovering and hesitating between decisions, moving from one interest to another without establishing or fostering growth of roots, a firm stand. When Bobby trumpets around the house, stamping and stomping, he's asking to be put on track, any track, as long as he is encouraged and prodded to continue in the same directions—not pulled several different ways at once or left no alternative but to push in conflicting directions. Bobby's school situation with Mrs. Garlow (lioness) also is described in the report. We hope our implicit suggestion will be understood by Bobby and may clarify some questions or encourage him to raise some questions at the family discussion about rules to teach the bright-eyed baby elephant how to move within the structure he wants.

Bobby used the word "jabby" several times during the Vocabulary subtest. To him, "jabby" means something that can hurt you or be dangerous. Bobby's world is jabby to him in some ways; for the most part, he depends on himself to test out or explore the jungle. But without guidance from the little bird who can see ahead and has lived in the jungle, Bobby gets jabbed.

Michele Julin
Kathleen Curzie Gajdos

Graduate Students
Department of Psychology
Duquesne University

The Jabby Jungle

Once there was a bright-eyed baby elephant, strong for his size, who lived in the jabby jungle. If he saw a branch in the way as he lumbered along, he would say to himself, "I am a strong little baby elephant. I bet I can move that branch!" And he would. He liked finding things that he could do because it made him feel grown up, that he could take care of himself sometimes. He liked to see a job well done, so it often took him a long time, but he was proud when he was done.

The baby elephant had a little bird who perched on his back. He liked this little bird, and she liked the bright-eyed baby elephant. She often rested on his back and thought that she should shoo away the little bugs that might annoy him while he was plodding through the jabby jungle.

When she sensed trouble ahead, she would chirp loudly, with screeching sounds, and become fluttery and flighty; this would make the baby elephant jumpy, and he would begin to trumpet loudly and stomp from side to side, flicking the little bird off his back. Then she would fly away for a little while, and the elephant wouldn't know that she had gone. He could hardly tell whether the bird was there or not, because she was so light and he was often too busy exploring the forest and moving branches out of his way.

Other times the little bird would go away because she had things to do by herself while the baby elephant was busy with other friends. The little baby elephant would go with his friends to learn the ways of the jungle from the likable lioness who shared her wise stories. She knew the ways of the jungle and set limits and rules for the baby animals. She showed them how to live by rules in order to be safe and happy.

The little elephant, so strong, enjoyed her teachings, and although he moved slowly sometimes, as elephants do, he learned quickly. When he lumbered slowly along, the lioness would gently prod him to keep up, and he could follow her firm directions. He and his animal companions knew that by following what the lioness said and did, they would learn how to make the jabby jungle a safe place where they could someday move by themselves.

The baby elephant needed the little bird whenever he left his friends and the lioness. He looked to the little bird to help him remember the rules he had learned from the lioness, because little baby elephants can't always remember.

But the baby elephant would often be confused and not know quite where the flighty little bird could be. Sometimes the little bird was perched on his back so lightly that the baby didn't even know it. One day the baby elephant wanted the little bird to guide him, and got so confused that he threw his head back and trumpeted as loud as he could, and stomped and stamped shaking his jungle home, so that she would know where he was and that he was lost and needed help. Usually when he did this the little bird gave him some peanuts to calm him down or flew away for a little while. But this time, instead of flying away or giving him peanuts, she flew in front of him where he could see her. The little bird looked at the bright-eyed baby elephant and noticed that he was not so big. A baby elephant is strong, but the little bird had realized how important she was to him and how he depended on her to guide him firmly through the jabby jungle. She had lived in the jungle longer and the baby elephant trusted her to see ahead for him. The little bird saw that she should be a guide in front of him on the tip of his trunk, so that he could listen to her and follow her.

Sometimes she would still fly away to her other tasks, and he would be off with his friends. But when he wasn't with his friends and the lioness, the little bird tried to make sure that she gave him directions so that he always knew where he was and wouldn't get lost in the jabby jungle anymore.

Comments

This assessment illustrates the usefulness of a flexible approach to referrals. Rather than construing the referral as a request for separate appraisals and reports, the assessors saw an opportunity to go to the heart of the referral issue—Barbara's relation with Bobby. When they discovered Marlan in the home, they included him in the assessment. The counselor who made the referral readily encouraged this approach, although previously she had thought that assessments could only appraise single personalities. This flexibility was possible because the graduate students viewed themselves not as testers but as assessors. They properly saw their task as helping the counselor and the Harrells in their efforts to enhance Bobby's growth through Barbara's development. Testing was helpful as an access to Bobby's and Barbara's approaches to tasks, ways of dealing with others, and their levels of effectiveness.

To find out whether Bobby was in fact getting along well at school, the assessors went there to watch him in that environment and to talk with school personnel. Granted, the pressures of time often require that these inquiries occur less directly, for example via telephone consultations. But the visit to the school was helpful because it showed that the same Bobby who could be problematic at home functioned cooperatively at school. We see how the two environments participate differently in the evolution of Bobby's comportment. I use the word *see* purposely; we can picture process—how Bobby can change from a bellowing, demanding boy at home to a quietly happy follower at school. It is within this process that we can identify what I have called the "pivot points" at which movement can be smoothly redirected. Therein we also see that Bobby's comportment is not simply a reaction to external stimuli; we see how Bobby and his environment flow along together in unity.

This process of flowing in unity is difficult for authors to express because our language is so linear and partitive. Then as readers, when we are removed from the actual behaviors and environments and are present only to records and reports, we think about what we read in terms of categories and constructs. We then integrate the secondhand data in terms of cause and effect. Here, for example, the assessors might have concluded from school records that "Bobby reacts well to a structured environment." That conclusion, of course, would have been correct but not particularly helpful. Most such correct conclusions are truisms. Individualized description tells how the generality is true of a particular person, and where within that person's movement through particular situations a pivot might be initiated, by either the client or other persons. For example, from the report we see that Bobby and his mother could readily learn to recognize the early stages of stomping and trumpeting as signs that he is becoming lost. Bobby can learn that at these moments he can forthrightly seek direction from his mother, his teacher, or other experienced persons. Now those persons are less likely to be put off by the boisterous nature of those requests, which indicate a change of course. Moreover, the adults now know that the object is not to stop the noisiness, nor even to find something new for Bobby to do. Instead, they try to understand where he was going and what he was trying to do, and to help reconnect him with familiar landmarks, rules, and tools.

The report, excerpted here for reasons of economy, accomplished the above points by virtue of its integrated presentation of family members in relation to one another and of Bobby in relation to different contexts. That report was lengthy—12 double-space pages preceding the fable. The fable then served many functions. It is not just a simplified report for a child, but also is a compact, vivid reminder for adults of the report's themes. Experienced from a fresh perspective, those themes strengthen and enrich readers' understandings. The playful literary device, at least in the present case, helps readers to appreciate both Bobby's and Barbara's circumstances without holding either to blame. In the fable each can see his or her responsibility for future comportment. The condensation provided by the fable encourages focused reflection and planning, while the imaginary quality encourages affective recognition of what it may be like to be that baby elephant and flighty guide.

Bobby understood the report, asked questions ("What's lumbering?"), offered elaborations, and was thoroughly pleased that adults could understand his travels through the jabby jungle. The counselor reported that she could use the fable in family therapy as well as in her work with Barbara.

Child Guidance Center Referral: Richard Ferris (6 Years)

Rick Ferris had been brought to a local child guidance center toward the end of his first-grade year. Until that time, his parents and teacher had thought that as he matured his indistinct speech and shy ways would ameliorate. Instead, according to Mrs. Ferris, his speech had remained "garbled," he had become "aggressive and disruptive at home," and he had "regressed academically" (reading readiness scores had fallen during the year). The clinical child psychologist who supervised the two graduate student assessors asked them to (1) explore the extent to which Rick's misbehavior might be frustration at not being able to communicate, (2) assess Rick's general abilities, especially in regard to how well he could be expected to achieve in school, and (3) note any indications that Rick's difficulties might be neurologically based.

To provide information pertinent to all these concerns, the assessors wrote a lengthy report. They emphasized that their observations had taken place in only one setting (the Center) for only one session, and that they were not trained to answer the diagnostic questions, but that they hoped their detailed description could serve as a point of comparison for other evaluators (pediatrician, speech therapist, developmental disabilities specialist). The following excerpts illustrate the power of an individualized assessment approach—even with a shy, troubled, inarticulate six-year-old.

Excerpt from the Report on Richard Ferris

. . . .

First Impressions

When we entered the waiting room of the center, Rick's soft "hello" was blocked by his fingers in his mouth. He turned away shyly as if there were a slight danger approaching, and wandered toward his mother, taking shelter by leaning close to her skirt as she stood over him. As we waited she tucked in his shirt while turning him around. Rick was brought into our room alone, seeming uncertain as he wandered over and sat down. He moved as if the situation were not a place where he could be assertive and take a firm stand. When he sat down his arms were tucked in as if there were nowhere else they could extend with certainty. Rick's nonassertive style also appeared in his words, which could hardly be heard and were difficult to understand. As we began to address him, Rick found something to hold onto, a rock, and he clutched it tightly as we talked.

Rick without Guidance

We asked Rick to copy some geometric designs (Bender-Gestalt), and he politely agreed. He held the pencil very tightly (so much so that it flipped out of his hand upon occasion) and pushed down hard, his whole body moving into each stroke, after which he'd look up at Cathy (the administrator). In looking up so frequently, Rick seemed not so much to be seeking approval or validation of his efforts, as to be keeping tabs on the situation during his bold extending of himself. His activity seemed to involve significant risk for him. Rick's left hand continued to hold tightly onto the rock and his toes tapped on the ground in an up and down motion (seemingly searching for a base). As a consequence of his holding onto the rock, the paper slid around on the table, and his preoccupation with Cathy served to break up his vision of the cards and his work. Also contributing to Rick's not seeing his work fully was his head's intermittent shying down or away, at which times his mouth sometimes opened showing his twisting tongue. Rick continued to work without pause, his gestures bold but shaky.

The drawings Rick produced were twisted and inaccurate. Their order on the page seemed to be random; sometimes they almost ran into each other; a couple of figures were rotated (#A, #1) and a couple were incompletely executed (for example, too few dots on #1). Eventually (at design #6), Rick put the rock down and at our suggestion held the paper. This helped to some extent, but even the last few figures wavered off course. The best way to describe these figures might be to call them "garbled," for they look much like Rick's speech sounds.

Our Intervention: Dormant Possibilities

At this time I was interested to know the extent of Rick's capability of appraising the accuracy of these drawings, assuming responsibility for his errors, formulating how they came about, and carrying out the activities necessary for copying them more correctly. Moreover, I was interested to see if Rick would, if he felt our interested concern and knew precisely what was called for, assume a more direct and active role to meet the task more successfully.

After he was finished I asked Rick if his first design looked like the one on the card, and he answered "no." I said, "Can you move the card to make it look more like yours?" He replied "yes," and with a slight smile turned it vertically without looking up. I continued, "What if I put this card back the way it was and gave you a new piece of paper, could you draw it the way it was?" He nodded his head and—sure enough—he did it almost perfectly, this time the diamond meeting the circle (both well formed) quite precisely. During this work Rick was holding the paper with his left hand and resting his feet on the floor. His hesitance to move out actively into the world was evident, as he twisted his hands together with the pencil while pondering what he was about to do. (This twisting was very much like twisting his tongue when he turns his head away, opens his mouth, and garbles his speech.) However, as he redrew some of the other rotated and more garbled designs, Rick seemed to become more at home and at ease. In facing the situation now he did not look up at Cathy nor turn his head down or away but concentrated closely on the work. Rick demonstrated during this time that he could recognize all the discrepancies between his original drawings and the cards as well as formulate, to a certain extent, how his errors were made (for example, not watching himself). His performance on the second attempt was far superior to his original attempts and turned out to be more accurate than the average for his age.

In this interaction, Cathy and I did not direct Rick but simply asked him questions about accuracy and whether he could be more accurate. After his more successful attempts we told him he did good work but we did not overwhelm him with praise. Our straightforward and structured participation was essential to Rick's straightening out his garbled efforts. However, as Rick began to experience success, he became more confident on his own (without even looking up). This experience was strengthening and uplifting for Rick and set the tone of the rest of the assessment, although further problems and difficulties were by no means absent.

In situations that were well defined and in which Rick could accomplish what was asked of him, he became engrossed in the activities. Here, extending himself into the world did not seem too risky for him. For instance, in drawing predetermined marks into designated forms—stars, squares, circles (Coding, WISC), he set to work in a sure and effective way, leaning back occasionally to breathe deeply. Similarly, when Rick was asked to find the missing part of a picture (Picture Completion, WISC), he remained intently interested with a single-mindedness that earned him his highest subtest score. When he couldn't find the missing part, he straightforwardly concluded, "I don't know." At one point Rick set out to go to the bathroom and also to show me where it was, and he marched along like he was on top of the world; he knew exactly where it was.

After two hours of hard work, Rick remarked that he liked "the copying" best. It seemed to have been an opportunity for him to take the time to change an uncomfortable way of handling a task in the face of significant others. As Rick left us, he took the lead and marched his family out the door like a little general—quite a contrast with his original shy wandering to his mother's side.

Rick in the Face of Risk

Sometimes when the situation called for a more independently derived understanding and for self-initiated activity, Rick's style changed distinctly. He defined brave as "going somewhere and buying something alone"—indeed a dangerous task for him. In these circumstances, after an attempt, Rick would either move around in the same way he came into our room originally—a kind of wandering (for example, turning away from a difficult block task and wandering "aimlessly" to the toys), or he would leap into the risky task as if his mere lunging movement would magically get him through (examples: the original Bender, scattering of blocks, becoming violent with toys).

During the times when Rick literally turned away from the task and wandered to the cupboard, he seemed to have no plan of action. He opened the cupboard as if hoping something would grab his interest. His own agency seemed abandoned as whatever struck him invited his activity. Rick initiated very few conversations in our time with him, again showing his hesitance to engage in complex activity in which he would be "on the line." Even when we addressed him, his voice wandered in a shy, slightly fearful way. Often times we would guess aloud at a word, and Rick would seem caught by it and would repeat it, rather than persist in trying to communicate his own original idea. Sometimes his speech faded away. Apparently, rather than face the risk of self-initiated action, Rick, in his wandering style, turns from the possibility of entering danger and latches onto whatever grabs him.

When Rick neither directly faced nor purposefully turned away from risk, he impatiently and impulsively acted without organizing himself. This took the form of a relatively blind attempt to face the task or an attempt to destroy it. Rick drew designs in whatever spaces caught his attention, and his effort was slap-dash, as if he hoped it would somehow magically save him from danger. Often Rick did not integrate the material in front of him, as when he looked only at the card and not at what he was drawing. At other times he tried to do two things at once in an impatient, lunging effort to assert himself. In trying to count a row of blocks, Rick rushed in with both hands, trying to count from both ends at the same time, tangling him up completely. Rick's disorganized (garbled) speech is a combination of his wandering style and of this abortive attempt to engage in a risky activity. His mouth begins to twist as he becomes more anxious and the words become unclear. On other occasions he seized upon a part of the situation and became fascinated with it without seeing the whole, as he did on the Block Design, turning one block around and around without any movement toward integration of the design (he then put the block in his mouth and wandered off to the toys). These rough, twisted, magical, and/or impulsive attempts to assert himself in the face of possible failure are, of course, ineffective.

Possibilities of Change

With a bit of help, but mostly with our straightforward concern, Rick began to develop approaches that were more effective for his purposes and with which he could be more at home. When we could not understand Rick, we asked him to clarify himself and he usually did so without becoming frustrated. Also, when he gave short, incomplete answers he gladly elaborated when asked to. He picked up suggestions very rapidly on many tasks. When he was trying to count with both hands at once, I said "slow down and see what you want to do first," and he paused and began counting with one hand. Another time he attempted in a rough and impatient way to balance a rock on a block tower and I said, "How come it keeps falling?" He smiled and then did it gently and successfully. We discussed with Rick several ways he came to err—such as not watching his hand while drawing. He said he only realized it was wrong after it was done, and we asked him how he could be sure it was right. He then did it again, watching carefully. This carefulness then carried over into the rest of the drawing tasks. After a long time at trying to assemble parts of a puzzle (Object Assembly, WISC,) and becoming stuck on a few parts, he said, "I can't do it." I got down on the floor with him and, looking at the other pieces, said, "Have you tried everything?" Rick then brought them into the picture, eventually putting the puzzle together.

. . . .

Frederick J. Wertz   Kathleen M. Doria

Graduate Students in Psychology
Duquesne University

Comments

Other sections of the report indicated that Rick scored in the Bright Normal range of intelligence on the WISC, and that abstract thinking was not impaired. For example, Similarities was one of his highest WISC subtests, and when asked, he said he could imagine Bender design No. 6 as a kite, bees, or a flock of birds. In addition, the report indicated that at various points in the assessors' work with Rick, his speech became clear and distinct. In consultation with the clinical child psychologist, the authors of the report concluded that in all likelihood Rick's difficulties were not due to any neurological deficit or damage, or to mental retardation, but rather could be understood psychologically in terms of his responses to unfamiliar situations that he was required to assertively structure himself.

Because his fearfulness and his subsequent wandering and lunging had developed within his family, the assessors recommended therapy sessions for the family as well as for Rick. Separate suggestions were presented to parents, teachers, and the future therapist. In essence, the various suggestions encouraged replication of the assessment circumstances and interventions through which Rick had found it possible to be direct, clear, and relatively independent. The assessors recommended that after such changes were in place, and Rick was accustomed to them, a referral for evaluation of developmental disabilities be considered. Just because Rick's behavior could be understood psychologically did not preclude neurological weaknesses that could be complicating his growth. An instrument such as the Illinois Test of Psycholinguistic Ability (ITPA), even if it did not indicate a specific learning disability, might provide clues as to the most effective modes of presenting material to Rick (visual, oral, motoric).

This report answered all the referral issues by making Rick's world visible to us. We saw process—the coming into being of Rick's wandering, being grabbed, lunging, garbling. We became aware that Rick's problematic comportment was at once a bodily, verbal, experiential coping with interpersonally risky situations. In short, we were present to structure—to the mutuality of context, experience, action. The consequences of this structural presence were powerful. Deficits and abilities as such disappeared as focal issues. There was no speech problem leading to "frustration"; rather, garbled speech was one of Rick's ways of getting through dangerous situations. Rick did not "have" a problem; he and his social environment co-created problems. Through the structural perspective we saw how adults could intervene to create opportunities for Rick to maintain an effective course or to find his way back from his wandering.

Rather than focusing entirely on end products (developmental level of Bender, IQ, and the like), the assessors were also attuned to the total situation—of which they too were a part. They observed the process of Rick's comportment unfolding in different ways with different outcomes. They re-presented the concrete whens and when-nots of Rick's various comportments. Those descriptions included the assessors' immediate reactions, evolved impressions, and the interventions through which they explored Rick's comportment and his viable options. Especially through the explicitation of the contexts in which interventions were effective (for example "our straightforward and structured participation"), Rick's parents, teachers, and therapist see how they too can step into Rick's life constructively.

Summer Camp Reports

At a summer day camp that enrolled children with physical, intellectual, and interpersonal problems in addition to its regular campers, I consulted with the camp staff in regard to supervising one of the special youngsters. One summer a community mental health and mental retardation center sent 21 youngsters to a four-week camp session, with a request that we provide brief feedback on how each child "looked" while at camp, and on what kind of counselor supervision might be required for the next summer. The idea was to help therapists, family, and teachers to see what difficulties the youngsters continued to experience in a different environment and, more important, to see how adaptively the youngsters grew in that environment. The camp was different for these particular children partly because their immediate staff and fellow campers were not informed that they were special in any way. Most of them remained unidentified as diagnosed children throughout the camp season, even though Mary Harrison and I, along with other senior staff members, made suggestions to counselors about these youngsters as well as about other campers.

Report to Bomburg Valley CMH&MR Center:
Behavioral Excerpts

Jack Tacaks (10 years)   Chieftans   July 15–August 9, 19____

Items of Concern
   • When uncertain of what was happening in a group activity, and when he felt that he had been unfairly ordered to do something, Jack rebelled. On these occasions he has threatened to throw rocks at another child (he

did not follow through, however), has instigated a runaway group, and has loudly muttered "shit," "pee on you," and suchlike.
- Jack's persistent mask-like grin contributed to an uncertain distance between himself and both other campers and staff.

Positive Items
- Jack responded very well to being offered concrete alternatives to assignments (such as helping to set the lunch table rather than gathering up athletic equipment).
- Jack took considerable pride in being genuinely needed. He threw himself into doing a good job with some volunteer "helper" projects (camp maintenance and clean-up).
- At first Jack seemed confused by the staff's consistent positive attention even in the face of his "rebellions." However, he soon formed first-name relations with the Chieftan counselors and with several staff persons outside of his own group. He seemed to revel in staff persons' follow-through on promises (providing a missed breakfast, asking the outcome of a project, and so on.)

At camp, Jack requires attention from assigned counselors who can provide a consistent relationship as well as general supervision.

Mary Harrison
Counselors' Consultant

Constance T. Fischer, Ph.D.
Psychologist

Report to Bomburg Valley CMH&MR Center: Behavioral Excerpts

Carolyn Meuser (10 years)   Chieftans   July 15-August 9, 19____

Items of Concern
- Carolyn did not seem to form friendships with her peers; she instead attached herself to a counselor.
- Initially, she frequently sought attention by tattling, complaining of not feeling well, and hitting some other child. Each time the situation she created was one in which she became the loser.
- Carolyn seemed fearful of trying herself out in the various activities. She instead often made remarks about other children's achievements, either derisively or enviously.

Positive Items
- Carolyn approached people through physical contact, and gradually came to ask directly for favors and attention without being negative and without converting the physical touch into a pulling.
- On several occasions toward the end of camp, Carolyn was able to admit a mistake (such as appropriating another child's craft project) and to entertain ideas of how she could work her way out of such a situation. She seemed unused to being presented with constructive face-saving alternatives but she was tentatively eager to try them out.

At camp Carolyn seems to require the sort of individual attention that provides continual recognition, physical affection, and gentle redirection.

Mary Harrison
Counselors' Consultant

Constance T. Fischer, Ph.D.
Psychologist

Comments

These two selections are reminders of three points: First, assessments do not necessarily require the use of tests. Careful observation across varying situations can provide equally useful data. Second, it is not necessary for assessors to individualize every assessment by collaborating with the subject, outlining an overall portrait, detailing the unfolding of process, or itemizing suggestions. Third, even within brief "feedback" reports, an individualized framework can guide the construction of remarks so that they evoke a sense of the particular person.

The CMH & MR staff was pleased with these feedback reports. The reports were brief enough to be read and utilized quickly. The concrete details lent themselves to comparison of comportment at home and at school. The camp's emphasis on possibilities for growth rather than on diagnosis and limitation encouraged a similar emphasis at home and at school. Moreover, the specification of positive events within their contexts encourage therapeutic staff and parents to recreate these positive options for the youngsters. The CMH & MR staff told us that they were amazed that such brief reports did not condense observations into judgmental or diagnostic terms. They were even more impressed by the hints for constructive intervention that were inherent in the contexts accompanying described comportment.

Special Education Referral (IEP):
Megan Ryan (9 Years)

Public Law 94-142, the federal legislation assuring handicapped children of quality education in a least restrictive setting, mandates that an Individualized Education Plan (IEP) be drawn up for the handicapped child. The year-long goals and shorter term objectives are to be specified, along with means and criteria for measuring arrival at the goals. In general these plans have been a boon to the involved youngsters. Their educational strengths and weaknesses are assessed, and the former are systematically called into play to assist in developing the weaker areas. Teachers are accountable for reaching goals. The individualizing traditionally is in terms of standard educational tools, however, rather than in terms of who the child is as an individual. For example, an objective might be stated as, "Reach average fourth grade vocabulary by the end of the year, as measured by the Metropolitan Achievement Test. Means: Dolch cards, New Word Club, and third grade Bobbs-Merrill reader for successful experiences while reading at home with parents."

As in the above examples, despite the word *Individualized* in the term "Individualized Education Plan," the IEP rarely addresses the child as a particular person. Nor does it address that child's specific situations at school and at home. Contributing to this problem is the underuse of the detailed medical, family history, educational testing, and psychological testing data that all too typically remain undisturbed in the respective specialists' files.

A school psychologist, Lois M. Love, and I had often commented both on the nonindividualized aspect of IEPs and on the other utilization of filed data. Eventually we devised a Child Study Form. The form brings together relevant background information, which school specialists summarize in everyday language, focusing on whatever is directly pertinent to developing the IEP. As needed, a child's team members sometimes summarized another specialist's report, to avoid bureaucratic inefficiencies.

The child's IEP team (for example, regular teacher, resource teacher, school psychologist, parents) work from the Child Study Form's summaries to document legal criteria for 94–142 assistance, as well as to develop educational goals and statements about how this particular child may be understood and addressed. Under "Team Meeting Summary," we expanded the IEP into two segments, the Remedial Education Plan (the traditional IEP) and the Individualized Intervention Plan. The latter alerts teachers and parents to what it might be like to be in the child's situation, and shows how educational principles could apply to this particular child. The headings of the Child Study Form are presented below.

Identifying Information
Reason for Referral
Past Interventional Efforts
Background Information
    Physical Appearance
    Health
    Motor and Athletic Development
    Social Relationships/Emotional Development
    Educational Development
        Achievement tests
        Classroom performance
Family Situation
    Family members
    Preferred person to contact regarding this child
    Developmental history
    Paternal family
    Maternal family
    Siblings
    Family supportive factors
    Family complications

Summary of Psychological Assessment
Team Meeting Summary
    Introduction
    Diagnosis
    Recommendations
    Remedial Education Plan (goals and objectives by subject areas)
    Individualized Intervention Plan (critical incidents and interventions)

The Individualized Intervention Plan arose out of Mrs. Love's observations of Megan Ryan in several settings at school, and through discussion with the parents and with other team members. Together, they agreed about critical times when one could tell that Megan was in trouble, what they thought was going on for her at those times, and what one could do to bypass or restructure those moments. Mrs. Love and I summarized the results as a series of Critical Incidents with accompanying Interventions.

The excerpts from the Child Study Form, which precede the Individualized Plan, provide some background on Megan and demonstrate that IEP documents do not have to be filled with educational and psychological jargon. Classroom and resource teachers later expanded the educational plan to include their respective teaching methods and criteria for success.

. . . .

TEAM MEETING SUMMARY
Summarized by: L.M. Love, MS Ed., School Psychologist

Nine-year-old Megan has been making minimal progress in the fourth grade. Her parents and teacher requested an evaluation. The parents are positive toward the assessment and are eager to help in any way.

Megan's level of overall intellectual development is in the average range, but her general educational achievement is 1½-2 years below age/grade level.

Megan's language skills are adequate, but her visual and auditory functioning are deficient. This circumstance now is adversely affecting further development of reading, writing, and spelling skills. The deficient reading limits other areas of learning, including social studies and science. Arithmetic is affected in the area of word problems.

Encumbered by the above difficulties, Megan has developed faulty reading habits and inconsistent word attack skills. The result is that much of her effort is directed to sounding out words in a slow, laborious manner that precludes understanding the meaning of what she is reading. When a passage is read to Megan, she comprehends at grade level.

During the present year, Megan has begun to engage in more behaviors that are self-defeating. She does not maintain attention to assignments, disturbs other students by entering alternative activities, and becomes distraught when she fails at play or at competitive class assignments.

Until now Megan's learning difficulties were undetected. Instruction therefore was not differentiated from that for typical learners, and it eventuated in a learning lag. In the face of this lag, Megan is experiencing failure and is developing an antipathy for learning. She has experienced little satisfaction related to school, and hence has not been developing positive learning attitudes.

Megan requires a highly individualized program to ensure successful learning. Work will have to be given at an easier level than her customary assignments. Reading should be required in small units and for short drill periods. Activities should be designed so that reading becomes personally meaningful and purposeful.

Megan should be placed in a smaller group, where her attention can be gradually lengthened as she develops satisfactory reading habits. She requires individual reading and writing instruction and practice. Adjustments will have to be made in independent arithmetic work when story problems are assigned.

Megan apparently has come to feel inadequate in many situations. She has made comments comparing herself unfavorably with her older brother. She has learned to avoid situations that seem too difficult, and hence has not had opportunities to correct her feeling that she is unable to handle difficult circumstances. She has preferred to remain dependent and be rescued by an adult.

Megan requires opportunities for satisfying social experiences. When possible, she should work in small cooperative groups in the regular classroom, so that she can respond personally to other children, rather than on a competitive basis via independent assignments. She needs a secure group where she is not embarrassed to try, and where the teacher demonstrates confidence in Megan's competence. Games and play should be utilized to facilitate learning in a variety of ways and to relieve tension around school work. These efforts will create a happier school experience for Megan.

Diagnosis [Provide legal criteria if appropriate.]

Megan's difficulties qualify as a learning disability. An educational lag has been identified as significant in relation to her age, grade level, and overall intellectual level. Visual and auditory deficiencies in processing information have been documented. Secondary to the learning disability, Megan now engages in disruptive classroom behaviors, but more often withdraws. She expresses feelings of failure and inadequacy.

Recommendations

Megan requires an individualized reading and educational program that can best be implemented and monitored in a Resource Room Setting. The Resource Room teacher will work closely with Megan's regular teachers, assisting them with the attached educational plans.

REMEDIAL EDUCATION PLAN
Recorded by: L.M.L.

Subject Area: Reading

Year's-end goal: Megan will read with smoothness and accuracy. She will comprehend material written at the third grade level and will apply these skills in all subject areas.

Short-term objectives:

• Megan will acquire and use word recognition and structural analysis skills.
• Megan will identify details in stories, select main ideas, sequence events, draw cause-and-effect relationships.

. . . .

Subject Area: Organizational Skills and Self-Direction

Year's-end goal: Megan will identify for herself when she has lost the concept being taught and will choose tactics to redirect herself to her work.

Short-term objectives:
- Megan will ask directly for assistance from appropriate persons rather than waiting for help or engaging in other behaviors to avoid school tasks.
- Megan will redirect her attention to school tasks with no more than two interventions from the teacher.

. . . .

INDIVIDUALIZED INTERVENTION PLAN
Recorded by: L.M.L.

Critical Incident—Independent Work
   During independent work time, Megan begins working along with the other students. However, in this instance, she does not understand the written directions. She moves about in her seat, half-heartedly raising her hand, then sits waiting for assistance. If the wait is more than a few minutes, she becomes distracted from the work. She tries to enlist the attention of nearby students by showing them a toy or an article from her desk. In the absence of redirection from the teacher, Megan continues to play with objects, annoying other students until an outburst occurs.

Interventions
   1. After students have read the instructions, ask one to explain the directions to the entire group. This will probably help other students in addition to Megan as they process the instructions through a different modality and in student terms. When Megan seems to have understood on her own, she could be asked to provide this group instruction, thereby adding prestige to her class involvement.
   2. A "rescue team" of two or three students can be designated to whom Megan (and others) can go when stuck on an assignment. The teams can be established in accordance with individual strengths.
   3. Design Megan's assignments so that small units are presented one at a time. Tasks will be more easily achieved when the amount of work is not overwhelming. Worksheets can be folded in half so that only one part of an assignment is visible.
   4. If the above measures still leave Megan not understanding a concept, provide alternative tasks that she has previously mastered. Then re-teach the unlearned concept. Megan wants to learn but feels threatened and confused by possible failure. She must begin where she succeeds. If provided with a task at mastery level, she can learn to follow through to the next step. Through this process she can assume increasing responsibility for her school work. She will learn that she does not have to avoid difficult work by withdrawing.

Critical Incident—Reading
   Megan tries to avoid oral reading, finding it embarrassing to read aloud. When she must read aloud, she reads in a slow, plodding manner, laboring over most words. She glances to the teacher, as if silently seeking her assistance. The longer she is asked to read, the more distressed she becomes. Comprehension has become secondary to getting through the words.

Interventions
   1. Limit oral reading initially to individual instruction times, to eliminate embarrassment in front of other students. Establish with Megan the purpose of the reading instruction period. If the goal is comprehension, select a short

paragraph at her independent reading level. Allow her to read alone to the teacher, or into a tape recorder, to establish an effective reading rate against which she can compare progress.

2. When instruction is in the basic skills of word recognition and structural analysis, establish with Megan that the purpose is to learn to decode words. Help her to keep charts of her progress.

3. Spend part of each instructional time in interpersonal conversation. Relate recent happenings in class or at home to the reading material or to Megan's general growth.

4. When Megan does read before a group, assign her mastery level material so that she can read with confidence before her peers.

Critical Incident—Playground

Megan joins in free play on the playground when invited, but seldom participates in structured games. If chosen for a team, she begins to play, but when accused by teammates of incompetent playing, she ends up crying and leaving the game.

Interventions

1. Youngsters who are less comfortable in group structured play could be given 5 or 10 minutes of formal instruction and practice in rules of the game and skills prior to team selections.

2. If Megan does leave a game in tears, allow her to go to a place that is comfortable for her. Give her time to regain composure and then assist her in sorting out her options.

. . . .

Comments

The above excerpts illustrate that not only psychological assessments, but also educational records and plans can be individualized. Legal requirements and concerns for a child's growth can be addressed simultaneously when specific events are addressed. The Child Study faced facts (for example, 1½–2 years learning lag) without positing undemonstrable neurological factors. By using descriptive words, such as "deficient" and "difficulty," rather than hypothetical, technological terms such as *deficit* or *disability* (except to meet 94–142 legal criteria), and descriptive terms such as "overall intellectual achievement" instead of *native ability* or *intelligence,* the assessors enhanced the possibilities of constructive intervention and growth.

The Critical Incidents served several functions. They render the child's world visible; they disrupt adults' slippage into perceptions of the child as "bad," "dumb," or "trouble-making." The next time we witness the critical event, we see the trouble in the process of unfolding, and we are reminded of the IEP—its purpose and its suggestions for intervention.

These excerpts reflected collaboration among the child's adults to gather information, to understand the child, and to devise a responsible, individualized education plan. What was not evident in the excerpts was Megan's participation. In fact, Mrs. Love typically includes not only the parents but also the child in the IEP meetings. The child's presence and involvement makes several contributions. All parties, most of all the youngster, perceive that youngster as presently handicapped but as capable of helping him- or herself to grow. Understanding what his or her adults are up to enables the child to cooperate more fully, and to question and offer suggestions, not just during the team meeting but in class and at home. Often the child corrects adult misperception, for example, "Well I don't care if Mrs. Hauser likes me; I don't like her—she calls me 'honey' and says I'm 'sweet.' Couldn't a different aide work with me?" Finally, when the youngster is present, all parties are more likely to remain mindful of the child's life rather than stepping into bureaucratic processing of the numerous mandated forms.

Residential Treatment Facility Referral: David Massey (13 Years)

From time to time I hear from professionals who have encountered one of my articles on individualized assessment. Benjamin G. Lewis, Ph.D., is a clinical and child psychologist in independent practice in Ukiah, California.

In his work as a consultant with a residential treatment program, Dr. Lewis was asked to assess 13-year-old David Massey, who had recently been transferred from on-campus residential treatment to an off-campus group home. The referral asked how David was doing and how the staff could understand and work with him. Dr. Lewis preferred to meet with David and write his report before reading David's records so that he could bring a fresh view to the staff conference. If it turned out that by not looking into the records first he had neglected to explore some area, he could meet with David again. At a staff conference, the experiences of David's teachers, house managers, consulting psychiatrist, therapist, and other workers would be woven together with Dr. Lewis's report into a coherent understanding of David. Then, with David present, a detailed treatment program would be written out. In the report *DOB* is the standard abbreviation for date of birth and *DOA*, for date of admission. The report appears in its original, unedited form, except for changes in identifying information to protect privacy.

June 15, 19 ____

PSYCHOLOGICAL EVALUATION

Re: David Massey
DOB: 2-12- ____
DOA: 6-18- ____

Fascinating is the word I think of for David in the way that I am drawn into his world. He allows me to do this but is clear that it will be on his terms. This he expresses not in any assertive manner but more in the aloof position he takes. In fact, David appears mild mannered, even submissive, yet in his quiet way he is assertive; that is, expects to get his way. Of course he expects to control this situation with me as well and is reluctant to give up his position when the dictates of the situation (and me) so indicate. He responds best to my interest in him but with a friendly, firm control. I have the feeling that if I treat him right, he will deign to share his time and thoughts with me.

Contributing to the above impression is David's appearance—an olive skinned young man with dark brown hair, and eyes and manner that are both serious and matter-of-fact. His voice likewise—deep in tone with not too much fluctuation, has a matter-of-fact, monotonous quality. It is an indication of his degree of involvement in his activities as will be pointed out later.

David let me know from the opening activity of drawing that he was an unusual child. Even the way he held his pencil was different. He would rotate his drawing in his mind, making a mirror reversal of the design I would present him—very unusual. He didn't seem to think so but was surprised to find that I did. Through his drawings he tells me other things about himself: that although he may feel inadequate he can be quite expansive. Yet another contradictory polarity exists between control over his actions and his impulsivity. He lets me know more fully about some of these qualities when he enters into the play situation. Even before he had the play material set up, David had in mind what the plot was going to be: "The devil's gonna try to get the animals." We seem to have something in common since we saw each other at the movie "The Black Stallion" the day before. For a moment it looked as though he would follow up the theme of the play since he was fascinated with the horses. This was not the case, however, because David has a mind of his own and certainly imagination of his own. He soon took over the play not just as director but as leader of the characters in the play, doing so with decisiveness. He becomes more animated as he speaks through the animals' actions and as the scene becomes more assertive as they try to capture the devil. He shows his identification with the devil in the way of being sneaky and clever in tricking others. "He's like a ghost" he repeated a couple of times. And now his voice became more animated as he laughed and talked as the devil. The monotone was gone and the intensity of his actions came through. It was as though he was saying with conviction, "You (adults) can't trick me. I'm stronger."

The following day David continued on this theme but this time through the picture stories and with the powers of a witch instead of a devil. He gives us some understanding of the genesis of such a fantasy system when he begins his first story with "that food's no good—won't make us grow. Let's go. Mother won't tell us what to do 'cause she mostly don't tell us what to do." His lack of trust in adults taking care of him leads him to find ways to care for himself.

When he encounters a frightening world, he must invent further powers. This he does in an unusual approach to the pictures when he weaves a story in sequence from one card to the next. At times it was obvious this was difficult for him to do, but regardless of the discrepancies that he would see in the pictures, he would pursue his theme: how to remove the power from the non-caring, frightening parent and give it to the child. This must have some deeply cathected meaning to him since he arbitrarily forces this theme on all of the pictures regardless of my encouragement not to and of my questioning him. For example, when the distortions became increasingly obvious and he was trying to carry through the mistreated chickens from the first card to the last saying "the chickens are trying to get the witch's power." At this point I asked "what are those?" and he answered "apes." My intrusion bothered him very little: "I could say bears. They're bears. They're helping the chickens get the witch's power cause they don't like the witch at all." This was the first indication to me that now he could not even keep the cast of characters straight since the bears were initially on the witch's side. This matters not at all to David. By this time he no longer needs the picture. He has taken off on his own story and he makes no effort to comply with the reality of his surroundings— he doesn't even go through the motions as he did previously. However, it is obvious that he is aware that I did not go along with him and now the mumble comes back to his voice as if he had been hiding this fantasy in his own private world, and by divulging it there is a threat of loss of his own power, which makes him aware of his helplessness. As he said in one point in his story: "the genie tries to attack the bear 'cause a lot of people try to get his powers. It got him furious so he gets ate." For those of you wondering how the story turned out, the witch never finds her power and those who are on her side turn against her. It is implied that since the children do not lose their power, it remains with them after they had taken it from the witch.

If you recall I mentioned David's dividedness in the dimension of control and impulsivity: in the devil and the good horses, and of course, in the baby chicks and the witch. Now we see this same theme continuing even into the Rorschach where on two occasions a discrepancy in a minor detail of the blot allows him to see the symmetry as different. For example: "a seal and a man" and later "a bear and an anteater." This kind of reasoning from detail and imposing arbitrarily his own unique configuration is typical of David, suggesting that he is inclined to arbitrarily make judgments based on a minor fact that he may see as significant and then rigidly hold to his view. That there is a rigidity about this is reflected in the certainty with which he views his percepts, indicating a lack of distance from the cards. To him they are not ink blots, they are what he describes them to be. David seems to be pretty much at ease with his idiosyncratic way. At least, the ease with which he describes shading in the blots is an indication of this, or that his anxiety is well bound in a fixed defensive pattern.

My impression has been that David has gone through an autistic phase in his development in which many of the matters he now speaks about in symbolic form were held more quietly within him and they are, at this stage of his development, more blatant and have a fixity about them that promises a continued similar defense pattern. My suggestions for working with David are based on this impression.

The danger in working with David would be in getting caught in his world and not holding sufficently to one's own. He already knows his "powers." Remember that they exist to protect him from the fear of no adult care. He needs to know that adults' "power" in the sense of their responsibility, caring, and greater knowledge is something he can depend on. Without this he must continue to build his own world and power.

The fact that David is willing to share his inner world is a positive indication of moving toward an outer world. To over-praise him for this move could lead him to further cathect this stage and contribute to his aloofness, rather than allowing him the next step of sharing others' worlds. He could be a very unique individual—alone with his uniqueness.

As the above implies there is a danger for this child in being a "good training case." To bring out those factors that would make for good training could be detrimental to David.

We saw the leadership qualities in David, at least in his fantasy world. Can these be used in the living situation with his peers?

The dramatic ability shown by David could be used as a therapeutic asset in helping him to role-play and thus learn certain social actions.

David is bright and verbal so that talking therapy may appear indicated. However, the material he has to work through is of such a primitive nature that likely play therapy would be required.

Should things get rough for David in the confrontation that he is needing to face, we have some indication of compulsive defenses that could be called into play and strengthened.

Benjamin G. Lewis, Ph.D.

Comments

Despite the absense of headings and the unrevised work-a-day dictation, the story of Dr. Lewis's encounter with David unfolds clearly. One source of that clarity is the report's disciplined selection of specific events, which are presented in implicit dialogue with diagnostic and treatment issues. Another major positive feature is that through this report we became acquainted with an understandable youngster. We have a strong sense of who David is—of where he is coming from and of his current concerns. We see the serious limitations of his present options, but we also see that there are ways to meet and engage him.

David's records attest to the helpfulness of this individualized assessment. The background documents furnished by David's residential facility indicate that his established DSM II diagnosis was latent schizophrenia with organic brain syndrome (documented by an EEG consistent with susceptibility to seizures). David had spent most of his life in a series of foster homes. After two years he had formed no strong relations with peers or adults in the program, actively irritated other youngsters, at other times shut out both peers and adults, and often exhibited inappropriate affect and thought disorganization. He was enuretic when not medicated. The house manager's report mentions David's "problems with basic techniques relating to cooking, chores, and personal hygiene, requiring constant repetition of demands and explanation." This report goes on to say:

> His interactions with his peers in the house are negative, argumentative and unyielding. He spends time in covert activities, which arouses the tension and frustration level of the house. He compounds his problems by attempting to place the responsibility of his negative behavior elsewhere.

From Dr. Lewis's report we can imagine how all these problems could be true of David. But we also see an understandable youngster. We see something of what his struggles are about, how adults are likely to perpetuate David's power plays, and that adults can bypass that perpetuation. At the staff conference, others presented the "when-nots" of David's problematic comportment. The ensuing treatment plan included provision of some backyard space in which David was to be trusted to work by himself, opportunities for David to carry out responsibilities with adults observing but not hovering, and immediate, quiet but firm interventions to preclude development of squabbles and stand-offs. A treatment review two months later attested to dramatic changes. These, of course, were not due solely to the psychological evaluation, but it was an important aspect of the staff's finding access points to work positively with David. The concluding paragraph of the treatment review:

> Incredible progress has been made with David and by David in most of his documented problem areas. He is no longer a constant management problem for the child care worker staff. He is well on his way to attaining grade level in school. He does not use repulsive behavior to keep the world or adults at a distance. David has begun to accept himself and make the best of what he has. Peer interactions are more appropriate. At this point, Dave has laid to rest the following comment which echoed the staff consensus of him two years ago: "David continually challenges one's capacity of control."

Dr. Lewis refers to the style of individualized reports as "prose." As he became more certain of himself and more willing to share his ideas, he could then write in "prose" rather than in the specialized language of testing. Because the primary readers of David's report were professionals and paraprofessionals all working together, he incorporated some of their shared language, such as *cathect.* Even though the readers share a general theoretical orientation, however, David's comportment with Dr. Lewis remains the clear referent of all the report's conclusions. Dr. Lewis says, after writing hundreds, perhaps thousands, of reports,

> I don't recall receiving such positive response as I have since adopting this [prose] style. It's not that there is always agreement, but that the readers appreciate the style. They look forward to the next "short story." Enthusiasm about the report invites discussion regarding its content.

Juvenile Detention and Rehabilitation Center Referral: Colleen Olsen (14 Years)

The author of the following report, Amy Lamson, Ph.D., is also author of a book on the *Relationship between Diagnosis and Treatment* (1978). She values both individualized assessment and the mental health field's accumulated knowledge about patterns of psychopathology. That knowledge alerts us to compare the assessee with relevant patterns, thereby learning more about the person than if we relied only on our own data. Knowledge of patterns, both normal and clinical, alerts us to likely points of access for intervention and to difficulties we should take into account in assessment and in treatment planning. However, Dr. Lamson also believes that assessments should address a person in his or her particularity, that the ways in which that person both is *and is not* representative of a diagnostic category should be presented, and that if the assessment is to be maximally helpful in bringing about positive change, the person should be a collaborative participant—discussing data and implications directly.

Dr. Lamson is a clinical psychologist in a juvenile probation facility in California. The juvenile justice system required a diagnostic understanding of Colleen Olsen's behavior—was it related to brain damage, or to psychosis or to something else, or was it another aspect of her already identified delinquency? Dr. Lamson explores these issues systematically and forthrightly, and provides the required bases for her conclusions. She includes her encounters with Colleen outside of the formal assessment, treating them as of the same order as assessment events. The setting is a juvenile detention and rehabilitation center.

Psychological Evaluation

Name: Colleen J. Olsen
Birthdate: 2-4-____   Age: 14-2   Requested by: John Arrow
Date seen: 5-17-19____   Timothy Palmer
Place seen: Girls' Unit, Juvenile Detention and Rehabilitation Center

Reason for Referral
    This evaluation was requested to determine if there is a serious pathology underlying Colleen's behavior. She has an explosive temper, and a package of fecal matter was found in her room.

Behavioral Observations and Data from Interviews
    When Colleen first arrived in JDRC, she appeared so poised and composed, she looked much older than her 14 years and I wondered whether she was a new Volunteer in Probation. Although on occasions she has since exhibited gleeful spirits in the manner of a younger child, there is still something about Colleen that seems older than her years. Whether it is the fact that she has been on her own and self-supporting for a long time or that she presents a picture of herself as supremely self-satisfied, she does not exhibit the floundering, searching quality of most girls her age.
    Colleen has been consistently eager to talk with the psychologist (myself). However, she has not used the time to discuss any problems she may have. Rather, she has delightedly related her past experiences in an apparent effort to re-live the fun she had. When confronted with difficulties she is having on the unit, she has repeatedly passed them off as inconsequential. When it was pointed out that if she kept up the way she was going she would probably have extra time at JDRC, she laughed and stated she had already had two weeks added. On the other hand, when it was suggested that perhaps she likes it in JDRC and wants to stay a long time, she adamantly insisted that was not true. Recently she related several promises of rewards from her mother and her PO

if she does better in the program. When asked if she plans to try to do better, she answered, as if that were a ridiculous question, that she would be crazy not to, now that she had been promised those things.

When Colleen first heard that she had been referred for testing, she seemed opposed to the idea. However, the very next day she started asking when she would be tested. It appeared that she had decided that this would be another arena for her to get attention and that she would revel in it. On previous occasions she had stated that she is "weird . . . crazy . . . not like other people," and she warned that the tests would show how weird she is.

After the evaluation, Colleen was told that the tests did indeed show that her thinking is different from others, but the problem is not so much that she is disturbed, as that her values are different, and she does not want to go along with the rules of society. She heartily concurred. When possible reasons why she became this way were suggested to Colleen, she strongly indicated that it was not because she was not taught right from wrong. She believes it was because she did not get enough attention from her mother to make it worth her while to go along with her mother's teachings. She feels her mother always favored her younger sister but had little time for either of them because she was always involved in getting married or getting divorced. When it was pointed out that she would have to change her thinking, at least to some degree, or else she would be in serious trouble the rest of her life, Colleen said she knows that and she is determined not to be locked up again.

Colleen expressed a lot of warm feelings for several girls she has met in Juvenile Hall. When one of these girls was suicidal, Colleen offered to speak with her to cheer her up. During several meetings with this girl, Colleen made many appropriate gestures and remarks to reassure her that she is cared for and to point out how foolish it is for her to think of killing herself. However, it was obvious from Colleen's reactions on another day when she did not see the girl, that her interest in others is rather short-lived and that she is basically self-centered.

After the incident in which fecal matter was discovered in her room, Colleen stated that she could not wait the hour until the rooms would be opened and she could go to the bathroom. She felt it was better to go on the paper rather than press her "E" light and risk having a lowered grade. It was difficult for me to believe that her judgment was that poor and I suspected that her defecating on the paper reflected a deeper motivation. I pointed out to her that she would not have that dilemma again because she was now in a room with a toilet. During a discussion in her room, my suspicions about deeper motivation were confirmed when I noticed a smell in the room and saw some fecal matter in the toilet. She denied that it was hers and insisted that it had been in the toilet before she was placed in that room. When these incidents were discussed again after the testing and it was suggested to her that they symbolically represent her desire to "shit on society," she laughed in agreement. It is obvious, however, from other behavior and remarks that these incidents also reflect an anal preoccupation. She is so messy and dirty in her room and on her person that other girls refer to her as "scuzzy." In addition, one day at lunch while I was eating cheese, she commented that cheese causes constipation.

Tests Administered

WISC (partial), Bender-Gestalt, Rorschach, TAT, House-Tree-Person, Animal.

Test Findings

Colleen's prorated IQs based on six of the ten subtests were as follows: Average Verbal (106), Superior Performance (121), Bright Normal Full Scale

(114). Her high Performance IQ was due to a high score on Picture Completion, a test of visual alertness. Her other Performance subtests were all in an average range. Her Similarities and Vocabulary subtest scores were in an average range but her score on Comprehension, which tests practical judgment and understanding of rules and behavior, was significantly higher. Evidently, Colleen is skillful in scanning her environment for important clues and is shrewd in practical matters. Her responses on Comprehension also indicate that she knows the difference between right and wrong, though she does not necessarily do what is right. In response to the question about what you should do if you find a wallet in a store, she said: "Turn it in to Security or take it to Security. That's what you're supposed to do. (laugh) I'd keep it."

Colleen's Bender-Gestalt drawings were very neat and well organized. They gave no evidence of organicity or impulsive tendencies.

Colleen's projective test responses reflect deviant thinking, attitudes, and feelings. Instead of seeing the usual Rorschach percepts of animals, people, and objects, she saw all kinds of bugs (for example, squished bug . . . swarm of dragonflies") which frequently are associated with frustrated needs for nurturance, as well as with acting out and psychopathic tendencies. Her TAT stories are similarily filled with maladaptive themes. One boy is "mad at his violin . . . 'cause he couldn't play anything right." A girl "really hated school . . . and wants to stay home." After suffering some losses, another girl "decided there wasn't anything left to live for so she killed herself." One little girl "didn't like to do anything she didn't want to. She was a brat."

Violent tendencies were also evident in one of her Rorschach percepts and in two of her TAT stories. "He really wanted to kill this guy." "She was about to scream. He threw a sack over her head and started strangling her." Colleen's most striking TAT story, however, was one which vividly demonstrated the shallowness of her feelings. She described a couple whose newborn grandchild died. "The old lady started crying, the man hugged her and said it would be O.K. They went home to bed and in the morning they forgot about everything."

Colleen's rather grotesque human drawings appear to be intentional caricatures of people rather than serious drawings. They seem to reflect a sneering, rebellious attitude toward people. Her choice of the animal she would most like to be ("A tiger, 'cause tigers are big and real majestic and pretty much rule where they go") is a further demonstration that Colleen wants to be a law unto herself.

Although Colleen gives evidence of faulty reality testing in her decidedly deviant thinking, she does not appear to be psychotic. Her responses on the Rorschach during testing of the limits, and her house drawing, indicate that she is fully capable of perceiving and behaving in conventional ways. Furthermore, she gives absolutely no evidence in any of the tests of the marked confusion and disorganization evident in psychosis. In other words, it appears that Colleen's deviant behavior is fully under her control.

Summary and Conclusions

Colleen is a 14-year-old girl of Bright Normal intellectual potential who has exhibited markedly deviant behavior. Her remarks and her test responses indicate that her deviant behavior is due to her antisocial values, rather than to any significant emotional disturbance. There is evidence in her social history that she has been hurt in the past due to insufficient nurturance and that these unfulfilled dependency needs are at the root of her antisocial thinking. However, it is apparent that she has succeeded in pushing these feelings aside and that she is very well defended against feeling pain. As a result, Colleen is a poor candidate for traditional psychotherapy to change her behavior. Nevertheless, the situation is not entirely hopeless. Colleen is a clever girl who cannot help but see the wisdom of modifying her behavior, at least to some degree, in order to avoid punishment. In addition, when sufficient rewards are held out to her she can be motivated to behave better. She has recently begun to see her mother as a more giving figure. If her mother continues to show interest in Colleen and to offer rewards for Colleen's good behavior, it is very possible that Colleen will begin to behave in more socially acceptable ways. To this end it is recommended that Colleen and her mother participate in counseling aimed at improving their relationship.

                                        Amy Lamson, Ph.D.

Comments

This succinct, to the point, balanced report presents a nonjudgmental, vivid sense of Colleen. She makes sense to us. We see her positive potential, but we also see the seriousness of her sociopathy ("antisocial" orientation). The brevity, clarity, and vividness of the report are due in part to Dr. Lamson's presentation of test data as firsthand events, that is, as selected instances of Colleen's comportment. There is no test-by-test overkill, obfuscating jargon, or refuge in theoretical constructs. We know the everyday life events as well as the test findings that led to the conclusions.

Dr. Lamson was not afraid to integrate activities that are too often maintained as separate roles for different professions: history-taker, assessor, therapist, family consultant. Nor was she afraid to move beyond her office to be with Colleen in her room or to eat lunch with the Center residents. In all these settings, Dr. Lamson inquires directly about Colleen's understandings, and integrates these into the assessment report. She knows that to help Colleen to help herself, her understandings must be directly addressed and taken seriously. But in this process Dr. Lamson remains clear about her own, broader comprehensions, through which she challenges Colleen.

A follow-up letter from Dr. Lamson reports, "Through counseling with her mother, Colleen made some dramatic changes in her outlook on life. These were reflected in a subsequent testing where she gave many high-level Rorschach percepts. She was placed in the Center one more time after her return home, but has been staying out of trouble for several months since then."

Probation Referral: Douglas Whitman (16 Years)

The concluding report in this chapter illustrates a different format: occasionally the report is written in the form of numbered suggestions with accompanying rationales. The graduate student who assessed Douglas Whitman had discovered by the end of the assessment sessions that his test data added little to what Doug's helpers already understood. Rather than go through the motions of making independent discoveries via testing, the assessor chose to cite test comportment only when it filled out the rationale for or extended current staff efforts to be of help to Doug. This format would be helpful to the judge, who would have to think in terms of options. In this instance, inclusion of more test findings would have added little, except the risk of obfuscating the conclusions.

_____

Dates of assessment: December 9, 12, 13, 19_____
Date of report: December 17, 19_____

Psychological Assessment of Douglas Whitman

Referral
    Doug is currently on probation for having broken into a Fullertown drugstore with several friends. As part of the conditions of his probation, Doug has been forbidden by the court to be in the company of his co-defendants and must be off the streets after 9:30 P.M. Recently Doug was found in the company of his co-defendants after his curfew (at 10:30 P.M.). He was referred to the Fullertown Mental Health and Retardation Clinic for assessment, with judgment by the court on his probation violation to take place in January.
    Mrs. Borckovitch, Staff Coordinator at the MH/RC, has asked me to work on an assessment with Doug in the hope of finding ways of breaking through the pattern of recidivism which seems to be emerging.

Assessment Opportunities
    Wechsler Intelligence Scale for Children (WISC-R), Bender-Gestalt, Thematic Apperception Test (partial), mutual discussion of my impressions.

My Impressions of Doug
    In spite of his size (5'10"), age (16 later this month), and considerable composure and poise in the face of the uncertainty and stigma for him of a psychological assessment, my overriding impression of Doug after our first session was one of a likeable little boy. This impression materialized for me most vividly while Doug and I worked on various parts of the WISC-R. In particular, I noted his willingness to guess at answers, his obvious smiles and pleasure at getting answers right, and his vocal displeasure with himself when he couldn't answer a question, or when he knew his answer was wrong. Doug was immediately willing to attempt tasks with which he had difficulty, at the same time enlisting my aid in a childlike, unembarrassed way. On the Arithmetic section, which involved reading problems aloud, Doug looked up to me for help on words he didn't know. This unusual childlike enthusiasm, friendliness, affability, and ease has been noticed by several other people who have worked with Doug. His probation officer, professionals at the MH/RC, and his Volunteer in Probation all seem to agree that Doug can be a likeable and enjoyable person.
    However, when we spoke of the "trouble" Doug was in and when I asked more personal questions about his family, I had the impression that Doug had formed a wall of pat answers between us. Much of the enthusiasm, ease, and open expression was flattened out. Although Doug initially painted a picture in short repeated sentences of a loving and comfortable home life, in another session he came close to tears in relating his perception that his family, particularly his mother, wanted to get rid of him, and wanted him to be

sentenced to a term in jail. Despite his pat answers about his crimes and sophisticated sociological rationales for his not being sentenced, Doug admitted being terrified of the prospect of a jail term.

Through the three sessions that we spent together I developed a perception of Doug as being at odds with his world much of the time. His lying (which I have described as pat answers) is a form of self-protection, which occurs when he feels that something about his conduct, if revealed, will lead to punishment or reprisal by an angry adult. Pat remarks are his way of attempting to get people to like or accept him in spite of his behavior. Although Doug and I did not talk directly about this aspect of his pat answers, I believe that they arise in part out of alienation: a sense of being unknown and unlike other people. The only adult Doug expressed some feelings of similarity to was his Volunteer in Probation, Mr. Sallis. I had the impression that pat answers also may function for Doug as a way of claiming the concern and affection he misses. For example, he blithely told me about unnamed friends who help him to stay out of trouble and who visit him at his house, only to leave at the time of his curfew. I wonder if Doug's friends do show the concern and affection for him implied in this account. Surely, Doug must wish someone would. I think he believed that if he told me that he had such friends my opinion of him would be improved.

Suggestions and Their Rationales

Suggestion 1. Doug should continue to see his Volunteer in Probation, Mr. Sallis, as often as possible. The topics of their meetings should be at least partially set in advance and the time formalized in terms of a definite hour and day of the week. Taking into account the limitations of Mr. Sallis' time and the importance of Doug spending time with sympathetic adults who can help him understand what is happening in his life and ways of planning for the future, I would suggest that an additional Volunteer in Probation, preferably a man, spend time with Doug every week.

Rationale: Doug never knows when he will see Mr. Sallis. For Doug this seems to mean that he has nothing certain and enjoyable in his life to which he can look forward. In order to increase the consistency and possibility of satisfying experiences in his life, I believe that it would help if Doug and Mr. Sallis attempted to set a schedule for their times together.

Doug and I talked about his need and desire to "stay out of trouble." But, as with other goals in his life, Doug has no clear sense of the procedures leading to its accomplishment. For example, Doug would like to find work as a bricklayer, or some other skill offering union wages, but has no sense of the difficulty or of what's involved in union work. Mr. Sallis could point such things out to Doug and help him move through the step-by-step processes involved.

Spending time with Mr. Sallis, whom he likes and admires, would also present Doug with an alternative style of life to his own. Perhaps Mr. Sallis could help point out to Doug the real consequences of his actions and increase Doug's sense of being in control of his own life instead of having things just happen to him. (Doug anticipates that he will get a prison sentence not for what he has done, but because he got caught and the judge, he believes, doesn't like him. He tends to blame his present situation on other people and circumstances.)

Doug tends to give up when he encounters some obstacle to achievement. On the intelligence test this often occurred when his method of breaking down problems into units small enough for him to deal with was thwarted. At these times, though, with any encouragement and pointing out of his steps and missteps, Doug was often able to proceed. I believe that he responds to complicated, confusing situations outside of our assessment in the same way.

Suggestion 2. It would help Doug if he could have a job (or jobs) which he could do every day after school and on weekends when he is not in the detention center. We spoke both of volunteer work and of jobs for which he would be paid a salary. Good work experience might increase his confidence and self-worth. Volunteer work in which he is helping other people would be particularly helpful. Since Doug perceives the detention center as a place from which he emerges frustrated and angry, I would suggest that work might be offered as a form of "alternative service" with an explicit understanding that unexcused absences from work would have to be made up for by time in the detention center. At first, Doug might test this out by missing work, but if the consequences were immediate and clear I believe he would come to develop the sufficient, immediate personal reason he needs for doing something well. With time on the job the benefits for Doug of this kind of work might emerge.

However, if a full-time job or apprenticeship in which Doug could learn a skill can be found, I believe that he should take it. In the meantime, since Doug will be sixteen this month, perhaps Mr. Sallis or someone at the clinic could guide him toward obtaining a social security card.

Rationale: Doug's interest in working conscientiously and successfully at a job seems to be associated for him with the meaningfulness of the task in terms of personal gain. For example, we spoke of his drawing geometrical designs (Bender-Gestalt) as meaningless to him, resulting in his not copying the designs with precision. Similarly, Doug spoke of not caring about how carefully he cleaned up around the house unless someone was coming over. The ideal work situation would be one in which Doug worked around other people, and where he could see that his contribution made a difference. His boyish enthusiasm, likeability, and willingness to ask questions would get him off to a good start. But his supervisor, Mr. Sallis, and perhaps others would have to help him keep sight of where his work was getting him.

Doug's score in the low Average range on the intelligence test was much higher than it had been on previous administrations. This may reflect Doug's increased comfort and sense of belonging at the school he is now attending, Wrights High School. The vice-principal there, Mr. Donatelli, reported that Doug has not presented any serious problems this year. He genuinely seems to enjoy his classes at Wrights and referred laughingly to how his teachers in social studies and science would be upset with his not remembering the capital of Greece, or what a barometer was. In this circumstance, his grades well might improve from his record of Ds and Fs. Since only 50 percent of the persons with an IQ of 100 or lower graduate from academic high schools, however, C's in competitive standard courses would be superb for him. If Doug does remain in high school it is important for him to be in one of the vocation-oriented tracks. However, the abstract meaning of a high school diploma is too distant. The immediate monetary rewards of work might well give Doug the incentive he needs to perform up to his capabilities.

Doug brought up the possibility of jobs before I had a chance to suggest it. He explained the motivation for his robbery of the Fullertown drugstore to be getting money in the only way available to him. Doug also mentioned wanting to help out his mother at home.

I agree with Doug that having a job(s) would be important for him in many ways. I told him that having something to do was an important way of staying out of trouble. Throughout the time we spent together Doug often referred to the environment in which his crimes were planned as "just sitting around with some friends." Similarly, on the Vocabulary section of the WISC-R Doug defined join in terms of "having something to do." Doug's tendency to go with whatever else is happening can lead him into constructive or destructive behavior, according to what is going on around him. His difficulty making plans and his desire to be a part of something would seem to suggest his crimes were adventures for him in which he went along with the group. In a work situation Doug might become involved with a group with more constructive values.

At times, while working on a problem on the WISC-R, Doug would give up. With encouragement he would return to the task and finish it. This, plus his allusions to his family wanting him to be "sent away" suggested to me that Doug has very few experiences in which he can feel some sense of accomplishment, worth, and success.

Suggestion 3. and Rationale: Would a prison sentence have the desired effect? I doubt this since Doug blames his circumstances on bad luck. Whatever lessons he would learn probably would have more to do with becoming more devious or with the advisability of staying away from authorities. Confinement also might disrupt his relationship with Mr. Sallis—which seems to hold the greatest possibility of rehabilitation at the moment. Part of Doug's attachment to Mr. Sallis has to do with the latter's not challenging Doug's pat answers or likewise talking down to him. Doug responds negatively to punishment, but does gradually learn through encouragement and positive example.

Steven Hesky
Graduate Student in Psychology
Duquesne University

Comments

Several features of this report might be adapted by other assessors. The author distinguished explicitly his direct observations and his inferences and projections ("I developed a perception," "I had the impression," "might well give Doug"). He specified the issues that were and were not explicitly and collaboratively discussed with Doug ("when we spoke of the 'trouble' Doug was in," "although Doug and I did not talk directly about this aspect of his pat answers"). Finally, the author integrated data provided by Doug's other helpers (the vice principal's review of academic records and his impressions of Doug's behavior, the multiple affirmations of Doug's affability). This integration provided the MH/MRC staff and the judge with a cohesive picture that was preferable to separate, lengthy reports of the various professionals' records. Of course, to arrive at integrated suggestions, the assessor had to go beyond his tests to talk with those other professionals. The resulting report was one that Doug's helpers identified with, which in turn encouraged future cooperation in Doug's treatment.

This report's format foregoes the drama of test-based data unfolding toward conclusions and subsequent suggestions. What is gained is a sense of the obviousness of the suggestions. In many ways the suggestions are standard for cases like Doug's, but here the reader sees how they are relevant for Doug in particular. The suggestions would not be mistaken as soft-hearted appeals for liberality. Doug was not presented as a poor misguided child, nor as a sick child who should be excused. On the other hand, he was not presented as essentially evil or deviant. The reader sees that the affable boy, the kid with pat answers, the youngster who blames others for his own troubles, and the youngster who wants to belong and to achieve are all Doug. The Suggestion/Rationale format shows readers that there are ways of helping him to avoid a recidivist career. Current helpers are reminded of the particular ways in which they can best assist Doug.

Questions and Responses

Question: Do field assessments that involve children require that the graduate students be alerted to developmental norms—sequential stages and age expectations for specific tasks?

Response: Yes, for these assessments, as well as those dealing with radical psychopathology, graduate students require special guidance. The specific danger here is that assessors not trained in child psychology mistake age-appropriate behavior (like the two- to three-year-old's negative assertiveness) for maladjustment, or fail to notice the absence of stage-appropriate activities (like the chumhood of 10- and 11-year-olds).

Question: Is the student-instructor ratio very small in your assessment classes? Do the students receive one-to-one guidance?

Response: There are 20 graduate students per class. I teach two other courses every semester, and fulfill the usual responsibilities of directing dissertations, serving on departmental and university committees, advising students, and so on. Hence I provide only occasional face-to-face supervision of a specific assessment. However, a teaching assistant, usually a graduate of the previous year's M.A. class, spends 20 hours a week reading and writing comments directly on the assignments, observing and videotaping assessment sessions, and meeting with the students. I too read and write commentary on every written assignment. We write numerous remarks in margins and in the text, pointing out the positive impacts of organization and wording, and suggesting alternative formulations. Tables 5.3 and 5.4 were developed from this feedback process. In addition, half of the weekly three-hour class is spent in small-group discussions led alternately by the teaching assistant and myself. The discussions usually focus on specific issues that have arisen during assessments. The students also receive guidance from professionals in the field settings, although that instruction is not usually directed to drafting of the report.

I do review reports before they are returned to the field setting, and I do ask authors if they would like to do some editing prior to publication, and/or if they accept my minor editing. But the thrust of the reports and their development are strictly those of the authors. The creativity and effectiveness of our graduate students' reports lie in the students' freedom to make use of their personal presence to the client. Our students are expected to develop technical expertise in administration and scoring, but they work within a framework that encourages disciplined attention to personal presence, context, and process. One cannot function as an "objective" technician throughout the assessment and then expect to "interpret" scores and test productions in terms of a client's life. One cannot get to individual process from end products.

Question: Suppose the assessor simply doesn't have time to write a separate version of the report for the child. Moreover, if a youngster is mature enough to make use of a report, isn't he or she old enough to be shown or be told about the adult version?

Response: Frequently it is possible to talk through a report and its suggestions with a child as young as five years, ideally in a joint meeting with the parents. What is important is that all parties, including the youngster, have a shared understanding of the assessment findings and of the purposes of interventions, and that the youngster be engaged as an active participant in any efforts toward change. This purpose, of course, does not necessarily require a separate report for the child. Nevertheless, time is well invested for the long run when the assessor devotes extra effort to assuring that findings and suggestions have been communicated effectively to all parties, including the youngster. Seeing the report in a different form, the one presumably written for the youngster, also helps the adults to understand its themes more thoroughly. When separate suggestions are written to different parties, and all are read by all parties, readers see how they are all parts of a cooperative endeavor. We should remember that efficiency of effort is calculated not only in terms of immediate time expended but also in terms of long-range quality of outcome.

Question: Does the development of metaphors and fables require special literary skills?

Response: Many of the graduate students are more adept at such writing than I am. But when one is not constricted to a psychometric orientation or to a particular theory of behavior or psychodynamics, then unifying themes occur more readily. Likewise, when one is not thinking primarily in terms of established categories, imagination and prior personal experiences are more likely to come into play, helping one to see the client in richer, more flexible ways. However, it is rare that a referral issue and the client lend themselves to being addressed in terms of an overarching metaphor or single fable. The authors of the Iron Bunny and Jabby Jungle reports did not write their other reports in these formats. My own use of such imagery usually appears only here and there in any report, serving to unify just a few of the report's themes.

Question: Wouldn't it be best to conduct all assessments in the clients' own settings, for example the home and school?

Response: Yes, in most cases that would be ideal. Time constraints, however, usually preclude the travel involved. Nevertheless, the field-visit ideal guides my interviews and collection of information. My questions to parents, youngsters, teachers, or whomever, are guided by imagining what might appear if I were visiting. For example: "If you are watching *Sesame Street* in the living room, where is Mommy?" I have learned to telephone involved adults, such as a teacher or a father who could not make it to the clinic, to ask that person to extend my view—especially into contexts and when-nots. These procedures are usually sufficient.

A field visit is more economical than a series of office visits: (1) when the youngster's adults have not perceived contexts or variations in comportment, and hence cannot help the assessor, and (2) when assessment is for the purpose of developing interventions to be carried out in the field. Christopherson (1972, 1976) sends pediatric teams into the home to help parents establish their infant's habit of sleeping through the night, to help parents toilet-train their toddler, and to help a family develop good working relations with their problematic adolescent.

Question: In the Rick Ferris report there are no actual measures of fear and risk. Isn't this report subjective?

Response: Yes, the report is subjective, in that Rick is presented in large part through the assessors' experiences with him. This very feature is the report's special strength—through the assessors' experience readers have access to Rick's world. Rick's unfolding comportment becomes visible and his world becomes imaginable through the assessors' presence. Process was observable as variations and unfoldings of comportment in relation to interpersonal and physical contexts. An example is Rick's going through the second Bender differently under different circumstances. Note that the authors did not posit fear and risk as explanatory constructs; rather, they directed readers' gaze to phenomena that might be named variously by different witnesses. The mother might remark, "Yes, he is skitterish just that way when . . . " A child specialist might say, "You know, I wonder if we're seeing an autonomy-shame struggle."

Personal (subjective) presence is primary data, no less valid than test productions. The latter also require someone's presence and are subject to different descriptions and namings. The point is that Rick's report was not *merely* subjective. The *events* named as risky and fearful were presented. Prior and future observers can verify and modify this report's picture of Rick.

Question: In the camp reports, why did you use the title "Behavioral Excerpts" instead of something more usual, like "Behavioral Sample" or "Report of Behavior"?

Response: The title was intended to disrupt expectations of antiseptic, clinical observations (of children already identified as "disturbed"), and to direct attention to moments from the child's ongoing life.

Question: Don't the child's helpers object to time-consuming tasks like writing summaries for a team meeting and designing an individualized intervention plan?

Response: Helpers become more cooperative as they discover that their participation makes a significant difference. It is bureaucratic busywork that people resist. Moreover, because teachers' training has not included this kind of individualized intervention, this is precisely where we can make a unique and substantive contribution. Written notes and critical incidents and interventions can help teachers to review, modify, and expand their work with the youngster on their own. When teachers still have reason to consult with you, that consultation will not have to start "from scratch," but at a level where progress is already under way. You will not be consulted out of helplessness over a bad or incapable child, but out of a desire to continue interventions after growth or after the child's responses to the planned interventions have indicated that fuller understandings of the individual child are called for.

Question: Do you think that diagnoses such as "psychopathy" and "antisocial behavior" are political?

Response: Some people argue that such labels excuse us from examining the alienating factors of our society. The literal meanings of the labels (*psychopathy:* disease of the psyche; *antisocial:* opposed to society) do encourage us to think in terms of inherent defect on one hand and willful malevolence on the other. In either case we may fail to take preventative responsibility as a society, and we may fail to see the diagnosed person's possibilities of positive growth. However, the comportment patterns we have named *psychopathy* and *sociopathy* do exist and will continue to evoke naming. Creating less biased names will not change the fact of their existence nor dissuade us from pretending to explain by labeling—especially with so-called antisocial personalities, in that these people strike us as troublesome rather than troubled. From my perspective, our alternative is to develop a human-science approach to comportment, one that explicitly recognizes that all events are co-created by the person and circumstances. This approach holds individuals responsible for their participation while also looking for helpful points of intervention into that process.

Question: Is that why diagnoses are not made for many of the youngsters in these reports, even though most of them seem diagnosable?

Response: In some instances, the graduate student assessors wrote descriptive reports, leaving it to the clinic's professionals to determine whether and what nomenclature should be applied. However, diagnosing tends to undercut efforts to understand how the particular youngster exemplifies and lives the identified condition. The goal should be to understand the youngster and to find entry points, whether environmental, medical, or interpersonal, for encouraging growth. Diagnosis is supposed to serve that goal. If the goal is met without resort to formal diagnosis, then even if the youngster is eminently diagnosable, the label would serve no positive purpose. However, there definitely are times when ruling out certain diagnoses ("no evidence of psychosis") and affirming others ("does meet criteria for learning disability") are clearly helpful to all parties.

Question: Do you mean more by the term "process" than the phase during which an end product was being produced?

Response: The confusion probably has to do with our Western inclination to think in terms of mechanical production. I use the term *process* to point to human ways of going through situations, leaving a trail of achievements behind.

That human way inevitably involves purposiveness—always being up to something and on the way, that is, besides being propelled by, also perpetuating, and perhaps redirecting one's biography. Actually, the "something" one is up to is always many things, some focal, some habitual, some never recognized, all fluctuating and reforming with progress and circumstance. The human way of progressing involves immediate holistic experience of one's environment, rather than a series of responses to discrete, independent stimuli. Finally, the mutuality of experiencer and experienced participate in one another, rather than only interacting. Psychologists will do well to reflect on this mutuality and to develop language more appropriate to human comportment than are the static conceptions we borrowed from the physical sciences.

CHAPTER 8

Clinical and Diagnostics Reports of Adults

In its broad sense, *psychodiagnostic* has always meant clinical anaylsis of the dynamics and meanings found in a particular instance of psychopathology. *Diagnostics* is sometimes also understood more narrowly as a selection of the closest-fitting nosological label. The reports in this chapter are all of the first sort and sometimes of the second sort also. The writing of these reports required a knowledge of psychopathology and of diagnostic systems. Even if the reader has not yet received such training, however, it will be apparent that an individualized assessment framework is applicable in clinical as well as counseling assessments.

Clinical reports differ from counseling reports in that they are written primarily for other professionals. These professionals make decisions such as whether to prescribe major or minor tranquilizers, whether to deny child custody, whether to seek a reduced degree of murder charge, whether or how long to incarcerate a convicted rapist, whether to grant guardianship of a father to his daughter. The reports in this chapter are directed to these decisions, and hence are relatively less focused on the clients' co-creation of their situations or on possible intervention points within their styles.

Nevertheless, each report says more than the referral asked for. Reports should be written for future as well as immediate readers, because later readers often work directly with the client (in contrast to the persons who make a single decision about the client). To the extent that future direct work with the client was anticipated, the reports included more detail about style, intervention points, and suggestions already made to the client.

When clinical reports become lengthy in their descriptions of the life data to which test scores and diagnoses refer, conclusions should be written straight to the point so the busy reader will be assured that the report is directed to the referral. Readers unfamiliar with descriptive reports may confuse length with nonprecision. Hence, individualized reports require special discipline. The commentary on several of the reports in this chapter suggests how some of these lengthy reports might have been written more effectively. These cases encourage reflection on the range of formats and writing strategies possible in individualized reports.

However, not all clinical assessments need be highly individualized. To emphasize that point, two brief report letters are included in this chapter. They also illustrate the point that not all assessments require a battery of tests. One letter reports principally on a Rorschach, and the other on an interview.

The clients' written commentary is often included when the client is about to enter a treatment or therapy program. In most of the cases in this chapter, however, clients were not available for follow-up in time to read and comment on the report before it was due to be mailed out. Every client participated collaboratively during the assessment, however, and was told how the report would be written, which examples from the assessment session would be included, and what conclusions or recommendations would be made. Each of my clients was told about the notation that I stamp on every report: "Contents have been and may be shared with the client." It was understood that the client had the right of access to the report at any later time. Finally, I gave each client my business card with a number to call if questions or additional remarks occurred after the assessment session.

I wrote all but one of these reports in my private practice. Another of my clinical reports is available in Tallent (1976). It addresses a psychiatrist's inquiry as to whether a young man might be a suitable candidate for psychoanalysis. There is room for improvement in all these samples, which were written under the usual time pressures of clinical practice. Typing and spelling errors have been corrected, along with several awkward sentences. Otherwise, these reports are representative of applied human-science clinical psychology. All names of persons and places and other potentially identifying information have been changed for the protection of clients' privacy. My reports were typed on letterhead stationery, which included my name, degree, clinical specialty, address, and phone number.

Competency to Enter into Contracts: Harold Brooks

Reports should be written with the concerns of multiple readers in mind. The Harold Brooks report addresses the lawyer's and judge's concerns about whether Mr. Brooks was capable of negotiating his financial and legal affairs by himself. The report was organized in terms of Pennsylvania's criteria for contract competency: memory, comprehension, and judgment. The Conclusions section includes precisely the information that the judge was required to take into account. The rest of the report provided details the lawyer would need if the judge questioned the conclusions. It happened that the judge required "a doctor's" direct testimony, which was given from the witness stand in three yes-no responses to the judge's questions about who prepared the report.

Mr. Brooks's daughter, who was seeking to become his guardian, also received a copy of the report, which was written in a manner that would enable her to understand the actual behaviors to which the legal category referred. Finally, the cover letter suggested that if she later found it necessary to place her father in a nursing home, the report might be of help to that staff.

> CONTENTS HAVE BEEN AND MAY BE
> SHARED WITH THE CLIENT

Competency Assessment

HAROLD BROOKS

Birthdate (reported): October 3, 18____
Age: 80 years
Date of Report: September 15, 19____

Referral

Wisconsin officials recently contacted Mrs. Marjory Hapchack (352 Locust Drive; Pittsburgh 15235) to ask whether she would take her father (Mr. Brooks) from a nursing home there into her own home. Although she had not seen him since her parents' divorce when she was a small child, she agreed to give it a try. He has been with her for about 2½ months. She feels that Mr. Brooks has adjusted well and is happy in her home, but that he does require full-time supervision.

The present assessment was requested by Ms. Lorraine Spivic, Mrs. Hapchack's attorney, pursuant to the latter's inquiry as to whether she might obtain legal guardianship of her father. In particular, the referral question as I have construed it is whether Mr. Brooks can handle his affairs by himself— whether his comprehension, memory, and judgment are sufficient for him to make decisions in his own best interests.

CONCLUSIONS

From a psychologist's perspective, it is clear that Mr. Brooks is not competent to handle his financial or other contractual affairs. With supervision he gets along fairly well in his daily activities; but severe memory impairment precludes his understanding presentations that involve several steps. In a matter of minutes he often forgets both new information and the goal. On other occasions he may recall portions of such material, but not consistently enough to count on. Mr. Brooks is not as forgetful about habitual forms of conduct; his social comportment and self-care remain more consistent and more effective than his abstract comprehension and judgment.

This condition is not unusual for persons of Mr. Brooks's age. It is typically associated with arteriosclerotic advances. Some days are better than others, and what is forgotten one day may be recalled the next, but the overall condition is not reversible.

These conclusions were drawn from, and are consistently supported by, each of the assessment findings presented below.

Assessment Situation

On September 7, 19____, I spent two hours with Mr. Brooks in his daughter's home. We met in the living room, where I conducted a modified mental status interview and administered the Information, Comprehension, Digit Span, and Picture Arrangement subtests of the Wechsler Adult Intelligence Scale, the Level II Reading section of the Wide Range Achievement Test, and the Rorschach.

So as not to upset him, Mrs. Hapchack had not told her father that I was coming. As he came into the living room from the breakfast table to be introduced, he mentioned to his daughter that he didn't have his shoes on, but quickly accepted her reassurance that that was all right. He struck me as a slight, spritely fellow of about 5'4", who looked ten years younger than his reported age. He sat down comfortably in an overstuffed chair, appearing very much at home. He chatted affably, waiting for us to explain my visit. Although toward the end of our second hour he did ask if we would be done soon, he remained alert, responsive, and socially appropriate throughout our session. Mrs. Hapchack retired to the kitchen, where she watched but did not intrude. She noticed when Mr. Brooks required handkerchiefs and when he was looking for cigarettes, and helped him. She also helped him to explain that he suffers from emphysema (which was readily apparent), although he calls it by a spinoff name and believes it to be black lung disease. Mrs. Hapchack's manner was one of an attentive mother, respecting a youngster's efforts at independence.

Mr. Brooks readily admitted to memory difficulties, and explained to me that they were to be expected at his age. He gamely answered my questions, without embarrassment at the gaps in his current knowledge. He accepted my explanation of my presence (that his daughter wanted to know if he was in good enough shape to look after his own financial and legal affairs, or whether she should be appointed to do that for him, and that I was a psychologist who would write a letter to Mrs. Hapchack's lawyer about my own impressions). In fact, he elaborated upon why that was "fine" with him, indeed advisable. However, he also asked me three times later, "Now, what are you doing here?" (The question was followed by, "Oh yeah, that's right. Well, that's fine with me.")

Assessment Findings

Memory. Mr. Brooks encountered severe difficulties in remembering both recent and longer range events. Examples: He could not remember President Carter's name, and did not know what month it was although he had just read about both in the paper. After I provided this information, he later recalled the President's name but again could not recall the month. In his efforts to make sense of things despite memory gaps, he often made up reasonable information (technically, this is called "confabulation"). For example, he told me that his doctor from Wisconsin had examined him here in Pittsburgh last month. At times it was difficult to know when he was confabulating and when not. For instance, he spoke of having been mayor of a small town, but this appeared to be a reference to his nursing home.

At other times Mr. Brooks gamely tried to figure out things he had once known, but settled for inappropriate approximations that appeared to follow proper form. An example is that when asked how many weeks are in a year he responded, "265 days in a year except leap year." While reading WRAT words to me, he frequently introduced extra syllables. On the WAIS Arithmetic subtest, he recalled and followed the proper mathematical operations, but substituted new numbers for those in the original problem.

On the other hand, Mr. Brooks correctly recalled information such as the distance from Paris to New York, and the location of Brazil. He also repeated seven digits forward (which is about par for adults). On the WAIS subtests, he often earned full credit for more difficult items after missing easier ones. This kind of sporadic loss is typical of many neurological conditions.

Comprehension. Mr. Brooks appeared to understand brief explanations and instructions. He asked pertinent questions before responding to instructions for the various subtests, and usually started off correctly.

However, he frequently forgot what he was supposed to be doing, and either substituted something that made sense to him or reverted to very concrete, sometimes personal, responses. For example, he strayed from his answer to the question, "If you were lost in the forest in the daytime, how would you go about finding your way out?" to tell me about how he had to walk three miles to school as a youngster. On the Picture Arrangement subtest, while rearranging a series of scenes into chronological order, he stopped midway and simply described what appeared to be happening in each of the scenes I had laid out. On the WRAT he read discrete words at a sixth grade level, and scored in the Average range for persons 75 years old on the Verbal portion of the intelligence test. (There are no norms for persons 80 years old.) However, his score on the intelligence test would place him only at the 25th percentile of 16-year-olds. It is clear from his correct answers to some difficult items that at one time he functioned at a much higher level. Now he no longer remembers what he once knew, and he often does not sustain an initially correct comprehension.

Judgment. Difficulties in remembering and related difficulties in maintaining a goal-set (as reported above) do, of course, preclude complex decision making on Mr. Brooks's part.

He was, however, clear and consistent about his own immediate desires, such as food preferences and his preference of living with his daughter rather than in a nursing home. He often challenged his own answers (saying "No, that's not right, is it?") indicating that he does take critical stands, evaluating matters for himself. His social comportment, as noted earlier, was appropriate and pleasant. He cooperated throughout, foresaw some of my needs, for example, waiting for me to finish writing before continuing to speak; and he waited until the assessment was completed before he joked with me about whether I was available for marriage. He struck me as a trusting person, and as unusually patient with his mental difficulties (although understandably irritated about his emphysema).

In short, Mr. Brooks's judgment was poor when it involved retaining new information for several minutes while also trying to work with that information toward a goal. Habitual forms of "social judgment" were relatively unaffected. Mr. Brooks's impaired judgment, as I saw it, did not derive from emotional upset or from delusions or other nonorganic disorder.

(The Conclusions section appears on page one.)

Constance T. Fischer, Ph.D.
Clinical Psychologist

Comments

Note that the report's conclusions were specifically restricted to a "psychologist's perspective." Only the judge could make a judicial determination of competency. Acknowledgement of such distinctions is correct, courteous, and prudent.

Knowledge of patterns of brain-damaged test comportment was necessary for the assessor, but in the report, jargon and unexplained test signs were bypassed in favor of examples and everyday characterizations. Confabulation was mentioned—and explained—to indicate that the picture was a formally recognized one. Because it also served to characterize many of Mr. Brooks's coping efforts, the term confabulation would help lay readers to recognize this pattern in varying contexts. Any psychologists who might read the report in the future were given adequate test-referenced data for forming professional judgments.

No effort was made to convert "memory," "comprehension," and "judgment" into verbs, as is advocated elsewhere in this book, because these nouns are legal terms that had to be addressed directly. Readers who might take these abstractions as capacities, rather than as outcomes of admittedly impaired approaches, are presented with descriptions of what the nouns point to in terms of Mr. Brooks's comportment.

Emotional Stability (for Child Custody): Jane Anne Cronkite

The assessor should be forthright with the client about such personal matters as attempting suicide or being an inadequate mother. Neither of these issues was new or shocking to Jane Anne Cronkite. In fact, she was relieved to speak of them and to discover options.

Because no diagnostic category was requested, none was presented. Instead, the report tries to give the husband's and wife's respective lawyers a detailed sense of this woman's situation, her part in it, and the points at which they might constructively intervene. The report was written with future therapists also in mind.

This example includes more personal history than most of this chapter's reports. In private practice, where no one else (such as an intake worker) is responsible for obtaining a history, the assessor must be sure to look into relevant background. Often the combined social history and clinical interview is adequate for answering the psychologist's questions. Tests were utilized to help Mrs. Cronkite see concretely and from a new perspective just how she was contributing to her difficulties, and how she might try out alternatives. These concrete descriptions also helped to convey the same points to recipients of the report.

The report ends with a recommendation that information about the father should be obtained before custody decisions are made. We should be mindful that assessment of an individual provides only part of the picture.

November 17, 19____

Psychological Assessment

JANE ANNE CRONKITE

Referral
    In September of this year, Mrs. Cronkite's husband, Baxter James Cronkite,
left her, took their three children (8 months, 3 years, 5 years) away, and left
them with his mother and her second husband. Mr. Cronkite is now attempting to gain legal custody of the children because he feels that his wife, who has
in the past cut her wrists on three different occasions, is too emotionally
unstable to care for the children adequately. His attorney, in agreement with
Mrs. Cronkite's attorney, Mr. Randolf Larrup, asked me for a psychological
assessment of Mrs. Cronkite's "emotional stability."
    During my meeting with Mrs. Cronkite, this general issue differentiated
into three questions for me: (1) Might she again do physical violence to herself?; (2) Does she undergo mood swings, especially depression, which could
preclude attention to the children?; and (3) Does she "have it in her" to give
her children the warmth and consistent responsiveness that seem necessary
for development of a sense of worth and security—which in turn allow children to grow into warm, responsive adults?

Date of Assessment Meeting: November 12, 19____

Techniques Used
    Interview, Bender-Gestalt, partial Wechsler Adult Intelligence Scale,
Rorschach, Thematic Apperception Test, drawings, and mutual discussion of
my impressions.
    Mrs. Cronkite at Different Phases of the Assessment
    Although I arrived at my office nearly half an hour early, I knew at once
that my appointment must be with the woman already waiting in the hall. She
was sitting with one leg tucked under her and the other braced around the
chair leg. Her arms tightly circled a sweater and large purse on her lap, and
her knuckles were white as she clutched an umbrella handle. Once in my
office, Mrs. Cronkite reassumed a similar position, until I offered to put her
things on the coat rack. Stocky if not plump at 5'0", she was plainly dressed
and groomed. This, together with her obvious nervousness and acceptance of
direction, gave me an impression of both openness and vulnerability.
    I began by telling her bluntly that the attorneys had asked me, as a
psychologist, to try to find out if she might be too emotionally unstable to care
for her children adequately. After explaining that this was about all I knew, I
asked if she could tell me concretely what it was that her husband was
reacting to. I suppose that in a way she demonstrated the answer when she
finally let loose a torrent of tears and confessed that she didn't understand.
She struggled to tell me the bitter things that didn't seem to hang together for
her: "They say I'm suicidal"; "Baxter says I'm a slob, but I'm not. I'm sloppy,
but that's not the same as a slob, is it?"; "They say I'm an inadequate mother—

but I take good care of my children. I feed them good, and the babies always have a dry diaper. I love them. But I don't know those other things—but I do tell them stories, and with the babies I can tell them I love them."

As I began to understand, I directed the discussion from within Mrs. Cronkite's own perspective. Then, when no longer left all on her own to account for herself, she began to relax. Eventually she shared both the humor and pain of her experiences. As we moved on, I became impressed with her candor and her willingness to try to find ways of understanding her life. At the end of our meeting, I overviewed what would be in this report and despite its unflattering aspects, Mrs. Cronkite agreed with it, clarified some points for me, and made some other cogent remarks. Although she failed to imagine any ways she herself could correct her own situation, she was eager to consider my suggestions.

Background Given by Mrs. Cronkite

The following information was pieced together from remarks gathered here and there throughout the assessment session. Mrs. Cronkite, now 27 years old, first married when she was 17, after a life of being shuttled among stepmothers and foster homes. At that time she had completed the tenth grade with a C+ average. (She later passed a high school equivalency test, and took business school courses as well as beautician training.) By the time her child was two years old, she was divorced, and had given her ex-husband custody of the boy because she felt his paternal grandmother could provide better parenting than she could. Mrs. Cronkite described herself at this time as being both a "spoiled brat" who was trying to find a good time, and a confused, lonely girl with no happy memories and little knowledge of life. Her father, a real estate broker, sent her to a psychiatrist, who apparently believed that it was necessary to sit in silence until Jane Anne decided to speak. Subsequently, she has sought outside help only once: during the rocky beginning of her present "shotgun" marriage, she went to her husband's post chaplain. He in turn spoke with both of them separately, and their life seemed to smooth out for a time.

While staying with his parents during her husband's overseas tour about four and a half years ago, Mrs. Cronkite cut her wrists. She did so again on two later occasions, each time when she felt alone and unable to reach anybody—when there was nobody to take her seriously on her own grounds. She feels that at no time did she intend to kill herself; she writes these events off as ineffectual attempts to win attention, "but they don't get you nowhere; they don't work. It could only hurt me now—they wouldn't let me have my children."

Although she obviously wishes desperately that her husband would make her happy, she said not a single thing against him. Although she sees him as the person who could make things right, she doesn't seem to blame him for the way things are. "I just love him. I want him to be my husband." As we talked, Mrs. Cronkite discovered that she had married a man much like her father, a man who puts his job before all else, who doesn't know how to make a house full of people into a family, and who either doesn't know how to love or how to communicate that he does. When I asked if Mr. Cronkite plays with the children, if he provides the kind of care that he sees as deficient in his wife, she looked puzzled, and said, "Well, whenever I'm sick he feeds them and puts them to bed." Apparently he spends most of his time, including evenings and many nights, at his office. Even now, he is living with his employers in their apartment. Mrs. Cronkite feels that these people detest her as a "dumb broad" and that they have urged her husband to leave her. In the meantime, he has continued to drop by to see his wife, sleep with her, and to explain that he has "mixed emotions." He has not visited the children, however, and he has refused to pay rent on the apartment in which he left his wife. She is now pregnant and is arranging for movers prior to threatened eviction.

She doesn't know where to go, since she has no close friends, and doesn't know whether she will be able to have the children with her or whether she should merely obtain a room for herself. Nevertheless, she somehow seems buoyed by the fact that now that the court is involved, maybe she and her husband will get a new look at their lives and maybe a new start. Recently, "Baxter lit a cigarette for me—the first time in six years! And he kissed me goodnight." Finally, Mrs. Cronkite feels that she's more mature now, and that although she didn't grow up until after she was an adult, she is now resigned to the necessity of relying primarily on herself.

A theme that runs through this account is epitomized by what she described of her relationship with the children. She spoke of being able to tell the baby that she loves her, of being able to tickle her and tumble with her. To a lesser degree she can also share herself with the three-year-old son. But she says of the five-year-old boy with whom she was pregnant when she married: "Sometimes I watch him, like when he's at the table eating. And his face is sad and lonely, and I want to tell him I love him. But I don't know how." Indeed, she says that she's even stricter with him. When I asked if she knows how to show her love to Baxter, she tried to speak of what she says to him and how he shrugs it off. Then she remarked helplessly that having not received love, she has been uncertain of how to help others to receive it.

I pointed out that there seemed to be a significant danger that her children, too, might be growing up without learning how to be loved and loving, and that they might indeed wind up like their parents. Mrs. Cronkite acknowledged this as a vague but persistent fear.

Mrs. Cronkite as Seen through the Tests

The following examples of Mrs. Cronkite's behavior during testing should serve to fill out the above picture. After she had copied by hand a series of geometric designs (Bender-Gestalt), I pointed out to her that she had begun with great care, rendering precise reproductions. Then the designs became progressively less accurate until she spontaneously asked to start over, only to follow the same pattern. She agreed that she behaves similarly in the house. Doing things well is important at first, so long as somebody else cares; but when left on her own with no encouragement or appreciation, she lets things slide. For example, Baxter says she is a slob for not washing the windows or keeping the cupboards neat; but he doesn't help or compliment good work. In contrast, there's an obvious need to take care of the children; and besides, in some ways they notice; so she works harder for the children.

Mrs. Cronkite recognized the intelligence test (WAIS) as being a school-related examination, and immediately protested that she hates exams. On the first section, which asks mostly for geographical, historical, and other school-taught data, she was so "shook up" that she missed things she knew and scored far below average. She admitted that only since Baxter and the children left has she been reading newspapers. For the most part, she seldom discussed things with him because "he's the big businessman who knows everything," and she's always wrong. She also feels he doesn't want, or doesn't know how, to talk about more personal matters.

On the second section of the intelligence test, which requires knowledge of cultural expectations as well as a sense of personal responsibility in solving everyday problems, she became more comfortable and scored above average for adults her age. When given the opportunity to try herself out where she knows things can be worked out and that the atmosphere is friendly, Mrs. Cronkite has been fairly confident and efficient. She can be strong and can persevere.

When I asked her to tell me what the inkblots (<u>Rorschach</u>) reminded her of, she was remarkably imaginative, frank, and open. Sometimes she spoke of beautiful colors and pleasant objects—good signs for a person hoping to change her life constructively. However, her responses were predominately sad, frightened, resigned: for example, she was repeatedly reminded of stab wounds, blood flowing, and things dying. When asked if she knew why I was worried about these responses, she immediately said that I was afraid she would cut her wrists again. She is very much aware of this possibility, but treats it as logically impossible; suicide wouldn't work, so she won't try it. On the other hand, she doesn't know what will "work."

Finally, I asked her to make up stories about some rather ambiguous drawings (TAT). Her stories were filled with the quiet joys of everyday family life—people just doing things together: eating, dancing, talking, being in love. From what she says these are the same things that occupy much of her time in the form of daydreams. But in her stories there were also themes of being the perpetual loser to stronger persons, and of suicide. About the latter story, Mrs. Cronkite was greatly relieved to hear that she is not the only person to tell such a story to that particular card. Indeed, while dismayed to be looking at herself in these ways in front of another person, she also seemed to have gained some reassuring perspectives and awareness of personal options.

CONCLUSIONS
1. <u>Mrs. Cronkite should be regarded as suicidal.</u> She could again cut her wrists if she again feels that it would be the only way to be taken seriously. <u>Presently she desperately needs to be taken seriously,</u> and to feel that she has some control over her life and relationship with her children and husband. Right now, <u>circumstances are not on her side</u> (she lost her husband and children, is losing her apartment, has nowhere to go, and is pregnant). <u>This is a critical time for intervention and support.</u>

2. Mrs. Cronkite has acknowledged that often she rests, naps, or daydreams as a way of coping with her despair, and that she thus indeed <u>fails to give as much attention to the children as she should,</u> especially <u>to the older boy.</u>

3. As to the final referral question, it seems clear that this woman in her present circumstances is <u>not providing her children with the open warmth and consistent responsiveness ideal for their own growth into warm, responsive adults.</u>

4. However, she is deeply concerned about these problems with the children. Now that she is familiar with the possibility of psychotherapy or marriage counseling with persons who would help her to express herself, she is eager to begin, and hopeful of personal growth. <u>She does love and care for others; but she has not had the guidance, structure, and support that have been necessary for her to function appropriately as wife and mother.</u>

<u>Is Mrs. Cronkite then an emotionally inadequate mother?</u> Yes, in the sense spelled out above in points 1-4, but not so dramatically that we could say that the children would necessarily be better off without her. Since there are no absolute criteria for this question, we must ask a second: Should Mr. Cronkite have custody of the children for their sake?—<u>Would the children be significantly better off in their father's custody? I don't know; but there may be grounds for doubting it.</u> From his wife's account, I am led to wonder whether he may be short on the human care and responsiveness necessary for being a concerned, constructive husband and father. Further, one wonders about the adequacy of grandparents for raising little children, especially when it was the grandmother who raised an apparently insufficiently caring Mr.

Cronkite. One also wonders if Miriam, Duane, and Billy would not find themselves repeating their mother's life-time query: "I always wondered where my real mother was and why my father didn't come to my birthday party."

5. In short, it seems highly advisable that Mr. Cronkite, too, participate in a psychological assessment so that recommendations can be based on this fuller understanding of both parents.

6. Furthermore, if Mr. Cronkite can come to see it as promising, psychotherapy especially for his wife and at least joint marriage counseling seem to be the soundest recommendations for their welfare and that of their children, even if they eventually decide to separate permanently. Mrs. Cronkite is in definite need of some such immediate support, especially in view of the increasing pressures due to pregnancy in her present circumstances. She is the kind of person who could profit from consistent help. I will be glad to provide a list of mental health facilities and of independent psychotherapists.

Constance T. Fischer, Ph.D.
Clinical Psychologist

Comments

The content of this report seems appropriate, but its form could be improved. Conclusions should be less discursive.

On her way out the door, Mrs. Cronkite said, "You know, I feel so relieved and hopeful. I don't have a 'self-destructive tendency' after all. I've just been trying to kill myself." Collaborative contextualizing allowed her to discover her freedom—her part in what was "happening to" her. Nevertheless, before writing the report, I called the lawyer to emphasize my concerns about a suicide gesture, and to ascertain that someone would be looking after her.

I told Mrs. Cronkite what I would write in the report and reviewed with her the individualized suggestions we had developed during the WAIS and Bender. For example, when she gives herself a chance, as on Comprehension and the beginnings of the Bender, she indeed knows what to do and can imagine for herself what she would like the outcome to be. When she feels alone and unsure that she is "doing okay," she can seek direct assurance as she used to do with a hallway neighbor. We talked about replacements for this neighbor (who had moved), including a counselor or therapist. In retrospect, it is apparent that these suggestions should have been in the report, so readers could reinforce and extend them. Mrs. Cronkite, too, should have been given a copy of these suggestions, both as reminders and as a form of support.

Recommendations should follow conclusions so that readers do not have to search for them within the Conclusions.

Organic Factor in Murder: Thomas James Sutherton

This is a second report in this chapter to present the "conclusions" section on the front page. This practice is particularly helpful in clinical and diagnostic reports when the primary reader wants answers to specific questions in order to make decisions. The reader may choose whether to read the rest of the report for elaboration. This arrangement also encourages the writer to organize the report with a tighter story line.

The Sutherton report was written directly for the referring psychiatrist and parties involved in a murder trial and sentencing procedures, but it was elaborated for later use by prison assessors and counselors and by a parole board. The assessment went beyond the narrow referral question about organicity (brain damage) to explore alternative understandings of how the murder might have come about.

The psychiatrist made the referral on the outside chance that Mr. Sutherton's alcoholism might have produced a pattern of diffuse brain damage, which would have been an extenuating circumstance. In Pennsylvania, however, perpetrators are held responsible for crimes committed under the influence of drugs or alcohol.

> CONTENTS HAVE BEEN AND MAY BE
> SHARED WITH THE CLIENT

November 29, 19——

Psychological Assessment

THOMAS JAMES SUTHERTON

Referral
    Determined that his girlfriend of several years would not stand him up again, Mr. Sutherton, by his own admission, intercepted her in a parking lot and shot her to death last April. His attorney, Jonathan S. Coombs, requested a general psychiatric evaluation from Dr. Samuel Wright. As part of that evaluation, Dr. Wright arranged for a psychological assessment; he was particularly interested in any signs of brain damage that might have ensued from Mr. Sutherton's at least five-year history of alcoholism (substantiated by medical records of hospitalizations for detoxification).

Identifying Data
    Mr. Sutherton is a 31-year-old blue-collar worker with a tenth grade education plus GED. He is Caucasian, divorced, and has no children. At the time of the shooting, he was living with his mother.

Assessment Opportunities
    MMPI and 16 PF (personality tests mailed into the Greenwich Detention Center), Wechsler Adult Intelligence Scale (partial), Bender-Gestalt, Rorschach, TAT, and discussion of my impressions with Mr. Sutherton. We met for three and one-half hours in Dr. Wright's office on November 19, 19——. Mr. Sutherton was brought there in handcuffs from the Detention Center.

CONCLUSIONS

There are no indications of brain damage, nor of any grounds for an insanity defense. Mr. Sutherton is not antisocial or sociopathic. The dominant picture is of non-specific character disorder which has led to alcohol addiction. By his own acknowledgement, Mr. Sutherton has been a chronically shy and "nervous" young man who values quiet, routine, and solitude. He has felt most secure working by himself, living with his mother, and being around groups only within the sort of structure provided by his social club (Rod and Gun). He has drunk to quell anxiety. He generally has withdrawn from confrontations, thereby allowing resentments to dissipate over time. A long series of disappointments, repeated betrayal by his girlfriend, inexorably increasing debts, all in the context of alcoholism, preceded the shooting—an incident most unlikely to happen again unless extreme circumstances again led to sustained, confused, helpless resentment.

Mr. Sutherton should be considered SUICIDAL. He is despondent, agitated, brooding, and remorseful. He admits to fears of going crazy, an abortive suicide attempt (prior to his divorce), wondering if the shooting wasn't somehow supposed to have been a murder/suicide, and to having investigated all available avenues of suicide within the center (without finding a feasible one).

He is terrified of large prison settings—with their noise, confusion, and crowding. He is hopeful that at the prison to which he anticipates being sent he might take a course in wildlife management and eventually be allowed to do forestry work. He made no rash promises about overcoming alcoholism when eventually released, saying that even now he misses his beer. But he noted that he's been dry (while in confinement) for longer than ever before, and that AA has made a lot of sense to him.

Mr. Sutherton is also frightened of group confrontational therapy (sometimes used in prisons). He and I agreed that the most beneficial form of counseling for some time would be low-key role-playing of ways he might be quietly more assertive and thus less nervous and resentful. Alcoholism, not murderous impulses, is the key problem. Even with the difficulties that alcoholism presents, Mr. Sutherton has a lot going for him: pride in doing a good job, sensitive and empathic relations (with persons with whom he feels safe), intellectual brightness, and a certain independence even within his withdrawal.

Outward Appearance

Mr. Sutherton arrived at the office wearing a pullover sportshirt and slacks. His nails were carefully manicured and his beard and hair neatly trimmed. The apparent pride contrasted with his hunched shoulders, downcast gaze, and alcoholic's reddened nose and lower face. His arms were the slender ones of a nonlaborer. He typically sat slumped back in his chair and almost always awaited instructions before speaking. Yet he was alert as he watched me closely under his eyebrows, sometimes shifting to an erect position. He maintained his own council while figuring out complex problems in his head, and at other times quickly produced answers to test items.

As time went on, even between almost inaudible sighs, he smiled a bit and spoke aloud his puzzlement over some of the test problems. Occasionally he shared a wry association (for example, in answer to "What is the Vatican?" he said "That's where the Pope's in confinement"). He never sought my sympathy nor excused his crime. He acknowledged the slight edge of bitterness that crept into his voice just a couple of times. Although not interested in answering more than I asked for, Mr. Sutherton did answer all my inquiries with increasing detail and straightforwardness.

Mr. Sutherton's Viewpoint

Based on material that emerged at different points of the assessment, it is my impression that Mr. Sutherton sees himself (even while drinking) as a reliable, steady person under most circumstances. He has been trusted on night shifts to work by himself. Employers and family see him as capable and push him to set higher goals (college, supervisory positions), but he prefers and enjoys blue-collar work and resents being pushed. He is nervous under close observation or other pressure. He resents being made to look "dumb."

At his club, members seek him out to hear their sides of disputes. He listens, forms his own opinions, but rarely speaks. When he does, he sees his remarks as bringing the disputants back together peacefully. He feels he understands people rather well, if not necessarily sympathetically. He befriended a 20-year-old mentally retarded youth, and has protected him from the teasing and humiliation of other men. He takes the youth fishing, and has taught him to bowl ("He surprised a lot of people!"). Mr. Sutherton loves the woods, fishing, and hiking. He reads fairly broadly, but prefers hunting and woodsman magazines.

He has drunk alcohol as a means of staying with groups in social settings, of relaxing at home, and to quell "nervousness." He prefers beer to liquor, which upsets his stomach. Upon questioning, he admitted that he does feel that if his wife had not divorced him, he might have gotten along all right—drinking, but not at the cost of his employment. Similarly, he thinks that if his girlfriend had not urged him to leave AA and to resume drinking, he might have stayed dry. He had been drinking heavily over an extended time prior to the shooting; he does not remember getting the gun or going to the parking lot. Nevertheless, Mr. Sutherton has not excused himself.

Elaboration of Findings

No brain damage. Upon my request, Mr. Sutherton had mailed me a background on his history and situation. It was nine pages long, articulate, well-organized, detailed, and with no spelling, writing, or grammatical errors. He scored in the upper 15th percentile on the intelligence test, with no difficulties with memory (short-term or long-term), spatial relations, abstract thinking, or verbal functioning. There were no tremors here or on the Bender-Gestalt.

The errors that occurred on the Bender were due to being anxious rather than to organic impairment. For example, he copied the Bender designs in one-third the usual time, agreeing afterward that he often races through stressful situations just to get out of them. Similarly, not copying all the dots was like getting up and leaving when he becomes nervous, or like quitting his Army course in Morse code when he couldn't stand the instructor's watching him. Similarly, figures that touched or overlapped on my cards were left separated in Mr. Sutherton's copies. When asked if there were other times that he doesn't like things to touch, he readily acknowledged that he prefers for people to keep their distance. He hasn't liked even an admired supervisor to touch his arm reassuringly. His wife slept on a separate floor of the house. Their communication was such that he was surprised that she had decided to divorce him.

Personality. Mr. Sutherton's responses to the Rorschach (inkblots) and TAT (ambiguous pictures) are significant. His response times to the first three Rorschach cards were about ten times longer than the average; he looked at the card from each side, and decided what all his responses would be before speaking any of them. When I later clarified that this was not necessary, he readily spoke his percepts as he saw them. He agreed that typically he is his own man in this way—not speaking until he's sure of all he has to say. But I find no evidence of neurotic conflict or other repression. His only unusual responses to the cards had to do with hunting—once he explained, I was easily able to understand his perspective. Mr. Sutherton is not autistic or otherwise out of touch with "reality."

His fears of going crazy are related to recollections of what I would call alcoholic fogs (times when physical reality seemed dreamlike, vague) and a psychiatrist's once asking if he had ever seen things that weren't there. In addition, upon admission to jail, he experienced rats trying to pull the covers off his feet, even though he knew there were no rats. This may have been an incident of DTs or related alcoholic perception. Finally, he fears that the shooting itself and the suicidal thoughts are evidence of his going crazy. He appeared vastly relieved when I assured him that although he was "crazy" to have gotten himself into such a mess, he is not crazy in the sense of being insane.

On the Rorschach, his emphasis on movement and physical tension (for example, a man holding up game with each arm, a barking dog, an eagle flying, an arm pointing) together with his visions of natural landscapes (a lake filling with water, familiar mountains with a valley between) generally have been found to bespeak a yearning for peace while experiencing a painful stuckness, a tension without a readily achievable goal. Mr. Sutherton acknowledged such pain only with a downcast glance at me and a slight nod. He then spoke only fleetingly of his various physical pains (kidney and stomach problems, sinus condition, bad back)—which were also reflected in his MMPI profile. The latter are probably alcoholism-related physical symptoms exaggerated by his unspoken concern for himself.

His stories to the TAT cards were unconflicted; he readily identified possible contradictory features, either letting them be or integrating them into a consistent story. The characters in his stories took responsibility for themselves and planned ahead even where they were very limited by circumstances. Mr. Sutherton grinned when I handed him the last card, saying that I had finally given him one that wasn't morbid (I had to agree!). On this card he told a story of a man in a rope-climbing contest, a man who looked happy because "if he didn't win, he was pretty close."

Suicide. It is precisely persons who remain alert and concerned even while also despondent, as in Mr. Sutherton's case, that often carry out pre-meditated suicides. In addition, he fits the picture of persons who attempt suicide after a severe loss, in this case that of his earlier reputation as a reasonable person and of his girlfriend ("I think of her a lot; I miss her.").

Therapeutic considerations. Mr. Sutherton agreed that the kind of assertiveness practice that would be helpful to him both during and after his prison term is the sort that would serve him when someone steps in front of him in a check-out counter line. He told me of an incident at his club when a woman employee unplugged the TV set he was watching. He felt she must have known he was there; but he simply went home to drink and refused to go back to the club for several weeks. He told me this story both sheepishly and with frustrated resentment. It has been in the face of an accumulation of this sort of event that Mr. Sutherton has sustained his alcoholic drinking. That combination eventually culminated in his shooting the girlfriend.

Constance T. Fischer, Ph.D.
Clinical Psychologist

Comments

This report was written prior to publication of DSM III. By the latter's criteria, Mr. Sutherton clearly would fall into the new category, "avoidant personality disorder" rather than "nonspecific character disorder." In this case the revised system is more helpful than the old.

Although suicide was not mentioned in the referral, it turned out to be an issue—obviously an important one—and the report addressed it directly, incorporating this finding into the Conclusions section. There the word *suicide* is typed in capital letters so that it will not get lost or forgotten among the other themes. *Suicide* also appears as a subhead later in the report.

Comparative Diagnosis: Marsha Jacobs' Rorschach

The following letter is included in this chapter to underscore the point that individualized descriptions are not always necessary or appropriate. This letter was sent to a psychiatry resident, Dr. Deniston, who was assigned to a woman whom I had assessed earlier and who had recently been admitted to her unit in a psychiatric research and diagnostic institute. Because she had already observed Marsha's various moods and behaviors and had interviewed her at length, Dr. Deniston did not need a portrait of Marsha. We had discussed my impressions of Marsha and were in agreement that if there is such a phenomenon as "schizoaffective" process, then that term applied better to Marsha's present state than did her prior diagnosis of schizophrenia. We were in agreement that her dynamics also seemed to fit a "borderline personality" picture. Consonant changes in medication were ordered on a trial basis. I volunteered to review the Rorschach I had done with Marsha earlier, to see if it would throw light on our conclusions about Marsha in particular, and about the nature of what has been called "schizoaffective disorder" and the more recently publicized "borderline personality." In terms of treatment, we wanted to be sure that we had not overlooked any indications of schizophrenia. Our interest in the other two diagnoses were professional curiosity; in this instance treatment would be similar in either case.

Marsha was 25 years old. She had been in psychotherapy more than four years with two therapists, and then, two years earlier, had been hospitalized briefly for the same complaints with which she had now admitted herself. These were daily panic attacks, insomnia, and recurrent thoughts that became insistent enough to be intrusive—feelings of being persecuted and fears of hurting her mother and herself. Her present private practice psychiatrist had diagnosed her as schizophrenic, although he had been maintaining her on imipramine (which is not usually used in connection with this diagnosis).

For about a year before the current hospitalization, Marsha had continued to obtain prescriptions from the psychiatrist but had discontinued psychotherapy. Her family referred Marsha to me for psychological assessment several months before the hospitalization, and afterwards I talked with them about the advisability of consulting with the psychiatrist, about other community resources, and about how it is that effective psychotherapy can require so much hard work and time. The diagnostic possibilities I had in mind when I administered the Rorschach were the same as those Dr. Deniston now entertained: schizophrenia, schizoaffective disorder, borderline personality, generalized anxiety disorder, and panic disorder.

Dear Dr. Deniston:

I have reviewed the psychological testing I did with Marsha Jacobs. There's nothing really new here, but perhaps a review of the Rorschach would be of interest through its abstracted picture of what we have seen more directly.

The Rorschach was given on January 23, 19____, on a day that Marsha reported being tired from attending a Steeler victory party. She had had no "anxiety attacks" that week.

The general Rorschach picture (Exner system) was of a person with remarkable resources (bright, flexible, sensitive to others, empathic, sense of humor, energetic, quick to organize—to see relationships). But the picture also was of a person experiencing needs in a painful way. Her scorings are of the sort that have correlated empirically with very strong affectional longings, with sadness, and with feelings of being boxed in—held in check. Similarly, although she gave many responses involving animals engaged in activities, the majority of the humans were passive—waiting for things to happen or undergoing others' actions. It is as though there are bodily and conceptual senses of things that could be done, but that these are unavailable to the full person.

Her general approach to situations was sampled as strongly ideational (here, attuned to motives and possible outcomes). And she gave an unusual number of responses that correlated with a reflective, putting-things-in-perspective attitude. But her pattern also indicated that when overtly affectively engaged she was likely to respond at a gut level rather than in a moderated way. Further, one would predict that at those times she would be more idiosyncratic in her perceptions, in ways that could lead to poor behavioral judgment.

However, there was no thought disorder, and her F+% (perceptions shared by most people) was within normal limits (albeit just barely). Even where her responses were idiosyncratic, she was aware of this, and of how most people might respond. On the other hand, she allowed herself to give a significant number of responses involving unrealistic relationships (fish dancing in a garden, pigs flying, etc.). These were given in a self-aware, playful way, but nonetheless were given.

As for content, there was a notable number of so-called "counterphobic" responses (for example, sad clown, funny creatures). There was a back and forth movement between peaceful, pastoral, religious, and cooperative scenes on one hand, and scenes of struggle on the other. For example: people relaxing together, then bulls confronting each other, followed by joyful dancing. There were several sexual responses (more than is typical, except perhaps for therapy patients—who are a bit freer with such material), but mostly they were ones that are often given: for example, naked female African dancers, a vagina, a lipstick print.

In summary, at that point (January 19____) the Rorschach showed a person with many resources, but also a conflicted, suffering person who was aware of many options but unable to pursue them comfortably. Deeper depression and agitation, and self-defeating outbursts or misjudgments were clearly future possibilities. From the Rorschach alone most interpreters would not think of psychosis as a strong probability (even though a merit of the Rorschach is its access to such pathology). With the details of Marsha's prior hospitalization, many clinicians would then address the possibility of stress converting the picture to a transient one of acute psychotic proportion (rather than of some form of schizophrenia involving long-standing thought disorder). Psychoanalytically oriented clinicians would probably think in terms of borderline personality.

The MMPI profile was consonant with the above summary. According to Marks, Seeman, and Haller (1974), persons with Marsha's profile have been diagnosed as neurotic (dissociative and mixed) as often as psychotic (schizophrenic and manic-depressive).

Through discussion with Marsha, I could see that there were pervasive or, at least, ever-lurking concerns about dependence and sexual preference, and there were overlappings in the meanings of affection, lust, and violence. But these were co-present with developmental achievements and integrations that are atypical of the chronic schizophrenias. It seems to me that this picture and the Rorschach and MMPI pictures are indeed consonant with our discussion of both schizoaffective and borderline personality diagnoses.

I hope these remarks have been of some assistance.

Sincerely,
Constance T. Fischer, Ph.D.

Comments

Although the Rorschach letter does not come close to describing the Marsha I knew as an individual, it addressed issues that were important for predicting if and when she could return to work, which medications might help relieve her distress, and so on. Although this letter is more abstract than the other reports in this chapter, its organization in terms of differential diagnosis responds to Dr. Deniston's questions. Even though the report is not individualized, it describes the findings in terms of research patterns rather than diagnostic theory. For example, "unrealistic relationships (fish dancing in a garden . . .)" might have been labeled as "primitive fantasy." The "self-aware, playful" delivery might have been called "childish." These interpretations, a direct translation into a currently prevailing theory of borderline personality, would foreclose exploration of Marsha's individuality and discourage alternative reflection on the meaning of "schizoaffective disorder."

If this letter had been intended for the entire staff or to be filed as a psychological report, I would have spelled out the specific ways in which Marsha both fit and exceeded the "schizoaffective disorder" and "borderline personality" categories, and I would have included representative examples of my general statements.

Marsha gave her permission for me to share the Rorschach with Dr. Deniston. Marsha and I had discussed aspects of the Rorschach when we first used it, but I had not written a report. I did not share this letter with her, but if she ever wished to see it, my copy was available to her.

Physical Rehabilitation Center Evaluation: Florence Harris

A graduate student wrote the next report as part of her fieldwork in a comprehensive physical rehabilitation center, which provided short-term medically supervised evaluation and treatment, and referred patients back to community resources for follow-up care. A Morrow Center psychologist instructed the graduate student to use a specified battery, to limit her report to three pages maximum, to focus on test results because these were familiar points of reference for all staff, and to use the standard report format (including headings such as Test Results, Adjustment to Disability, Motivation, Personality, Goals and Recommendations). The Morrow medical psychologist supervised the evaluation, and I supervised the report-writing.

The student provided the information that the center required for decision-making in the familiar form that served its efficiency requirements. Yet she did not have to compromise her interest in providing a sense of what the patient was like as a person during the assessment. Institutional constraints should never preclude an individualized approach to assessment.

Florence Harris, the patient, had developed Guillain-Barré Syndrome—a nervous system disorder, which in this case involved partial paralysis of all four limbs. Other medical problems included hypothyroidism and a hearing loss. Mrs. Harris improved, although slowly, while at the center. The present testing was part of the predischarge re-evaluation. Facilities closer to her home were to continue her treatment on an outpatient basis.

Morrow Physical Rehabilitation Center

Psychological Report

Name: Harris, Florence

Age: 49

Education: 9th grade

Date of Admission: 8/28/19____

Date of Report: 3/15/19____

Case No.: TN-32-54

Admission Diagnosis: Guillain-Barré Syndrome

Sponsor: Middle States Insurance

Referred by: Dr. Termon

Tests Administered:

Wechsler Memory Scale (WMS)

Hooper Visual Organization Test (HVOT)

Wechsler Adult Intelligence Scale (WAIS), verbal scales only

Reason for Referral: Psychological Re-evaluation

Test Results

Behavioral aspects of neurological impairment have improved to an overall "mild" degree by Morrow Center norms. There are definite residuals, but also clear progress since the tests were administered last September. Mrs. Harris's WMS improved from Dull Normal to Average (a gain of five points) and the HVOT improved from Moderate to Mild Impairment.

The WMS Memory Quotient was 94, which is in the Average range. Mrs. Harris repeated rote memory material efficiently; she responded quickly and correctly on digits, alphabet, and counting backwards tasks. However, mild impairment was evident as she struggled to recall two paragraphs of logically related material, and as she was unable to complete the more difficult mental control materials. Mrs. Harris was well oriented as to person and place, but was confused about date and time. She was unaware of current events not directly related to her immediate plans (for example, she sometimes did not know the name of our mayor or governor).

On the HVOT Mrs. Harris scored 21.5, which indicates mild impairment in planning and visually organizing. She failed several times to synthesize the disassembled pictures.

The WAIS Verbal IQ was 81. Mrs. Harris struggled most with the Similarities and Arithmetic subtests (scaled scores 5 and 2) where abstract thinking and mental computation are required. Again in contrast, her level of immediately recalling digits was good (scaled score 12). Similarly, Mrs. Harris had difficulty on the Comprehension questions that were not related to her personal experience (finding one's way out of a forest, child labor laws, proverbs); nevertheless, her score was close to average. Throughout the testing, Mrs. Harris dealt best with familiar materials and information— things that she could work with concretely, in a habitual, direct manner. Tasks requiring extrapolation into personally unfamiliar situations, and ones requiring logical abstraction were most difficult for her. For example, she did not find effective ways of solving arithmetic word problems or of identifying shared properties of items such as "eye-ear" on Similarities (WAIS).

Mrs. Harris's hearing loss seemed to fluctuate: She did not appear to hear me from the left side (she was not wearing her hearing aid). But it was often difficult for me to judge whether her several off-target anwers were due to mishearing or to her difficulties in thinking conceptually. For example, she answered "clothes" when asked what was alike about an axe and a saw, and explained the reason for child labor laws by saying, "People should take care of their own children."

Adjustment to Disability

Mrs. Harris struck me as generally pleasant and cooperative, passively preferring to await instructions. Her hair had been neatly styled, her fingernails had been manicured by Center employees, and she proudly mentioned that she has maintained a weight loss of 48 pounds. She generally sustained a good mood during the assessment, but because she tired easily, the tests were administered in two 30-minute sessions. Both her movements and her speech were slow, giving the impression of weakness. Her eyes and head oscillated slowly, as though she were sleepy.

Nevertheless, she is highly motivated in the area of physical rehabilita-tion. She spoke openly about the onset of her illness, the paralysis, her recovery thus far, and the difficulties in regaining strength, especially on her left side. She seemed eager and somewhat impatient: "I want to get better . . . I can't wait"; "I'm not going to feel sorry for myself, and I don't want my family to have to take care of me." When asked to reproduce a figure on the WMS, she was determined to demonstrate her improved right hand strength by grasping the pencil with her spoon holder. However, the attempt failed.

On the other hand, Mrs. Harris did not acknowledge impairment to memory and thinking. When she did not know an answer, she avoided the issue by answering too quickly, or by mentioning her hearing loss or tiredness. When pressed, she became agitated—tearing, breathing heavily, and protesting that she was tired. On the Comprehension and Similarities subtests of the WAIS she insisted on her (incorrect) answers by repeating them forcefully. On the HVOT she insisted that the disassembled block was a circle.

Suggestions

There are no indications for changes in present treatment and planning. However, future caretakers (including her family) should be alerted that Mrs. Harris's face-saving efforts cover over significant hearing and memory/conceptual impairments, and that these efforts may be very constructive ones for now, ones that allow her to maintain her determination and courage in regard to her physical rehabilitation.

Carline Goodwin
Graduate Student
Department of Psychology
Duquesne Univeristy

Comments

The center staff members were pleased with this report. The headings were familiar enough to help readers find what they were looking for, while the format innovations provided that information in an integrated but streamlined form. Staff appreciated the assessor's brevity. In particular they appreciated that Ms. Goodwin had not reviewed generalities about their kinds of patient (need for structure, function of denial, and so on), which all the staff already knew. They also noted with approval that the assessor had not burdened them with individualized description that they did not need for their primary tasks of decision making and record keeping. They liked the personal touch of referring to Mrs. Harris by name (rather than "the patient," which is used in many medical settings) and the concrete examples of her appearance, comportment, and test performance.

Unlike most intellectual and neuropsychological evaluations, this one does not refer to memory, organization, ability, and so forth, as though these were entities within the person. Rather, the report refers to performance on "rote memory *material,*" or "mental control *material.*" Its references to planning, recalling, and organizing keep the coping patient in sight.

However, I would prefer that the center reports contain a more complete Referral section for the benefit of later readers—who too often do not have access to a complete medical record, and hence do not know the entire context of the evaluation. I would also recommend the addition of a section written for the patient's later helpers (usually the family and family physician). Most instructions to outside helpers are oral and therefore subject to forgetting and to confusion, especially as one party interprets to another and that person to another. A section on Suggestions for Discharge Adjustment could be duplicated for family use.

Presentence Assessment (Rape Conviction): Mark E. Pallard

The defense attorneys in this case advised me that the format of my findings was important because the particular presiding judge on other occasions had openly expressed impatience with technical data and explanations of their meaning. He had been know to interrupt such presentations with requests to "Get to the point; what's your conclusion?" In addition, the attorneys were concerned that the judge might see their client's imposing, apparently macho appearance in court as contradicting the testimony of their character witnesses. I was asked if I could prepare a nontechnical report of my findings that could help the judge and prosecuting attorney understand how these different profiles could indeed belong to the same man, and whether it would be possible for this man to have raped the plaintiff.

The local newspapers had been running stories about women having been raped by men who had been arrested and/or convicted for prior rapes or attempts, but who had been found not guilty, had been given short terms, or who were on parole. Even more than usual, a judge would be obliged to consider whether Mr. Pallard might be one of these repetitive offenders. Nevertheless, when imposing sentence, most judges also take into account any evidence of remorse as well as a reasonable possibility of treatment or other circumstances mitigating against future offenses. Therefore, in this report I addressed these issues directly. At the same time I did not recommend particular action to the court. Although it is part of the assessor's job to render the defendant's situation understandable, and in that sense one becomes the defendant's advocate, the assessor must not join in the adversary system of the courts. The assessor does not take the side of the client and the defense attorneys against the prosecution, the judicial system, or society at large.

The report on Mr. Pallard includes a brief Technical Appendix for the referring psychiatrist, who had some familiarity with psychological tests and had requested that I include such information for his own edification. The appendix also reminds the reader that although the report presented its findings in terms of life events, those findings were influenced by the multiple perspectives afforded by a battery of standardized tests. If the prosecution had so requested, all test profiles and protocols would have been made available for examination by another psychologist.

Psychological Assessment

MARK E. PALLARD

Referral
One year ago Mr. Pallard was charged with having driven a waitress to his home and there repeatedly beating and raping her. He denied all criminal involvement, but was found guilty in a nonjury trial. Attorney Harold Berman then requested that psychiatrist Samuel Popovich conduct a presentence evaluation. The present report was requested by Dr. Popovich as part of his evaluation of Mr. Pallard's character and personality, and of the likelihood of his committing the charged or any future violence.

Before this psychological assessment was conducted, attorney Berman had obtained a retrial, at which Mr. Pallard was defended by attorney David Rogers. Mr. Pallard was found guilty, but of fewer charges. I attended a portion of that trial, but my testimony was disallowed after probative challenge by the prosecutor. This report is now being written to serve the upcoming presentence proceedings.

Date of Formal Assessment Session: March 10, 19____.

Date of Report: August 9.

Actuarial Data: 41 years old
                Second marriage; two children reside
                   with ex-wife
                7th grade education
                Mechanic, recently with supervisory
                   responsibility; with same automotive
                   company for 14 years

Assessment Sources
Last March I met with Mr. Pallard in Dr. Popovich's office for 3½ hours and interviewed him intensively in conjunction with use of the Wechsler Adult Intelligence Scale (partial), the Rorschach, and the Bender-Gestalt. I previously had obtained through the mail answer sheets to the MMPI and 16 PF objective personality tests as well as a taped personal history. In addition, during the ensuing months I received a lengthy call from Mr. Pallard and, at his request, one from a personal friend of his who is a counselor. I also read the transcript of the original trial, and attended an afternoon session of the second trial.

During the assessment session, Mr. Pallard held back in a few areas, but overall shared quite openly, as will be seen in the Personality section below.

Conclusions
The following conclusions are drawn from highly consistent findings throughout all the tests and the other assessment opportunities. (1) Mr. Pallard very clearly is not a criminal personality (character disorder); (2) He

does not fit any of the several patterns of rape repeaters; (3) He is not the sort of person who would plot (premeditate) and then carry-out a kidnap-rape; (4) He is not an "explosive personality," who loses control with minimal provocation.

(5) It is possible that he could indeed retaliate angrily and forcefully if he found himself being made a fool of by someone he had been given reason to believe that he could count on. His general temperament is an energized, affable, peace-seeking one. Being thought well of, being trusted, and being able in turn to count on others are terribly important to, and a source of vulnerability for, Mr. Pallard. It is possible that, if led on over the course of that August evening, but then rudely rejected—he could have struck out at the plaintiff and forced her into sexual intercourse. Once having so reacted, however, this man does not seem to me capable of continuing to beat a person. (If initial physical blows and forcible intercourse did occur, the plaintiff could, of course, nevertheless continue to feel intimidated.)

Personality

The test data are highly consistent and are consonant with Mr. Pallard's history and with my interview observations. They reflect a complex and troubled man. The following description presents behavioral examples of the personality patterns identified with the tests.

On one hand, he is the man I later also saw in the courtroom: six-feet tall, well filled out (200 pounds), strong, his dark hair and square face seeming to emphasize the intensity of his bent-forward listening and fist-against-palm frustration with the opposition's arguments. I had not been surprised to learn from him that he had played semi-pro football. Nor that in younger years on a couple of occasions he fought with his fists rather than lose his job to co-workers who attempted to undermine his efficiency and to blame him for broken equipment. All of this fits with his being a self-made man, one who has "made it" despite having only a seventh-grade education and only a fifth-grade reading and writing level. He shares many interests and values of lesser educated manual workers—allegedly including a surly response to police who searched his apartment.

On the other hand, he is also a man who drove a BMW and wore a blue suede sports coat and coordinated clothing to our assessment session. He carried himself well and expressed himself fluently. He jogs and works out regularly in a spa. He voiced great pride in these accomplishments, along with his reputation as a highly responsible worker. By his account he has typically held a part-time job in addition to his full-time employment, throwing himself energetically into the work at both settings. He is proud of working as a house and grounds man for one of Harrisburg's leading families. He respects education and authority, especially that of professionals. Early in our session, and then from time to time, I experienced Mr. Pallard's social ease, genuine affability, compassion for his wife, and consideration for myself. At these times I was aware of the openness of his face, his relaxed posture, and ease of eye contact.

Between these two aspects of Mr. Pallard is another. My first introduction to it was a halting, soft, trembly voiced audiotape Mr. Pallard sent me in lieu of the written background information I had requested that he send me prior to testing. The tape was accompanied by a misspelled, laboriously lettered note saying that due to his poor writing he thought it would be easier for me to listen to the tape. He then followed my request line-by-line with a self-conscious but complete history. Later he told me of bandaging his hand before going to the bank to fill out forms, so that people would not see his poor writing for what it was. During the assessment session, at times he hyperventilated and anxiously grasped the arms of the chair, particularly as I questioned him about his first wife's demands upon him and about any similar patterns in his present marriage. (I suspect women tend to perceive him as strong, and then sometimes reject his needs for support.) When I pushed him into explaining why he did not want to have more children, his body sunk deep into the chair, his eyes were cast downward, and he struggled to explain that he fears that somehow he had passed on bad futures to his two youngsters. Mr. Pallard, for example, was born with a congenital deformity of both little toes, and one of his sons is plagued with health problems. He also spoke with anguish of not knowing his middle name until the Marines informed him of it, and of how he has taken special care that his children know who they are, both literally and in a more general sense. Then as he spoke of his sternness with his nephew and niece, and of how the latter nevertheless tells him she loves him, he broke out sobbing.

Later, I interrupted the Rorschach to say that I felt he probably had been worried about his sanity since the alleged rape incident, and that although I deemed him "crazy to have gotten into this mess," he was not in any sense insane. He was visibly relieved, and confessed that since the incident he has suffered nightmares, sleepless nights, and distressed awakenings in which he pounded his body in frightened attempts to disprove its seeming hollowness. It was during this discussion that he admitted that whatever his degree of legal guilt, he was wrong to have driven the waitress to his home when his wife was out of town, and that God was now testing and punishing him—not so much for this incident as for all the wrongs and deficits of his total life. A bit later he admitted to finally comprehending how his brother could have committed suicide a few years ago, and to contemplating means to his own suicide.

In conclusion, Mr. Pallard is all these identities: a laborer quick to impatience with interference and with a street sense of justice; a self-made, suave, controlled, aspiring, accomplished man; a warm, caring, concerned family man and admirer of socially responsible professionals; and a fellow of above average intelligence, but who today probably would be classified as having a developmental disability (reading and writing). He has strived painfully and pridefully to hide this disability, but it has been one source of Mr. Pallard's strong sense of vulnerability and of his quick anger at being made to look foolish. He is a complex and troubled man, but not one of criminal personality.

Mr. Pollard already has suffered in multiple ways for his involvement with the plaintiff: lawyer fees, extreme stress on his marriage, public disgrace, fear for his sanity, suicidal ideation. He was clearly suicidal when I saw him in March. Although he never admitted to me any attack on the plaintiff, and although he is angry about what he sees as her refusal to acknowledge her own culpability, I found him to be clearly remorseful for his involvement.

These circumstances significantly decrease chances that Mr. Pallard would again become violent with an unconsenting woman. I believe future attempted rape would be unlikely. Specifically, the extended and public nature of the court proceedings have confronted Mr. Pallard as never before with his sensitivity to being made foolish and with the negative consequences of becoming physically angry in response. In addition, Mrs. Pallard is now, after their having struggled together over her husband's unfaithfulness and her ensuing humiliation, a stronger source of support. Mr. Pallard feels that this holds for the extended family, too.

In addition, actuarial statistics indicate that men of Mr. Pallard's age and stable work history rarely begin to commit repeated crimes of violence; rather, any such prior patterns begin to peter out. This prediction, of course, is not guaranteed; it is an estimate based on the psychological assessment and on research data. It remains true that Mr. Pallard does not like to confront his personal day-to-day difficulties, especially with people closest to him. However, I believe he would abide by, and profit from, court-ordered psychotherapy, which would strengthen the above prediction that there is little chance of another sexual offense. In many of my assessments of convicted rapists, I have not seen reasonable ways of protecting society aside from incarceration; in this case, from a psychological perspective, that does not seem necessary.

CTF:cit

Technical Appendix (from March 10, 19____)
> Fast response times to Rorschach and Bender
> Large B-G drawings (one per page); accurate
> Bright Normal range on WAIS
> Rorschach: striving seen in high content range, and in reference to trophies, mansions, and the like. Shading and inanimate movement predominate, reflecting depressive tension, stuckness. Perceptual accuracy and organization/integration strong.
> MMPI: high ego strength (K), energy; follows rules and wants to be thought well of, but can't always put himself in others' shoes; high subscription to "male" values (for example, Mf, Pd).
> 16 PF: trusting, group-dependent, outgoing, polished; concrete, stubborn, easily upset.

Comments

The judge imposed a lighter jail term than anticipated by most participants in the case, but at this point did not order psychotherapy (which might be posited as a later parole condition). While deciding whether to challenge a procedural aspect of the trial, Mr. Pallard's lawyers agreed that in the meantime they would strongly encourage him and his wife to enter joint or individual psychotherapy. I had declined the Pallards' earlier request that I be the therapist. I did not want to compromise my assessment testimony by becoming more involved with them. Moreover in forensic assessment, anything the client divulges to the therapist can be examined in court once the client has agreed to allow that professional to serve as a witness. That circumstance is not conducive to effective psychotherapy.

Mr. Pallard and his extended family were in court when I testified about my assessment findings. Despite the testimony's publicly divulging previously hidden, negative aspects (learning disability, fears of insanity and of being defective, positive possibility that he could have raped the plaintiff, and so on), the Pallards told the attorneys they were grateful for the testimony's sense-making. The report did not attenuate the seriousness of the crime or of Mr. Pallard's responsibility, but it did render it understandable, and did not reduce him to a set of traits or labels. Although the rape, whatever its circumstances, remained highly reprehensible, Mr. Pallard emerged as comprehensible—to himself as well as to others—and hence rehabilitable, in his own eyes as well as in the eyes of family and community.

Psychological Component of Pain: Fred S. Barnard

This diagnostic assessment again illustrates how the report can be written for multiple readers, in this case the referring psychiatrist, the court, and any psychologist hired by the hospital's attorneys. Like most of the other diagnostic assessments in this chapter, this one renders the client understandable in an everyday way while providing the mental health specialist an implicit dialogue with the presence and absence of various clinical patterns. The Technical Appendix and Reference Notes are primarily for psychologists, but they also help other readers to be assured that additional evaluators would come to similar conclusions.

> CONTENTS HAVE BEEN AND MAY BE
> SHARED WITH THE CLIENT

December 12, 19____

Psychological Assessment: FRED S. BARNARD

Referral

About 1½ years ago, as part of an effort to better his blood circulation, Mr. Barnard underwent surgery ("stripping") on veins in both legs. While recovering in the hospital, Mr. Barnard fell to the floor when a chair in which he had been placed collapsed. Despite a subsequent occipital neurectomy, Mr. Barnard reports recurrent dizziness and blackout spells, headaches, and a sensation of pressure where his head was struck, as well as penetrating pain in the same place—as though in the form of a nail. In addition, he reports pain and numbing of his legs due to continuing circulation problems. Mr. Barnard attempted to return to work, but could not tolerate the pressure of his helmet.

Mr. Barnard is suing Lorreville Hospital for negligence. His attorney, Mr. Arthur Randall, requested psychiatric evaluation by Dr. Samuel Wright, for whom this psychological assessment was conducted. The referral issue was the extent of any psychological aspects of Mr. Barnard's pain and incapacitation.

Identifying Information

54 years old

Married (2nd marriage)

High school education, plus
    2 years night school

Steady work history: lathe and
    drill press operator; tool crib
    and receiving clerk

Active in union affairs

Address: RFD #3
Box 40A
Lexington, PA 15644

Opportunities for Assessment
    Minnesota Multiphasic Personality Inventory, 16 Personality Factor Test,
and essay (all mailed in from Mr. Barnard's home); Wechsler Adult
Intelligence Scale (partial), Rorschach, Thematic Apperception Test; brief
interviews with Mr. and Mrs. Barnard together both before and after the
testing session. The assessment meeting took place in Dr.Wright's office for
three hours on December 8, 19____ .

CONCLUSIONS
    The assessment data consistently fit <u>one</u> of the well-known male
"conversion" patterns. This pattern involves a man who has worked especially
hard and taken great pride in that work all his life. He has been an upright
citizen, outgoing, and sociable. He has been determinedly self-sufficient,
sometimes to the point of achieving beyond what is expected of his general
ability level. He is not an introspective person, and believes simply that he will
be justly rewarded and taken care of by virtue of working extra hard and living
properly. It is precisely this person who is most devastated by an injury or
disease that seriously disrupts the above way of being a man. It is as though
"the rug were pulled out from under him"—leaving him disoriented and with
no place to stand. He had not developed reliable ways other than direct action
to cope with adversity. He won't allow himself to cry or to give in to
depression. In this circumstance, he focuses on the physical ailment as <u>the</u>
source of his distress.
    Earlier, he would have subordinated pain to his work; but now the pain
stands out and is experienced more fully. When such a man believes that he
can no longer be the kind of person he feels he has to be, then the physical
disability becomes emphasized as an honorable reason for his change. This
reaction is <u>not</u> malingering; and the pain is real (even though another person
might not be as disabled by it). More generally, Mr. Barnard's pattern has
sometimes been referred to as a "conversion pattern imposed on an organic
disorder"; the proposed revision (1980) of the American Psychiatric
Association's Diagnostic and Statistical Manual names this circumstance
"Psychological Factor Probably Affecting Physical Disorder (316.10)."
    In Mr. Barnard's case, this picture is complicated by an additional
uncertainty. He is vigilant in his attunement to signs that he might black out
again. He not only fears further injury to himself in a fall, but also is greatly
threatened by reminders that he is no longer in control of his life. These
apprehensions probably exacerbate whatever neurological symptoms he may
suffer. Mr. Barnard's old ways of coping, in the present circumstances, actually
place greater emphasis on his experienced symptoms. That is, he pulls in,
grits his teeth (so to speak), and determines to live through adversity. But
with no physical activity to which to devote himself, and with the constriction
of his old hopes, plans, interpersonal relations, and general responsivity, his
problematic body has become more focal. He struggles gamely, but is
experiencing more difficulty than is visible to many observers.
    Mr. Barnard differs from some conversion patterns in that he does not fit
the psychodynamic picture of a person whose illness serves as an avoidance of
a conflictful situation while also providing special solicitudes from family and
friends. He does enjoy the attentions of his wife and the consideration shown
by his friends, but probably no differently than most of us would. Because of
this difference from some conversion patterns, I estimate that without the
additional trauma (physical and psychological) of his hospital accident, Mr.
Barnard might well have found gradual, more or less effective, ways of
adapting to his circulatory problems. That is, he might well have bypassed
classification as totally work-disabled.

I did not examine Mr. Barnard for brain damage, but his performance on intellectual tasks was consistent with that of a person coping with the arteriosclerotic changes that have been established medically.

Finally, I anticipate that once the various uncertainties hanging over him (lawsuit, application for social security, medical verdict on his neurological problems) are settled, even if with the worst outcomes from his perspective, Mr. Barnard will begin to adapt more constructively. That is, the stress of these uncertainties probably aggravates his condition. This does not mean that he has been feigning in the meantime.

Elaboration of Assessment Data

Interview. Physically, Mr. Barnard reminded me of a Norman Rockwell "average American man"—average in height and weight, wearing slacks, open shirt, and white belt, looking clean-cut and alert in his shortish, graying hair and clear glasses. He sat forward and was eager to cooperate. Until I interrupted, he often spoke sociably of persons in his community, his union activities, singing in barbershop quartets, etc. He often quoted his father and Will Rogers. He told with pride of building his own home (personally digging the foundation), and of editing his union's newsletter for years. Similarly, Mr. Barnard said he had worked for seven straight hours to complete the tests I sent him. He mailed them back to me neatly filled out, carefully stapled, and accompanied by leftover sheets of the notebook paper I had sent him. This sort of unrelenting good citizenship frequently has been associated with conversion diagnoses for men.

Eventually Mr. Barnard spoke of his frustrations: no longer being able to work on his car (can't keep his head bent over), requiring three days to mow his lawn, no longer being able to take his wife to socials. Unlike many men diagnosed as hysterical conversion reactions, however, Mr. Barnard did not call on me to feel sorry for him, to blame employers or doctors, to affirm his righteousness or his religious or civic beliefs. Toward the end of our three hours together, he stood up several times to help the circulation in his legs. His discomfort appeared genuine.

MMPI and 16 PF. Both of these profiles were those of persons who have endured medically substantiated pain and who prefer to focus on specific physical pain rather than to allow other kinds of psychological anguish (see References in regard to MMPI). The profiles were also those of persons who are orderly, conventional, and outgoing.

WAIS. At one time, Mr. Barnard probably functioned in the Bright Normal range of intelligence (60-65th percentile); he scores in the mid-Average range now (50th percentile). He must have had to stretch to take night college courses and to edit the union newsletter. When I commented that he sometimes used the wrong "big word," he sheepishly told me that a woman relative of his has long said that his is a case of either "too little or too much education." Similarly, sometimes his way of answering questions was an effort at sounding educated or bright: Question: "What is the Book of Genesis?" Answer: "I do not know; I am not a Biblical man." In answer to "At what temperature does water boil?" he gave answers on both celsius and Fahrenheit scales, and explained that both were at sea level. In answer to "Why do we pay taxes?" he said, "We are obligated in the privileges we receive from paying taxes . . . the privileges we endure . . . parks and living in the United States."

His decrease in Performance subtest scores in comparison to Verbal scores is even greater than expected for his age. Nevertheless, he worked diligently on Block Designs until he got them correct (without credit, because of time-overrun). Mr. Barnard said that he has experienced similar situations at home: He has trouble concentrating, often having to reread directions several times; but he does finish whatever the project is (for example, putting toys together for his grandchildren). These difficulties often have been found to involve both general anxiety and cerebrovascular difficulties associated with aging.

TAT. Here Mr. Barnard readily pointed out the hostile, sexual, and conflictual themes many people avoid. I took this as partial evidence of his not being a traditional repressive hysteric. He preferred, though, to come up with positive outcomes on most of the stories, and agreed with me at this point that he tries "to make happiness" and that he refuses to be depressed or "feel sorry for myself." However, he also admitted that he does feel "cut down something fierce" and is distressed by mounting bills.

In one story (card #5—the woman looking into a room through the door—which often elicits paranoid themes), Mr. Barnard told of a mother going up to an "attic which used to be used as a child's study room . . . . The children have left . . . . They're in school or away. She is looking for something they have requested by phone or letter. She will find it." As he told the story, I experienced Mr. Barnard as longing for the familiar and the lost, but in a reconciled/optimistic way. It is this sort of finding that leads me to expect a better adaptation of his ill health after current uncertainties are settled.

Rorschach. Here I found a sense of impotence and perplexity in the face of things that don't fit. Mr. Barnard was constricted in his approach to the inkblots, giving only 16 responses (Beck administration), taking a long time to answer, trying to fit percepts together, but eventually giving up and seeing mostly animals and anatomy. There were no people and no directional activity. Even so, once again the personally familiar showed up: his living room mantel with Christmas stockings hung up, and driftwood like that at his camp.

The content of his percepts was mostly passive; the only movement was on the part of animals and clouds. He was more drawn to the dark and the vague than to color. His preoccupations led to anatomy responses (for example, lungs, backbones) that do not match most persons' perceptions. In general, the Rorschach showed Mr. Barnard to be more withdrawn, pained, perplexed, and self-absorbed than is apparent from the way he speaks about himself.

Summary: Discussion with Mr. and Mrs. Barnard

As they developed, I reviewed my impressions with Mr. Barnard. Later I briefly shared them with Mrs. Barnard. He was relieved that "nothing's wrong with me" (that what has happened to him does make some sense, and that it has happened to other men, too). He responded receptively to the following analogies: Hearing people cough in church leads one to ask his throat if it feels tickly—and lo, it does! When one has a bad cold and has to stay in bed, all the aches and pains seem bigger than life. When his first wife left him, he developed a temporary ulcer and tremor, but then he had his work to provide continuity and purpose. Now he does not. After a heart attack a man at first is wiped out physically and psychologically, but with time he grows stronger and finds modified ways of getting things done; eventually he no longer appears as an invalid to friends. Mr. Barnard himself provided an additional picture: suddenly finding himself as though 65 years old—forcibly retired, trouble concentrating, weaker, and so on, but robbed of the intervening years of income and gradual adjustment. He had no difficulty understanding that his personal reaction to pressures might be aggravating his symptoms.

I did not take time for Mrs. Barnard to talk-out her own perplexities in the face of her husband's problems. She struck me as an earnest, trusting woman, but one understandably in need of some supportive discussion from her husband's doctors. I explained that the above findings were only my own, and that they awaited other evaluations for a full picture.

Technical Appendix

16 PF Standard Scores (Form A)		MMPI T-Scores	
A	8	L	56
B	7	F	50
C	6	K	57
E	5		
F	5	Hs	79
G	8	D	56
H	6	Hy	82
I	4	Pd	50
L	4	Mf	65
M	3	Pa	53
N	10	Pt	50
O	7	Sc	55
Q₁	5	Ma	63
Q₂	6	Si	40
Q₃	8		
Q₄	3		

WAIS Scaled Scores

Information	12
Comprehension	11
Digit Span	7
Block Design	7

Reference Notes (Re MMPI Conversion V)
Bradley, L. A., Prokop, C. K., Margolis, R., & Gentry, W. D. Multivariate Analyses of the MMPI Profiles of Low Back Pain Patients. Journal of Behavioral Medicine 1978, 1, 253-272. (See pp. 270-271 re groups Bm & Bf & Df.)
Marks, P. A., Seeman, W., & Haller, D. L. The actuarial use of the MMPI with adolescents and adults. Baltimore: Williams & Wilkins, 1974. (See p. 43.)

Constance T. Fischer, Ph.D.
Clinical Psychologist

Comments

The constructive individualized intervention helped Mr. Barnard to understand and begin to come to terms with his part in what had "happened to" him. After the assessment I asked the referring psychiatrist if he could arrange a discussion including Mrs. Barnard, to alleviate some of her concerns. For example, I had mentioned to them that I imagined their sex life had been nil since the accident. They were both greatly relieved to learn that such a circumstance was understandable and not necessarily permanent. However, the psychiatrist forgot to invite Mrs. Barnard to participate in his concluding discussion with her husband. When the psychiatrist acknowledged this omission, I realized that I should have taken more time myself, or more appropriately, I should have encouraged the Barnards to request a conference with their family physician. The assessor should not go beyond his or her training into other disciplines' realms, but it is also important not to define one's responsibilities too narrowly.

Suicide Potential: Rosemarie Stefanik's Interview

This final report is included as a reminder that referral requests for assessment often can be met without use of tests. Here, a collaborative interview was sufficient. In other cases, review of records, visits to the client's home or work environments, and other direct observations may be used instead of (or in addition to) test materials. Mrs. Stefanik's case, like that of Marsha Jacobs, also illustrates that not all assessments require a full report of what the assessor has learned about the person. Nevertheless, life events and their contexts are the primary data of the report, which in this instance is a brief letter for the therapist's records and my own.

December 10, 19___

Johnathan R. Atkins, Ph.D.
Suite 204, Ardmore Building
1870 Hopkins Boulevard
Pittsburgh, PA 152___

Re ROSEMARIE N. STEFANIK

Dear John,
    The following note serves as a record of the information we discussed yesterday over the telephone.
    At your request, I met with Mrs. Stefanik yesterday morning for the purpose of assessing suicide potential. As it turned out, use of tests was unnecessary since during our discussion of the referral, Mrs. Stefanik acknowledged that she has been giving increasing thought to actual means of killing herself. Her method is one of high lethality, namely a revolver, but she has not yet obtained one. This acknowledgement occurred after our discussion of her being depressed, and after my statements to the effect that although she most probably worried that these thoughts might mean she was going crazy, that neither you nor I saw her as being insane or insanity-prone.
    She then agreed that talking to her therapist (you) directly about her suicide fantasies would more likely decrease than increase chances that she would act on them. She also agreed to accept your earlier recommendation of a psychiatric evaluation for medication. I assured her that the physicians with whom you work prescribe in a conservative manner and prefer to remove medications as soon as feasible.
    Mrs. Stefanik and I then spoke with you on the telephone from my office, and you two arranged an appointment for a meeting later in the day.

Constance T. Fischer, Ph.D.

Questions and Responses

Question: As an expert witness, shouldn't you restrict yourself to test data and direct extrapolation from norms?

Response: No. Expertise is the *specialized comprehension* that one's discipline affords of even everyday events. The task is to help the jury and judge to understand how the person could have behaved in a given way and under what circumstances that person might behave in the same or other ways. Sometimes tests are not necessary; an interview and review of records may be sufficient. When tests are used, the assessor's work is unfinished until relevant behavioral instances of test findings have been described.

Question: Marsha's Rorschach letter was very different from the other reports. Was that because the Rorschach reveals dynamics that are not visible through direct observation?

Response: No. Rorschach scores, like those from any other test, show us an outcome from how the person approached a task, in this instance one involving ambiguous visual material (the inkblots). Although the outcome here involves the client's cognitive/affective/behavioral choices rather than a performance level, in either case scores are summaries of sampled, actual comportment. Dynamics *are* more readily apparent through the Rorschach than through many other test materials, but dynamics are not something underlying or causing comportment. They are the vacillations, the multiple pulls and pushes, that occur during the cognitive/affective/behavioral choosing. As always, inferences can be made from a direct sense of what it is like during the tests to make the various choices, as well as indirectly from what we have learned was true of other persons whose choices were similar.

Question: Do you really believe in conventional diagnostic categories?

Response: I take diagnostic categories seriously but not literally. I take them seriously in that they are the best cumulative knowledge that several professions have developed over many years of research and practice. They are practical because they orient participants to the general issues and parameters of a particular case, such as permanence of a condition, irrelevance of logical arguments to a patient, or probability of a person's functioning within the law. Diagnostic categories are useful for communicating across professions, for example, to insurance companies for reimbursement for treatment, or to school boards to indicate that a child has met legal requirements for placement in a special education class. Moreover, categories help us to be explicit about our understandings of pathology; research and experience can then lead to revision.

However, to take diagnostic categories literally would mean to regard them as having an existence apart from mental health professionals' efforts to organize data and to think about clients. I do not regard psychiatric and educational categories strictly as states of nature. Categories are *tools* that help us organize observations and formulate questions. I am aware that categories reflect cultural and scientific values and biases, that they are subject to political and personal abuse, and that we may trap ourselves into thinking restrictively when we entertain diagnostic questions. If I nevertheless decide that a diagnostic decision is useful in a particular instance, then my report ought to indicate how the client exceeds as well as exemplifies a particular category. The point is that diagnostic systems should serve people—not the reverse.

Question: But do you take psychopathology itself seriously? Somehow most of the people in these reports don't appear to be as disturbed as their diagnoses would suggest.

Response: I do take disordered and restricted existence very seriously. Making a diagnostic abstraction concrete and showing the ways it is true of a particular person does not render the problems less real. What it does do is to disrupt totalizing views of pathology. Presentation of when-nots and what-elses in addition to instances of pathological experiaction, all in mundane detail, opens the way toward constructive change. Moreover, as experienced clinicians write and read such individualized accounts, the details across cases sometimes gestalt in new ways, leading to revised comprehensions of that type of pathology.

The experienced clinician indeed reads reports with an eye toward how the material matches known diagnostic patterns (just as the assessor writes the report with that question in mind). When the reader is not a clinician, however, the danger of not taking the psychopathology seriously in individualized accounts can be significant. Our reports should try to make it clear to such readers that just because the difficulty now makes sense to us does not mean that the client can be expected to behave in liberated, responsible, reasonable ways. Understanding does not by itself render the difficulty less limiting, troubling, painful, or dangerous for the person or for the people around him or her.

PART THREE

SOME PSYCHOLOGICAL TOPICS RECONSIDERED

NOW THAT the basics of individualized assessment have been presented, it is appropriate to reconsider several psychological topics from the perspective of a human-science psychology. These chapters encourage readers to develop further their own theoretical foundations for their individualized assessment practices.

Chapter 9 presents six separate topics, each intended to clarify or expand earlier ideas, or to indicate connections between individualized assessment and broader aspects of human-science psychology. Some topics are offered matter-of-factly, some are playful, and one requires the reader to be open to alogical thought. The subjects range from individualized assessment's differences from psychotherapy, through exercises exploring reality as it evolves in the realm between perceiver and perceived, to qualitative program evaluation and qualitative research, and to the relations among rapport, privacy, and intimacy in the assessment situation.

Chapter 10, "Ethical Dilemmas in Standardized Testing" of children, shows some ways in which using standardized tests need not be at odds with individualizing assessment. At the same time, the chapter argues against allowing ourselves to slip into predominately technological attitudes.

Chapter 11 explores the character of facts and of their description within an individualized assessment report. This exploration is undertaken through a comparison of the works of the representational painter Andrew Wyeth with our individualized assessment descriptions. Both sorts of description turn out to be disciplined and personal. The differences between artist and assessor highlight the assessor's special responsibilities.

The final chapter summarizes human-science theoretical foundations exclusively, through the now familiar question-and-response format. Again, readers are encouraged to formulate their own responses, pose additional questions, and thus contribute to the development of a theory and practice of individualized psychological assessment.

CHAPTER 9

Further Aspects
of Individualizing Assessment

THIS chapter is composed of six independent sections, each elaborating an aspect of individualized assessment that was only mentioned in earlier chapters. The first section briefly expands the point that although assessment may be collaborative and interventional, it is not psychotherapy. The second section is playful and yet probably more profoundly foundational than any other presentation in the book. It invites the reader to explore reality as it evolves in a realm between perceiver and perceived, and to discover how being attuned to that reality allows language to speak beyond the constraints of everyday positivism (that is, the assumption that only physical things are real, that they are clearly separate and distinct, and that all practical knowledge consists of facts about these things). The third section is also playful in form, but addresses the more mundane (although timely) subject of program evaluation. Specifically, an allegory illustrates that just as a human-science approach to individual assessment allows integration of qualitative and quantitative data, so too the same approach can be taken in program evaluation. The next section is a reminder that individualized assessment requires not just theory, techniques, and natural science research, but also research carried out within a human-science orientation. Illustrations are provided for such research on how patients live their low-back injury, on being in privacy, and on being criminally victimized. The privacy findings and then the last two sections address the special relations that occur during individualized assessment; specifically, the relation between assessor and client, their relation to the assessment events, and the client's relation to his or her life as it is explored during the assessment. These relations—rapport, shared privacy, and witnessed intimacy—turn out to be quite different from what they are traditionally thought to be. As with the other chapters, this one ends with a question-response section, this time broken into subsections for each of the six topics.

Interventional Assessment Is Not Psychotherapy

The first task of assessment is to develop an understanding of who a client is—of how that person has been co-authoring his or her life. The second task is to develop suggestions for improving that authoring. If the suggestions are to address this particular individual, the assessment will have to engage the client actively and intervene in the client's life in three ways: First, the very fact of being assessed is likely to change a person's understanding of him- or herself. To obviate the likelihood that clients will experience the testing and findings as evidence of forces beyond their control, the assessor can engage clients as active participants in the assessment process. Second, deviating from standardized administration, the assessor occasionally interrupts the client to explore his or her customary (and alternative) ways of doing things. Third, as a means of jointly tailoring personally viable alternatives, the assessor guides the client in trying out these options, sometimes with test materials, sometimes in imagination, and sometimes by role-playing. It is this third form of intervention that may be confused with psychotherapy. The difference is that of purpose. The assessment intervention is in the interest of assessing and in developing individualized suggestions for bringing about change. Psychotherapy is one vehicle for pursuing that change, following assessment.

Clients do leave individualized assessment sessions feeling better about themselves. In the assessment session, they have been dealt with respectfully—as particular individuals who are capable of exploring and changing their own lives. With surprise, relief, and pride, these clients have reached new understandings of old puzzlements and problems. They leave with concrete, personally viable suggestions, many of which they have already tried out and modified in one way or another during the session. They may also have developed a long-range plan for further exploration, perhaps with the assistance of a psychotherapist or counselor.

But this process is not *psychotherapy*. Generally that term refers to an extended process that includes exploration of conflicts, styles, and meanings that are not readily grasped by the client. Psychotherapy requires not only more hours than are typically allotted for assessment, but also a relatively protracted span of the client's life. During this span the client tries out new understandings and comportments, not only in therapy but in a wide range of other situations. Psychotherapy's task is to bring the client through these attempts and through concomitant efforts to integrate his or her past, to a comprehensively restructured life in which he or she lives more freely and responsibly.

Individualized assessment's constructive interventions—the trying out of alternatives—are more akin to short-term counseling about daily life and decisions than to psychotherapy. In the interventional aspects of both counseling and assessment, the professional serves as a consultant, providing certain information, exploring different perspectives on past situations, and perhaps suggesting some options for the client's future. Although complex, ambiguous levels of one's life are usually addressed (directly or indirectly), what the client carries away to work on are suggestions about comportments that had been habitual or taken for granted, or about which he or she had been uninformed. These suggestions are tailored to the client's present readiness as starting places for further exploration. In contrast, our suggestions to the client's other helpers (such as vocational counselors or psychiatrists) may address options for long-range treatment or planning. For example, during an assessment the client might discover that although she resents her supervisor's criticisms, she had also set herself up for them by not checking out expectations in advance. The assessor might suggest to both the client and her other professionals that this discovery is typical of certain life patterns of resentment, and that these could, or perhaps should, be explored in therapy.

On the other hand, I have carried out collaborative assessments over half a dozen sessions as a form of short-term therapy. Some of these interventional assessments might more accurately be called counseling; some might be called crisis intervention; and a few were psychotherapeutic in the strict sense. The latter dealt directly and swiftly with critical dynamics with which the clients had already grown more or less in touch but had not yet faced directly. In these infrequent but greatly rewarding cases, the clients initiated restructurations of their lives through the assessment-for-psychotherapy sessions, and then went on, independently, to consolidate and further develop these changes. But although these clients and I knew that we were attempting radical changes, and that our sessions were meant to be therapeutic, the point still holds true that interventional *assessment* is not psychotherapy.

Sometimes at the end of the assessment process, I have contracted with a client to continue the sessions as psychotherapy. On the other hand, I do not always go through an initial formal assessment phase with my psychotherapy clients, and I do often use test materials within a therapy relationship for exploratory and interventional purposes. (I did not use tests for this purpose before I developed individualized, collaborative methods of assessment because standardized procedures might have disrupted the therapy relationship.)

When the number of sessions is to be limited, as is almost always the case with assessments, the assessor must be especially sensitive in approaching areas of concern to the client. If I am not going to be there later (as a therapist is) to help the client find viable options and gain reasonable closure, then I do not involve the client in exploring issues that are not central to the referral, and I do not end the assessment sessions until we both feel that we are in general agreement about my response to the referral issue(s).

The neophyte assessor sometimes tries to be "therapeutic" by helping a client to feel comfortable, "normal," reassured, unthreatened, and so on, or by offering resolutions. When these efforts are at the expense of systematically exploring how the client copes with situations, then they undermine the assessment's efforts at understanding and its search for viable options. What is more, these "therapeutic" efforts sometimes say to the client that the professional has judged him or her to be fragile or otherwise incapable of coping with ambiguity and stress. Insofar as the client respects this judgment, it is damaging. In short, the assessor should remember that his or her primary goal is *assessment*. Although an individualized assessment is necessarily helpful for the client, efforts "to be therapeutic" during an assessment typically are conducive neither to growth nor to effective evaluation.

Going through Words to the Between[1]

Mental health professionals and consumers alike are becoming increasingly aware that diagnostic labels (like "mentally retarded" or "schizophrenia") should be taken seriously but not literally. That is, they do indeed point to distinguishable patterns of behavior, thought, and affect. But these patterns exist as much in the eye of the beholder as in the labeled persons. The labels neither point to real entities nor are they merely words. The diagnosed condition exists between the labeler and the labeled person.

But most of us think of words as things that *we use,* much as we use labels. We manipulate them to our own ends. However, we often allow ourselves *to be used by* words; we let ourselves assume that nouns always refer to real things (trees, cars, aptitudes). In addition, we assume that the rules of syntax and grammar reflect *one* true order of reality. So we are careful, for example, to use nouns and pronouns as subjects and objects of sentences, modified by adjectives but not verbs.

The following exercise will help us to explore reality as a *lively process between* the perceiver and the perceived—that is, as being neither in the perceived nor the perceiver but in between. The title of this section, "Going through Words to the Between," describes how we shall go about this exploration. We shall (1) explore via (through) words, using them as orientation and jumping-off points, and we shall (2) go beyond words as they customarily function to a richer, fuller sense of reality as an experience in which perceiver and perceived, and subjects, objects, and verbs, interpenetrate one another. Let's begin with an excerpt from the report on Robbie March (Chapter 2):

> We (Mrs. March and I) entered through the recreation room, where my first view of Robbie was at his full set of drums, enthusiastically and loudly producing what seemed to me as high quality music. Turning off the amplifier, he looked me over and grinned broadly during a comfortable introduction. That image of an alert, energetic but relaxed, smiling youngster has remained with me as representative of Robbie.

Freeing the words

Now let's remove capital letters and punctuation, and thereby begin to let words flow.

> we entered through the recreation room where my first view of robbie was at his full set of drums enthusiastically and loudly producing what seemed to me as high quality music turning off the amplifier he looked me over and grinned broadly during a comfortable introduction

Next, let's pause here and there in our reading, sometimes going back to repeat a phrase. There is no right or wrong way. The goal is to let the words enrich our sense of the situation.

[1]This section is an elaboration, albeit with my own understandings and modifications, of a Duquesne University doctoral seminar presentation by Patricia Deegan and Kevin Jones. They cite as part of their inspiration James Hillman's (1977) "An Inquiry into Image."

we entered through
the recreation room where my first view
my first view of Robbie
view of Robbie was at his full
full set of drums enthusiastically and loudly producing
producing what seemed to me as high
as high quality
high quality music
turning off the amplifier he looked me over
he looked me over and grinned
over and grinned
grinned broadly during
grinned broadly during a comfortable

Now let's see what further meanings might be found in the original image. By playfully mixing modifying phrases and disregarding rules about parts of speech, we come to such statements as:

When the volume is turned down I am looked over
I am overlooked when the volume is up
Robbie is recreating in the room of my first view
Robbie grinned over
Enthusiasm is for Robbie a loudly producing, a musicing with quality.
He enthusiastically drums the high quality of his musicing when in the
    fullness of his roomy recreation.
When there is room, Robbie produces high quality.
When we enter his roomy recreating and view first his fully drumming, we
    have entrance to his view.
Robbie low volumes himself for our introducing comfort.
Robbie's off turning for mother is high quality music.
When looking over to mother, Robbie turns off his enthusiastic producing.

There are, of course, other possible variations, including some that are not particularly illuminating. (One produced in the seminar was: "Introducing comfort is a grinning broad!") Still, the exercise attunes us to themes that do not appear until later in the report, such as Robbie's enthusiasm, his looking to adults, his mother's wish to tone down his drums. Instead of a sentence-by-sentence view of the Marches, we have a rich, vibrant, holistic sense not only of the recreation room scene, but of Robbie's situation in general.

Even in the original report, my choice of words and juxtapositions was meant to re-create an image that would help the reader to hear the words more freely than usual. For example, I used the phrase, "enthusiastically and loudly producing." Grammatically, I ought to have said "enthusiastically producing loud music." But at that moment in the recreation room, *loud* was not just in the music. It was in my ears and in my taken-aback blinking; it was in his mother's unspoken desire for quiet. *Loud* filled the room. Robbie *was* loud; he *was* loudly producing.

I see now that I was attuned to more than I knew when I chose the term "recreation room" rather than "den" or "family room." Robbie was indeed into re-creating and recreating.

The original report also refers to "a comfortable introduction." By convention, I should have said that each of us seemed comfortable during the introduction. But experientially the comfortableness was indeed among us, not in each of us. The comfort was in the introduction of which we were all a part.

Implications for assessment

Of course this use of words to encourage productive images is relevant not only for writing reports, but also for the assessment process; one must allow oneself to be attuned to the "between" during the assessment if the later descriptions are to evoke the richness of the earlier scenes. Usually in retrospect I see which images best represent (re-present) what I have come to understand about the client's situation. But in the meantime, I try to be attuned to what is going on between (or among) us, and I jot down words or phrases to help me re-create these impressions later.

In an assessment class, during an oral reading of an *Alice in Wonderland* excerpt by Patricia Deegan and Kevin Jones, I wrote:

> Pat directing, but waiting for agreement from Kevin
> Kevin waiting but clear about direction
> Class waiting for direction, withholding judgment

In our different ways we were all waiting, seeking direction (orientation), and directing. But at the time, I did not know that I knew it. I did know to scan the situation for how we were relating to one another, and I knew to look for the dynamic quality of that relating—to a person's being engaged in more than one thing ("directing, but waiting"). As an assessor, too, I try to thematize perceived meaning and locate its sources. I may not see relational and dynamic qualities at first, so I may, for example, jot down "angry." As the session goes on, I try to locate where I recognized that anger, and I may find that it is in the client's tightly folded arms, in my tightened abdomen, in the now more careful quality of my inquiries, and ultimately in the still unclarified differences in our purposes for being together. This sort of attunement allows me to see interpersonal process—how we together participate in the evolution of a situation.

Later, when writing a report, "going through words toward freed meanings" can help one to capture and evoke this mutuality of assessor and assessee, and of subject, object, and verbs. I wrote these free variations after the classroom exercise mentioned above:

> waiting for agreement, Pat directed
> while agreeing with Kevin, Pat waited to direct
> Pat directed, "wait"
> when Pat directed, Kevin waited
> while directing, Pat agreed to wait with Kevin

Words are about a whole situation, not just separate parts. If we let words move around, breaking out of habitual and logical form, we allow ourselves to articulate what we were only implicitly present to. Allowing meanings to emerge in this way may seem somehow suspect; but note that there is a truth to each of the above Pat and Kevin variations. They cohere. Think too of those times when you have written a sentence only to discover that the same word showed up several times (for example, "He was just trying to be just"). It is not merely recency of word use that leads to this apparent redundancy. As it happens, the author of the above example also meant "he was justly trying." The word applied to the situation, not only to one part of it.

Another example may be more directly applicable to the assessment circumstance, where one is focusing on only one person (the client), using oneself as an access. Prior to another reading from *Alice in Wonderland,* an entire class was instructed to jot down notes. I wrote:

reading hesitantly, but surely
anchored but in motion
touching base with text and body
knowing our uncertainty, but sure of worthwhileness

Prior to free-varying, we shared our jottings. Our wordings and the order of what we observed differed, but themes were readily recognized. As we read aloud, each of us was asked where attunement to Pat Deegan's reading had been located. That meanings were between Pat and each of us, and not just in Pat's behavior, was readily apparent. For example, her "reading hesitantly" was in my cocked head and my leaning forward while waiting for the reading to straighten out. And "but surely" was in my confidence that the reading would eventually go well; "surely" was in my pencil poised expectantly. The "between" is not confined to verbal expression; the between is also the mutuality of our possibilities for action.

Following this exercise, each of us was clearer about what had been visually observed, and what had been going on between Pat and us. We were then better prepared to write a description of the sort that would be appropriate in an assessment report. Mine read:

Pat reads hesitantly, losing her place, apparently aware of our uncertainty. But her solid stance, continued reading, and straightforward gaze at us bespeak sureness of the project. She seems both self-conscious and eager to move on: she pushes up her sleeves, shifts weight from foot to foot, fingers the text.

When a report writer has been freed to speak of the between, to break out of subject–object separations, the concrete descriptions and commentary allow the reader to go beyond categories ("personality disorder," "confident woman," "FS IQ=97"). Through grounded but enriched description, the reader is in vibrant touch with processes that precede and exceed names.

Program Evaluation: The Helicopter Pilot and the Parkway Driver

Mental health and other service delivery programs funded by various levels of government are under increasing demands for accountability. In particular, programs are being called on to show that they not only are being run efficiently and honestly, but also actually accomplish what they were funded to do (for example, decreasing crime or suicide levels or increasing rehabilitation or employment rates). The federal government mandates that a certain percentage of Community Mental Health and Mental Retardation funds be spent on program evaluation. The Joint Commission on Accreditation of Hospitals (which also accredits CMH&MR programs) requires extensive record-keeping to demonstrate that meaningful services have been planned, shared with the client, and then actually delivered. State and local governments add their own requirements. This all bodes well for the taxpayer as well as for the client.

Evaluation of effectiveness, however, is more easily mandated than executed. The field of "program evaluation" is a new one, thus far drawing heavily on statistical data collection and analysis procedures borrowed from business and from the social sciences. Similar to psychological and educational assessment, in the absence of well-established ways of studying process—what individuals experience and do as they go through situations—program evaluation has forgone such qualitative assessment and instead turned to quantitative measurement of outcomes. These established procedures are helpful in looking at what quantities of people are served where, and at what proportions of them appear to be better off for having been served. Statistical techniques also help us to see patterns of service usage (for example, in terms of neighborhoods, ages, and referral sources of clients), and which program components are overused or underused. But how can we find out how these patterns happen? How shall we determine which variables to measure? On what basis shall we estimate which changes should be made? How do we know what the numbers mean in terms of citizens' lives? What personal experiences and outcomes are hidden within cost effectiveness ratios, service unit frequencies, and discharge rates? This matter is complicated still further in that it is difficult to decide upon measurable criteria for program effectiveness. For example, how shall we measure effectiveness of drug addiction counseling, when our professions are not certain about what the stages of rehabilitation and growth are, and how they might differ for different styles of being in trouble (for example, ways of being addicted)?

In addition, service providers—therapists, counselors, caseworkers, nurses, social workers, supervisors, and so on—are frustrated by the record-keeping demands of auditors, monitors, and evaluators. Despite bureaucratic constraints and frustrations, and already being overworked, they genuinely try their best to serve the people who come to them. To be told that one must not only do one's job but also document it client-contact by client-contact, often taking ten minutes out of every hour, can be infuriating. Fury turns to demoralization when the worker suspects that the data sheets, rating scales, and report categories simply do not allow what is meaningful about the service to emerge. From the provider's perspective, not only is all this recording time-consuming at the expense of service, but it is unlikely to demonstrate service effectiveness.

Both evaluator and service provider are calling for more meaningful measures, for ways to investigate and report not just output categories but processes. The guiding principles and the assessment practices of the prior chapters are useful for assessment not only of individuals but also of programs. However, rather than make a point-by-point comparison, I proffer some vignettes to explore ways that quantitative mass data and qualitative individual perspectives can be mutually informative.

The helicopter pilot and the parkway driver

The quantitative perspective is that of the traffic-watch helicopter pilot; the qualitative perspective is that of the automobile driver negotiating a parkway. The pilot observes, counts, reports, and predicts, all in terms of numbers. Through these activities he can also intervene, if not control. For example, the helicopter pilot notes an accident at a tunnel and predicts within how many minutes the traffic on the parkway will be backed up to a certain exit. He advises motorists by radio which alternate routes to take. The pilot might also report his observations on traffic flow at various hours to the city planners or to the transportation office for their consideration in developing traffic policy. Here, then, we have an example of the efficacy of a quantitative approach; the distanced overview of frequency, rate, and outcome is appropriate and useful.

When might the automobile driver's experiential perspective also be efficacious? Suppose the pilot, while visiting with colleagues, complained that he felt frustrated, that despite his advice to motorists, almost all of them persisted in remaining on their course. The colleagues might suggest a radio feature along the lines of a "man-in-the-street interview." The subsequent person-on-the-parkway interviews might reveal, for example, that most drivers figure they are better off staying where they are since others listening to their radios will now clog the alternate route. A few drivers might say they prefer to get to work late, excused by the traffic delay. Many probably would say something like, "It's well and good for the pilot to advise taking another route, but I have only the vaguest idea where it is, let alone how to get to it from here. I'd probably get lost, and waste as much time that way as sitting here in the traffic. Besides, it's less embarrassing to say that I got stuck on the parkway than to admit I got lost trying to find the alternate route."

With the benefit of these insights into what it is like to be a driver, the pilot might assure drivers in his next broadcast that only a certain percentage of car radios are estimated to be tuned to his station, and of those only a fraction typically attempt the alternate routes. He might also advise the city council or county commissioners that a public information media blitz might improve traffic flow. Public service TV spots could show diagrams of the city's beltway system, which is made up of pre-existing roadways connected by colored markers. Perhaps testimonials could be given by citizens about how one actually can follow the markers, that the signs are there when you need them. Each community newspaper could print a map showing that area's alternate routes, and so on.

Another time the helicopter pilot might note that during winter, even in dry weather, the traffic slows down inordinately from summer rates, and that drivers change lanes erratically and sometimes stop suddenly in the midst of the parkway. He might note that this traffic pattern correlates with increases in temperature following frigid periods, and that it reaches its peak when winter too has peaked. He might suggest research into winter-fatigue effects on the populace's mental health. He might even speculate about an interaction effect of industrial pollution and temperature. Upon leaving his helicopter and getting into a car himself, however, he would quickly discover what any resident of Pot-Hole City could tell him about: Chuck holes caused by repeated freezes and thaws interrupt the flow of traffic.

In part, the allegories are reminders that our basic behavioral-science research, and its application to program evaluation, for the most part have been limited to natural-science laboratory methods. For example, researchers often posit hypotheses, frequently of causal relations, and they count the results that follow the experimental intervention; or as in the example about erratic driving, they count some ongoing data and correlate them. Within these efforts, all too often our laboratory tradition leads us to restrict our reflections about what we ought to measure prior to laboratory-type research. Too rarely do we venture into the field to talk to our subjects (the drivers in the allegories). Although we know about this problem, we persist in our old ways. Of course, there often are needs for immediate data analysis that cannot await development of qualitative methods nor even extensive interviewing. Still, we ought to be developing ways of assessing individuals' experience with their service system and then basing our generalizations and experimental research on such assessments.

In short, the allegory serves to remind us that neither quantitative data (the statistics of the pilot and of laboratory-type researchers) nor qualitative data (the experience of the driver, and of clients, service providers, and other participants) is more real or more valid than the other. Each offers a different perspective, useful at different stages or for different purposes. If we look carefully at programs, environment, and physical structures on the other hand, in terms of *how people go through* them—*what it is like* for the client, provider, administrator, and so on—then we will have a sense of the living structure. In that way we will know more about what to quantify if we wish to do so. Qualitative information gives us knowledge of the *processes* through which quantifiable *outcomes* develop. For example, quantitative data such as increased school truancy rates can indicate areas that might profit from qualitative research into the experiences of the participants. Knowledge of either kind of data may be used to change the circumstances that lead to both.

Granted, the person-on-the-parkway analogy to a direct question interview within the mental health system is unrealistic. Very often people cannot say why they do or do not do certain things. In fact, "why" usually is not an appropriate question. For example, during an assignment for a qualitative research course two of my graduate students found that clients from a local community mental health center could not say exactly why they failed to show up for therapy after completing intake interviews. But when asked what it was like to go through interviews, they talked about how they had never before revealed so much to another person, and about how they had surprised themselves both by their own teeth-gritting courage and by what they learned in the telling. They went on to remark that one really could not go through something like that again with another stranger (the assigned therapist). An occasional subtheme was to the effect that after being so intimate in one's revelations, the suggestion that one should now go to see another therapist was like having one's lover say he/she was busy but one could go out with the lover's roommate. People *can* tell us what it is like to be in their situations. We can help them begin to say "what it's like" by mentioning some of our own (pilot-like) observations about program structures. For example: "I've noticed that there are no signs outside the building," or "The records show that most of the people who come here are retired . . . ?" We also can mention the subject's behavior (for example, "You seem more animated when you speak of your last session . . . ").

Program evaluation

To meet record-keeping and evaluation requirements, it makes sense to begin with the familiar and available: the quantitative. For political survival, we revamp and extend existing data forms first. However, these changes should not be made only in terms of regulatory agencies' categories. Staff members who have been required to use the forms should be asked for suggestions, from their experience of *what it's like* to use the old forms. For example, a therapist might note that it seems inefficient to fill in "diagnosis" on a client's form after the computer already has that information. Someone else might report that five-point scales do not allow differentiation from session to session. The staff should be assured that record-keeping requirements will continue to change in a sustained effort to identify and reflect whatever is critical for effective client service. True, service providers still are not pleased by the time required for this paperwork, and perpetual changes in requirements and procedures can seem like so much more bureaucratic hassle. But morale grows gradually as workers experience themselves as constructive parts of a demonstrably successful effort to provide services that work.

After evaluation and delivery staffs have developed these dialogal procedures, then clients too should be consulted (as in the above graduate student interviews of intake clients). The term "dialogal procedures" refers to a collaborative meeting of different perspectives, with the intention of developing new knowledge. The idea is to go beyond cut-and-dry checklists and direct questions (such as "Where did you find out about our service?") to inquire about "what it is like" to come here, to go through this service, and so on. As the client/resident/consumer describes what it is like for him or her, we have a glimpse of what happens—of process. For example, a methodone program client may describe how his therapy group has become his family, how it's really great to have people who always stand behind you even when you fail. After hearing variations of this account from other clients, we may hypothesize that for at least a segment of the methodone clientele, this situation may be a weak link in the treatment process. That is, it may be that otherwise well-progressing clients return to drug use just at the point of terminating the program, in order to retain their newfound families.

By looking together at the situations of the various participants (administrator, provider, evaluator, consumer, citizen), we can develop a sense of the structure of the *living program*. We can identify in what ways and up to which points a program is working, rather than being stuck with statistical data which seem, for the most part, to say that a program is never working as well as it was supposed to. Usual conjectures about poor success sound like rationalizations rather than points of entry for future efforts. From qualitative data (concrete descriptions of "what it's like") we can specify our new understandings of client–staff situations and indicate at which points we could now alter procedures.

In sum, quantitative measures provide overviews of categories and outcomes, which can serve as points of departure for exploration of what is actually happening to people. These qualitative data may then suggest more appropriate categories and outcomes for quantification, which in turn may lead to program innovations that make a difference to people's lives. Qualitative data are not merely subjective; quantitative data are not more valid nor more explanatory. Statistics answer the "how much" question; qualitative description addresses the questions of "what" and "how." Pilot and driver offer different perspectives on the same phenomena. Program monitors and evaluators, as well as assessors, would do well to maintain contact with both perspectives.

Human-Science Research

All responsible assessors make use of empirical research, including frequency data (such as dropout rates from intake interviews at a mental health clinic or percentage of juveniles with 4–9 MMPI patterns who nevertheless have no history of delinquency), descriptive data (such as characteristics of successful middle-level managers, or results of a questionnaire asking about problems of employed mothers), and hypothesis-testing data (such as experiments derived from theories of field-dependence, or outcome studies of lithium treatment of different categories of depression). Such research is used to correct or expand one's general conceptions, to guide one's thinking about specific clients, and to provide clients with information required for informed decision-making. However, just as individualized assessment makes use of some views and practices that differ from those of our strict natural science tradition, so too it also makes use of research conducted from a different perspective.

Rather than researching only from the observer's point of view, which traditionally has meant looking at physical—measurable—outcomes, human-science research also investigates the subject's perspective. A rigorous approach is being developed at Duquesne University. At this stage in our efforts to develop qualitative research methods, we typically ask subjects to write a detailed description of what it was like to be in a particular kind of situation. (For example: Please describe a situation in which you were in a state of privacy. Describe some specific ways in which your life is different than before your back injury. Please describe the time you were criminally victimized.) Subjects are asked to leave aside any explanations or conceptualizations, and instead to help the researcher to know what a particular situation was like. After reading the description, the researcher then asks the subject open-ended questions about missing or unclear aspects of the experience. The resulting transcription is divided into units that can stand alone—that is, that do not require surrounding material to understand the subject's orientation at that moment. A unit could be a sentence or a paragraph or more. Then the researcher addresses a specific question to the units, one by one. For example, what is the nature of consciousness here—what was the subject attending to? How did the world appear? What was the subject's participation in that attending? Or, how did this patient go about his life before his back injury, and how is he trying to go about his life now? Or what does this description say about the way this person goes about his or her daily life and about how the victimization enters and affects that way of living?

The researcher's answers to the question are written for each unit, staying as close as possible to the subject's own words, and dropping out any material not relevant to the question. These paraphrasings are then pulled together into a synopsis of the subject's description. After following the same procedure for additional subjects (perhaps half a dozen to several dozen, for each of several comparative groups), the synopses are collapsed into a structural summary that is necessarily more abstract, but that holds for each case and remains as concrete as possible. Just as clients become co-assessors, so subjects often become co-researchers as they discuss the faithfulness of the synopses and structural summary to their original experience. [See Fischer and Wertz, 1979, for variations of steps in qualitative analysis; see Fischer, 1984b, for comparative utility of qualitative and quantitative analysis.]

When interviews have been conducted carefully, these research results necessarily include subjects' phenomenal experience, its evolution, and its interface with other events. The following examples show that these features are particularly relevant for individualized assessment.

Being in privacy

The following is a very condensed structural summary of descriptions of moments of "being in privacy." A decade ago it helped me to answer my questions about how it was that even though I openly discussed my impressions with assessment clients, and they openly explored very personal material with me, I rarely felt as though I was intruding upon their privacy. The reader may wish to recall a recent moment of being in privacy (for example, writing in a journal, working in the garden) before considering the following structural summary:

> In summary, privacy is when the watching self and the world fade away, along with geometric space, clock time, and other contingencies, leaving an intensified relationship with the object. The relationship is toned by a sense of at-homeness or familiarity, and its style is one of relative openness to or wonder at the object's variable nature [Fischer, 1971b].

Next is a similarly condensed structural summary of disrupted privacy. Again, the reader would find it helpful to recall a recent incident in which privacy was invaded or disrupted.

> In summary, disrupted privacy is when attention is jerked from its prior object and shifts repeatedly among the intruder, self as caught by the other, and the peripheral world, as well as the lost object. There is a jarring aura of control being still out of grasp, with return to privacy being in the hands of the intruder. Relations are now in the styles of task, manipulation, or withdrawal. Time is lived in that future to be somehow achieved, or in a helpless, fixed present or past. Both time and space thrust forth as inescapable contingencies, limitations to be suffered or reckoned with. As attention flits among its three focal objects, affect varies with felt ability and desire to do something about each of them. Specifically, the intersection of ought-must (do something) with uncertain-can't is the location of such affects as irritation, anger, and impotent, frightened rage where the focus is on the intruder). Where oneself is the object (at the same intersection), the affect is unease, embarrassment, or shame as one finds oneself fixed. Finally, where the prior object is sought, the affect includes agitated despair, inadequacy, or anxiety. [See Fischer, 1971b, for the original study, including some individual synopses; see Fischer, 1975 and 1980, for additional synopses and social policy implications.]

Reflection upon this summary indicates that being in privacy is quite different from secrecy or even from guarding something private. It turns out to be a state of consciousness—of attending—in which one is unmindful of external matters, or at least does not feel called on at that moment to contend with them. Instead, one attends to a new sense of reality's richness. The collaborative aspects of individualized assessment occur within a state of *shared privacy* wherein both participants allow the referral issue and related matters to unfold in a new light and in their own right. External judgments or other objectifications are not salient.

Following this understanding, I then began to conduct assessments so as to nurture shared privacy, for example, by more carefully grounding the referral issue from within the client's perspective. I found that from within the open, nondefensive stance of shared privacy, clients were more insightful and more resourceful than had been thought. I was encouraged in my fledgling efforts toward sharing reports with clients and toward advocating client access to records. I realized thematically that people attend to matters more creatively and less defensively when they are not dealing with secrets and with the private, but rather are attending undistractedly to new understandings. Moreover, during this kind of attending, a sense of connectedness, of oneness, is enhanced. This research encouraged development of my individualized assessment practices and led to additional studies.

Living low-back injury

A psychologist colleague, Mary Anne Murphy, had found that she and the medical staff of a physical rehabilitation facility typically agreed on differential psychiatric diagnoses of men who continued to experience back pain after physiological indices had cleared. But she also found that differential diagnostic agreement about both psychophysiologic and "conversion" patients frequently did not lead to differential understandings or treatment plans. We undertook a human-science qualitative research study of those two groups as well as of a control group of men ("organic backs") whose recovery from back injury was not accompanied by "psychological overlay" (Murphy & Fischer, 1983).

We discovered that recovery had to do with continuing one's life as the kind of person one had seen himself as being. The men identified as "organic backs" found that although they would not be as physically able as they had been, and although the injury continued to be a source of occasional discomfort, they nevertheless could pick up their lives where they had left off. Often they had to accept a less demanding job, but each remained essentially the same person he had been prior to the injury. In contrast, the two problematic groups of men could not find a way to accommodate their prior existence to a partially disabled back. Both of these groups insisted that their backs were only temporarily sick, albeit with publically evident pain, and that there was no need to make accommodations; as soon as they recovered, they would be back at their old demanding jobs. Both problematic groups indeed had been extraordinarily hard-working, physically able, upright citizens, pillars of support for their families and communities. Now, being temporarily sick was the only way they could continue being themselves; they could not conceive of themselves as permanently partially disabled. With no realistic future to work toward, the present pain and disability became focal. This understanding on our part, replacing the older notions of secondary gains and unconscious symbolism, opened the way for more effective counseling.

In addition, we differentiated the "conversion" group as men who, utterly confident in their own rectitude, blamed others (mostly doctors) for their continuing illness, and became all the more determined to return to (and only to) their prior style of life as soon as the pain allowed. In contrast, the psychophysiologic group was a bit more introspective, for example, sometimes wondering whether they might have been to blame in some way for the accident or their nonrecovery. They alternated between determining to exercise their backs into whatever health was possible, and insistence that full recovery would occur medically, to be followed by return to their old life situations. These men probably thereby maintained continued bodily stress on the injury.

Of course, these ways of living back injury are not exclusive; the "conversion"—psychophysiologic characterizations may be regarded as reference points that may be of assistance in individualizing understandings of each patient. We proposed differential comprehensive rehabilitation programs and counseling strategies for these two groups. We also developed comparative clinical descriptions to assist diagnosticians. So in this case, qualitative research has been of direct assistance to assessors in recognizing the ways patients participate in their problems.

Being criminally victimized

For several years I advised interns who were conducting qualitative program evaluation studies for our regional Governor's Justice Commission. We often wondered what life experiences lay behind the volumes (literally) of crime statistics. Eventually I received a grant from the Public Committee for the Humanities in Pennsylvania to study the experience of being criminally victimized. The following presentation, one of several forms of our results, is organized in accordance with the temporal order of the experience.

> Being criminally victimized is a disruption of daily routine. It is a disruption that compels one, despite personal resistance, to face one's fellow as predator and oneself as prey, even though all the while anticipating consequences, planning, acting, and looking to others for assistance. These efforts to little avail, one experiences vulnerability, separateness, and helplessness in the face of the callous, insensitive, often anonymous enemy. Shock and disbelief give way to puzzlement, strangeness, and then to a sense of the crime as perverse, unfair, undeserved. Whether or not expressed immediately, the victim experiences a general inner protest, anger or rage, and a readiness for retaliation, for revenge against the violator.
>
> Later as life goes on, the victim finds him/herself pervasively attuned to the possibility of victimization—through a continued sense of reduced agency, of the other as predatory, and of community as inadequately supportive. More particularly, one continues to live the victimization through recollections of the crime, imagination of even worse outcomes, vigilant suspiciousness of others, sensitivity to news of disorder and crime, criticalness of justice system agents, and desires to make sense of it all.
>
> But these reminders of vulnerability are simultaneously efforts toward recovery of independence, safety, trust, order, and sense. One begins to get back on top of the situation through considering or taking precautions against crime, usually by restricting one's range of activities so as not to fall prey again. During this process, the victim tries to understand not only how a criminal could have done and could again do such a thing, but also how he or she (the victim) may have contributed to the criminal's action. Also, one's

intermittent readiness for retaliation provides a glimpse of one's own potential for outrageous violence. The victim thus is confronted with the paradoxical and ambiguous character of social existence: the reversible possibilities we all share, such as being agent or object, same or different, self-disciplined or disruptive, predator or prey. One may move from this encounter to a more circumspect attitude toward personal responsibility.

However, the person's efforts toward such an integration of the victimization are not sufficient. The environment must over time demonstrate that the victim's extreme vigilance is no longer necessary. And other persons must respond with concern and respect for the victim's full plight, including his or her efforts toward sense-making. All three components are essential for recovery of one's prior life as well as for development of a fuller sense of responsibility, reciprocity, and community. But no component is guaranteed. The absence of any of them eventuates in a deepened victimization of isolation, despair, bitterness, and/or resignation [Fischer & Wertz, 1979].

A lengthier version of our findings includes illustrative quotations from victims (Fischer, 1984a). Both forms have been used by intake assessors and therapists in evaluating clients' phase and course of recovery from criminal victimization. Often clients are greatly relieved, upon reading our structural summaries or synopses of individual cases, to recognize their own experience. That recognition helps to undo a sense of isolation. Moreover, these clients see and affirm the victims' active participation in coping with what happened to them at the time, as well as their continuing responsibility for pursuing their own recovery. Policemen, lawyers, judges, and other concerned citizens have reflected on the study and remarked on its social policy implications (Fischer, 1984b).

In summary, empirical qualitative research can:

1. contribute to general foundations for individualized assessment practice
2. provide leads for exploring a particular client's experience
3. provide concrete descriptions of pathological or trouble patterns of life, for use directly by clients as well as by human-services professionals
4. point to the broader social significance of a client's experience
5. contribute to general foundations of program evaluation

Rapport as Mutual Respect for the Limits and Possibilities of Perspective

In our social lives we recognize that before we can settle down to working cooperatively with another person, we have to get acquainted. So we observe and "make small talk" until each has a preliminary sense of the other's rhythms, style, background, interests, and relation to the joint project. This preparatory social activity clears common ground on which each differentiates and maintains his or her own stand. Imagine two faculty members beginning work on an assigned task (each with characteristic postures, distances, gestures, and cadences):

A: Good day to be working on class schedules!
B: It's a lousy day for anything . . . I detest Pittsburgh winters!
A: Well, I enjoy the fresh snow, but not all this sleet, slush, and dirt.
B: Snow's okay until I get out of my front door. You must not have to drive to work!

After further "socializing" and tentatively delineating what they want to accomplish, the professors find that they anticipate and respond to one another with a certain harmony, affinity, and mutuality. We speak of this relationship in an everyday sense as "rapport." Within it, the participants can cooperate toward their common goals despite gaps in their knowledge of each other and of their project, and despite implicit recognition of the probability that differences of opinion and other obstacles will arise. Through the ambience of rapport, they can become forgetful of themselves as individuals as they focus on their unfolding work. Unexpected developments can be received confidently with creative openness.

When this process breaks down, the partners progress through a dialectic of personal differences and sharedness, sometimes in rough and strained ways, until once again they find that they can anticipate and respond to each other in harmony as they go about their joint project. En route they have in effect acknowledged both (1) the inevitability of some differences in background that indeed "make a difference," and that (2) these differences have to be taken seriously if they are to be either transcended or lived with. When the task involves mutual creative exploration of one partner's life, as in collaborative teaching, counseling, assessing, and so on, rather than a relatively technical job like developing a class schedule, then rapport definitely is a necessary condition for looking and exploring *together*.

Scientistic transformation

At least implicitly human services professionals, of course, have known all this. Most test manuals and assessment courses include early sections on "establishing rapport." However, psychology's historical effort to model itself after the physical sciences too often has resulted in a scientized transformation of rapport's meaning. (*Scientize* is my own neologism connoting the *sanitizing* interest of *scientism*—the view that all science is by definition physicalistic.) When psychologists have strived for laboratory-like objectivity, thereby presumably removing themselves from the complexity and ambiguity of everyday mutuality, they have curtailed rapport.

When this process occurs, rapport—both conceptually and in practice— becomes a unilaterally established condition, monitored and manipulated by the professional. This so-called rapport has been established to serve the *assessor's* ends, ends of which the client is largely uninformed and for which he or she is merely the source of data. In abilities-testing, for example, the traditional goal of establishing rapport has been to elicit the client's best performance on that particular test. In projective testing and counseling settings, the purpose has been to elicit optimal spontaneity and candor, so that underlying problems will emerge more directly. The assessor is supposed to ensure that the client is motivated but not too anxious, interested but not engrossed to the point of inefficiency, comfortable but not overly relaxed.

The neophyte tester or counselor generally is instructed to establish rapport by appearing friendly but professional. "A friendly, cheerful manner helps to relax the client." "An organized desk assures the client of your efficiency." "Explanation of the use of scores will imply the seriousness of the test." "Intermittent approval and encouragement maintain motivation."

In short, our formal literature and all too often the practicing clinician have participated in the scientistic transformation of rapport into a one-way relationship, namely a condition in which (1) the *assessor's* goals, theoretical orientation, and data are primary, (2) the assessor is a standardized technician rather than an experienced partner, (3) the assessor analyzes the client's actions into separate abilities and dynamics, and (4) the assessor manipulates these "variables" to achieve optimal performance and data.

We professionals nod affirmingly when we read reminders that the client should be approached holistically. But when we begin to follow the methods set forth by our testing tradition, we often find ourselves thinking and working analytically in terms of defense mechanisms, abilities, response hierarchies, and of lowering anxiety, increasing motivation, and so on. As in daily life, this does not happen so readily if we are primarily interested in *understanding and collaborating with* the other person. It is when we feel that we *have to do something* about that person, especially if it first requires solving a problem, that we stop participating with that other person in a common world and scrutinize him or her in hopes that we will uncover a trait, dynamic, stimulus-response sequence—something to get hold of, to use in explaining the problem and deciding what else *to do*. This problem-solving is also an effort toward scientistic categorical clarity, precision, and control. Moreover, we often find ourselves pulled into this unilateral analysis by the client's expectations that we experts should take charge.

Before going on to specify the consequences of this transformation for both client and professional, let me affirm that positivistic science did not introduce it, but rather formalized an everyday process. Think of the two faculty members assigned to work out the departmental class schedule for the next semester. Their work flows as one of them sketches out a master diagram of available class times, while the other brings in coffee for two on his way back from collating data on past registration for each course. The freshman and sophomore slots take shape through unspecified but shared expectations (for example, that the two of them make a good team, that once they get started they'll work it all out, and even that freshmen and teaching assistants for intro courses should be the ones who fill the 8:00 A.M. classes).

When it comes to obstacles where differences in background and values are involved, the colleagues pause to attack the problem logically, asking respectfully what each other's information base and assumptions are. If clarification and compromise do not work, they may for a while shift the attack to each other, explaining away the opposition. "Just because your undergraduate training emphasized Experimental doesn't mean that's the only way to produce rigorous students!" "Not everyone can be as casual as you are and still learn systematically." Perhaps part of the common ground on which they will come together again will be the conclusion that students' complaints about not having enough course options are a function of undergraduates' immaturity or lack of discipline.

This everyday experience of the transformation of being-with into coping-with and back to collaborating-with illustrates that even though most of us do not take the textbooks literally in their advice about manipulatively establishing and monitoring rapport, in the absence of an explicit alternative to that advice, when we have trouble "making sense" of a problem, we typically fall back into that formally sanctioned and already familiar mode of coping: distancing, analyzing, maneuvering.

Consequences of unilateral rapport

When rapport is conceived as the client's readiness to produce for the assessor (rather than as a mutually working relationship), it is exclusively the *assessor's* responsibility to provide tests or questions that systematically tap into the areas that may be relevant to the presenting problem. It is then also only the assessor's task to make sense of the client's productions. What with the tests and interview already aimed at component parts of personality, and the professional in a task orientation and on the spot to come up with explanations and recommendations, the assessment is bound to become that coping process of distancing, directing, and partitive analyzing. In this circumstance the client is unlikely to contribute his or her own reflections and questions, and the assessor will have difficulty relating test data to the client's personal situation.

More specifically, once the client has been evaluated in an analytical way, neither the evaluator nor the recipients of a report can add up the categories to summarize the integral being who initially walked into the office. When findings deal with parts instead of persons, their usefulness is limited, and they may even be harmful. Imagine what happens to the youngster who returns to class characterized as "of Bright Normal intelligence, but difficult to motivate because of a tendency to distrust." If rapport is something established by the assessor in order to elicit optimal responses from the client, the assessor's formulations of these productions are bound to be mechanistic. This circumstance is all the more true of problematic clients.

Unilaterally established and monitored rapport can also lead, on the client's part, to self-protective distrust and restriction, which are hardly conducive to optimal performance and candor. For example, in the interest of increasing motivation, relaxation, and cooperation, the assessor tells a child that he is going to play games, but later the boy discovers the assessor's hidden agenda. Think of your own experiences of being interviewed, only to discover that the interviewer's show of interest in your comfort and relaxation was obviously in the service of some other specialist concern. When rapport is regarded as a unilateral arrangement, the client is less likely to explore the context of the professional's observations and conclusions. That is, the client is less likely to try to understand for himself or herself the necessarily relative and restricted character of the assessor's impressions.

When clients give themselves over to the assessor defensively or passively, they are altogether too likely to experience themselves as emitting responses instinctively, magically, or automatically for the expert's analysis. To the extent that they experience themselves as having no control over the traits, abilities, dynamics, and so on uncovered by the assessor, even if the latter does not divulge actual scores and conclusions, the clients' efforts to take active, directive responsibility for their lives are already attenuated.

When rapport is conceived as the client's readiness to produce material for the assessor, both persons focus on these productions and on the expert's possible explanations for them. Each is self-conscious about how these explanations might reflect on his or her own competence. However accurate such conclusions might be, that focus precludes the self-forgetfulness that is necessary for *looking together* in alert but receptive appreciation of the multifaceted realities of the client's situation. For example,

Assessor: As we spend more time together, I discover that your stare seems to me less threatening than vigilant.

Client: . . . Maybe that's what an employee meant when he said he had to get to know me before he felt he could trust my supervision. He said at first he thought I was out to get him.

Assessor: Oh, now I see how that could happen. Here with me, at first I assumed that you were angry about being referred by your boss! I guess your stare is many stares.

Client: Even for me. Maybe it wouldn't be quite so troublesome if I talked with more than my eyes—like now.

This looking together is also a looking toward open-ended understanding, and toward the possibility of the client's changing his or her previously taken-for-granted participation in creating situations. Although reflective and problem-oriented, this approach is nevertheless appreciative of the fluidity and ambiguity of human reality; here that reality is not converted into logical categories for the sake of (artificial) precision. Neither party feels inadequate or mystified that the situation is not neatly "cleared up." This mutual openness and cooperation is present in everyday instances of rapport in which the partners look together toward the evolving project rather than looking at each other. This process is severely restricted in situations guided by laboratory notions of rapport.

Finally, when rapport is unilateral rather than mutual, the assessor's opportunities for discovering his or her own taken-for-granted assumptions and participation in creating the assessment situation are severely restricted. Not only are the opportunities for correcting otherwise repetitive misguiding assumptions limited, but the assessor's chances for expanding personal as well as professional growth are lessened.

A return to rapport as a relationship

An alternative conception of rapport already has guided the above critique. I propose that rapport be regarded as *a relationship in which client and assessor have found that they share certain understandings that serve as common ground for joint, give-and-take explorations of the client's situations and options. This exploration is carried out through mutual respect for the limits, openings, and ambiguities posed by each other's perspectives.* By "perspective" I mean the way a person experiences a particular situation, coming to it from a personal history and going through it en route to present goals. Although this "way" may change even during the assessment session, at any particular point the person has no alternative to living the situation as it is experienced.

By "respect" in the above conception of rapport, I mean acknowledgement of the awesome power and complexity of another person's perspective. Through that perspective, a newcomer is seen as friend or foe, as understanding or as judgmental. Accordingly, that newcomer is or is not allowed access to the individual's personal life. If the client is to expand or otherwise modify his or her experiaction through the assessment session, the professional must begin where the client is and work from there. But if the client is to take an active part in this process, thereby taking responsibility for guiding his or her own course and helping the assessor to know when the discussion is off base, that client must recognize that the assessor's perspectives are limited, too. If this mutual respect for the limiting power of perspectives is to qualify as rapport, however, these persons must share common ground from which they explore openly and creatively the goal of new understandings and of new experiactional possibilities for the client. These moments are characterized by a certain mutuality or harmony that is absent from a stand-off or from an uncreative working arrangement.

An everyday example of the evolution and function of rapport as mutual respect:

Fourth grader: No, I'm not going to do book reports! They're too hard. You always give them back to do over. I don't know how. You don't know how hard it is.
Teacher: Yes, they are hard at first. I know you've been trying, Mark. Sometimes it's hard for me to try to help, too.
Fourth grader: Not as hard as it is for me.
Teacher: I guess not. Maybe *you* could help me, though. I know that you read well, and that you tell the other children all about your books. I can't

figure out what's hard about writing it down. Is it that some of the words are too complicated to spell?

Fourth grader: But you said we just had to *practice* book reports; the spelling doesn't have to be all right!

Teacher: That's true. Then I'm wrong about the spelling being what's hard about book reports. Help me figure this out. What's it like to start the report?

Fourth grader: Well, I don't know if I can get done by recess, and Tommy won't wait for me.

Teacher: Oh, so you rush and then I tell you to be neater and to say more.

Fourth grader: Yeah, it's sorta like that!

Teacher: Well, Mark, suppose you work on your report this afternoon if you need to. Just put it in your desk at recess.

Teacher and student have moved to common ground and an implicit goal, and from that point to Mark's accepting the invitation to share and explore what he senses neither of them quite knew before, and finally agreeing to a concrete proposal.

In short, rapport is not so much a *precondition* for assessment as a way *of working together*. One does not initiate this kind of relationship by trying to make the client comfortable, "establishing eye contact," making a point of exhibiting concern, and so on. Instead, the assessor begins the working relationship by being straightforward in the effort to understand the other's perspective—his or her purpose for being there, understanding of the issue, and so on—and in letting the other know about one's own purposes and what one does or does not understand. The motivation, comfort, and concern typically associated with rapport will fall into place as aspects of mutual respect for one another's limits and potentials as they pertain to resolving the assessment issue.

This type of rapport in the interest of a collaborative, interventional assessment is more akin to counseling or therapy than to a presumably objective and non-influencing assessment. I say "presumably" because, in fact, an assessment situation cannot be objective in the traditional sense in that the subject experiences the assessment process according to his or her own history and goals. Likewise for the assessor. There is no one true subject, but a subject and an assessor co-creating their understandings of each other. In actuality, for the physical sciences, too, there is no object in itself, but an object-as-experienced-by-the-scientist. Assessment that is grounded in a human-science psychology acknowledges its own inevitable influence, tries to be aware of it, discipline it, and direct it toward the client's growth. Rapport established in the interest of laboratory objectivity also influences the client, but in restricting, objectifying ways, and without formal cognizance of that influence.

This notion of rapport as a relationship has been revived in the hope that it may help clinicians bring their conceptions and procedures still closer in line with their intuitions and practical experience.

The next section reviews rapport understood as perspectival relationship, and then explores similarities and differences between two additional critical relationships that occur during individualized assessment.

Rapport, Privacy, and Intimacy

When I first began to work collaboratively with assessment clients, I discovered that one of the basic issues that I had to make sense of for myself was that of relationships—those between client and assessor, and between the client and his or her life as it emerged during the assessment.

My training in standardized administration had not addressed relations as such. The assessor had been instructed to establish and maintain rapport, which did sound relational, but upon closer reading the process turned out to be a unilateral effort to place the assessee in a state of maximal responsivity to the tests. Assessees' relation to tests had been addressed only in terms of the "stimulus qualities" of test materials, which were said to elicit response tendencies or personality dynamics. Virtually nothing was said about clients' relations to what they were revealing, discovering, and sharing about themselves. Eventually I came to think of the relations that obtain during individualized assessment as *presences,* that is, presence to one another, to observed events, and to clients' recognition of essential aspects of their lives. The following brief presentations on rapport, privacy, and intimacy describe what I came to know about these relations.

Rapport

I kept notes and reflected for about a year on those assessment sessions in which an optimum working relationship had been achieved. "Optimum working relationship" seemed to be the equivalent of rapport in the more traditional, unilateral assessment situation. Many of the more usual features associated with rapport turned out not to be essential to the working relationship. These features sometimes occurred, but not across all cases. Examples: making the client physically comfortable, motivating the client, initial exchange of small talk, assessor statements demonstrating concern or understanding. Instead, what occurred in all cases of rapport during collaborative assessments was a sense of common cause, and within that relation a mutual respect for the power and limits of the other person's perspectives. There was a give-and-take harmony, in which each knew that the other could be counted on to do his or her part in the assessment, all the while being mindful of the other's sometimes different perspective. Each participant knew more or less what the other's purposes were in regard to the assessment. Each sensed that "where the other was coming from" was both that person's access to understanding and a limitation to communication. Each knew that whether or not one agreed with or valued the other's perspective, a productive session required that it be taken into account. This understanding of rapport clearly exceeded the earlier unilateral conception, and therby could encourage assessors to think of the assessment relationship as a dual one. It also became apparent that rapport in a collaborative assessment is not established prior to assessment, but gradually builds during the work of exploring and making sense together of the referral issue.

This understanding of rapport was also helpful in explaining to humanistic colleagues and students of those years that rapport did not involve proclamations of equality between participants, liking or approving of the client, confession of one's own feelings, nor siding against the establishment. Conceiving of rapport as mutual respect for the power and limitations of perspective continues to be a helpful reminder that although we may use "objective tests," there is no single truth to be revealed, and that understanding the client's viewpoint is critical to productive assessment.

Privacy

The empirical study of being-in-privacy and of experiencing the disruption of that state indicates that privacy is not the hiddenness or guardedness we often associate with that word. Rather, it is a mode of consciousness, an intrigued attunement to phenomena in their own right, without self-consciousness, defensiveness, calculativeness, or maneuvering. True, concern for possible intrusion, whether physical or judgmental, must be absent for a state of privacy to exist. But that state itself is not defensive; to the contrary, within that state phenomena can be comprehended and appreciated in new, deeper ways. During psychological assessment, the phenomena to which client and assessor are present are instances of the client's comportment and their place within the client's life. Any calculating and analyzing are in the interest of openness to that life.

The particular kind of privacy that occurs during collaborative assessment is that of shared privacy: The participants together observe while phenomena begin to appear differently in response to open inquiry and exploration. For example, client and assessor together see that rushing through the Bender was unnecessary, and that perhaps the client's rushing through office work is similarly a personal style rather than a demand of the job. The use of tests, so long as this use is individualized, does not intrude upon privacy. To the contrary, tests allow both participants to witness unfolding comportment, rather than focusing on the person as object. The latter focusing, which often occurs during unilateral evaluations, is likely to result in defensive self-consciousness. Even though personal material is shared in a collaborative relationship, neither participant thinks in terms of privacy being intruded upon. Shared privacy is not a constant presence to assessment events, however. As in all situations, attention shifts and vacillates. In addition, from time to time the client ponders whether the assessor understands one's situation well enough to risk disclosing certain issues.

This understanding of privacy has been helpful to new assessors in that it makes explicit how one can explore personal matters and yet not pry, offend, or hurt the client. This explicit understanding is also important in that it enables the assessor to specify to others, who wish to continue constructive working relations with the person, the assessment conditions that allowed unselfconscious, and open, intrigued consideration of assessment events.

Intimacy

The above understandings of rapport and privacy resolved, at least roughly, my own questions about the nature of the relationships through which the results of individualized assessment evolve. Colleagues and students, however, asked how it was possible to maintain a professional stance during what seemed to be an intimate relationship with clients. I did my best to explain that one's professionalism was not altered, but eventually I realized that I should study actual instances of intimacy rather than talking in terms of assumptions and conceptions. I obtained written descriptions from research subjects of "an experience of intimacy and the situation in which it occurred." Study of these descriptions and later discussion with the subjects revealed that intimacy is presence to an event that places one focally and awarefully in touch with the core of one's being. The event and the critical aspect of oneself to which it points are of the sort one has cared about deeply, if not thematically, and in regard to which one remains vulnerable.

Examples from research subjects: (1) A young man holds and reads a valentine poem he has composed for a woman friend, and realizes that the feelings it expresses are truer and deeper than he had allowed himself to know. In this moment, he also realizes that he wants to share their lives in a permanent relationship. (2) A married couple had brought a kitten home from a pet shop several days ago. They had enjoyed caressing it and caring for it—naming it, setting up its food station and litter box, watching it tumble about during its play. But they were also worried because it hadn't eaten. It was as they looked into each other's face upon hearing the veterinarian's terminal diagnosis, that they realized how deeply their affections had been tapped, that together they would again risk such affection, and that it would indeed be a risk. (3) A woman had told herself and her friends that she had applied for reinstatement to a graduate program only to demonstrate to her husband that this is no longer an option, that the faculty long ago had rightly judged her to be an unsuitable candidate. The day after receiving word of her reinstatement, she joyfully shared with a friend her relief, excitement, and plans. Later, she spoke of how important the graduate program had always been to her and admitted that, despite her protestations, acceptance by the faculty and later by the profession were critical to her sense of herself.

Reflection on numerous other reported instances further revealed that:

What we call intimacy is an open, acknowledging presence to essential aspects of one's journey through life. In the face of a concrete event, there is an unexpected sense of coming home to one's self, and of the giftedness of that return. There is quiet wonderment and reverence within an aura of gradual unfolding and then of profound immediacy at witnessing and owning without defense, a continuing, inevitable, perhaps universal, and yet also uniquely personal theme. There is awareness of vulnerability both in owning this deep caring, and in continuing—as one must—to care. The moment is recognized as an occasion for reaffirmation and/or for reflection on one's nonconsonant actions. Intimacy is thus a presence to one's own life, to one's simultaneous innocence and responsibility.

That presence may occur in solitude, but often the co-presence of a knowing witness intensifies the significance of the moment. Intimacy may also be co-presence to the mutuality between or among lives. Poignance is intensified by a progression of symbolic ceremonial events (as at weddings) or of a progression of hurdles (as at Olympics competitions or in daily struggles); in all cases, risk, vulnerability, and commitment are highlighted [Fischer, 1982].

This description of intimacy helps to identify some mistaken assumptions relevant to collaborative assessment practices. First, intimacy is *not* a relationship between the assessor and client, although the assessor may witness the client's recognition of something as reflecting an essential aspect of his or her life. Second, intimacy is indeed a recognition about one's own life, and not necessarily a divulging to someone else. Intimate presence is more likely to occur for a client within a collaborative assessment than in a standard evaluation.

The constituents of intimate presence are built into individualized procedures: One's concrete actions, viewed openly within shared privacy, are explored in terms of their meanings for who one has been and how one continues to author his or her life; the sequence of tests and discussions builds a sense of inevitability of recognition; and the presence of a witness (the assessor) intensifies the significance of choice points. Professionalism comes into play as the assessor's responsibility to know when mundane testing events have put the client in intimate touch with his or her life. Care must be taken not to rush past these moments, but instead to assist the person to integrate them into the assessment and into action plans. Note that intimacy is not a goal of assessment, but rather a mode of presence on the client's part during the assessment, one that is likely to occur when that person genuinely explores who he or she is—where he or she has been and is going. I think that all of my individualized assessments have involved intimate insights. They are momentary recognitions that vary broadly in depth, cognitive thematization, and frequency. A lengthier presentation on "Intimacy in Assessment" appears in Fischer (1982).

When we examine rapport, privacy, and intimacy from an experiential perspective, we discover that they are not so much variables or even states of being as intermittent modes of presence—respectively, between assessor and client, between these two participants and the assessment events, and between client and an essential meaning of his or her life as recognized in an instance of assessment comportment. In the assessment context, rapport is necessary for shared privacy, which is necessary for witnessed intimacy. Understanding these relations is important for effective individualized, collaborative assessment: (1) When appropriate, we can better foster these attitudes, thereby allowing relatively open self-exploration; (2) we can be more mindful of the nature of the situation in which such exploration took place, and how it might differ from the client's other situations; and (3) we can see more readily beyond test products, and beyond presumably hidden secrets or dynamics, to process—to persons' relations with their ever-unfolding worlds.

Questions and Responses

Assessment and Psychotherapy

Question: Doesn't a psychotherapist continually assess clients' progress, as well as reassess initial understandings of clients?

Response: Yes, of course. And at some points it may be done collaboratively, and occasionally it may involve use of tests. But for the most part, it is a reflective activity. The therapist must be disciplined in choosing when to pursue such reflections rather than attending more directly to the client. It is still the case that assessment is not psychotherapy, and vice-versa.

Question: Couldn't assessment intervention be regarded as akin to therapy inasmuch as it is similar to behavior modification assessment and intervention?

Response: There indeed are several similarities between behavior modification and interventional assessment. Both engage in joint exploration with the client of the when/when-nots of problematic behavior, both heed the client's preferences for method of changing comportment, and both regard their activities as sufficient for resolving many problems. However, both behavior therapy and interventional assessment differ from psychotherapy, where deeper restructuration of the person's life is the goal.

Question: Isn't your distinction between counseling and psychotherapy artificial, and doesn't it promote divisiveness between the two professions?

Response: My focus was not on that distinction, and I may have made it sound like an either-or matter, which it is not. But I'll stand by my earlier remarks within their context, and simply add the following. Many persons with counselor degrees and titles have also been trained in psychotherapy and in fact do psychotherapy. Similarly, many clinical psychologists engage in counseling. So long as the professional is appropriately trained, and is clear about which intervention is being undertaken, I have no concern about who does which. Both professionals, if trained, can use individualized assessment as a springboard into counseling or psychotherapy.

Question: Do you specialize in assessment rather than therapy?

Response: No. I have seen myself as a generalist clinician. More of my hours with clients are spent in therapy than in assessment. My experiences in each domain inform the other.

The Between

Question: If free variation of words is more expressive than standard English, why not include free-varying exercises in assessment reports?

Response: In addition to being expressive, we must be efficient and clear about what we wish to communicate. Free variation helps the assessor find the best examples to re-present clients' rich participation in their situation. But I think that our language license should not go much further than I went in the

Robbie report, so that the form of our writing does not distract readers from its content.

Question: Do you go through free variation for every assessment? Isn't it terribly time-consuming?

Response: Free variation is a training exercise, which I presented here as a further illustration of the approach and attitude of a human-science psychology. But many times during a session or later while writing the report, I informally explore "the between" to develop its meaning or to find the best language for evoking it.

Question: What did you mean when you said, "At the time, I didn't know that I knew it"? You have to know what you know to write it, don't you?

Response: I meant that I didn't know it in a reflective, aware, explicit way. Moreover, the effort to express first-person meanings (the client's and the assessor's) is a creative act, a bringing into being, a shaping. In contrast to technical and habitual language, such expression is not merely a mirroring of an established reality or a matching of words to things. Finding expression for lived meanings precedes and allows reflection, both imaginative and deductive. First-person experience and efforts toward its expression vary with context and purpose; there is no pure knowledge for which the right words are awaiting application. Yet sincere expression is coherent—it speaks a reality that resonates among participants. For example, Robbie, his parents, and I all recognized the Robbie I described even though the description was new to all of us.

Question: Will psychology require a new epistemology in order to develop and utilize the reality available in the "between"?

Response: Yes. Such a theory of knowledge is not yet well established. But phenomenological philosophy is a philosophy of science and of meaning and already provides the foundations for an epistemology appropriate to human-science psychology. The major authors are Husserl (1913/1969, 1954/1970), Heidegger (1962/1927), and Merleau-Ponty (1942/1963, 1945/1962); also relevant are Habermas (1968/1971), and Radnitzky (1973). Polkinghorne (1983) overviews contemporary post-positivist, human-science systems of inquiry.

Question: The description of Pat reading hesitantly is also a description of your presence to her. Was that intended?

Response: I did not work at putting myself into the description, but that outcome was both inevitable and desirable. It was inevitable once I pursued "the between." It was desirable in that, although Pat is properly the focus of the description, the reader can see something of the perspective from which she was seen in that particular way.

Question: To what extent should clients be involved in program evaluation?

Response: Clients should be involved not only to contribute their perspectives on the system, but also to gain personal benefits. Client participation in evaluating a program is an important occasion for self-evaluation—for seeing how far one has come, where else one wishes to go, and what one might do to aid the system in becoming more helpful.

Question: How does this approach to program evaluation differ from systems analysis?

Response: In two related ways. First, systems analysis is more like the helicopter pilot's view. It is an external view of what appear to be sequential interactions of physically identifiable, interdependent, but separate parts of the system. A human-science approach accepts that view as one valid perspective, but also addresses (or at least is mindful of the importance of) each "parkway driver's" particular experience in its own right.

Second, the human-science approach views structure (here, the program) as a simultaneous shaped-shaping, and as mutually implicatory of the experiences and actions (experiactions) of all participants. This second point was not explicit in the parkway allegory. This living, ever-changing structure is difficult to describe—which is probably one (very good) reason that we move back and forth between quantitative and qualitative data; the former summarize physical events and give us a sense of consensual knowledge and clarity, the latter provide meaning and inspiration.

Question: Doesn't the pilot–driver analogy of the quantitative-qualitative perspectives break down in that the quantifying pilot is also an experiencing person?

Response: Yes, in that even though the pilot can be impeccably objective (for example, operationally defining each unit of measurement as the stuff between front and rear bumpers), he may draw his hunches for hypotheses from his nonwork existence as a citizen driver. But no, the analogy does not break down, in that all categories for quantification are proposed by people, who inevitably arrive at their proposals through life experience and intuition as well as through controlled observation and logical deduction. We would do well to acknowledge this inspiration and incorporate it explicitly and systematically into our research.

Human-Science Research

Question: Are you implying that it is necessary for assessors to conduct their own qualitative research?

Response: No. I cited my own research partially because I am most familiar with it, and because it is representative of one of the two major qualitative research approaches. Although these approaches are relatively new and are just beginning to accumulate a body of findings, that beginning is well established. In the Psychology Department at Duquesne University, following the lead of Amedeo Giorgi, we have spent nearly 20 years developing empirical phenomenological research methods consonant with our philosophical foundations for psychology as a human science. About 60 doctoral candidates have contributed empirical dissertation studies. Some of these, along with theoretical studies, appear in the four volumes of *Duquesne Studies in Phenomenological Psychology* (edited by Giorgi and colleagues, 1971, 1975, 1979, 1983) and in the *Journal of Phenomenological Psychology*. Colaizzi's dissertation is available as a book (1973). Similar research is being conducted by deRivera (1981; 1984) at

Clark University and by Keen (1977) at Bucknell. A group of scholars, principally at the University of Michigan and the University of Alberta, have established *Phenomenology and Pedagogy,* a journal that includes empirical phenomenological studies.

The second major approach is that of the phenomenologically oriented ethnomethodological sociologists. This group has been researching the implicit order in the ways people together create their social worlds. *Human Studies* publishes some of these projects; others may be found in edited volumes, such as Psathas, 1973 and 1979. Dialectical psychologists thus far primarily have criticized and reinterpreted traditional research. Their work can be found in *Human Development* and in Riegel, 1978, 1979. Geographers, too, have been conducting phenomenological reflections and studies; for example, Buttimer (1972, 1976) and Seamon (1979, 1982). Outside of these formal research alternatives, social scientists in general have been turning to qualitative case studies, such as Lifton's work (for example, 1979) and Levinson's *Seasons of a Man's Life* (1978).

Question: In the three studies you mentioned briefly, aren't the findings limited to what the subjects already know?

Response: Yes and no. Yes, in that the first line of interest is indeed the subject's perspective, rather than other factors such as physical environment or physiological processes. It is also true that articulate, expressive subjects facilitate this kind of research. And at least through the level of a structural summary, most subjects recognize the findings as familiar. But those findings were not previously explicit, especially not in holistic form; they were unavailable for use by either subjects or researchers. Moreover, depending upon the researcher's questions, previously unnoted aspects become visible. An example would be the back patients' participation in the continuance of their "illness."

Question: But don't your results depend on the instructions you give the subjects, the interview inquiries, and the questions you address to the transcript?

Response: Yes, of course. That is necessarily true of all research. In the traditional paradigm, the hypotheses, experimental design, and statistical tests determine the form of findings. The point is that all researchers should remain aware of this participation in findings, and should choose their questions with circumspection. At present, human-science researchers are posing questions that give us access to individuals' co-authoring of their lives, and that access is central to individualized assessment.

Question: Doesn't your human-science research emphasize what you call "lived world" at the expense of other factors like physical environment or genetic endowment?

Response: Yes, but this research is not seen as a replacement for research into the neurology, physiology, and so forth, of human comportment. Qualitative research must be still further developed, then truly integrative studies may be pursued. These would be fully "human-science" studies. In the meantime, it remains true that insofar as physical matters make a difference in the living of one's life, that difference shows up in qualitative descriptions.

Rapport

Question: Would you agree that rapport is not a once-and-for-all phenomenon, and that an effective session might include argument, impatience, and even permanent disagreement?

Response: Yes. Respect for the inevitability of differences in perspective is also a recognition that the process of clarifying and working through those differences is sometimes a jarring one for both persons. But it is the assessor's responsibility to invite the client to meet on common ground again so that even the differences can be explored jointly in a relatively open way. Sometimes the experience of having stuck through the confrontations together serves as that shared experience.

Question: Technical efficiency and objectivity evoke respect from the client and allow the interviewer to observe more keenly. Aren't these important components of rapport?

Response: Yes, the client must see that the assessor is competent in these basic ways if he or she is to take the tests seriously. But if scores are to be obtained from a cooperative client, and especially if the client and assessor are then to jointly explore the client's circumstances and options, a strictly technological attitude is not sufficient.

Question: Is it really necessary for the assessor to share his or her life with the client?

Response: The mutuality referred to is not a sharing of lives but of their goals for the client, of common ground in the assessment situation, and of awareness of the limits and possibilities posed by personal differences. Sometimes sharing the source of my personal perplexity about what a client tells me helps to clarify how the client's situation differs from my expectation: "I find myself wanting to help you get the answers right and to reassure you that you're doing okay; but the women at work don't seem to feel that way?" "When I was in school, you had to be in one of the cliques to be anybody. Is it the same in your school?" The client comes to know the assessor's life insofar as it is apparent visually, through the assessor's questions, and through what the assessor does and does not understand.

Question: How can one respect a rapist, a drug pusher, a mugger?

Response: If the assessor cannot get past abhorrence, then his or her perception, the working relationship, and the report will necessarily evolve from a context in which the client could not cooperate or explore options. If this assessor cannot find someone else to conduct the assessment, then at least he or she should specify that the report is limited to a judgmental profile of the client. But the respect we have been considering does *not imply reverence or even approval.* Consider the respect I have for a growling German shepherd guarding a gate I want to get through. If I have my wits about me, I know that I can't just charge through the gate or even try to pat the dog's head. I may stay around until it gets used to me, or offer it food, or call someone who knows us both. My respect for the growling dog is my acknowledgment that I have to take its perspective into account if I'm going to deal with it effectively. The assessor respects the *fact* that in terms of affecting the client's experience and behavior, the professional's reality (situation, perceptions, beliefs) is no more valid than the client's. It is the *client's* reality that presents both limits and access for the professional. Arcaya (1973) has written a clear, effectively illustrated account of how the probation officer and his or her client can work together despite their different realities. He describes this process in terms of active listening, responsive talking, and contextualizing of language.

Rapport, Privacy, and Intimacy

Question: Surely during the assessment session there must be periods when the assessor and client are not in that shared privacy state? Surely there are many moments when the client feels defensive, or at least is not all that open even to himself or herself, and when the assessor does think in terms of categories and is perhaps judgmental about the client?

Response: I am in complete agreement. "Shared privacy" describes a general attitude that evolves for both participants in regard to how they approach the client's assessment comportment. The term also describes specific moments of looking together and coming to new understandings. Privacy as presence is certainly not a constant state.

Question: Doesn't privacy in the usual sense of hiddenness become an issue when it is time to discuss how the findings are to be reported? That is, aren't other peoples' potential judgments regarded as intrusive, as disrupting privacy?

Response: Yes, very often. But privacy is a condition of assessment, not a goal. We are not interested in perpetuating privacy for its own sake. What is important is that the reporting be done in a way that helps others understand the client's situation, so that any judgments will respect the client's perspective. Then such judgments, although they may not be welcome, are more unlikely to be alien, arbitrary, or destructive. Moreover, discussion with the assessor about coming to terms with others' anticipated reactions can be a productive experience for the client.

Question: Aren't the popular notions of intimacy also valid—like "intimate relations" referring to sexual encounters, or "an intimate dinner" referring to a private, candlelit rendezvous?

Response: Dictionary definitions of intimacy mention *close, friendly, thorough,* which are indeed consonant with both my description of intimate moments and with the popular uses. Not all sexual or candlelit encounters are intimate, however. When they are, there is mutual recognition between participants that something central and vulnerable in each has been witnessed by the other. In other encounters, one or both may recognize that only one person has been in touch with a core aspect of himself or herself. Distinctions like these are important for understanding the modes of presence, the relations, that do and do not occur during collaborative assessment.

CHAPTER 10

Ethical Dilemmas in Standardized Testing: Toward Reflective Involvement

TODAY, the phrase "ethical dilemmas in standardized testing" appears straightforward but dull. Less than ten years ago it would indeed have been dynamic because of its apparent contradiction: The primary ethics of testing *were* standardized construction of tests, standardized administration, standardized interpretation, standard report writing, and maintenance of closed files. Ethical issues had to do with deviating from these procedures, intentionally or unintentionally.

The goal of standardized testing, of course, has been to obtain measures of the child[1] that could be compared against those of his or her age group. A standardized test, whether for use with groups or individuals, has been scientifically constructed and demonstrated to be reliable and valid under specified circumstances. Graphs and tables indicate the range of scores that were obtained. Testers are trained to judge whether these norms are appropriate for new test takers and to keep abreast of emerging research. They are trained also to administer the tests according to the manual's explicit instructions, so that each test taker has been exposed to the same testing circumstances, and the resulting scores can be interpreted in the standard way. Historically, the testing movement rightfully has taken pride in its scientific character: No matter which test administrator gave and scored a test, the measured results would be as similar as possible for a given child (this is, in fact, the basic definition of an objective test).

Ethical Dilemmas in Standardized Testing

Today, it is just this allegiance to standardized procedures that raises ethical questions. Ethics are the formal, well-established standards that a profession follows in order to protect and promote the welfare of its clients and of society. Dilemmas arise when a client's welfare seems to bring established standards into conflict. Such conflict is most likely when scientific knowledge, technology, and social consciousness evolve beyond a profession's established

[1]This chapter is a modification of a chapter in Mearig's (1978) book *Working for Children: Ethical Dilemmas Beyond Professional Guidelines*. The emphasis on children has been retained because our special concern for children helps us to see general moral and ethical issues more clearly.

ethics. The Karen Quinlan case is an example: Medicine now can keep bodies alive even when all human capacities are gone. Today's doctors must decide case by case whether it is best to uphold their pledge to maintain life.

Partly because of changes in the philosophy of science, partly because of humanistic psychology's teachings, and partly because of research on testing of minority groups, but mostly because of protests by those minority groups, users of psychological, developmental, and educational tests sometimes find themselves in conflict about whether clients' welfare is best served by standardized testing. In particular, we are increasingly aware (1) that tests are subject to discriminatory use, (2) that rather than being value-free, they inevitably reflect cultural and scientific values, and (3) that too often we have given more credence to test technology than to directly observable behaviors. We have given location on the bell-shaped curve priority over individualized understanding and helping.

Today's ethical dilemmas in standardized testing can be grouped, overlappingly, as struggles of a new consciousness that questions earlier versions of *objectivity, professionalism,* and *efficiency.* These groupings highlight different aspects of a general tension: A technocratic attitude versus involvement. Somehow we must provide assessment services despite the apparent contradiction between preserving objectivity, professionalism, and efficiency and still attending to the client's individuality. Examples submitted to me by practicing professionals and graduate student interns illustrate these dilemmas.

Dilemmas of Objectivity

1. Often, even as I gain clinical skill, I find that standardized administration of tests gets in the way of working effectively with personal material. To obtain objective scores and to ensure that a child's energy is concentrated upon responding to the test items before he or she becomes fatigued, I am supposed to proceed systematically according to the manual, but I'm sure that sometimes the scores aren't as helpful to the youngster as my immediate response might have been. For example, just yesterday during a Wechsler test, a fifth-grader began to elaborate upon the fact that the bigger boys pick fights with him; but I felt that I had to move him along to the next Wechsler Comprehension item. When I brought it up later, he wouldn't talk about the fights. I had lost a chance to explore part of the referral issue—"Mark's social wariness." On the other hand, it was also important to get as valid an IQ as possible, and I wasn't sure that this would be possible if he became emotionally involved in the fight discussion. I just don't know where my greater responsibility to the child lies, so I usually take the conservative course of sticking to the standardized procedures. Yet I'm not certain if that's the right thing to do.

2. My supervisor says our job is to provide accurate measures on the children and to indicate to which established categories they belong, since other people who work with the children and also locate services and funding for them best understand their needs in terms of categories. He says that it's

up to the child-care workers to use that information responsibly. But sometimes I think that for the child's sake it would be worth the risk of overstepping professional boundaries to add my comments about possible misinterpretations or about the best ways to use our measures for a particular child. He says that would just be my subjective opinion, which has no place in objective records. I see his point, but somehow it still seems like a "cop-out" from an opportunity to be more helpful to the child.

3. Well, I personally think it's unethical to objectify a client through overly rigorous standardized assessment. You can't see the kid as an individual if you treat him like all the others. And standardized results can't say anything about his uniqueness; they just say how many standard deviations he is from an average. But I'm in a bind here, because I don't think it's ethical just to go in and make decisions based only on my own impressions without test scores as supportive data. And I guess for the scores to be useful they have to be valid, which, according to the manual, means derived in a standardized manner. There must be a middle road, but I don't see it.

The issue in all three cases is whether the professional can be *objective and involved* at the same time. The answer is yes, and the dilemma dissolves when we reexamine the meaning of objectivity. In general, objectivity assures that observations are not *merely* subjective, that referents and procedures can be readily agreed upon and shared by different people. That assurance is what standardization provides. In a still broader sense, objectivity is the assurance that many perspectives on empirical touchpoints have been taken into account and have converged in a consensus. What we sometimes forget is that the final converted test score is only a summary, an average compared to other averages, of right-wrong judgments of specific behaviors. This distanced, general, and abstract quality of test scores should not be mistaken for a sign of a reality more basic or more valid than firsthand observation of the effectiveness of particular behaviors. Averages are generalizations, and they do not generalize beyond the specific kind of circumstance in which the data occurred. This assertion is true for the individual child as well as for group norms. Test scores represent the effectiveness of a person's solving particular problems. In the case of the traditional intelligence tests, for example, that set of problems was put together by middle-class, academic, white social scientists in a capitalistic society. The test makers valued efficient production, one-truth answers, and Aristotelian logic. In short, tests do provide objectivity via their standardization, but that objectivity is inescapably limited: Tests necessarily call for particular values and for only selected aspects of the test taker's effectiveness.

I believe that assessors are obliged to provide not only publicly available— objective—grounds for their testing conclusions, but also correctives to the limited perspective of the standardized test. These correctives may require assessment of areas not found on the test. Sometimes the assessor intervenes during testing to explore how the child is missing certain items or to investigate the circumstances in which the child performs more happily or more effectively. Often the assessor must assist score users to understand the limits of the particular scores and the advisability of additional information. In short, assessment is more than testing; the assessor must be more than a technician. The assessor must be *reflective* about the assessment profession's procedures, and the assessor must be *involved,* again in a reflective way.

So in response to the above dilemmas, I would amend technological objectivity with broader involvement. When Mark introduced the problem of those bigger boys who pick fights, I would have encouraged him to talk about it. The ultimate purpose of applied testing is constructive intervention—helping the child toward fulfillment. Why not begin that process during testing by tailoring the assessment and helping Mark to be a part of it? Moreover, for most purposes, an estimate based on additional items or other subtests will place Mark in the same range as the foregone IQ; besides, ranges or percentile bands are more reliable than a specific number.

As for offering unsolicited assistance to those who use scores, I am all for it. We are partly responsible for the uses and abuses of our assessments. Consumers should be helped to use scores in a less absolute way. Information on the circumstances of testing, information on limitations of the test for particular uses, and additional observations on the child help the recipient make more reflective use of scores.

Standardized findings can be set apart from personal or speculative observations by labeling the latter as such—for example, "assessor's comments." We can provide other workers with the data they request in ways we believe are most helpful to the client.

By now, the third case seems artificial. We rarely have to choose between strictly standardized procedures and personal impressions. Neither is adequate by itself. Each is a way station, not a final destination. When the assessor relates test scores to his or her own perspective, then both objectivity and the client are better served. However, impressions should be documented, so that they, too, are available for examination. For example, concrete behaviors, interchanges, or the assessor's personal responses could be described. This kind of involvement helps to individualize the assessment, which, in turn, encourages the child's helpers to see new possibilities. Otherwise, they may see scores as ceilings or limits rather than as present locations or starting places. This danger exists when classification by score replaces team conferences, and when the report is written in third-person, objectifying terms as though there were no historical context for the tests in general and no specific situation that gave rise to this particular assessment.

Dilemmas of Involved Professionalism

1. The medical doctor in charge of our unit in the hospital routinely makes out a referral for "WISC IQ and WRAT" (Wechsler Intelligence Scale for Children and Wide Range Achievement Test). He seems to think that numbers in the child's record fulfill his obligation to be sure every child has been assessed. My problem is that, as an assessor, I know that this referral is often inappropriate; other tests are often more useful for a particular child. But our director of psychological services says that our obligation is to

provide the doctor with what he needs for his own purposes. At first, I tried to give the tests the doctor wanted and then add whatever else I felt was helpful for the particular child. But there just isn't time to do both. Besides, with most of our children, attention span and interest preclude extensive testing at any one time. Anyway, in my opinion the scores themselves aren't all that helpful for treatment planning; they usually don't add to what the ward staff already knows from interacting with the youngster. And yet, the ward staff seems to feel that test results are the assessor's basic contribution into the multidisciplinary team. I think they feel more secure about their own judgments if they jibe with my scores.

2. Something that happened last week is still bothering me. I was supposed to do a "standard battery" on a five-year-old orphan whose foster parents of six months had brought her back to our agency complaining that she just didn't "fit in" and that they'd rather have a lively boy instead of this quiet girl. In order to give us time to investigate the situation, my boss had promised the foster parents that he would not yet tell Marie why she was being tested; she was told instead that she was being brought in for a "doctor's check-up." But respecting confidentiality in regard to the foster parents meant that I had to be devious with Marie, and I think she knew something was wrong and probably felt that she was defective. I wish I could have been more honest with her to help her cope with what was going on.

3. Some parents came in and wanted to see their son's counseling file. I explained that this file included the psychiatric consultant's notes as well as the school psychologist's results, and therefore the Buckley Amendment did not apply. They argued that the writer's profession should not limit parents' access to documents that were influencing their son's welfare. So I also explained that laypersons would be confused or misled by the language, scores, and concepts written by and for professionals. I also felt that it would be damaging to both the youngster and the parents to see some of the labels and psychologisms in the record. I know I had both law and ethical standards behind me, so why do I feel uneasy and defensive every time parents question me about access to the counseling files?

The major assumption in these instances is that professionalism requires uncritical adherence to intra- and interprofessional traditions. Traditions do embody a certain working wisdom, and client welfare does require cooperative relations among professionals as well as a judicious approach to innovation. To me, however, the above examples involved protectionism rather than responsible professionalism. In each case the clinician has neglected to examine the grounds for established practices and to clarify his or her understandings of the meaning of tests. The responsible professional places the client's welfare first, with personal confidence in one's procedures—confidence that comes, in part, from periodically questioning their contemporary salience.

In the above example, I would take the position that it is the assessor who carries primary responsibility for the selection and use of tests developed by our profession, and I would, in fact, begin to use whatever developmental and educational tests I thought would serve the child best. But also I would have to take further initiative, namely, addressing the situations of the other workers. I would have to take into account their desire to feel as competent and comfortable with the new measures as they were with the old ones. Therefore, I might continue to provide WRAT and Wechsler estimates at first, while gradually familiarizing the staff with additional measures. Through my way of speaking about tests and direct behavioral observations, I would help the staff see that scores are not absolute. I would help them develop their own senses of how scores are people-made aids or tools rather than states of nature or final results. Finally, by providing examples of how assessment can address children's actual lives, I would encourage the staff to pose their referrals as questions about a youngster's life rather than as requests for scores. We have become servants of the tools when "results" cover over more of the individual child than they reveal.

The example of the foster child Marie illustrates how easily we can forget about the individual child and about our personal responsibility when we think in terms of professional roles. The assessor in this case has created an unnecessary bind; one does not have to pit allegiances against each other. Instead, I would matter-of-factly explore with Marie her concern about being brought in, and I would help her to face the possibilities of the foster parents' wondering whether they were a good fit for each other. I would explain that I am not a doctor (physician), that I am not looking for things that are wrong, but that I want to get to know her to see if that might help her foster parents do the right things. In short, I would take an honest middle ground. Later, I would explore with my boss whether our office might formulate a policy of not confronting youngsters prematurely but also of letting guardians know that neither they nor we should deceive their children.

About the third case, the problem of closed files: I do think we are obliged to abide by laws and formal policies. But I do not believe that psychiatric or psychological records should be exempt from disclosure, and I have worked within the system to change that convention. In the meantime, in this case I would advise the parents of their options. For example, they could request that an independent practitioner evaluate the files and advise them about whether anything should be challenged or amended by additional assessment. Of course, I am assuming that the school staff has already discussed with the parents the general relevance of the file for the student's progress. Parents should be advised also about the status of any recent court cases pertaining to right of access, and of the existence of relevant advocacy groups.

The responsible professional examines the rationale for closed files and works to change protectionism from within the system. For example, I stamp my reports "Contents have been, and may be, shared with the subject." I can do this because my reports contain no jargon (unless parenthetically explained), no opinions that have not already been shared with the client, and no scores that have not been translated into classroom or everyday behaviors. In other words, I recognize that jargon, conceptions, and scores are tools that I use, but my results should consist of concrete suggestions for working with a particular child in a particular situation. Reporting on tools and categories alone is reporting unfinished business.

Moreover, the child, parents, and teachers can help to make sense of test data, and hence of the child's situation, when the assessor already has identified similar instances from home and school. These joint efforts also help the assessor to correct his or her own mistaken assumptions, and to develop a richer sense of the relationships between test comportment and other comportment.

Finally, I talk to assorted staffs and to school boards, lecture to my students, publish in education journals (Fischer & Rizzo, 1974), and write chapters, like this one, about alternatives to closed files. In this process I not only influence others but also develop and adapt my own ideas while learning from others' efforts. Such interchange is necessary for genuine professionalism. In sum, the responsible professional person questions traditional ethics and looks for constructive means of meeting their underlying intention of protecting client welfare.

Professionals are responsible not only for their personal competence, but also for that of their profession at large. (See your own association's code of ethics.) We must be concerned with the competence of members of other professions also when the child's welfare is in question. A professional dilemma arises, for example, when an assessor believes that another helper is misusing tests. Incidents like these are all too frequent: An inexperienced special education teacher interprets House-Tree-Person (HTP) drawings literally from a manual ("dark lines equal hostility"). Or a pediatrician, not trained in a test's standardization, does not take into account that parts of the test were developed in different eras with somewhat different implications; perhaps, too, he or she gives credit on the test for the first emergence of a behavior, before it is clearly developed, thereby falsely raising scores and expectations. Or a nurse administering the Denver Developmental Screening Schedule does not evaluate whether the mother is answering questions according to what she thought should have been the case or to what actually was the case. Or a school psychologist interprets statistically nonsignificant scale differences as evidence of learning disability. Or an audiologist's technician administering the Peabody Picture Vocabulary Test falsely concludes that a deaf child is retarded when, in fact, the technician had not seen to it that the youngster was attending to the visual instructions.

It is our moral and ethical obligation to go directly to such colleagues and share our experience with these complex instruments. Sometimes it is helpful to refer the colleague to textbooks on psychological testing or to specialized works such as Palmer's *The Psychological Assessment of Children* (1983) and Sattler's *Assessment of Children's Intelligence and Special Abilities* (1982). If necessary, we must then go to that person's supervisor or eventually even to his or her association's ethics or peer review committee. Of course, professionals must be tactful and helpful rather than merely critical. The welfare of future clients may require a good working relation between you and the problematic professional. Nevertheless, future children can also be helped by working through the dilemma involving the present child. The goals usually are not so mutually exclusive as to justify taking no action.

Dilemmas of Efficiency

1. I know that assessing twenty pupils a week does necessitate one- or two-page, often test-oriented, reports. I've learned much more about each youngster than I have time to write up. And I know that since the brevity of the reports makes the findings seem absolute, they may be misleading. It's demoralizing to all of us, knowing that there is usually so much more we should check into and report. But I don't see any other way. These kids have to be processed, and the county is not about to pay for more assessors.

2. We run a standardized screening program for developmental disabilites. It's really quite sophisticated, and we've been able to identify and help many disabled youngsters. Since this technology is available, I think we are morally obliged to use and even to extend it. But many of the teachers and many of the ethnic families strongly oppose the whole program, protesting that our tests are racially biased, and that labels and developmental classes hold their children back. Granted, there are always a few false positives, but the numerous correct identifications seem to justify the program. Moreover, even the so-called false positives could use some help, or they would not have scored so poorly on the tests, even if they do perform better in some other situations. Although I can make a strong case for the program as a whole, I feel somehow responsible for the youngsters who perhaps would be better served by some other kind of specialized screening or norms.

3. We're required by state law to keep records of each student's potential and present achievement. Standardized tests are considered to be the fairest way to compare children, so no one can complain about teacher bias. But I often feel that our records are too test-oriented. They're good for tracking progress or pointing out possible motivation problems, but I wonder if the lawmakers realized that our careful records don't help teachers or parents to develop more effective programs for the individual child. It seems to me that the students would be better served if we sacrificed group testing and just concentrated on developing constructive individual programs for children identified by their teachers as not keeping up or not moving ahead as well as they could in the classroom. But our director says that this wouldn't be efficient and wouldn't meet the state law.

Efficient recording of mass data seems to be winning out over service to individual children in all three of these examples. Records have become more important than education or intervention and scientific form or appearance more important than practical function. How could we have taken such a position? The historical reason is that in our earlier positivist, operationalist understanding of science, we thought of scores as more objective and even more real than actual experience and behavior. But now we recognize that scores are derived data secondary to behavior and experience. We realize that assessment is more than testing, that it requires person-to-person evaluation of the child's perspectives, situations, and options, as well as test scores. Moreover, service requires going beyond assessment of the present to individualized suggestions for the child's future.

Therefore, my resolution to this last set of dilemmas is to look for ways to deal more directly with the lives of children, reminding myself and others that scores and categories are unfinished beginnings rather than satisfactory assessment or record keeping. True, we still have to be as efficient as possible, especially for monetary reasons. For example, we might use scaling devices into which we could enter brief phrases describing behavioral instances that illustrate or contradict a child's score on the scale. A full range of scales could include such neglected areas as comportment outside the institution or clinic setting and, perhaps, self-responsible behaviors. Where life examples had not been filled in for various acceptable and unacceptable reasons, the readers would see that these records were incomplete, in contrast to the more typical assumption that a few test scores tell the basic story.

A national project on the *Issues in the Classification of Children* (Hobbs, 1975a,b) led to Public Law 94–142 regarding handicapped children's special needs. Schools now are required to write out an individualized program for each child with such special needs. Thus, a boy's record might go beyond traditional diagnostic categories to include, for example, that he requires "dental work, extra reading assistance for a year, and a volunteer big brother." Nevertheless, reconceptualizing overall classification schemes so that they preserve the individuality and specialness of each child remains a challenge for professionals in children's services.

Many assessors are already developing ways to render evaluations more relevant and to involve more persons as helpers. One productive way is by serving as consultants to the critical adults in children's lives. Brief interviews with parents and teachers, for example, can provide concrete life instances of the comportment that occurred during testing as well as the opportunity for mutual development of specific suggestions. Brown (1975) brings parents into the assessment setting to participate in administering tests. Behavior modifiers are training groups of parents to participate in the assessment process at home. Besides being relevant and saving time, such procedures go a long way toward returning responsibility and initiative to parents and children. Again, I believe that we are obliged to present fellow workers, the public, and our legislatures with piloted alternative practices and conceptions, and with specific suggestions for implementing them. Granted, such changes require greater skill and reflection than does score-oriented testing, but no more than should be expected of a professional. Competent students and professionals have been able to develop such practices in spite of their initial time-consuming struggle with the problem of working efficiently while still respecting the individuality and complexity of the child.

Short-range efficiency and cost-effectiveness, with their over-reliance on scores as the basis for placement, often are not in the long-range interest of the child. When a child has been insufficiently understood as an individual, education and treatment programs may fail to promote his or her development. In these cases, the purpose of testing has gone unfulfilled, and chances are that the underserved children will require longer-term professional attention. Children's welfare *and* strategic efficiency require that we take the time to go beyond scores to understand the individual child who earned them.

Responsible professionals therefore ask themselves, case by case, whether scores are appropriate and sufficient to promote a youngster's welfare. I have found that as long as I have presented useful data and suggestions, many situations have not required scores and sometimes not even categories. When all efforts to change another worker's overreliance on scores to the detriment of a child have failed, I have found that personal, direct proposals to take the problem to our area's peer standards review committee have sent the offender to our assorted standards publications for clarification. In the process he or she discovers that technological efficiency is not adequate to assure professional and ethical comportment, and change ensues. However, I should acknowledge that my interventions have been effective partially because of my reputation as a person who is familiar with developments in research and standards and who is involved in my professional associations' governance.

If this discussion sounds remote, let me remind the reader that Mercer (1973; 1975) showed how California Chicano children have been shunted into relatively unstimulating classes for the retarded on the basis of IQs, even though most of these same children were found to be functioning at nonretarded levels when evaluated in terms of after-school job performance and home responsibilities. Also, until recently, deaf children were expected to be intellectually below average. Today, they are not because the dynamics of their language disabilities are more fully understood and handled. Other handicapped children continue to be misassessed. For example, boys with Duchenne muscular dystrophy are frequently diagnosed as retarded when, in fact, they may be reflecting a limited learning environment or reacting to the emotional components of the disease.

There are two main points in these examples: (1) Test conditions are necessarily artificial and may provide inadequate overlap with the profundity of a child's resources or with his or her effectiveness in everyday life. (2) The American Association on Mental Deficiency (AAMD) and many state standards formally require that adaptive social and emotional accomplishment be included in determination of retardation. We know this, but often practice as though we do not, despite well publicized articles such as Bersoff's (1973) presenting rationale and procedures for psychosituational assessment. Through our IQ-oriented technology, we have created and perpetuated many cases of retardation. To function as mere technicians is not only unethical; it is destructive.

Although I may have to work within restrictive policies or laws for a while, I cooperate with colleagues to develop system-wide alternatives that meet the spirit of regulations and thus allow the latter to be changed. Efficiency and scientific form are not worthwhile in themselves; we are better off without them if they are not in the service of children's individual welfare and growth.

Summary

Procedures that work against the best interest of the child as an individual are unethical. Standardized testing becomes unethical when scores are taken as more real than daily behaviors and experience, and when they are presented as though they were independent of dimensions such as cultural values, historical context of test construction, the specialized, contrived nature of testing, the personality of the tester, and the child's sense of the situation. The danger is that scores will be seen as underlying causes rather than as extracted aspects of the child's complex, total existence, and that they will thus be taken as levels of capacity rather than as sampled areas for investigation or encouragement.

The dilemmas presented in this chapter showed workers caught between older traditions and emerging changes in our understandings of science and social responsibility. Ethical resolutions acknowledge new developments and strive to develop practical procedures based on those developments. In other words, they adopt neither a functionary nor a rebellious stance, but instead are responsibly reflective about earlier goals and emerging understandings.

My own solutions acknowledged the inevitable human involvement in testing and encouraged innovative intervention in the interest of service to the individual. All of these resolutions in one way or another rejected subservience of the assessor to tests and sought to promote recognition of the child's life events as the primary data and focus for concern.

Questions and Responses

Question: Isn't there a danger of overinvolvement?
Response: Yes, but that possibility is disciplined by recognition that involvement is a corrective only to the narrow, technologized senses of objectivity, professionalism, and efficiency. Our involvement should be guided by a reflective respect for the functions of objectivity, consensus, standards, and expediency.

Question: You do see a place for standardized testing, don't you?
Response: Yes. I teach my students standardized procedures, and to deviate from them only for very particular purposes. Even individualized assessment occurs against a backdrop of normative expectations. Also, there are times when a case calls for careful comparison with earlier scores, and standardized procedures are then necessary. An example would be assessment of recovery from brain trauma.

Question: Then you do believe that test findings like trait profiles and IQs are useful as such?
Response: Yes, so long as they are understood as statistical comparisons with particular groups of people who answered test questions in ways limited by the form of the test. Such test findings should be understood as leads for investigation of actual life situations.

Question: Wouldn't the issues raised in this chapter apply to work with adults too?
Response: Definitely.

Question: When you talk about different persons' perspectives on a child's behavior, are you saying that there are no facts independent of perspectives, that there is no truth in itself?

Response: Yes, in the sense that facts are always facts for someone, and every someone co-constitutes—participates in the forming of—his or her perceptions. Facts are not merely made up, but certain values, interests, backgrounds, and purposes are necessary before particular facts are formulated. This knowledge frees us to be responsible for what we test for, for the form of our data and categories, and hence ultimately for our impact on children.

Question: I can see the usefulness of describing everyday behaviors, but is such description scientific and professional?
Response: Derived, numericalized aspects of the person may be scientific, but they also are inherently artificial and incomplete. Especially in applied settings, there are more useful forms of being scientific. We can meet the requirements of scientific objectivity by specifying procedures, context, and empirical referents, all in everyday language.

A major issue is that we have to "dare to be ordinary" (Mann, 1971)—to make our data available, to be accountable in terms of everyday events and meanings. The more "ordinary" we become, the more we can offer uncommon opportunities for clients to participate actively in guiding their own growth.

Question: How much agreement is there among professionals about what you've said in this chapter?
Response: There are still test theorists who would say that traits and capacities are real factors that tests merely tap into. And there are some people who believe that testing technology should be separate from the broad and more involved task of assessment. But my impression is that by now there is a general theoretical thrust in the direction of this chapter. Many practitioners are not sure it is practical, or even possible, to individualize assessment in institutional settings. Others are not sure that they personally can learn these new skills and responsibilities.

Question: You seem to imply that assessment should be helpful in itself. Isn't this confusing assessment with treatment?
Response: Testing already intervenes and influences; I'm saying that we should make that inevitable involvement be a positive one. Moreover, testing is likely to be restrictive or destructive if it is not part of an individualized assessment of where the child can go from that point.

Question: Did you mean to imply that we are responsible for educating the public about the uses and misuses of tests? Can we be held accountable for what other people do with our materials?
Response: Yes. And yes we should be held accountable if abuses go uncorrected.

Question: Aren't there times when we should protect our profession's image instead of agreeing with criticism?
Response: We should respond to criticism honestly. But yes, the welfare of present and future clients demands that the public respect our competence as well as our self-criticism. We should help the public to see that competence.

Question: Why don't our manuals and codes spell out exactly how to use standardized tests ethically?

Response: The broad principles presented in our ethical principles and standards of practices are in fact consistent with this chapter. However, our knowledge and conceptions change. Overly specific statements would preclude development of innovations. Formal ethical principles provide reference points from which we may work out each case anew, always in the face of an evolving social consciousness and scientific advances. Every day I struggle with ethical decisions—with balancing established practices (objectivity, professionalism, efficiency) against concern for what I think might be best for each client. Similarly I must balance what I see as the client's immediate welfare with that of my facility, the community, later clients, and so on. Ethical conduct is a matter of reflective involvement, not of compliance with technical criteria.

CHAPTER 11

Description as Re-presentation:
A Hermeneutic Reading of
Andrew Wyeth's Art

I think one's art goes as far and as deep as one's love goes. I see no reason for painting but that. If I have anything to offer it is my emotional contact with the place where I live and the people I do.

Andrew Wyeth
(In Meryman, 1968)

THIS chapter studies Andrew Wyeth's painting in relation to the work of assessors. The comparison serves three purposes: (1) to indicate the kinds of presence during assessment necessary to writing a descriptive report later, (2) to encourage reflection on the nature of description, and (3) to explore implications for report-writing.

Human-Science Assessment and Andrew Wyeth

Everyday events, described in their own right, are the primary data of individualized assessment. This type of description is representational rather than quantitative or categorical. The client is represented—presented via a sample of assessment moments and of similar daily events; he or she is represented by being re-presented. Particular instances illustrate the client's general difficulties (for example, being brain-damaged, depressed, retarded, anxious), but in ways that also illustrate the individual's particular manner of living these difficulties. The sample also includes instances of the client handling situations effectively. These re-presentations of assessment events specify the assessor's presence to them at the time as well as his or her current reflections on them. The assessor chooses examples that various readers could recognize both from past experience with similar clients and from their own lives.

Individualized—re-presentational—description is an art rather than a technology in the following senses: The assessor uses his or her own life as an assessment instrument. The assessor addresses events in their particularity, beyond their membership in given classes. He or she communicates not only by reciting facts and conclusions, but also by evoking readers' experiences. The individuality of both assessor and reader is involved. This chapter, then, explores these and other similarities between the assessor's descriptions and those of an artist. The chapter presents a hermeneutic "reading" of Andrew Wyeth's paintings.

In traditional hermeneutic reading, scholars have addressed biblical or classical works, taking into account their historical contexts. In a hermeneutic approach one does not ask what the author (in this instance, artist) "really" intended or achieved, but rather how that person and we are in touch with similar truths from different vantage points. In this study we deepen and develop our understandings of our own efforts, both through discovery of similarities and through articulation of divergences. We do not attempt to do justice to the other's work itself; instead we focus on its implications for our own work. (See Sardello, 1975, for a lucid discussion of this form of hermeneutics.)

Andrew Wyeth is an American painter, primarily of landscapes and people, often referred to as a representational artist. His works are technically realistic, almost photographic in their detail. Yet Wyeth's paintings are not merely photographic; they are also composed, simplified, orchestrated. He is best known for his dry brush and tempera works. The former are first painted via washes of color and then detailed by use of a dry brush. For tempera, the brush is dipped in a mixture of egg yolk, distilled water, and natural pigment. Although difficult to work with, this medium allows strokes to build upon one another. The brush is splayed out so that the bristles create blades of grass, fabric texture, woodgrain. The viewer senses smells, textures, sounds; one feels drawn into the work, personally present to the scene. Wyeth's representational painting now is recognized as disciplined creative art. What touchpoints might there be between his and our own attempts at re-presentation?

The Particular and the General

The reader may want to look through some of the collections of Wyeth's paintings available in book form (See Corn, 1973; Hoving, 1978; Meryman, 1968; Wyeth, 1976). One can, however, understand this chapter just by following the discussion occasioned by Wyeth's work. As a first exercise, consider "Wind from the Sea." This painting presents a section of a darkish room, almost filled by a worn, transparent curtain fluttering into it from a window looking out on a flat landscape. Ask youself, "What is it that I recognize here from my own life? When have I been here?" People generally respond to this question bemusedly but readily:

1. This is my grandmother's farm. Even with the breeze lifting the curtain, the air is hot and dry. The days go by slowly yet too rapidly. Out here is the wheat field, and the [hired] hand's tractor trail.

2. It puts me in mind of this beach house my folks used to rent in New Jersey. Yeah, you can see the sand disappearing out toward the bay. I loved the beach. The cottage was a haven from the city. It was also a prison when we kids wanted to play outside in the August storms, but our folks made us stay in. I wonder if it's still there; it was old even then.

3. This picture evokes the attic room in Lexington where I lived during part of my graduate school years. There was a large desk right here in front

of the window, and the only light was from a gooseneck lamp that balanced on a stack of books. I worked at this desk only late at night when there were still things to be done before morning. My bed was over here; and out there is Lexington—the hospital that way, the university this way—where my friends, accomplishments, history were. Somehow this scene also recalls the poem by Robert Frost ("Stopping by Woods on a Snowy Evening"), with the lines having to do with promises to keep, and miles to go before I sleep.

It doesn't matter what building Wyeth actually painted. Its particularity reverberates with moments in our various lives, and through (not despite) their differences, common, shared themes become available. Through farmhouse, beach house, and attic we all are in wistful touch with past longings, circumstantial restrictions, fragile durability, historical flow. True, some of us cannot quite place the painting at specific moments in our lives even though we can speak of these evoked meanings. Nevertheless, these are *lived* rather than abstract or philosophical meanings. A symbolic or abstract painting would not elicit the same sense that we know immediately, if inarticulately, what the painter and we are present to.

An implication for individualized assessment is that description is located not merely on paper but at the interface of subject matter (client), painter (assessor/author), and viewer (reader). As assessors we should be mindful of this multiperspectival constitution of meaning; we respect it both as a resource for enriched understanding, and as an inevitable limitation to understanding. That is, understandings are as rich and as limited as the client's, assessor's, and readers' common ground allow.

A further implication, then, is that most of the incidents depicted in the assessment report should be ones to which client and diverse readers would resonate readily. The readers' lives are a resource through which they sense what it might be like to be this client. For example, an assessor might choose to describe a client's spat with his wife rather than, or perhaps before, describing an otherwise similar jailhouse brawl. Likewise, one might present a client's pattern of relating to his girlfriend instead of or before presenting a comparable pattern of his relating to his homosexual lover. The idea here is not just to reach the reader through the commonplace rather than the dramatic or overly value-laden incident, but also to reach the reader through what is familiar. Thus an assessor might also choose to exemplify a process through instances that occurred while the client was purchasing a refrigerator for his home rather than while purchasing some sort of highly technical equipment for the laboratory.

In Wyeth's "Distant Thunder," the top third of the picture is a clump of spruces and a hazy sky; under this is a grassy field in which a dog rests and a human figure reclines with arms lightly crossed over abdomen, face covered by a floppy hat. A box of picked blueberries, a metal cup, and binoculars lie nearby. There is a bare and spindly area near the top of one of the center trees, just before its apex. When I first saw this picture, I was startled to find myself vividly recalling the pine grove off the thirteenth hole at the Ft. Benning golf course. As sixth graders, a friend and I used to pack our lunches and favorite books and spend a summer's day in and around our special place within that clump of trees. The smell of those pines, and the red, slippery Georgia clay, the deeply breathed, dry air, the deep-blue skies, and the peaceful exhilaration of our adventures in the woods all come back. Wyeth's center tree serves as what we might call a "concrete universal." Its particularity in this specific scene—that is, its concreteness—also conveys a sense of universality, of spruce trees in general.

As I look back into the picture, my Georgia days recede, and now I am more attuned to the picture in its own right. I see the tension between darkening sky and summer repose; I wonder if this young man used the cup for picking berries. I imagine that he . . . oh, no, it must be a young woman . . . was watching birds with the binoculars. I wonder if she will be awakened by tickly grass and little bugs, by nudges from the dog, by a call from an unpictured person, or by a sudden shower. Had Wyeth painted a prototypal spruce, its symmetrical proportions would not have evoked my relevant history—through which this painting reached me and through which I came to attend to it more carefully.

So too with our assessment descriptions. If the reader is to use his or her own life as a resource for understanding the client, and if he or she is to attend carefully to the histories and futures alluded to by the report's description, then the writer's representations must be concrete. For example, an assessment report re-presented a client as dressed in faded blue jeans with a "have a happy day" face sewn across the seat; it was not simply said (as was true at the time) that this client, a student, was dressed in the typical casual attire of undergraduates. Usually the assessor does not know at first what general meaning will evolve from such observations. Only after that evolution can one choose instances for the reader, examples that best capture the particular client's exemplification of a pattern. For example, upon first meeting the above client, the assessor did not know that for her the patched jeans would come to stand for the student's particular way of being both upbeat and cynical.

Painter and assessor occasion a reverberation between the lives of the viewer and the viewed, and they do this through selections of concrete detail. This is not an accumulation of detail, but a selection. Just as Wyeth in "Brown Swiss," a portrait of the Kuerners' farmhouse, best evokes the Kuerners' world by leaving out a couple of windows here and some cattle there, so too as assessors we provide theme and focus by omitting as well as by including certain details. The assessor did not describe everything the above student was wearing; to do so would not only be inefficient, but would also detract from the meanings she wished to convey.

Now we come to several points of divergence between artist and assessor. Although we both choose our foci, angle of viewing, background, highlights, and contrasts, the assessor's "artistic license" is much more restricted. Wyeth was free to shift from the red strawberries in his prestudies for "Distant Thunder" to the final blueberries. The assessor is not free to change what was actually witnessed. The difference is that the artist uses the specific to communicate a general truth; the assessor makes use of the general to communicate about specific instances, which must be reported factually.

A related divergence is that the artist can leave interpretation to the viewer, with only the (often enigmatic) title as a cue. "Distant Thunder" is meaningful to us before we read the title and thereby discover that the dark sky has to do with a threatening storm. We are already attuned to the tensions between repose and intervention, light and dark, past and future. It does not matter if we think the woman is a man. Reading the painter's commentary in a text, we discover that the woman is his wife, Betsy. Now the painting has a more particular meaning for us, but we still do not know its personal significance for Wyeth. In contrast, as assessors we must provide explicit commentary directly with the examples so the reader will know what we meant to say about this client in particular. Thus the assessor said explicitly in her report that the student's patched jeans were one instance of what she came to see as his being simultaneously upbeat and cynical.

Yet like the artist, the assessor drafts "prestudies" in the form of an outline of the report, with jottings about which examples to include. While writing, the assessor, too, discovers that a different example than a previously chosen one now works better (like blueberries rather than strawberries). The assessor too discovers fuller particular and general meanings than were thematic when he or she began to write. Whether as artists or assessors, we often develop richer meanings as we strive to express what we had thought was adequate meaning.

People and Territory

Wyeth's most widely known painting is "Christina's World." A slope of yellow-brown grass covers four-fifths of the panel; above this is another hazy, gray horizon interrupted by two weather-worn wooden buildings including a house on the right of the skyline. Across the incline are traces of a trail to these distant buildings. In the lower section, left of center is Christina, a dark-haired woman in a faded pink dress. She is sitting on the slope, facing the distant buildings, her thin arms awkwardly supporting her forward-leaning body. One can smell the dryness of the day, hear the soft crunch of late summer's grass and weeds, feel the resistance and support of the soil beneath Christina's palms, and recognize the topography of the field in her fingertips, hands, and body as she rises toward what turns out to be her home. In both individualized assessment and Wyeth's art, terrain and person imply each other; they are interdependent. There is no gait without ground from which to push off, no focal object without its background, no to-which without a from-which, no action without a context. "Christina's World" is Christina; Christina is Christina's world. Wyeth has said that were he to paint "Christina's World" again, he would do so by portraying her via the field; there would be no human form as such.

Indeed, many of Wyeth's preliminary sketches of the Kuerners (a couple living in a farmhouse near the Wyeths' Pennsylvania home) show Karl and Anna in assorted poses, gradually giving way to background emphasis, and finally being removed from the picture altogether. Even so, these still lifes and

landscapes are for Wyeth portraits of the Kuerners. As assessors we are reminded to represent our client's usual terrain as it is present in his or her
gait—the brisk walk expecting no obstacles, the bowed head that has weathered
storms, the shuffle that has accomodated many uncertainties. I am speaking
here of worlds as lived by our subjects. We have access to these worlds through
their similarity to places we've been, places that invited, repelled, accepted, or
restrained our own movement.

Not only places, but more discrete objects of the environment provide
access to another's world. "Groundhog Day," for example, is a still life showing
a table-top set with a knife, plate, cup, and saucer. Faded wallpaper frames a
window through which we see logs from recently felled trees. The wallpaper,
though worn, is a delicate floral pattern, and the wainscotting and sill have
been carefully repainted in white. The white kitchen table top is unadorned but
for the simple knife and worn, also white, plateware. The logs seen through
clean panes are heavy, with logging chains still attached; the jagged, sharp log
ends point past a barbed wire fence into the kitchen. Anna and Karl are present
through implied past and future action, and through the quality of that action.

"Groundhog Day" is not a picture of abstract symbols; it points to actual
action, to lives. The painting thereby evokes my own biographical presence (in
this case, the starchy dryness of Grandmother's Oregon wallpaper and, concomitantly, my parents' postwar Frankfurt home in whose attic my brother
and I discovered submachine guns, above the family dining room, aimed out
toward the dwelling's walkway). Through this biographical presence the painting
also puts me in touch with universal themes. These have something to do with
life's inescapable, enduring opposites: nourishment and destruction, safety and
danger, order and wildness, indeed life and death—all of this in its matter-of-
factness. After I read texts on Wyeth's relation to the Kuerners, the painting
also reminded me that they emigrated from Germany after World War I. Anna
became a shadowy recluse, Karl a self-sufficient landsman; together they maintained the farm. Anna left gifts from Wyeth unopened on windowsills; Karl
gave Christmas presents of handmade venison sausage to the Wyeths. The
Kuerners cleared the land, grew crops and livestock, raised children. Painting
and commentary enrich each other. Of course the painter's commentary is separate from the painting, usually appearing in such sources as a gallery booklet
or a published interview. The assessor's commentary is integral to the assessment report, appearing as the phrases and sentences that surround the re-
presented events.

Both painter and assessor attempt to utilize the universal, via evocation of
viewers' biographies, to convey what it may be like to be this particular subject.
For both, commentary accompanying concrete description is most useful. A
further point of these last paragraphs is that discrete objects of the client's
environment help the reader to enter her or his daily world, to imagine its
atmosphere, demands, invitations, constraints, its records of an accumulating
past. So in the report on Robbie (Chapter 2), I referred to his drums in the
basement, his report cards, the camp projects in the kitchen, the encyclopedia
and tape recorder in his bedroom, the model ship he built with his cousin, his

baseball team's photo, the family scrapbook of athletes' autographs. Of course it is not usually feasible to assess people in their own surroundings, but when we can, that assessment is richer. When we cannot visit our clients, we can still inquire into their environments.

Pursuing the notion of "lived world" further, let us continue the discussion of what both Wyeth and individualized assessors are in touch with as they describe. "Cooling Shed" is a vertical painting of a corridor within a shed where milk is water-cooled. The entire base of the painting is a dark brown, earthen floor, narrowing as it leads into the middle third and to the right, where it meets the open doorway of the cooling room. If the painting were divided into a 3 x 3 grid, this doorway (with its view of the cooling room) would occupy the right-hand column off the middle third. All the rest, above and to the left, is sunlit walls of whitewashed boards. Our eyes scan across these boards, past the open plank door, and into the sunlit interior of the shed: a whitewashed ceiling slopes above the cement water trough on which two up-ended metal buckets rest. A pink cleaning cloth hangs above the pails. We are again struck by the synesthesic quality present in many of Wyeth's temperas. We feel in our toes and heels the path giving way to steps made heavy by the weight of full milk buckets, even as we feel that ground providing a resistive/supportive pushoff to those steps. Concomitantly, in our nostrils there is a commingled odor of soil, dry wood, fodder, manure—all clean, penetrating smells. Where is the dividing line between person and environment? Where does one begin and the other end? Here, we are reminded that before we impose objectivistic order, separating person and world, that person *is* her or his living of her or his world. The primacy of that lived world must be respected if one is to understand and work with a person. The better one evokes that lived world through the assessment report, the better access readers will have to the client.

As we dwell longer with "Cooling Shed," our fingers want to touch the boards, already anticipating their grain, their dry roughness and wornness. Upon reflection we may realize that the dairy farmer usually passed this way in a taking-for-granted manner, only occasionally noticing these things. Although the painter or assessor may see and describe details that render the subject and the subject's world visible, the subject himself or herself may not have focused on these details. When describing a client, the assessor should be sure to indicate at what level of thematization the client experienced whatever is now re-presented.

Both Wyeth and the assessor liberate themselves from facts as finished, from events as determined, to see instead how they are chosen, achieved, and still unfinished. Within this attitude, even still lifes are lively. Thus in "Cooling Shed" we see not just the product of farm values of cleanliness, orderliness, and hard work, but the daily creative, perpetuating acts to which such abstractions point. In the scuffed baseboard we witness the farmer's looking ahead of himself, attending to tasks yet to be done even as he or she lugs something through the doorway. We see sturdy, careful construction in the plank door's architecture, and years of use in its warped, worn, off-center state. In the buckets balanced on the trough, we see this evening's chores. There is a combination of planned and of prechosen, repetitive, habitual action here; such is the nature of our daily lives.

Individualized assessment differs from art in its systematic rather than occasional or chance effort to engage its subject (client) in collaborative examination of the previously habitual, taken-for-granted living of situations. I can imagine the farmer looking at this painting (or reading my description here), and perhaps commenting that it is his wife who keeps the shed clean, while he is concerned with its function. Perhaps, viewing the painting and thinking of its contrast with the newly built shed years ago, he might comment that actually he has been thinking of selling the herd and tearing down the shed. Mrs. Wyeth has in fact reported that upon viewing "Groundhog Day," Karl Kuerner noted a hairline crack in one of the window panes, and hurried home to repair it. In these examples, we find intentions and process more readily available when we view environments as lived rather than as merely factual. And we find that when we (both artists and assessors) share our particular views with our subjects, they can clarify matters for us. They also can bring background into focus, reflect on it, and take new action.

However, neither assessor nor artist is limited to portrayal of the merely habitual. The power of Wyeth's paintings is largely their evocation of dynamics—the tension between what is given and what is possible. We find ourselves with certain bodies, pasts, sociocultural contexts, contingencies, and with the necessity of choosing their meanings and our future actions. Thus the power of "Christina's World" is not just its open-spaced, youthful future; it is also the contrast of those aspects with the thinness and awkwardness of Christina's arms—which imply what we later read: that Christina's legs have been paralyzed since high school. Similarly, "Hay Ledge" portrays brother Alvaro's dory resting incongruously in the hay loft. This Maine lobster fisherman placed it there without comment when he decided after their parents' death that he must become a blueberry farmer so that he could look after Christina. The painting calls forth both a sense of peace, stillness, different possibilities put away and taken up, and of things out of place, alternately given up and yearned for.

So too as assessors, we search for access to our clients' particular living of life's ambiguities—of each moment's necessity and possibility; past and future, life and death, public and private. And we search for ways to make these visible, to re-present them to our readers. Such dynamics do not underlie, but *are* the client's actions and inclinations, always in particular contexts. Specifying actual actions *and* terrain not only bypasses objectifying abstraction ("the trainee has passive-aggressive tendencies"), but helps the reader to imagine what it might be like to be in the client's situation. The reader then can understand personally as well as theoretically.

The individualized assessment might report that the above trainee, whose name was Barbara Martin, brought her roommate's mail up to the apartment for her, but let it remain out of view after watching the cat knock it off the end table. Likewise, the assessor might report that Barbara neglected to correct the practitioner's (mistaken) assumption that her MMPI and interest tests were on file in the University Counseling Center. The practitioner might also specify that both of these events had occurred when Barbara wanted to depend upon the other person for support (the roommate for friendship, for accompaniment to a "Management for Women" lecture, as someone to help plan a Christmas cookie baking project; the practitioner for sympathy and for his recommendations about whether she should change her graduate major to accounting and whether she should move back home with her parents). In both cases, however, the other person had ignored her unspoken but apparent request for direct assistance. She was uncertain whether she was dealing with friends or foes. This concrete description regrounds the earlier designation of "passive-aggressive tendencies." This description allows the reader both to see the pattern through which Barbara has become stuck *and* to consider points of access for intervention in her actual situations.

At this point I have introduced another divergence from Wyeth's paintings. Assessment description and commentary ought to present action portraits, descriptions that show the client shaping his or her world even as he or she is shaped by it. For example, Barbara Martin might be described concretely by the assessor as sitting with feet tucked under her chair, hands folded in lap, eyes glancing up from a downward gaze. The assessor describes his own presence as initially conflicted: desiring to reassure Barbara in a protective manner, and yet feeling manipulated by her implicit demands. He then finds himself being unusually directive in his questions and instructions. Later Barbara affirms that this scene was relevant to Personnel's referral question. She has complained that her supervisors leave her with less room for initiative than other employees are given. With the assessor's help, she begins to see how she has contributed to her problem. This joint participation in the evolution of her situation is easier to present through juxtaposed scenes and commentary (such as the above) than in a single painted scene. The report writer should choose instances that depict the evolution of these situations. Single-image examples and portraits may be accurate and even powerful, but they are limited in the extent to which they can evoke the person's ways of going about his or her particular life. They present only one instance, one context; without the company of other instances and contexts, they lead us to think of general types.

Wyeth's "The Drifter" is a portrait of a black man's head, chest, and wide shoulders. He is wearing an unzipped corduroy jacket over a shirt and a shapeless sweater. He appears to be in his thirties. He is facing the viewer but with eyelids lowered. His broad face is composed—attentive but inactive. As in most of Wyeth's work, the colors are earth tones: brown skin, the wheat-colored worn jacket, the rust-colored wool sweater. The bold portrait leaves room only for white-gray background. When flipping through the book in which "The Drifter" appears, I had often noted this portrait as another of those very realistic interesting faces. Only when I later read the commentary did I find that the subject was a merchant seaman, temporarily returning to Pennsylvania in the 1960s. The viewer can feel this man's steady breathing, sense his own sense of waiting while being on his way to unknown destinations. Wyeth is quoted as saying about this painting, "Perhaps to like it you've got to be somebody who feels the pathos of Negroes. And it has violence in it—yet repressed" (Meryman,

1968). Painter and viewer are in touch with the immanent surging of an awakening race. Still, just from the painting it is difficult to imagine how he might rise from his chair, speak, leave. Perhaps softly but purposefully? But then again, perhaps with growing impatience and awkward gestures? What objects will be in his way, will he use, will he take for granted? The assessor must be sure to go beyond evocation of types (of person or situation) to illustrate how this individual in particular circumstances sustains and exceeds as well as exemplifies the general pattern.

Creativity and Discipline

The creative artist, the one who surpasses technique, brings into being a variant view of truth. Art movements (such as impressionism or cubism) do not deal with revised technique for its own sake, but to show us that there is a different way of seeing and thinking about our world. They create new visions of reality; they disrupt our old assumptions. They transform our customary views as we find ourselves struggling to make this new view once again familiar. So too, the individualized assessor strives to present the client in a manner that conveys a transcendent reality, one that helps readers to develop revised understandings of the client. Transformative description goes beyond normative scores, history, diagnosis, biology, and environment, to present all of these in terms of the client's lived world.

Like art, the descriptions in our reports do not merely present factual data, but also evoke a personal sense of the subject matter. In each case, the viewer is aware at some level that his or her comprehension of the subject is his or her own, and likewise recognizes that the production too is perspectival—*a* view of reality presented by the artist or assessor. In each case, truth is respected as inevitably ambiguous, as dependent on access. Such humanly known truth is forever unfinished. Forever evolving vantage points, contexts, purposes all point to an order that can never be known in itself and that should not be accepted simply as "given."

However, neither Wyeth nor the assessor attempts to argue abstract ideas about truth in our descriptions. We may do so in art magazine interviews or in chapters such as this, but our respective workaday productions are applied creative enterprises rather than theoretical ones. It is the particular subject that we wish to present creatively, that is, by using our personal resonances in a way that encourages new sensitivity and understanding. Neither the artist nor the assessor wishes to proselytize on behalf of a theory, nor to allow our techniques to draw attention from our subject. Both abstraction and technique instead serve concrete presentation.

Such an accomplishment, however, requires the painter or writer to master traditional tools and techniques. The artist must be proficient with drawing, mixings of paints, recognizing proportion and perspective. The assessor must be knowledgeble about test construction, norms, recent theory and research, and patterns of pathology. He or she must be proficient at interviewing, involving the client, writing efficiently, answering the referral question directly, addressing the interests of potential readers, and describing the kind of person the client is while also evoking an individualized sense of that person.

Beyond technical proficiency, what sort of discipline—of principled effort and constraint—do both Wyeth and the individualized assessor bring to bear upon their work? It is a balanced tension between subjective involvement and responsibile reflection. Personal resonance allows access to others' lives. We must encourage this openness. But as artists or assessors our purpose is to share this sense of the subject's life with others and, moreover, to emphasize the subject we've come to know rather than our own meanings. The latter are a tool for understanding, not the theme. One first recognizes that he or she has been touched; then one attempts to get hold of that experience, to identify its personal and worldly anchorages. One further reflects on its significance for others, perhaps asking oneself questions about general structures of which this is an instance, or about how the experience might be relevant to viewers or readers. Finally, one reflects on ways to show what one was in touch with; ways to be true to one's personal inspiration while portraying the phenomenon in its own right and in ways that are likely to reach others.

Wyeth has described himself, for example, walking one morning through the Pennsylvania countryside near his home and discovering fallen apples touched by the autumn's first frost. He rushed home to recreate the moment, first by boldly sloshing color (browns and reds) on his paper. Then he began to shape the apples. "Cider Apples" is an unfinished result of this effort. One can see the bold washes of color that bespeak urgency, drama, depth. Many of his other paintings also retain traces of wild beginnings—splotches of paint on the margins of finished work, and on unfinished beginnings, color on top of color adjacent to color with form here and there hinting at a not-quite-captured mood.

Wyeth has said that a major reason for developing his use of tempera was the discipline it requires of him—in effect to go through mood or affect to the specific visible features that seem essential to it, and to then portray them faithfully, in detail. Interpersonal and existential meanings are recognized first in terms of how we find ourselves affected—what Wyeth, like many psychologists, calls emotion. As assessors, if we are to go further than looking for signs and symptoms and thinking analytically, then we must keep ourselves open to being affected by the client. For the assessor, the purpose of this openness is to get to know the other person's particular ways of going through this life we share. The assessor considers these understandings in terms of the referral issues and of patterns of pathology, environmental contingencies, and so on, and then selects examples for readers. The examples are chosen as those relevant to the referral and to recommendations, but concomitantly as those that might put the reader in affective touch with the client. The assessor chooses "concrete universals" that may resonate with the readers' lives. This process indeed requires discipline! One must restrict what one reports of his or her own experience to what is helpful to client and reader. The assessor should be directly evident in the report only as context, not as focus.

These moments when the assessor is affected are not usually full of drama and excitement; they are quietly poignant (like the cider apples or Kuerner's kitchen window). The imagery the assessor offers the reader is equally mundane:

> Mr. Buckham copied the Bender designs while sitting straight-backed, arms stretched out (left firmly anchoring the paper with fingertips, right firmly gripping the pencil). He drew lightly though, without retracing and without lifting his pencil, allowing the lead to skim over the paper purposefully, but warily. Between repeated glances at the stimulus cards, Mr. Buckham watched his productions emerge. I was reminded of a determined driver tentatively traversing icy, hilly roads.

Just a few such carefully selected examples go a long way toward grounding explications in the client's and reader's lives. Like art, our descriptions are creative, subjective, and disciplined; but they are not art. They do not present one moment as a total work, nor do they attempt to express even that moment fully. Ours is practical work; but it is mere technology if it is not also creative and subjective.

For Wyeth and assessor, selection is part of this discipline. Which visible objects or events best evoke for others what we saw? Wyeth returns to his subject many times, both to stay in touch with what moved him and to search for its worldly referents. He may attempt numerous prestudies (some in water color, some in ink, many in pencil). In his prestudies, we can see how he moves Karl Kuerner from one side of the room to another, how he concentrates for a while on Karl's sausages hanging from meat-hooks, then on a window, then on Karl's head. Finally the finished portrait ("Karl") is of Karl and of bare meat hooks.

So too the assessor scans through his or her notes and recollections, looking for essential and evocative constituents with which to re-present the client. We assessors cannot simply write out the Behavioral Observations section in terms of what we saw during the initial interview. At that time we did not yet know what fuller or more refined meanings we would see in those earlier behaviors. For example, what I initially see as a shy entrance into my office I later understand as also a calculative one. I must find examples that point to this more complex sense of the client's world. One must be open during the assessment to an evolving sense of the client's world. We cannot re-present what we were not present to. Ultimately, one should feel comfortable about the written report, but ought not ever experience complete closure; all individualized understandings are rightly ambiguous, unfinished. Each reader contributes to filling out meanings.

At other times it is through the artist's prestudies and the assessor's efforts to record a particular moment that they discover what was especially meaningful about that moment. Expression not only gives voice to thought; it also brings new meanings into being.

Discipline demands integrity. Wyeth's temperas are strikingly honest, straightforward, and yet full of complexity. They respect their subject without making judgment. Whether landscape, still life, or actual portrait, and regardless of factual perspective, they have the appearance of being frontal views, hiding nothing, emphasizing nothing; each detail seems to be there. In "Miss Olson" we see an older, heavier Christina gently supporting a tiny kitten on her chest, with closed eyes and head nodding downward toward the sleeping creature. The bottom of the picture (just below the kitten) shows Christina's aging rumpled cotton dress—we see the stressed stitches, the fading floral pattern, the thinning of the material. In the middle of the picture is Christina's head, nose a bit humped, narrow, and oversized. The lips are compressed. An ear shows through straggly auburn hair pulled into a bun on the back of her neck. Wyeth included the wart on her cheek and the lines forming in her face. The rest of the picture is brownish wallpaper—scarred, scratched, fading, torn. There she is: poverty, advancing age, wart and all. And yet, as I dwell with the picture, I find myself breathing quietly in unison with her, feeling her assurance, strength, substance, dignity, and more.

Would Wyeth have been more loving, more respectful of this dear and longtime friend had he omitted the wart, smoothed out the dress, deleted the tear in the wallpaper? No—he sees and accepts Christina as she is. She is not reduced to wart, age, or any other feature. Nor are these details meant to be symbolic or judgmental; they are visible aspects of a person who knows them well, and who would be offended by well-meaning alterations in the portrait. Moreover, they are our access to a dynamic sense of Christina, one in touch with power and care, beginnings and endings, motion in arrest. Here is non-dramatic drama. The lesson for assessors is that we too ought to respect and represent the client's mundane moments and aspects rather than emphasizing high and low points (strength, weakness; health, pathology). Moreover, if we care for the client, we ought to be straightforward in our observations, rather than avoiding or euphemizing on the one hand or objectifying and clinicalizing on the other. How observant and caring, for example, would you judge a counselor to be if you consulted him about applying to medical school, and he never mentioned your D+ average in life sciences? Or if he either announced that it didn't matter at all (when you know it does), or simply pronounced you deficient in scientific reasoning powers?

Honest details enable readers and viewers to know our subjects and our subjects to recognize themselves. Recall "Distant Thunder," the painting of a woman (Mrs. Wyeth) lying in a field next to a box of blueberries. She is stretched out on her back, with a hat covering her eyes. When Mrs. Wyeth comes across this painting, she may smile as she recognizes that floppy old felt hat from the summer of '61. It is neither flattering to her nor detracting, nor is it symbolic of anything. It is simply *hers* and it shares her history. In a similar manner, when clients read their individualized assessment reports (with nothing hidden), they often smile in surprised acknowledgment, nod, and say something like, "That's really me!"

Wyeth does not expect one image to tell all there is to know about a person or place. Each painting carefully portrays what Wyeth was present to at one moment of many possible moments. Through his paintings of the same places and people at different seasons and ages, we come to recognize them, to discover the familiar through its variations. As individualized assessors we present images of the client at different moments, selected to help the reader begin to recognize him or her through the similarity within variation. We too include adequate detail so that the client both exemplifies and exceeds convenient categories.

We might also say of Wyeth that he "respects the ordinary" and that he "lets people and places be." To do so requires care, which inevitably reveals the painter in the painting. Wyeth neither exaggerates his presence nor hides it. He simply presents the subject without compartmentalizing or judging. Individualized assessors do likewise. We must also at some point be explicit about the nature of our participation, however, and we usually must follow the descriptions with recommendations for placement or treatment, or with other suggestions.

Discipline requires the artist or writer to be true to ambiguity—to evoke the open-endedness of events and the relativity of comprehension. Looking at each of the paintings mentioned in this chapter, I experience a "You Are There" realism. I scan the picture for cues as to what has happened earlier and what might happen next. In "Wind from the Sea," for example, my gaze is drawn past the fluttering curtains and into the fields. My eyes follow the double-rut roadway to the left of the visible scene, where the fluttering curtain carries me back into the room. I am startled and frustrated to discover that the picture's boundaries prevent me from looking further into the room at furnishings, possessions, or the occupant; the margin cuts me off at the sill. Again I look outward, this time at the horizon's pine trees and gray skies. Then, dropping my gaze once again, I encounter the rutted road and follow it into obscurity where the foreground curtain again intercepts my attention.

Moving in and out and back and forth, one is in touch with history and possibility. Long ago someone hung these curtains; someone has looked out the window upon this scene thousands of times with varying moods and reflections; someone has gone forth countless times to somewhere (where?) on that road. One imagines this someone to be older, accustomed to routine, unpretentious. There is a sense of history completed, and of a future undefined.

The reader also looks beyond the printed words, seeking to understand more than is explicit. Assessment representations should occasion expectations, a search for confirmation and for details, and a sense of a still-open future. We achieve this in part by providing concrete images of the client, which the reader can project into other situations. We also do it by filling in background up to a point, and by showing the client in motion. The reader then imagines how this person might veer off in this or that direction. We do not totalize the client in our characterizations, but instead provide adequate situated detail for the reader to become involved in imagining what it might be like to be this client, and what his or her options might be. The future could provide continuity in any of several directions. The point here is not that our comprehension is deficient; it is not. Rather, our clients participate in making their futures. Shifts in their own reflections as well as external interventions may lead to shifts in course.

Artist and assessor must not give themselves over to merely categorical renditions, to portraits of permanence or predictability.

Even so-called "internal dynamics" need not be presented in terms of symptoms and test scores. Dynamics are the tensions and vicissitudes among multiple, sometimes mutually exclusive, possible futures. Dynamics are visible in a person's terrain, pathways, and junctures. "Hay Ledge" bespeaks Alvara Olson's putting away his dory—no doubt a resolute decision, but a still-living one. Artist and assessor must be careful not to petrify such tensions, but to invite the viewer or reader to sense the tension from his or her experience of similiar choices. The disciplined artist or assessor achieves a sense of process—of things in motion, unfolding, and shaping while being shaped. There must be an attunement to what photographers call the "critical moment." For example, which of a series of camera shots best captures a boxer's power, a racehorse's speed, a model's allure? What incidents, what postures, which quotations best evoke a sense of this particular client's ways of succeeding and of becoming stuck?

Process can be portrayed also in territory and objects. "Distant Thunder" invites me to linger in the grass, to feel its remaining warmth while the shadows grow cool. In the picture's silence, I listen for sounds, and now there are quiet rustlings in the trees, insect buzzings, and thunder in the distance. Through such sounds and sensations I am in the place of the reclining figure. I anticipate possible scenarios: for example, the dog becomes restless, moves about in its "nest," and then ambles over to nudge its mistress.

Wyeth can afford to spend time painting backgrounds. Indeed many segments of any of his pictures are themselves complete portraits. The assessor who includes too much historical and environmental background, however, risks an overly long report, a distracted reader, and the implication that the background totally explains the present and determines the future. Our assessments are not so much like Wyeth's completed pictures as they are like some of his prestudies and unfinished paintings. The subject is detailed in some sections, hinted at in others; surroundings are mostly sketched, detailed only here and there. In short, one of the most demanding tasks of the artist or assessor is that of selecting what to re-present so that the subject's participation in process is visible.

Some works come readily, not requiring prestudies, outlines, or written notes. Others require much reworking and perhaps are never satisfactory. Wyeth can put the painting aside, but the assessor usually must complete the report. In either case, technique should be mastered so that it does not distract from the subject. For example, Wyeth does not clutter his painting with extra texturing just to display his tempera skill, nor does he forget principles of lighting and balance; as an assessor one does not use jargon or overemphasize one's knowledge or write in convoluted or ungrammatical sentences. Except for commissioned paintings, the artist is typically free to paint whatever is inspiring or intriguing. The assessor is obliged to do the best that can be done with whichever client requires assessment. Moreover, the assessor usually has to settle for whatever can be accomplished within time constraints. Still, the individualized assessor's work always transcends technology in its creative, personal accomplishment.

Summary

This chapter compared some works of Andrew Wyeth with the written work of assessors. The purpose was threefold: (1) to convey a sense of the spirit with which one goes about describing a client's living of his or her world; (2) to reflect on the nature of description, and (3) to explore the implications of the comparisons for report-writing practices. Before this chapter concludes with its Question-Response section, its theoretical themes will be summarized.

What traditionally has been called "personality" is better understood as the ways a person moves through situations, shaping even while being shaped by them. These ways continue to evolve; they are forever unfinished. Comprehension of these ways depends upon observers' access: their interests, backgrounds, and so on. There is no single, true person or thing to be known "objectively." Truth is interpersonal. The effort to be objective by describing a person just in terms of standard categories (such as scores, labels, or levels) transforms ongoing life into limited and fixed stereotypes. Although such categories may be helpful to the assessment process, ultimately the client should be described in terms of direct interpersonal experience.

Re-presentation of such perception does not "wrap up" a case so much as open the way for still further development of understanding by readers, who bring their own lives to the report. Further, it retains a sense of ongoing process, of what could yet be. Finally, the re-presented person is allowed to exceed as well as to be consonant with general patterns of "personality."

Questions and Responses

Question: Are you saying that assessment is an art rather than a science?
Response: No. I'm saying that the professional practice of assessment is best based on a science that recognizes that human events are comprehensible in their own right, that we do not have to transform them into the categories of the natural sciences. Human-science practices require their own standards for objectivity, such as specification of what was visible and under what circumstances. Thus, the writer's description of daily life resembles both art and science.

Question: But aren't re-presentational descriptions always the assessor's own subjective interpretations?
Response: Yes. Any perception, including that of the scientist looking through a microscope, is subjective—interpretive—in that learning, past experience, and expectations come into play as he or she sees whatever is there as

meaningful. But note that *subjective* does not mean "merely subjective"—available only to this one person. And note that the meanings inherent in re-presentational description are not presented via a translation into a different area or level of reality, such as T-scores or hospitalese.

Question: Do the re-presentations in an assessment report serve as illustrations, or do they serve as evidence for the points you wish to make?

Response: Both at once. As an assessor I feel obliged to build a case for my conclusions and recommendations. Readers can then qualify these in accordance with what they saw for themselves in the re-presentations.

Question: Doesn't the assessor have to be a sensitive, mature, self-aware person?

Response: Yes, like teachers and therapists, assessors should be more than technicians and storehouses of knowledge.

Question: When is re-presentational description particularly appropriate?

Response: A report should include representative instances throughout when the readers are going to be working directly with the client rather than stopping with classification or placement decisions. These helpers are best served when they are provided access to the client's lived world—where they and the client will meet. Re-presentational description also can correct stereotypes (of "a schizophrenic" or "an incorrigible," for example) by showing the concrete, mundane, understandable ways in which the person exemplifies a technical category.

Question: Shouldn't some reports describe natural-science findings, such as evidence of brain damage?

Response: Definitely. Neuropsychological reports, for example, might serve primarily as decision-helpers. The report might help a physician decide whether to order a CAT scan or to undertake exploratory brain surgery. However, if the report is to be fully psychological, it should describe the patient as a person and in a way that helps people to address his or her particularity. It must also describe some of the specific daily-life limitations imposed by the brain damage. And it must describe how this person is living his or her brain damage, what this allows and disallows, and what options might be opened.

Question: Doesn't the assessor have to know about general types of personality or pathology before he or she can describe the particular way in which a person does or doesn't match that type?

Response: Inevitably our perceptions *are* in terms of what we're already familiar with and what we already know. As assessors we ought to be aware of known patterns and consider their relevance for this particular client. However, we also ought to allow ourselves to be present to the individual before we begin to make thematic comparisons. We remain aware that the patterns (types or categories) are not real by themselves, but are ways psychologists and their colleagues have tried to organize complex data. At certain junctures in our pursuit of knowledge, our psychological research ought to start with subjects' reports and behaviors and then find ways to summarize them all—rather than merely testing data against the hypotheses of existing theories. See Fischer & Wertz, 1979, for examples of qualitative research that moves from individual descriptions (in this case, of being criminally victimized) to general descriptions that hold for every case studied; see the *Duquesne Studies* volumes (Giorgi et al., 1970, 1975, 1979) for other examples.

Question: Can the assessor be positive of what the client's experience is, or can the reader of a report be sure what the assessor actually saw?

Response: No, but this uncertainty is not the result of deficient methodology, but of the character of human experience and knowledge. When we read a quantitative research report, there too we don't know exactly what behavior (and certainly not what experience) was observed and recorded in the form of check marks, scores, and so forth. At any rate, the assessor (or qualitative researcher) ought to make as visible as possible just what he or she observed.

Question: In regard to the Wyeth quotation that introduces this chapter, are you implying that love of one's client assures individualized assessment?

Response: No. But another's life can be best evoked when one cares for that other's difference, lets it be, and respects it as a variation of the life we all share. This care is an access to the other's life.

Question: Perhaps Wyeth's portraits "let people be," but aren't your assessments intended to intervene?

Response: Yes. The "letting be" refers here to our describing a person in terms of his or her own life, without at that moment imposing judgment. But as service providers, we are indeed obliged to ask about the implications, and work collaboratively toward constructive change. But here too, that care for the differences through which we recognize what it is to be human encourages circumspect intervention.

Question: Is it always possible to gain access to what we have traditionally called "intrapsychic dynamics" just through juxtaposing scenes or incidents that illustrate incompatible choices?

Response: I don't think there *are* any dynamics aside from inclinations toward and withdrawals from action. But these choices are not necessarily focal for the client, let alone clearly visible to the observer. Sometimes our clients don't lend themselves to portrait painting. Often I merely say that I *imagine* what may be happening, judging from what I have learned of other persons in similar situations. But never have I had no sense of a client's struggles. At a minimum I can portray what it was like for me to meet this person, and therein what it would be like for many others. I suppose that's what artists' portraits do.

Question: Haven't some clients given up struggling? Aren't some people just plain stuck?

Response: Definitely. However, even a status quo is a *sustained* status. Spinning one's wheels, digging in one's heels, going in circles, putting in time, and so on, *are* dynamic. Here, the person wishes both to continue on and *not* to get somewhere. Or as is more usually the case, the person wishes to follow incompatible inclinations, and perpetually stalemates himself or herself. When the person is stuck, that should be described forthrightly, but as far as is possible the perpetuation of the problem should also be described.

Question: Is the assessor supposed to be able to give examples of everything he or she has learned about the client?

Response: No, I don't see how one reasonably could. At any rate, I sometimes settle for stating a general impression, saying outright that I can't put my finger on just what I was responding to. If the point is central to the referral issue, however, I am obliged to work until I do know concretely where I can make visible what I "saw." Individualized reports remind me more of Wyeth's prestudies and unfinished paintings than of his finished works. We paint referral-relevant areas in detail, but settle for hints and sketchy outlines in other areas.

Question: Are you making a judgment about representational art as being more valid than expressionism, symbolic art, and so on?

Response: No. It's just that the realities and perspectives that they make available for us are not ones that are relevant for this book.

Question: Is there some existential significance to Wyeth's dark, somber painting that led you to choose him as the artist for this chapter?

Response: In most of his work Wyeth has preserved life's multiple tensions. In "Tenant Farmer," for example, there's a dead deer hanging by a rope from a tree next to a country house. The tree is barren; the ground and woodpile are snow-covered. The scene puts the viewer in touch not only with the past and with death, but also with the cycles of life, future growth, seasons, work, rest, nourishment. I don't find Wyeth's paintings depressive; I find them honest, detailed, yet respectful of ambiguity. They are personal yet transpersonal. We would do well to emulate these standards in our assessment reports.

CHAPTER 12

Theoretical Foundations: Questions and Responses

THIS final chapter addresses the most frequently asked questions about the theoretical underpinnings of individualized assessment. Some of the responses have been mentioned earlier in the text, many have been implied, and some appear here for the first time. The chapter is intended to encourage assessors to further articulate their own understandings, by comparing them with the responses presented here. The more explicit we are about our theory, the more likely we are to modify both theory and practice, thereby providing more consistent service to our clients.

Question: It seems to me that this book deals with the existential situations of individuals, but it does not seem to adopt the existential philosophy of despair. Is your approach to individualized assessment in fact existential?

Response: Yes it is, in that it focuses on how individuals experience their worlds and how individuals participate actively even in what happens to them. However, individualized assessment is of course psychological rather than philosophical. As assessors we are interested in individuals, not for the sake of exploring principles of existence, but to assist clients by presenting different perspectives, pointing out consequences of habitual comportment, and suggesting possible options. Existential writings have informed and sometimes inspired human services professionals, but commitment to any specific social or political philosophy does not necessarily follow. Similarly, the insights of existential philosophy do not necessarily lead to pessimism or despair.

Although phenomenology has been interested in the abstract ontology of Being, existentialism has been interested in the ontic problems of existing as a concrete, individual being—for whom everything has meaning, and who inescapably contributes to his or her own future. Existentialism is a philosophy of existence (from the Latin *ex-istere,* to stand out toward, to emerge, to become). Its developers have been concerned with the individual's continuous struggle to achieve a creative balance between acknowledging the immutable facts of one's existence (for example, gender, age, war, vulnerability) and daring to project one's self-made future. This struggle creates the tension of living both the necessary and the possible, or the tension of living both one's subject*ed*ness (objectness) and subjectness. Despite severe limitations to freedom, we nevertheless do participate actively even in the way we live our restrictions. We inevitably and continually play a part in what we make of our lives. This is the meaning of Jean-Paul Sartre's celebrated statement that "existence precedes essence," namely, that one must make what one will of one's own existence.

Hence also Sartre's (1943/1975) seemingly contradictory statement that we are "condemned to freedom."

Existentialism's beginnings are not only in the works of the French atheist philosopher Sartre (1905–1980), but also, for example, in those of the Danish Christian theologian Sören Kierkegaard (1813–1855) and the German social critic and philosopher Friedrich Nietzsche (1844–1900). They addressed the times within and against which they wrote from their individual pessimistic and sometimes anguished persuasions. In their various ways they stressed the anxiety and despair that attend an individual's efforts to make life meaningful in a world with no absolute, pregiven meanings. That is, not only are our daily accomplishments impermanent, but our ultimate progress is toward death, and we are responsible for making our own meaning of that too!

Acknowledgment of this circumstance, however, has not led all existential philosophers into despair. For example, Max Scheler (1928/1962) addressed the nature of sympathy and described human beings' fundamental mode as that of love. Martin Buber (1923/1958) stressed our possibilities for personal, open, sensitive, spiritual relations with fellow persons. Gabriel Marcel (1951/1978) has stressed the role of hope in transcending our difficulties. European psychiatrists were the first to see in phenomenology and existentialism helpful ways of understanding their patients' daily struggles, ways that encouraged therapist and patient to look beyond disease and causality models and examine also the patient's co-authoring of his or her life. From there, patients could be encouraged to take the initiative in revising the course of their lives. Some influential texts were those of Ludwig Binswanger (1967/1975), Medard Boss (1957/1963), Viktor Frankl (1946/1955; 1946/1959), and Jan van den Berg (1955). The American psychologist Rollo May, as chief editor of *Existence: A New Dimension in Psychiatry and Psychology* (1958), brought a variety of European existential psychiatric formulations to the attention of American clinicians. (See Fischer and Fischer, 1983, for the relation between existentialism and phenomenology, and how these philosophies can serve as a framework for psychotherapy.)

Question: The book strikes me as simply taking a consistent humanistic stance. Why don't you call your approach humanistic and let it go at that?

Response: The approach is, of course, humanistic in the broad senses of being humane, sharing the humanities' concern with the role of values in culture and history, acknowledging the power of a person's experience and will, and taking a holistic, growth-oriented stance. However, as it happened, I encountered existentialism and phenomenology before I discovered humanistic psychology, so in fact I developed individualized assessment within the context of those European philosophies. Other people, however, such as Ray Craddick (1972/1975) and Richard Dana (1966) began their correctives to traditional testing within more explicitly humanistic frameworks. Others, like George Kelly (1955), prior to the coalescence of humanistic psychology, had already taken approaches to assessment that were broader than the prevailing natural science paradigm. In short, one can undertake individualized assessment under several aegises, not just that of humanistic psychology.

Another reason for not labeling individualized assessment as basically humanistic is that humanistic psychology has become a partial corrective to traditional psychology rather than an alternative theory or approach. I prefer to ground individualized assessment in a human-science psychology, one that has an explicit philosophy of science, and that encourages research and theoretical integration of the findings of other disciplines. Despite significant efforts at developing and systematizing humanistic psychology (for example, Bugental, 1967; Severin, 1965; Sutich & Vich, 1969), it has remained primarily an attitude. Granted, it is a constructive attitude—a vigorous, helpful, affirmative commitment to human welfare—and it emphasizes possibility rather than limitation or necessity. Still, it has remained an attitude rather than a systematic approach for psychology.

A third reason that individualized assessment is not primarily humanistic is that many people believe that this attitude can be appended to other theories. For example, behaviorists (Avila, 1972) argued that they, too, could be considered humanistic insofar as they apply their system toward humane ends. Thus, characterizing individualized assessment as humanistic may inaccurately imply that it is merely good-hearted and growth-oriented.

Also, because in the early days much of humanistic psychology was largely a reaction against technology, quantification, experimental manipulation, medical models of mental illness, and so on, the term "humanistic" still implies to many people a rejection of traditional psychology. Just ten years ago many psychologists said that humanistic assessment was a contradiction in terms. Many colleagues who saw my work as humanistic could not comprehend that I took testing, diagnostics, psychopharmacology, and psychopathology seriously. But a hopefulness that does not take into account physical reality, limitations, and pain is an artificial hopefulness. Finally, I wish to avoid the unfortunate associations of humanistic psychology with numerous faddish, superficial, would-be therapies.

I will quickly if oversimply characterize the course of humanistic psychology, in order to provide a further sense of its relation to individualized assessment. Its greatest force and impact occurred in the late sixties. It had drawn support from phenomenology and existentialism, from Gestalt perceptual theory, Eastern religions, and from some of the more holistic early-day American psychologists like William James and Stanley Hall. In the 1930s, several leading American psychologists, such as Gordon Allport and Henry Murray, had stressed holism more explicitly and attempted to legitimize experience and ideographic methods, but their work was still primarily within the intrapsychic determinist orientation. It was not until 1955 that Hadley Cantril introduced the term "humanistic psychology."

By that time the movement had become a distinctly American one, a reaction had set in against what was seen as the elitist, authoritarian, removed concerns of behavioristic, materialistic academic psychology, and against the emphasis of applied psychology on abnormality and deficiency. Clinicians in particular were ready for Carl Rogers' optimistic "client-centered" approach (1942/1961). Shortly after, Abraham Maslow (1954/1962) bypassed the artificialities and fragmentizing of laboratory and statistical research to favor literature and field interviews. Moreover, his topic was the lives of self-actualizing persons, rather than traits, abilities, or dynamics of pathological or laboratory groups. Despite this radical departure from mainstream psychology, he offered a touchpoint for traditional concerns by specifying that a hierarchy of physical needs must be met before a person can develop toward higher human values and functioning. However, his appeal to students and younger psychologists, who are now teachers and leaders themselves, was his emphasis on human potential, growth, and community. It was probably critical for the movement that Rogers and Maslow in their early work wrote in optimistic, practical, nontechnical language that nevertheless provided explicit alternatives to traditional concepts and practices. When their distinctively theoretical work appeared, both the public and psychologists were more receptive to it.

By the late sixties, the humanistic movement was solidly established as a psychology of well being—of growth, becoming, potential, pursuit of goals, self-actualization, self-worth, self-fulfillment. It emphasized joy, spontaneity, ecstasy, love, transcendence. Its basic concerns were the inner person and higher human qualities, such as consciousness, creativity, meaningfulness, ethics, aesthetics, dignity, choice, and spirituality. By the beginning of the eighties, these concerns were widely acknowledged as relevant to psychology. Therefore, psychologists no longer found it necessary to specialize in humanistic psychology. At the same time, other schools of psychology had come of age and hence could afford to look for ways to accommodate some of the humanistic themes. In the meantime, most humanistic psychologists had discovered that their movement was not sufficient in itself, and that rapprochement with the new mainstream was possible, even though it remained necessary to re-emphasize humanistic themes from time to time. In short, humanistic psychology has completed much of its work, and it is time now for a scholarly and collegial pursuit of a scientific psychology designed to address human matters on their own ground. This human-science psychology, of course, also includes and perpetuates humanistic psychology's basic concerns.

Question: Of course, the next question follows directly: just what is human-science psychology?

Response: It is an approach that considers not only the characteristics that humans share with other biological organisms, but also those characteristics that have evolved as uniquely human. Among the particularly human characteristics are consciousness, language, purposiveness, and reflectiveness. Humans comport themselves in accordance with their experience of a situation's relevance to where they are going. But that experience is complex. At a particular moment, cognition and reflection may dominate, or may be only potential. The relevance, or meaning, of a situation is influenced not only by the subject's past, but also by his or her ways of moving through it to his or her various goals—which themselves vacillate in their salience, partially in accordance with interruptions from the environment. The methods of the natural sciences are not sufficient for studying these human characteristics, which do not lend themselves to physical measurement, for designing experiments in which conditions are presumed to remain constant, or for explanations in terms of preconceived variables. The term "human-science psychology" is meant as an explicit contrast to North America's historically dominant approach, which had been one modeled on the classical natural sciences. Textbooks refer to psychology as a "social science," but they do not say outright that sociology, psychology, and education have been modeled on the *physical* sciences, presumably the only way to be scientific. The term "human science" is meant in part to call that assumption into question. This questioning of our old allegiance to the natural sciences' paradigm is not restricted to phenomenological and humanistic circles. Precisely because psychology has come of age—having proven the rigor and efficacy of its method—it is now looking at its limits, and looking for ways to broaden its scope while still remaining scientific.

Human-science psychology, as it has evolved thus far, is scientific in that its qualitative, descriptive methods are designed to explore and share the order, the coherence or consistency, that holds for people in general, as well as for various subgroups of people. Human-science psychology is empirical in that it studies actual events as directly as possible, through subjects' descriptions and through first-hand observance. Its research methods are presented in detail so that other researchers can conduct similar studies, compare findings, reach consensus, and clarify differences. Through these studies, a coherent body of knowledge is now being developed. Practitioners of human-science psychology not only apply these research findings, but in their own practices are scientific in that they specify both the perspective through which they observed, including their own involvement, and just what they saw that others too could see if they looked in a similar way.

Human-science psychology is not new. In the nineteenth century, when academicians and researchers were formulating psychology as an area of study in its own right apart from philosophy, Franz Brentano (1838–1917) made a case in Germany that psychology should not be conceived strictly as one of the rapidly developing natural sciences. He argued instead that it belonged within the Geistesewissenschaft tradition, and should be pursued as a human science (see, for example, Rancurello, 1968). Later, William James, sometimes cited as the father of American psychology, was similarly inclined, but American psychology took up the major part of his *Principles of Psychology* (1890/1981), which dealt with laboratory-type psychology, rather than his other reflections. It was not until the 1960s that systematic critiques of our natural-science traditions began to appear among psychologists (for example, Bakan, 1968; Lyons, 1963). Since the mid-1960s, the entire psychology department at Duquesne University, all faculty and graduate students, have worked within a general project of developing psychology as a human science, with an explicit theoretical foundation, research methods, content, and practical applications. In 1970, Amedeo Giorgi published *Psychology as a Human Science: A Phenomenologically Based Approach*. A representative sample of other writing from Duquesne can be found in the *Duquesne Studies in Phenomenological Psychology* (Giorgi et al., 1971, 1975, 1979, 1983) and in the *Journal of Phenomenological Psychology*. Duquesne graduates are now completing their own books, for example, Colaizzi, 1973, and Romanyshyn, 1982. Many other psychologists also are contributing to the development of psychology as a human science (for example, Chein, 1972; de Rivera, 1976, 1981; Polkinghorne, 1983; Pollio, 1982; Rychlak, 1977).

Ideally, human-science psychology will not stand in opposition to its older colleague, natural-science psychology. Rather, psychology at large will broaden its base by incorporating human-science psychology's developments. Of course, individual psychologists will continue to pursue our subject matter from our favored perspectives, some attuned to individuals' lived worlds, others to behavior in relation to environment. But we should all be mindful that humans are not adequately described through either perspective alone.

The following points correct some frequent misunderstandings of human-science psychology. (1) It is not traditional psychology, with humane or humanistic intentions added on. (2) It goes beyond philosophical phenomenology by dealing with empirical matters in their own right. It is not just an "armchair" psychology, dealing only in "intuition," reflection, and so on. (3) Although human-science psychologists are at present concentrating on the uniquely human realm, they acknowledge that environmental and biological realms also guide and limit human possibilities. As our human-science research methods, data, and understandings grow, we can attempt to study just how all three realms participate in experience and action. (4) Human-science psychology is not opposed to laboratory research or to statistical analyses, so long as these methods are regarded as ways of describing human comportment, and so long as research into lived worlds is also acknowledged as a valid and related access to human events.

Question: The preface to this book says that its individualized approach is grounded in a European phenomenological philosophy of science. That sounds like a contradiction. How could phenomenology be a philosophy of science? Besides, the assessments took into account medical and environmental factors, not just the client's experience. In what sense is individualized assessment phenomenological?

Response: Let me address "phenomenology," and then say in what senses individualized assessment is consonant with phenomenology. Before that, though, I also want to point out that although my own route to individualized assessment was via phenomenology, the practices and general approach also are consonant with other contemporary post-positivist orientations, such as structuralism and systems analysis.

Etymologically and philosophically, *phenomenology* refers to the study of (*ology*) how things appear to us (*phenomena*), in contrast to how they could be thought of as themselves (*noumena*). Of the three distinct contemporary meanings of phenomenology, the first two are *not* foundational for individualizing psychological assessment. First, in medical practice and research, the phenomenology of a disorder refers to a pattern of apparently identical symptoms that may be due to different etiologies. Although attention-deficit disorders may look the same in many children, for example, for some the disorder may be due to a catacholamine imbalance, sensitivity to artificial food preservatives, or a congenital nervous system impairment.

Second, in North America, when clinical psychologists and psychiatrists refer to phenomenology, they generally point to experience in its own right, apart from its causes or from "reality." "The phenomenology of schizophrenia," for example, refers to the experiential world of schizophrenics, regardless of one's theory of schizophrenia. Psychologists such as Rogers (1964) and Snygg and Coombs (1949) were influential in establishing a legitimate place in psychology for this phenomenal world. Until recently, however, mainstream American psychology has been primarily interested in explaining the natural scientific causes of experience and perception rather than exploring the nature of human experience in its own right. This meaning of phenomenology is relevant for individualizing psychological assessment, but it is the third meaning that offers theoretical foundations.

This version of phenomenology is a philosophy most directly associated with the German thinkers, Husserl (1913/1969; 1954/1970) and Heidegger (1927/1962). Their critiques of the philosophies of the natural sciences pointed out that scientists have defined their task as the discovery of the laws that govern nature, as though these were knowable by humans and yet independent of human ways of knowing. Instead, sciences ought to take into account the structure and functioning of human ways of knowing—which are not separate from humanly known phenomena. Philosophical phenomenology is the methodical study of how things appear through consciousness, and hence also of the nature of consciousness. The epistemology and research methodology implicit in this position are a radical alternative to logical positivism in particular and to empiricism in general, which in one way or another have claimed to bypass human participation in science, and instead have attempted to explain all events exclusively in terms of classification and quantification.

Phenomenological psychology, being an empirical rather than philosophical discipline, does *not* pursue phenomenology's further interest in ontology. Phenomenological psychology instead has been interested in the "consciousness" of actual embodied beings—that is, a "consciousness" that is not necessarily cognitive or self-aware but always part of an individual's particular situation. Consciousness, body, and environment are distinguishable but inseparable aspects of a unitary phenomenon: the person's relations with his or her world—the world as he or she lives it, perceptually/affectively/behaviorally, and so on.

Those inevitable hyphens in phenomenological literature (for example "being-in-the-world") are intended to evoke a sense of a particular world with which a person is already in relation. At least in terms of what is knowable to that person, there is no independent, true world in itself. Likewise, the person does not exist apart from the world as he or she lives it. The term *intentionality,* as it appears in phenomenological literature, refers to this condition, namely that a person is always "intending"—referring to, being oriented toward. This being oriented-toward includes one's explicit and implicit purposes. Another frequent term in phenomenological writing, *structure,* refers to the mutual relationship of a person and that person's world in any particular situation. That relational, structural whole is the unit of study for a phenomenologically based psychology. The writings of the French philosopher-psychologist Merleau-Ponty (1942/1963; 1945/1962) have encouraged recognition of the coherence of such structures.

Of course the physical and biological realms are also real, and human-science psychology, being interested in actual lives rather than in philosophy per se, takes into account the medical, environmental, historical, and other aspects of a person's situation. These constituents predispose and limit; focusing on them helps us both to understand more fully and to find points of intervention. But as phenomenologically oriented psychologists, we are mindful that to understand how such constituents participate in a person's life, we must also look at how those predispositions and constraints are taken up by individuals as they continue their lives, pursuing projects in accordance with their perceptions and perceiving in accordance with their projects.

Individualized assessment, then, is phenomenological in the following major senses. (1) Its practitioners take into account that all knowledge is human knowledge; that is, that even our sciences are formed in accordance with human questions, ways of thinking, concerns, and so on. We do not simply discover data; we inevitably prefigure it through our interests and perspectives. (2) Individualized assessment respects the structural, unitary character of what we break apart for analytic purposes: experience, action, body, and environment. Von Eckartsberg's (1971) term *experiaction* evokes a holistic sense of the experiencing person traveling through environments. Biological and physical predispositions and constraints are not regarded as totally deterministic; instead they are seen as participating in the person's lived body and lived environments. (3) Individualized assessment takes into account the necessarily perspectival character of all perception and knowledge, whether those of scientist, assessor, or client. *Perspective* refers to cultural and historical context, methods of observation, personal history, present concerns, and so on. (4) Individualized assessment is phenomenological in that it addresses the individual as a particular individual in order to explore and describe that person's lived world. Rather than describing the person in terms of pre-established kinds of measurements and categories, the assessor tries, in the parlance of our times, to reach clients "where they are." "Where they are" includes clients' ways of taking up biological, environmental, and developmental givens, in terms of where they are trying to go. "Where they are" also includes what things look like from the clients' present stages in their travels. (5) Individualized assessment is phenomenological in that it attends to how assessees' approaches to situations preform what they can see and do. (6) Finally, given the above orientation, individualized assessment is phenomenological in that its practitioners are open to the development of methods of research and service that take into account humans' structural ways of co-determining their worlds.

Question: If knowledge is always perspectival, what becomes of objectivity? Does this mean that all our assessments are subjective?

Response: Yes, all our assessments *are* subjective, in that the client is inevitably seen and understood in terms of particular decisional concerns, the assessor's training and personal history, our social-cultural context, and so on. *Subjective* here implies recognition that humans (including scientists and assessors) are more than passive mechanisms; they engage the world actively, relating to it in terms of where they are going, of what they are up to. But subjectivity is not necessarily distortion; rather it is the starting point for accrued, consensual knowledge. It is only through particular perceptions that we discern shared meaning—themes known through variation.

"What becomes of objectivity," then, is that physicalistic methods of study are no longer seen as guaranteeing truth, nor even as more objective. Instead, we acknowledge the ambiguous, unfinished, always-in-transition nature of what is known. Being objective now involves two efforts: (1) respecting and being faithful to the richness of any subject matter, and being open to alternative perspectives on it—whether potential ones or those already taken by others; and (2) while still within that openness, trying in a disciplined, systematic manner to specify one's own access and perception and their relation to what others have reported. Other investigators, too, then can see how to make direct comparisons with their observations.

Although it also makes good use of measurements, this objectivity does not limit knowledge to prespecified, external criteria (such as cut-off points for diagnosing brain-damage). On the other hand, a merely personal viewpoint, such as a "feeling" that someone is masking depression, is regarded as only personal until the viewer specifies what was perceived and what his or her professional and personal points of access were. The subjectivity of our assessments, when properly disciplined, is also objective.

Discussions of the subjectivity within objectivity may be found in the following sources: Boelen, 1968 ("Objective knowledge can never be understood in terms of the external object alone"); Koestenbaum, 1971 ("Objectivity means objective to a subject"); and Strasser, 1963 ("Nothing is objective for us without us").

Question: Doesn't the collaborative aspect of individualized assessment assume that people have free will? If so, how can psychological assessment be predictive?

Response: Human comportment can be understood and anticipated because our freedom is limited, and because it follows known constraints. We certainly cannot simply "will" things to be one way or another. Even our capricious moments arise in particular, "predictable" circumstances.

We are free to the extent that we are not entirely determined by things and forces. It is for this reason that natural science methods are not sufficient for the study of human comportment. Effective study must take into account that people behave in accordance with their sense of the situation in which they find themselves. That "sense" develops in terms of their evolving goals. But goals are not projected out of nowhere; people's destinations are continuations of where they have been, with variations occasioned by obstacles and invitations. Through collaboration with clients, assessors refine their understandings and predict more effectively because their collaboration takes into account both (1) clients' sense of their circumstances; and (2) how clients take up those circumstances. The collaborative aspect of individualized assessment also increases clients' latitude—their options—by inviting them to explore viable variations of their past goals and paths.

We are free in that we each take up our situation in our own way, and with opportunity and reflection, we can change both the taking-up and the situation. But the other side of this freedom is that we have no choice but to take up our circumstances in our own ways, in accordance with who we are and where we are going. Although individualized assessment does not attempt artificially precise prediction, it does *anticipate* productively by being mindful of both sides of our freedom.

Question: Are tests necessary for assessing individuals as individuals? Aren't field observations and interviews more direct, and therefore more relevant; indeed, more valid?

Response: Tests are not essential to individualized assessment, but they certainly can be helpful. Testing is a more efficient way of getting to know a person than following him or her through assorted environments and circumstances. Beyond providing systematic samples of a person's comportment, tests help the assessor to focus, to avoid environmental distractions. Rather than everything seeming new to the assessor, only the client is new, against the backdrop of familiar tests. For the client, the tests are an opportunity to rediscover oneself. Normative profiles provide both assessor and client with additional perspectives, with surprises and slants to consider. From the client's side, test data present aspects of one's life usually taken for granted, but now thematic. The testing situation also affords the client time out from the full complexity of daily demands. It is an occasion for the client to contemplate, pull things together, consider alternatives. The testing session is a special situation but not an artificial one.

Table 3.1 reviewed many of the functions of tests in individualized assessment. In various ways the table pointed out that we have direct access to the client's life when we regard test scores as derived or secondary data, but as also being tools to help us explore the client's ongoing life. Moreover, comportment within the assessment session(s) provides a direct sample of the client's life. Within the context of shared assessment work and shared referents, client and assessor explore the relevance to the client's concerns of what they observe together. Regarding everyday life as the point of departure into tests, for the purpose of returning to that actual life with jointly revised understandings, renders tests as relevant as field observation. In addition, testing affords the advantages of normative comparisons, and when the assessment is collaborative, it affords focused experience and interventional opportunities, all of which are not as readily available in field settings, even when followed with discussion. Individualized use of tests is expressly calculated to increase relevance and validity of conclusions.

Question: I can see how test comportment, in the sense of directly observed behavior, can be regarded as an instance of how the client behaves within certain kinds of situations. But how can an assessor integrate research data on traits and factors with observations of an individual's comportment? I can write reports either in terms of my personal observations and discussions with the client, or in terms of scores on tests of abilities and personality traits, but not both at once. These seem like different levels of knowledge that don't go together.

Response: The way out of this common dilemma is to regard the life events that led to the referral, as well as comportments during the assessment, as the primary data. Statistical norms, lists of subtest factors, tables of traits, and so on, are ways of presenting performance outcomes from groups of people. These indeed are a different realm of data. To use them effectively in an individualized assessment, the assessor must be mindful of the assumptions and procedures through which statistically based information was gathered, and must ask to what degree it is pertinent to the client's present situation. The assessor must remember that a person's place within group-derived data is one type of information to reflect upon; it is not more basic, relevant, or valid than direct observation. Scores are not the "results" to be reported; they are sources for reflection and should result in new understandings of actual comportment. These new understandings of the ways a person is going about his or her life are the results; scores may be reported as secondary data that were useful in developing these understandings.

For example, Mr. Lipton's corporation wanted to know whether he was ready for promotion to a higher level of management. On the WAIS-R, he earned an IQ of 103; his critical thinking skills as measured by the Watson-Glaser were above average for the general population, but low for management norms. These scores placed Mr. Lipton well below average for persons in his present position, and way out of the running for higher positions. But I did not report this information until I understood its relation to how he had earned these scores and the relevance of that process to his current job success and future positions. It turned out that his success on the job, which was greater than would have been predicted by the intelligence tests, was related to the clarity of performance standards at work. There, he could readily tell when he had reached the designated standard. But on the WAIS-R, he was left on his own to decide when an answer was adequate; in that situation he earned many one-point credits where two were possible. Similarly, there was notable intra-subtest scatter—that is, he often received credit for items more difficult for most people than those he had just missed.

The subsequent "results" reported to the corporation were neither just direct observations during testing nor just scores and interpretations based on tables. Rather, I said that Mr. Lipton has performed creditably when clear criteria were provided for him, but that despite this prior success, he was likely to encounter more difficulty than his peers when his job required abstract thinking about goals, and when it required him to decide when a job was done well enough. I added that with opportunity for practice and help to understand why various criteria have been set, Mr. Lipton could develop a more independent, reflective, and hence consistent approach to the less structured assignments that are part of higher levels of responsibility.

I did not report that Mr. Lipton's "general fund of knowledge is lower than his comprehension of social relations." That kind of statement is taken directly from "cookbooks," tables, manuals, and handouts. It misleads readers to believe that the Wechsler tests were constructed to sample such "abilities" as "comprehension of social relations" systematically. Although the statement seems reasonable, the reader cannot use it to help Mr. Lipton since daily life referents are missing. Such reporting is unfinished business. The assessor has reported what he or she should reflect upon, rather than the results of that reflection. Interpretive tables—whether numerical, psychodynamic, trait, factored abilities, or whatever—should be taken seriously but not literally. In short, normative data are integrated into a report to illustrate the client's ways of going about his or her life. Simultaneously, such data serve as documentation of how the assessor's understandings were developed. Further documentation may be presented in schematic form as a technical appendix to the report.

Question: I can see how you use the Bender and the Wechsler tests in an individualized way. But how can you use the traditional Rorschach within an individualized approach?

Response: The Rorschach is a task similar to many others in a person's daily life. A person "walks through" the cards placed in his or her path, continuing along his or her way, coping with obstacles and opportunities in habitual manners. I do not look for underlying causes, traits, drives, and so on; these are only names that we have applied to patterns of observed behavior. Rather than describe a person in terms of these generalities, which risk "explaining away" actual comportments, I prefer to describe how, where, and when the person encounters situations like those presented by the inkblots. For example, I noted that Mr. Lipton looked for a meaning to an entire blot (W) but when nothing immediate—like a bat or butterfly—occurred to him, he addressed a segment of the card (D), and moved from there to find related meanings in other sections. In this additive way he generally accounted for most of a card, but the relationships among the parts were often tenuous or forced, such as: "Well, make this part be a lamp behind them, but I don't know what it's doing in a jungle."

Similarly, he had answered WAIS–R items in a fact-by-fact way that did not always add up to maximal credit. To describe the similarity between an axe and a saw, he said, "They cut. Both made of steel. They're sharp." Mr. Lipton did not abstract from these features the more essential commonality, that both are tools. Later discussion revealed that at work he likewise has earned a reputation for sticking with a project, segment by segment, until everything is done. He is respected for finishing assignments in a thorough manner. But now we could see how he had experienced difficulty in developing a training program to teach others his job. He just was not accustomed to looking for an overview, for basic principles, or for relationships.

Mr. Lipton's Rorschach included several *m* responses (inanimate movement). Above average *m* has been found empirically to correlate with feelings that things are situationally out of one's control, that one must await fate, like surgery patients just before their operations (Exner, 1978). Mr. Lipton had blithely told me at first that despite his difficulties in establishing a training program, and despite uncertainty about if and when he would be promoted, things were moving along just fine. This strong presence of *m* indicated to me that Mr. Lipton was after all appraising his situation more realistically than he had admitted. Now when I asked, he readily agreed that indeed his current situation was much like being in an airplane maintaining a holding pattern—that he was eager to move on, that there was nothing at the moment he could do about it, and that what happened next depended on circumstances and other people. The various blends, calculations, and ratios are signs of how the person progressed through the cards, that is, instances of his or her current ways of going through other, similar situations. Rorschach comportment is not similar to *all* situations, and reflection and discussion are necessary to reveal the differences. Discussion and reflection also help to clarify whether the person's present attunements are more situational than habitual.

Besides direct observation and discussion with the client, I often consult norms for the traditionally scored Rorschach. Thereby I have available about 60 years of Rorschach experience on the part of hundreds of clinicians and researchers. I find it particularly helpful to reflect on Exner's empirical research on the life circumstances during which people change their ways of going through inkblots. He has reported that attunement to achromatic areas (C′) goes up during a state of emotional constraint, such as occurs during Marine boot camp and divorce procedings. Hence in recent years I have usually administered a standard Rorschach, and when it was at all complex, I have scored it and drawn up a summary sheet. Exner's (1974) administration and inquiry procedures are efficient, and do not alienate the client. Hence I can complete a standardized Rorschach, and still have time to collaborate and to try out interventions with the client. The formal inquiry instructions not only facilitate scoring, but yield a personal sense of the client's experience of the cards ("I want you to help me see it as you did").

In short, to use the Rorschach for individualized assessment, I do not have to read a crystal ball, make symbolic interpretations, nor deal in intrapsychic structures as such. When a report says things like "this is a person who has rich inner resources and organizational skills, and whose preferred response tendency is for actional delay," the author is reporting unfinished business. That author has not yet found out what he or she is talking about, aside from what manuals say about interpreting the Summary Sheet entries M:EC, Z, and perhaps a:p. The purpose of a test is not to find out how a person performs on that test, but how that person performs in similar situations in ordinary life. This view is consistent with recent positions taken by Rorschach theorists, such as Exner (1980) and Weiner (1977). In addition, within individualized assessment's human-science psychology framework, test scores are regarded as providing another perspective and an occasion for questioning prior perceptions. Test data are not regarded as indicators of presumably underlying generative conditions or entities.

Question: I understand the use you make of projective materials, but what is your general theory of projective techniques? In particular, how can an essentially perceptual task, like inkblots and TAT pictures, reveal personality and predict behavior?

Response: Projective techniques are tasks for which assessees are given only general instructions and for which there is no right or wrong answer. As assessees we undertake the task in accordance with our understanding of the assessment's personal relevance, and within that framework bring to bear our knowledge, past experience, ways of approaching unfamiliar situations, and ways of continuing our progress through life. That is, since there are no right answers, as test-takers we respond in terms of where we have been and where we are going, in short, in terms of who we are ("personality"). *Projective* materials reveal our *projects*—what we are up to as we travel through life, shaping and being shaped by what we attend to. We avoid facing certain possibilities, become immersed in others, notice but do not speak of some, simply do not see others, and so on. Our choice of responses is guided by our attunement to features that are familiar parts of our lives, to possibilities for expansion, and to dangers to be avoided. The depth of who we are, of our personality, can be said to be horizontal—existing in our journeys, in our evolving relationships with people and things. Our future behavior, at least in similar circumstances, is foreshadowed as a continuation of our travel through the projective cards. Thus, although a human-science theory of projective techniques deals with the complexity and tensions of personality, it does not require constructs like "inner dynamics," "unconscious determinants," or "defense mechanisms."

To understand how a see-and-associate task can inform assessors about a person's "personality and behavior," we need only to recall that perception and behavior are abstractions from the unitary process of living our lives. For example, we perceive in light of what we are up to; that is, we know the world in terms of our actional past and projected movement. And just as we see in terms of our projects, so we comport ourselves in terms of what we see. No mechanisms are required to account for the relations among perception, personality, and behavior.

Question: But what about inner dynamics? These are real, although they are not always visible in a person's daily life. Aren't you missing dynamics when you insist on bringing test data down to terms of observable life events?

Response: Inner dynamics are indeed real, in two senses. First, we have all felt torn between two desires, both of which may be personal and not known to observers. Second, we all have observed someone else stuck between warring desires, perhaps resolving the struggle through self-defeating, otherwise inexplicable behavior.

However, there is a danger in accepting these impressions of dynamics as being totally "inner." The danger is that they become regarded as unconscious mechanisms, with lives of their own. "They" are then seen as causing or explaining action. For example, a student's demanding but then missing an appointment with me might be explained as a consequence of inner conflict. In turn, we assume that she would require therapy or other external direction to change her ways. Psychological assessment then would be aimed at evaluating the "inner dynamic" rather than the person's ongoing life.

Reflection on the initial impressions of the innerness of the struggle shows us that besides being personal and not necessarily directly visible, the struggle also involves things, people, and events with which the person is actionally related. That is, the desires are desires to *do* something, in order to get somewhere, have something, be someone. I can imagine that the student's desires might be to receive attention, warmth, praise, reassurance from someone important, while also being someone important, someone who does not need others. The action is relatively passive; but receiving and being *are* actional. The struggle was between a present, in which the past is still relevant, and a future.

"Inner dynamics" are seen as exclusively inner only when we fail to look at the full situations in which they occur. This failure is encouraged by the coherence, the repetitive pattern, of the struggle across situations; it is indeed possible to recognize the same struggle despite differences in its context and content. However, we are not being true to the actual state of affairs if we then say that the context and the content (the people, things, events that are the immediate objects of the struggle) were not essential constituents of that struggle. Recognition of the repetitive strain is important for effective assessment; but the work is unfinished if the actual life contexts and objects are not acknowledged as essential aspects of the struggle.

Question: Thorough approach to assessment requires a theory of unconscious motivation, defenses, and emotion. What has become of those in your individualized approach to assessment?

Response: We are continually and multiply motivated. That is, we are always up to several things at once, always trying to be many things, and always on our way to more than one place. But we usually are not conscious of all of our motives. I think of *unconscious* as a term that points to the broad range of "up to's" that we are not aware of at a particular moment. The following are examples of comportment being purposeful without the person having consciously decided on that purpose. (1) A man shifts positions in his chair, seeking bodily comfort, even before realizing that his legs are becoming stiff. (2) A woman chooses yellow wallpaper for her bedroom, without knowing that as an infant she came to associate yellow surroundings with the nursery that was quiet, warm, and responsive to her cries. (3) A professor is unfairly critical of the content of a poorly typed and unproofed term paper, not realizing that through prior experience he has come to associate this kind of presentation with careless thinking. (4) A receptionist scares off young sales representatives with the gruff manner that she assumed years ago to dissuade people from taking advantage of her; today she is no longer afraid of being exploited and does not realize that she is still being gruff.

Of greater relevance to the above question, of course, is behavior that reveals purposes a person prefers not to acknowledge. An example is the woman who went to a behavior modifier with the complaint that her marriage was in trouble because of her frigidity. Therapy progressed nicely through use of systematic desensitization, wherein the woman, relaxed in a prone position, was asked to picture scenes that were increasingly anxiety-provoking as they advanced along a hierarchy from nonsexuality to intercourse. The woman managed to remain relaxed until the intercourse scene was suggested, at which point she sat up and proclaimed, "I'll be darned if I'll give him [the husband] the satisfaction!" Here we see that what has been called "the dynamic unconscious" is not some sort of mechanism, but the conflict of a person unwittingly undertaking incompatible projects. In the example, the woman wanted to be a good wife—including being a lover—but she did not want to provide sexual satisfaction to her husband. As is usually the case, her way of defending herself from seeing the whole situation, being frigid, served its purpose but was self-defeating because it restricted her life.

Defenses are ways in which we manage not to acknowledge that some of our goals are in conflict. The more rigidly we adhere to our defenses, the more we restrict our lives. Among the best known patterns of defensive restriction are those we used to call neuroses. Of course self-deceptions are also part of our everyday lives.

The work of W. Fischer (1982; 1984) strikes me as the most promising approach to emotions, especially as it relates to defenses. He describes how we try to be certain kinds of people while the world both facilitates and resists our efforts. We find ourselves *affected* by these promotions and impediments to our progress. Our bodily exhilaration, weakness, and tension are the immediate, lived realm of affect. Especially when our progress is disrupted, we may attend to how we are bodily affected. Fischer reserves the word *feeling* for what we then focus on as we try to name or describe our state. He reserves the term *being emotional* to refer to the stance we take toward finding ourselves affected.

Consider my reaction when I find myself stuck in a parkway traffic snarl on the way to the airport. My fingers drumming on the steering wheel, my breath becoming shorter, and my abdomen tightening as though ready to push on ahead, all announce that I have been affected, that I want very much to be on my way, and that I am becoming frustrated in that endeavor. When I realize that I will miss the plane, I become angry and castigate the road system, the dumb drivers, and other scapegoats. Gradually, I recognize that my emotional castigating is a defensive maneuver that protects me from facing the fact that even while getting myself to the airport, I had been acting as though I did not have to take special measures like listening for traffic reports or leaving home early enough to allow for congestion. Being angry also lets me put off full recognition that indeed I have missed the flight, and that I must now decide "what to do about it."

If my motives were not incompatible in the first place (trying to be both a competent person going to important meetings and a person who does not have to take reality into account), I might have bypassed being angry. In that instance, following the initial frustration, I might simply have noted what a shame it was to have lost all that time, and started planning how to route myself back home and what to do about the missed meeting.

Being emotional is not always a negative stance. If I had been aware that I was not eager to catch that plane to go to a boring meeting, I might have found my body relaxing, and then I might have celebrated with a joyful exclamation that "Hah! I don't have to go after all!" In either case, the emotional stance can be both a defense against seeing my involvement in what "happened," and later a source for reflection about my assorted, previously unconscious, motives.

Individualized assessment practices are consonant with this theory of "unconscious motivation, defenses, and emotion." In individualized reports they appear primarily in the form of the re-presentational descriptions of comportment, insofar as those descriptions show the client being on the way toward multiple, oftentimes conflicitng, goals.

Question: You take a thoroughly holistic attitude toward personality, affect, and so on, and yet you also use intelligence tests. What is intelligence from a human-science perspective?

Response: I think of intelligence in its older, prepsychometric sense, as when we speak of "an athlete's intelligence" or "a statesman's intelligence." This usage is closely related to what we mean when we speak of personality in that it brings into focus what stands out for the athlete or statesman as he or she analyzes and maneuvers through situations. The term *intelligence* points also to the impact of the person's consciousness and actions. The "more intelligent" quarterback, for example, has read the defense more perspicaciously and passed for greater yardage than other quarterbacks.

Although most of our standardized intelligence tests were constructed originally with the intention of measuring an underlying capacity, they nevertheless lend themselves to exploration of intelligence in the holistic sense. To facilitate this holistic usage, and to avoid reification of IQ, I developed the following definition of what intelligence tests address (see Fischer 1969; 1973c; 1974).

Tested intelligence is
  the sampled
    effectiveness,
      expressed statistically in relation to age peers,
        of one's approaches
          to situations
            in which competence
              is highly regarded by our culture.
                Today our culture values
                  competence that deals with facts and logic.

Each phrase of the definition helps to prevent slippage into thinking of intelligence as an actual thing that presumably causes, drives, directs, or allows intelligent conduct. *Intelligence* is only a generalization from comportment that we characterize as effective. In the definition, the word *sampled* reminds us that the test items are a small sample of situations, and that the particular occasion during which one was tested was not representative of all such occasions. Being mindful of sampling encourages assessors to reflect about the relevance or nonrelevance of the test items to the client's life situation, and about the testing circumstances and interactions and how they might be relevant.

The phrase *effectiveness of approaches* alerts us to look not just at the outcome (right or wrong answers, total points), but also at the process through which the person arrived there. *Approaches* attunes us to the individual as a person coming to the test items proactively, but also out of a history. *Approaches* also reminds us of the dialectics of testing: The person approaches something in particular (the assessment project, specific items) with his or her own understandings, shaping and being shaped simultaneously, as well as sequentially. When we are interested in influencing the person's kinds or levels of effectiveness, we will be most successful by attending to and stepping into that dialectical process that involves both approach and specific situation. The word *situation* evokes a sense of the client's lived world; it disrupts any notion of the test items as stimuli for responses mediated by "intelligence."

The reference to effectiveness "expressed statistically in relation to age peers" reminds us of how IQs come about. Determining the IQ is like curving grades for a spelling test. The middle scores are assigned C's, the top and bottom spellers are assigned A's and F's, and so on. Neither IQs nor spelling grades measure inherent capacities or other entities. Intelligence tests, like spelling tests, are tests of achievement. Both are generally effective predictors of what can be accomplished next, and in this sense they are also tests of aptitude.

Finally, the definition points out that the socially valued competence sampled by intelligence tests is largely that of learning facts and dealing with them in a logical manner. Precisely because of the importance of this kind of competence in our culture, intelligence tests are helpful in sampling a person's problem-solving approaches. However, we should remain mindful that through our test construction and use, we perpetuate or revise what is thought of as "intelligent."

Question: Do you distinguish among intelligence, ability, aptitude, and achievement?

Response: Yes, certainly these distinctions are useful in their everyday senses. I think of *ability* as pertaining to demonstrated accomplishment in a very specific area, whereas *intelligence* (on the IQ test) refers to how one "reads" more or less cognizable situations and maneuvers effectively through them. Thus we might speak of someone as an intelligent sales manager, but also as one whose mathematical ability is underdeveloped. It is through observed accomplishment that we predict future achievement. What one has already done (achievement) one can do again (ability); we say that one is therefore ready (aptitude) to learn more advanced forms of the particular activity.

There is a technical distinction between achievement and aptitude, however, that should be honored. Within the testing tradition, especially in educational contexts, an achievement test is used to test individuals' mastery of course material after an entire class has been exposed to the same instruction. Aptitude tests make no assumptions about prior experience, and simply assess present readiness to go on to the next step of learning.

Few assessment professionals *conceive* of intelligence, ability, or aptitude as some sort of physical capacity inside a person. Nevertheless, in the absence of an explicit theory of accomplishment, such as that above, we often talk and act as if we do. For example, we ask whether someone "has enough" intelligence to do something, or we speak of someone "lacking" an ability ("He lacks social skills"). This shorthand way of speaking works well enough when we are making decisions about whether a person is ready to handle a task. But this languaging with nouns can undercut efforts to help a person develop. From an individualized assessment perspective, we would look beyond present levels of tested ability, to ask what else the person already has accomplished and under what circumstances. We would explore where we might step into his or her approaches to those tasks, to promote further accomplishment. Verbs, adjectives, and adverbs are the appropriate language for working with action, context, and process.

Question: I gather that you see your human-science approach to individualized assessment as being suitable for both normal people and for people who are pathological. Do you view pathology, then, as on a continuum with normality?

Response: All patterns of existence, whether disordered or not, are variations of our human situation. But I do not see what we call normal and pathological as necessarily being points on one or more baselines. One of our major difficulties in distinguishing normality and pathology is that we have defined normality as the absence of symptoms, rather than in its own right. I would prefer that we go ahead and follow our inclination to think in terms of categories, but that we broaden them: (1) ordinary existence—the norm; (2) extraordinary existence—ideal development; and (3) disordered existence—variations from the ordinary that are problematic for the individual or for his or her community. I would like to do away with both words in the term "mental health," because disorder is not primarily either mental or medical. Even though we are coming to see "health" as an umbrella term for both psychology and medicine, we readily revert to speaking of nonhealth as "disease," and look too quickly for medical explanations and treatment at the expense of attending to the person's world, choices, and life circumstances.

What we now refer to as "healthy" could be defined as optimum well being or readiness to fulfill optimum human potential. Our current loose use of *healthy* allows us to give a person a "clean bill of health" (absence of any categorized disorder) even if that person is unhappy, destructive, or rut-stuck. We should be as alert to possibilities for helping ordinary persons to grow as we are to identifying disordered persons. The inclusion of ideal forms of personality reminds us that normality and disorder are not simply natural states that we can name. They are inescapably formed by social/political/economic/religious values. We should be more explicit about these values, question them from time to time, and purposely plan our communities to enhance ideal personality and to impede disordered existence.

My own criteria for ordinary functioning include readiness to cooperate with other individuals and with society at large, in addition to readiness to understand and maneuver within one's community well enough to hold one's own. This readiness is based on exposure to, and respect for, differences. My notion of ordinariness is strongly influenced by American democratic ideals, including the assumption that the ordinary is socially viable. Of course there are many ways of being ordinary. I hope psychology will increasingly study the structure of these ways, rather than continuing to concentrate on statistical norms (IQs, divorce rates, MMPI norms). For example, some researchers are concerned with everyday affective states and emotional stances, such as being pleased with oneself (Mruk, 1981) or being jealous or envious (Titelman, 1977). These human-science studies include analysis of how people get into these states or stances, and of what becomes possible for them at these junctures. After we study the structures of these ordinary phenomena, then we can research how they sometimes become prevailing life styles rather than transitory moments. Whether these styles are lived in an ordinary or in a disordered way, we can understand the individual in terms of process. And we would recognize that person's possible pivot points into other states and stances.

Disordered existence is just that: life that is ordered, structured, so differently from the ordinary, the usual, that the person does not cooperate with others, or does not hold his or her own as a member of the community. This person may exaggerate or minimize some aspects of ordinary life (the continuum issue), or maintain a radically different pattern of existence. Disordered existence is always restricted existence—the person, for whatever reasons, is not as open to life's range of possibilities as most people are. To understand disorder, we should study the person's life holistically—structurally—rather than focus on symptoms. We could then discover if and when a person functions as most of us do, and whether those moments could and should serve as a point of expansion into more ordinary or extraordinary existence. Again, we would have to examine our values closely, to avoid promoting conformity at the cost of diversity and challenge.

We should be more keenly aware of the implicit criteria we currently follow in identifying people as pathological. In actuality, we identify as pathological those people whose differences from us are problematic to themselves or to us, especially if those differences occur in a recognized pattern. As our increasingly complex society requires even more cooperation and flexibility from its members, we are increasingly noticing, diagnosing, and studying patterns we call "personality disorders." People diagnosed in this way do not necessarily experience themselves as troubled, but they certainly trouble us through their drug and alcohol abuse, criminality, withdrawal, or erratic conduct. Studies of disordered lives from a more holistic perspective than we usually take would attend to the person's lived world, and to the when-nots as well as the whens of problematic conduct. Yochelson and Samenow in just such an attempt have provided a rich glimpse into *The Criminal Personality* (1976).

Extraordinary, or ideal, existence extends ordinary viability into greater depth and breadth of experience, openness, wonder, appreciation of others' circumstances, and a sense of connection with nature, with history, and with the future. Extraordinary persons take responsibility for their actions, while pushing the limits of constraints as they pursue the possible. I also think of the ideal mature adult as combining Maslow's self-actualizing person (1954) and Erikson's eighth stage of development (1959). Qualitative, descriptive research into patterns of disordered existence (Murphy & Fischer, 1983) and into ordinary affective and emotional phenomena (de Rivera, 1981) will test and develop these conceptions, as well as provide knowledge for individualized assessment practice.

Question: If "psychopathology" is in fact restricted or disordered existence, and if judgment of pathology necessarily involves social values, does that mean we should not use scientific diagnostic systems, like DSM III?

Response: No, it doesn't. But of course we must use any diagnostic system in a circumspect manner if it is to serve our clients well. We must remain mindful that the diagnostic system is a way of organizing our observations. Because the system is more or less scientific, we tend to see the categories (such as "unsocialized aggressive conduct disorder") as real in themselves. Then, instead of using the accumulated experience available through the system to alert ourselves to a possible pattern, we look for the "proper" label: "Is this patient actually a schizoid personality or a schizophrenic in remission?" Similarly, when we are not circumspect, we slip into circular reasoning, categorizing symptoms with a diagnosis, and then explaining the symptoms as a function of the category: "Of course he refuses to mingle; after all, he's an avoidant disorder." As Szasz (1970; 1974) has vividly argued, this attitude leads professional and client alike into underplaying the client's responsibility for his or her life.

There is a related danger of forgetting that a diagnostic system is supposed to be a tool rather than an end. We sometimes restrict ourselves to looking for, and noticing, only those features that are listed in the diagnostic manual. Not only is this a limiting attitude, it also emphasizes negative features. The "bottom line" of clinical records becomes a summary of evidence in favor of the chosen diagnosis. That evidence is expressed in terms of the manual's criteria (for example, "blunted, flat, and inappropriate affect were displayed") rather than in terms of actual events. Clinical records in particular, and diagnostic conferences to a lesser extent, too easily become places where professionals talk among themselves, solving the puzzles presented to them by their diagnostic system rather than exploring the client's world, self-direction, interests, and so on.

These negative functions of a diagnostic system can be avoided when we bear in mind that the system is something we constructed to help us observe, communicate, and reflect. The diagnostic system also serves positive functions.

It is a means of sharing the accumulated experience of generations of clinicians and researchers. The difficulties of using the system with particular clients alert us to false assumptions, or simply to gaps in our knowledge. These experiences then lead to research and revision of the system. Robert Spitzer, chairperson of the Task Force that produced the third edition of the *Diagnostic and Statistical Manual of Mental Disorders,* has said, "A major purpose of DSM III is to serve as the forerunner of DSM IV."

A systematization of what we know about so-called mental disorders allows the clinician to scan that knowledge to see if he or she has prematurely understood a client in terms of only one pattern. Schematization of present knowledge also helps professionals to consider what past and present thinkers have had to say about similar groups of troubled persons. We humans live our limitations and further restrict our existences in very complex ways; thorough consideration of this complexity is facilitated by a system of classified knowledge. That system is necessarily somewhat arbitrary and cannot provide a complete "fit" for any client. Most clients do not match criteria "classically," and all lives exceed the categories. That is, lives are fuller than just their disordered aspects. A diagnostic system is like a tour guide—highlighting familiar routes to frequently visited places, but not attempting to map the entire area.

A major positive function of a diagnostic system is that it facilitates communication among professionals. Because the terms have consensual meaning, they are shortcuts to more detailed discussion. This orienting function of diagnosis helps professionals and clients alike to see that a troubled or troubling pattern is not idiosyncratically chaotic, but has happened before to others. This knowledge assists both client and professional to realize that neither is helpless; both can cope with the difficulties. Indeed, formal classification schemes are intended as a preliminary phase of treatment—of doing something about the identified trouble. Finally, professionals are more readily held accountable for their interventions when others can ask questions in terms of a shared system of knowledge.

In summary, diagnostic systems are not counter to a human-science psychology or to individualized assessment, so long as we use such systems in pursuit of diagnosis in its larger sense of in-depth understanding. Etymology can be a helpful reminder in this regard: *dia* means "through" and *gnosis* means "knowledge." Circumspect use of a diagnostic system also requires that we remain mindful that its categories reflect our attempt to organize our observations and understandings. They are not natural entities existing independently of our concerns, values, and questions.

Question: This book has emphasized comportment as experiaction: the ways people live their worlds. You have said that physiology and environment limit and shape comportment. Just how do bioneurology, physical environment, and experience interact?

Response: Questions about how mind and body "act" on each other arise only if we have imposed a separation on what is first apparent to us as a unitary life. Of course human life does lend itself to distinguishing physical, biological, and psychological realms; they do function differently, but not independently. Thinès (1977), for example, has described the common subject matter of phenomenology and biology, namely direct observations of organisms as they constitute and adapt to their worlds. Merleau-Ponty (1942/1963) referred to the differentiable realms of the physical, vital (living), and human *orders*. He described the evolution of the vital from the ground of the physical, and of the human from the vital. But he also reminded us that what we might call the "roots" of each evolved order remain embedded in their ground, transforming that ground with their own growth and change, even while continuing to depend on and be limited by the ground. An example illustrates the point: Surgeons recognize that the biological heart of the man whose wife has just died is not the same as the heart of the man whose daughter is soon to be married. Here we see that interpersonal relations (human order) are also lived out biologically (vital order), that the biological state will be lived in the patient's mood and plans, and that both will participate in the man's psychological, biological, and physical survival or death.

My own major reason for emphasizing the holistic, structural unity of these realms is a practical one. Otherwise, when confronted with a problem, we turn to our analytic mode of dividing that problem into parts, and of then looking for cause-and-effect relations. Again, when problem solving, we are inclined to look for a past or underlying cause or source, and we regard the lowest order of biology or physics as most real or explanatory. For example, we too readily assume that *the* explanation for and treatment of major depression and schizophrenia will be at the level of molecular structures and metabolism. I, too, am eager to learn what happens at these levels, and I believe that such understandings could greatly benefit disordered persons. The drawback is that when we think reductively (looking to the lowest order for explanation), we fail to take into account the participation of the human order in the lower orders. Hence we also fail to appeal to the individual's own resources and responsibility. Specifically, we should investigate how the particular individual takes up the injury, disease, or problem into his or her continuing life. The man who is determined to return to his prior level of physical labor following an injury, for example, may indeed recover more fully than another man with the same injury. Or, his determination may keep the injured area under such stress that he remains disabled longer than a less determined patient.

The lower orders both limit and predispose events at higher orders, but they are neither unilaterally causal nor totally deterministic. Thorough remediation of a disordered life is achieved partly by attending directly to the realm in which the disorder originated, but also by bringing the other realms to bear as resources. Physicians treat Judith's epilepsy with Dilantin, for example, but we also help her to understand that epileptic neurological firing is most likely when a person becomes tense. We explore (psychologically) with Judith when and how she becomes tense, and help her, perhaps with the assistance of biofeedback, to develop ways of relaxing herself in potentially stressful situations. We also can influence the psychological level via the bodily level. The threatened dissolution of Richard's marriage is showing up bodily as headaches, sleeplessness, and so on, and behaviorally as poor performance at work. The most thorough resolution of his disordered life would occur through his facing his responsibilities for the marriage's difficulties, and either saving the marriage, or going on with his life, sadder but wiser. In the meantime, during the acute phase of his efforts to adjust, a mild tranquilizer could calm him adequately so that he could both function better at work, and face the marriage problems more effectively.

In short, I accept the mutuality of the physical, vital, and human orders rather than viewing them as interacting or viewing higher levels as being unilaterally caused by lower levels. Hence a search for mechanisms to account for interaction or causes is unnecessary. Rather, it seems to me that as each order takes up the characteristics of the lower order, those characteristics are transformed. Certainly we can and sometimes must study the physical, biological, and psychological orders one at a time, each in its own right. But our research will be most relevant to human existence when we also remain mindful of the "bigger picture," in which there is a mutuality among the physical, biological, and psychological.

Question: You have emphasized that individualized assessment requires that context be addressed. "Context" has meant not only physically visible environment and biological status, but also the momentary projects and perspectives of client, assessor, and other participants. You have also reminded us that projects and perspectives occur within an historical/cultural context. Do you have a theory of the relations between society and the individual?

Response: No, at least not at a stage that I could write about. But I agree that an explicit understanding of those relationships would benefit our assessments and interventions. Such an understanding is also essential for a thoroughgoing human-science psychology. The following writings on this matter are provocative for readers within a human-science orientation. Foucault (1970; 1973) looks historically at the ways we have constructed reality. Van den Berg's metabletics (1974) looks historically at how changes in consciousness have given rise to synchronous scientific discoveries and social theories. Sartre (1960/1968) has looked at more recent history in his development of what might be called an existential-dialectical theory of social change. Habermas (1968/1971) has been a leader of the critical emancipatory movement, which examines the assumptions underlying social belief systems in order to free ourselves for other options. Schutz's phenomenological social philosophy (1962; 1964) looked directly at the individual's relations with different levels of community. Phenomenologically oriented sociologists such as Garfinkel (1967) and Psathas (1973; 1979) are developing ethnomethodology, which looks, through direct observation, for the implicit social rules through which we comport ourselves and build our social systems. Sociologists Berger and Luckmann (1966) also discuss *The Social Construction of Reality,* and Berger and Kellner (1973) explore the relations of the contemporary citizen to our present world. Von Eckartsberg (1979), a phenomenological social psychologist, has developed methods of exploring the "eco-psychology of personal culture-building."

Question: Does individualized assessment require a different model of clinical training than the one we currently follow?

Response: Our scientist-practitioner model, broadly conceived, seems sound. Within it, graduate students are first oriented as scientists, learning to conduct as well as to evaluate research. Graduates enter their professional practice not only knowledgeable about clinically relevant research findings, but objective in their observations and disciplined in their pursuit of explanation and change. But the psychologist should be trained not only in natural science, but also in human science. I would like to see the science of psychology construed less narrowly. As it is, we too often slip into a technological attitude, unmindful of our participation in shaping our findings through the questions we do and do not ask.

Professionals can incorporate many aspects of individualized assessment into their practices, regardless of their theoretical training. However, it seems to me that consistent, thorough-going respect for and service to the individual require that the scientist-professional be schooled in what we might call radical (at root) reflection (bending back; see Fischer, 1976). The reflective psychologist is one who is aware that humans are the source of *human* knowing and acting. I would like to see our programs balance technological training with promotion of a reflective attitude: (1) promoting interest in the everyday world as our primary data, (2) exposing our graduate students more systematically to the arts and to philosophy as collegial and congruent efforts to comprehend the human order, (3) sensitizing assessors as well as therapists to themselves as their basic access to clients, (4) recognizing perspectivity and situation as essential to understanding perception and action, and (5) promoting inquiry into the body as simultaneously psychological and biological.

This reflective stance precludes certainty and final answers. It disallows practice based only on derived data and constructs. It requires acknowledgement that one's answers are always only partial and always subject to revision. It requires owning one's perspectives as one's own. This reflective psychologist version of our scientist-practitioner model admittedly is demanding. There are, of course, advantages to its disciplined circumspection. It enables assessors to address individuals in their particularity—within their own lives. I hope that this introductory book on individualizing assessment has shown concretely that this approach is not only feasible but rewarding to client and assessor alike.

Assessor's General Checklist

The following checklist was developed for graduate students in an initial assessment course. It addresses both basic and individualized procedures. Like most checklists, it is meant to provide a preparatory overview as well as a postassessment review. The checklist can be used also by established practitioners to reflect on their current practices. Readers may wish to insert additional items, such as their own weaknesses, peeves, or desiderata or those of their students or supervisees. The checklist can be used by oneself or by observers. NA indicates that the item is not applicable, and a check mark or minus sign indicates accomplishment or nonaccomplishment. In the latter case, notations about when within the assessment session the observation was made help both observer and assessor to recall the actual incidents. Likewise, the observer may jot down specific actions or words he or she might have preferred at those points.

Situating the referral with the referring party (usually by telephone or in person)

_____ The assessor ascertained what decisions the referring party must make.

_____ The party's terminology was clarified as to referents or personal meaning (for example, what does the party mean by *hyperkinetic,* and what history or behaviors led to consideration of that term?).

_____ The assessor explored the contexts of a problematic comportment, including its when-nots (for example, what else was going on when Mrs. Burkhardt began leaving her baby alone in the house? And when has she been appropriately conscientious in caring for the baby?).

First contact with the client (for example, telephone arrangements, information provided during initial intake, or information given to referring party to pass on to the client)

_____ The client was asked for his or her understanding of the assessment's purpose.

_____ A brief confirmation or clarification was provided.

_____ The client was left with the impression that further questions would be well received at the session.

_____ An estimate of the time required for the assessment was provided.

_____ The assessor's name (also pronunciation, spelling, title) was given to the client.

_____ The client was reminded to bring glasses or other necessary aids.

_____ Directions for getting to the assessor's office were provided.

_____ Each person was given the other's phone number, in case further clarifications or changes became necessary.

Preparations

_____ Prior to meeting the client, the assessor reviewed the referral and any other relevant data.

_____ If the assessor was going to the client's setting, travel time and directions were checked.

_____ A broad range of tests was readied, whether or not they all would be used.

_____ The assessor reviewed any tests he or she had not administered recently, to be sure of standardized procedures, times, and so on.

_____ Other materials were readied (sharpened #2 pencils with erasers, plain white paper for Bender-Gestalt and for drawings, red pencils for WISC-R, test forms, stopwatch, clipboard, and so on).

Physical arrangements

_____ Initial seating allowed client and assessor full view of one another.

_____ Physical arrangements were free of distractions:

_____ Seating was comfortable.

_____ Room was reasonably soundproof.

_____ Lighting was adequate.

_____ A smooth work surface was available.

_____ There was adequate space for supplies (out of the way but handy).

_____ Diagonal seating was available for test administration.

Situating the referral with the client (or with the client's guardians)

_____ The client was asked for his or her understanding of the referral (self-referral, or as made by another party).

_____ The client's terminology (his or her own, or that taken up from the referring party) was clarified.

_____ Contexts and when-nots of focal comportment were explored.

_____ Refinements or expansions of the referral were made in response to new information or understandings.

Rapport

_____ Respective and mutual purposes for the assessment were clarified.

_____ Important differences of background, perspective, and purposes were mutually acknowledged.

_____ The assessor went about the session in an efficient but thorough manner.

_____ The give and take of an effective working relationship evolved.

_____ The five counterproductive assessor comportments (Table 3.2) were successfully bypassed:

_____ No extraneous sociability

_____ No collusive or avoidant maneuvers

_____ No technician mentality

_____ No rescue maneuvers or doctor's advice

_____ No acceptance of opponent role

_____ The assessor was not an automaton; for example, admissions of a mistake, laughter, and suchlike occurred spontaneously, so long as they did not distract from the assessment project.

_____ The assessor used observations as an access to the client's world, rather than only as external evidence of client characteristics.

Standardized procedures

_____ Any testing that was undertaken was appropriate (it contributed significantly beyond the interview).

_____ Standardized procedures, where they were undertaken, followed manual instructions for the particular test.

_____ Deviations from standardized procedures were undertaken knowingly, and with particular purposes in mind.

_____ The assessor was clear about when he or she was deviating in order to better assess the present person, as compared to deviating to explore alternative future comportments with the client.

_____ Any deviations occurred when the client had been adequately involved, and could now explore effects of the intervention with the assessor.

_____ Where deviations occurred, their nature was indicated directly on the test forms.

Note-taking

_____ Taking notes was not at the expense of observing the client.

_____ The assessor did not rush into note-taking before a working relationship was established.

_____ The significance of the notations was clear to the assessor (as opposed to random writing in hopes that meaning would emerge later).

_____ Note-taking was nonsecretive; the client was allowed to read the notes if curious.

_____ Note-taking was unobtrusive (perhaps utilizing a clipboard).

_____ Notes are legible, for future readers as well as for the assessor.

_____ Recording of the client's responses (such as TAT stories) was efficient (for example, good judgment was exercised in selecting what to record; speed writing techniques were used).

_____ Recording was unrushed (for example, the client was asked to continue only after the assessor had caught up).

_____ Recorded responses also indicated parenthetically where the assessor had raised questions or encouraged further response.

_____ Notations included indication of their context (for example, recording behaviors directly next to the pertinent section of a test form, or indicating that a client's statement was in response to a direct question).

_____ Recording of test responses included samplings of linguistic style, and "extraneous" remarks en route to scorable answers.

_____ The client's own words for important issues were noted.

_____ The date and client's name, as well as any other required information (for example, assessor's name, client's age) have been noted on all test forms.

Responses to client's questions

_____ Answers to the client's questions were honest and to the point.

_____ The assessor listened for the concerns behind questions and addressed them.

_____ Answers were posed so the person could fully understand.

_____ Questions that the assessor said would be addressed later were indeed addressed.

Interventions

_____ Interventions into the client's ongoing comportment were referral-relevant.

_____ The client eventually understood the relations among the intervention, the referral, and nonassessment behaviors.

_____ The client participated actively in exploring the meanings of the disrupted behavior (for example, positive and negative outcomes of the habitual comportment, personal options).

_____ Subsequent efforts to develop alternative comportments were tailored to the particular client.

_____ Concluding suggestions were explicitly linked to the assessment discoveries.

_____ Any concluding suggestions for the client specified their purpose, pivot points (recognizable occasions when a shift from habitual behavior is called for), concrete actions, times, places.

Concluding the session

_____ The assessor checked notes and forms to be sure of having requisite information for further scoring, pursuit of other records, and report-writing.

_____ The assessor overviewed the findings and suggestions, as they will be presented in the report (if there is to be one).

_____ The closing was unrushed, and allowed the client to ask for clarifications, to disagree or raise additional questions.

_____ The client understood what was to occur next (for example, physician would arrange conference after remaining reports were completed; or the person should clarify specified issues with an attorney).

_____ Arrangements were made for the client to read and write comments on the report.

_____ The person understood that permission forms were to be signed for release of the report to specified recipients.

_____ The assessor asked for feedback about how the session might have gone better for the client (to learn more about the client as well as more about one's own impact).

Replacing materials

_____ All test materials were arranged in starting order (for example, cards in sequence, manuals in kits).

_____ Supplies were refilled, reordered, and refurbished as needed; test forms ordered when supply is low, pencils resharpened, card containers mended, pencil marks erased from stimulus cards).

_____ Materials were returned to their customary storage location(s).

Self-monitoring

_____ The assessor arranges for periodic follow-up of a sample of clients (with both assessees and report-recipients) for the sake of improving accuracy and service.

_____ The assessor periodically arranges to be observed during assessment sessions by colleagues or supervisors, directly or on videotape, for feedback on slippage from standardized procedure, bias, or blind spots.

WISC–R Checklist

T<small>HIS</small> checklist should be used in conjunction with the Assessor's General Checklist (Appendix A). This list is not comprehensive, but indicates frequent areas of difficulty. Both students and supervisors can use this list as a reminder that training in psychometrics and standardized procedures is essential for effective individualized assessment. Readers may wish to insert additional items, especially their own or their supervisees' problem areas, or develop similar lists for other tests. The checklist may be used for self-review or by observers. NA indicates that an item was not applicable in a particular case, and a check mark or minus sign indicates accomplishment or nonaccomplishment. Notations should specify actual errors and where they occurred.

General standardized procedure

_____ Testing supplies were placed so as not to distract the youngster, but were not hidden in a secretive manner. For example, the WISC–R case can be placed on a chair next to the assessor.

_____ Likewise, the supplies did not get in the assessor's way. For example, the manual can be propped to one side against the blocks box, so the assessor (but not the assessee) can read instructions, with hands free for recording and working with other testing materials.

_____ Subtests were begun at the proper level of difficulty (see item 5 on Information, for 8-year-olds).

_____ Subtests were discontinued after the designated number of sequential failures.

_____ The child was allowed to finish or to spontaneously stop working on a failed item. Otherwise the assessor's manner of moving on to the next item or subtest was considerate.

_____ The exact wording of the printed instructions was presented matter-of-factly but nonmechanically.

_____ Pronunciation of all items was correct, especially on Information and Vocabulary.

_____ Where repetition of an item was allowed by the manual, the item was repeated in full.

_____ Timing was accurate (beginning with finished presentation of the item, and ending with completion of the problem).

_____ Manipulation of a timing device by the assessor clearly indicated to the youngster that a subtest was to be timed.

_____ The assessor was familiar enough with the WISC–R materials to attend to the testee's comportment (even if the instructions were read from the manual).

_____ The assessor refrained from prefacing each subtest, and instead simply began it.

_____ The assessor refrained from nodding, and from saying "okay," "uh-huh," or "That's fine."

_____ Observation of the youngster was direct, matter-of-fact but non-judgmental—that is, evaluative but not categorical.

_____ The assessor paused long enough before going on to the next item to allow the testee to correct or to elaborate an answer that did not earn full credit.

_____ The youngster's responses were sufficiently clarified and recorded to ensure proper scoring.

_____ In response to the youngster's inquiries, honest reassurance was given that discussion would take place immediately after the test or subtest.

Subtest standardized procedure

Information

_____ Inquiry was limited to a request for a more complete explanation.

Picture Completion

_____ If the testee missed the first two items, the correct answer was provided.

_____ The first time (only) the testee mentioned an unessential missing part, he or she was told, "Yes, but what is the most important thing missing?"

Similarities

_____ Every item was introduced in the same manner ("In what way").

_____ If the youngster did not give a 2–point answer to items 5 or 6, the assessor affirmed any correct answer, and provided the full-credit answer.

_____ Ambiguous or unclear answers were clarified only by saying "Explain what you mean" or "Tell me more about it."

Picture Arrangement

_____ Instructions were repeated for each set of cards, for items 5–12.

_____ The order of the youngster's arrangement was recorded.

Arithmetic

_____ The problems were read clearly.

Block Design

_____ During initial instructions, the blocks were turned in the assessor's hand to show their different sides.

_____ Rotations of 30° were noted and considered as failures.

Vocabulary

_____ When a youngster misunderstood the presented word, the assessor said, "Listen carefully. What does _____ mean?"

_____ Requests for clarification were no more leading than "Explain what you mean" or "Tell me more about it."

Object Assembly

_____ The entire subtest was administered, regardless of failures.

_____ Pieces were laid out in accordance with the pattern on the Layout Shield.

_____ The youngster was credited with only those connections that were made within the time limit.

_____ Any pieces turned upside down by the testee were unobtrusively righted.

Comprehension

_____ Help (in the form of a 2–point answer) was given on item one, and only on item one.

_____ If only one point was earned on starred items, the assessor asked for an additional response, in the prescribed manner.

_____ A hesitant youngster was encouraged ("Yes . . . "; "Go ahead").

Coding

_____ A left-handed youngster was provided with an extra coding key.

_____ During verbal instructions the appropriate areas of the test booklet (the boxes or the figures) were indicated to the subject.

_____ Completion before the limit was timed accurately.

_____ Any skipping of blocks was noted immediately, and the youngster was instructed to "Do them in order. Don't skip any. Do this one next."

Digit Span

_____ Digits were presented with even cadence (one per second; no groupings).

_____ Both trials of each item were administered.

_____ If the Digits Backward example was failed, the child was assisted in accordance with the manual.

Mazes

_____ Two pencils with red lead and no erasers were available.

_____ The six permissible cautions were given as necessary, but only once each.

Recording

_____ Client-information was filled in on the cover sheet, at minimum the youngster's name, birthdate, and age at testing, along with the date of testing.

_____ Any circumstances that affected level of performance were noted next to those scores on the cover sheet. Examples: "John forgot his glasses." "Up to this point Mary Anne thought the testing was for purposes of removing her from her foster parents."

_____ The way in which an item was missed is clear; for example, blocks were correctly arranged but over time, youngster refused to try; a (specified) wrong missing part was named.

_____ Recording of responses and notes is legible.

_____ Recording was efficient; for example, where only one answer is acceptable a check mark suffices; abbreviations such as "DK" for "don't know" are standard.

_____ On the other hand, recording was detailed enough to allow someone other than the assessor to judge the accuracy of scoring.

_____ Recorded responses and marginal notes were complete enough to represent the youngster's language and problem-solving style.

_____ The assessor's repetition of instructions or items, requests for elaboration, and encouragement are indicated parenthetically within the recorded responses. For example: (repeat), (?), (enc).

Scoring

_____ Most items were scored during administration, for the sake of efficiency.

_____ Scoring during administration was not secretive, but did not result in the youngster's watching to see how each item was scored. (The test form can be attached to a clipboard angled to intercept the testee's line of vision; on the record form a slash line can be used in place of a zero.)

_____ The WISC–R profile was filled in.

_____ The profile's graph line (if used in place of a bar graph) was not connected across nonadministered subtests.

_____ Prorated (extrapolated) IQs were clearly designated as such. Besides the recorded mathematics, parentheses are a traditional indication of a prorated IQ, for example: (101).

_____ Scoring took into account regional expressions, and factual developments since the manual's publication.

_____ IQs were accurately calculated (recording of scaled scores; exclusion of Digit Span and Mazes unless prorated; addition; transposing of VIQ, PIQ, and FSIQ from the manual).

Individualized procedures (Many of these can be used in conjunction with standardized administration.)

_____ The youngster's approaches to all subtests were represented and notated. For example, a youngster might work his or her way to full credit on Vocabulary through added remarks, rather than through giving the essential meaning immediately. The answers should be recorded in sequence, and their character noted nearby on the margin.

_____ Wrong answers were recorded, as sample unsuccessful outcomes of the youngster's approaches to tasks. Such recording is particularly pertinent for Arithmetic, Picture Completion, Picture Arrangement.

_____ For any unusual sequences on Picture Arrangement, the youngster was asked to tell the story of the arrangement. (Usually, the sequence is reconstructed by the assessor at the end of the subtest.)

_____ Deviations from standardized procedures were noted on the front of the record form, as well as next to the relevant subtest(s), so that later evaluators would understand the circumstances under which the performance and scores occurred.

_____ If some subtests were deleted, IQs were not calculated unless they were based on the more stable (reliable) subtests.

_____ Deviations from standardized administration were undertaken purposely, with awareness of the value of the foregone standardized score, as well as with awareness of the cost of possible influence on later testing. In other words, deviations were not undertaken gratuitously.

_____ If only selected subtests were administered, they were chosen as representative of the life events relevant to the referral.

_____ Interventions were undertaken at points that allowed both the youngster and the assessor to see the effect of the youngster's previous and alternative approaches. (Usually the completion of a subtest is an optimal point for discussion and for trying out alternatives.)

_____ For an individualized assessment, where referral-relevant, the assessor varied the subtest instructions to explore the circumstances under which the youngster could succeed with previously failed material.

_____ The assessor had developed a stock of daily life or school tasks similar to those of each subtest, for the ages covered by the WISC–R. In this way, test performance served as an entry point for comparison and discussion of the youngster's effectiveness at school and home.

_____ Promised discussions or clarifications indeed took place, and in a manner that allowed the youngster to pursue his or her concerns to satisfaction.

_____ Even though the WISC–R was used, IQs were not presented in the text of the report unless such technical data were clearly relevant to the referral issues. (Scores should not become more central than the comportments from which they were derived.)

_____ Subtest scaled scores and IQs were made available to qualified readers who could use them in the youngster's interest. (These derived data may appear in a technical appendix; or a note on the report may indicate their availability, along with other test productions, in a specified file.)

_____ If IQs were reported, relevant circumstances were also reported. Examples: prorating, deviations from standard administration or testing conditions, special concerns on the part of the youngster (for example, a dying pet, misunderstanding of the purpose of testing).

_____ IQ was not reified; that is, intelligence was presented not as a capacity, but as a level of current intellectual achievement.

_____ If it was appropriate to present level of WISC–R performance, relative standing rather than absolute score was emphasized. For example, level can be presented in terms of national decile standing among age peers, and in terms of a range that takes into account the standard error of measurement.

_____ If relevant to others assisting the youngster, his or her effective and ineffective approaches to subtests were described, along with mention of the circumstances under which the youngster could learn to cope more effectively.

_____ Subtest names and IQ classifications were capitalized, thereby helping readers to see that the names referred to technical aspects of the test rather than to more inclusive everyday meanings. Examples: "Comprehension" rather than "comprehension," "Vocabulary" rather than "vocabulary," "Very Superior" rather than "very superior."

_____ If subtest scatter was analyzed, the actual subtests and similar everyday accomplishments were described. That is, subtest performance was not presented as evidence of vague, presumably underlying traits, such as "field dependence," "verbal reasoning," "social judgment." However, it is appropriate to use such terms to characterize specific accomplishments that have already been described.

_____ Reported WISC–R findings were clearly relevant to the referral issue(s).

Background knowledge

_____ The assessor was familiar with the construction and norming of the WISC–R, and took into account its standard error of measurement as well as any dissimilarity of the tested youngster from the normative groups.

_____ The assessor was familiar with research on how various groups perform on the WISC–R—for example, bilingual, minority, and handicapped youngsters.

_____ The assessor was familiar with developmental norms, both cognitive and social-emotional, and related to and evaluated the youngster in terms of these understandings.

_____ If not qualified to assess developmental slowness (for example, retardation, dyslexia, other learning difficulties) or restrictive psychological states (for example, avoidant, schizoid, or anxiety disorders), the assessor conferred with relevant professionals about an appropriate referral.

_____ The assessor was familiar with factor analytic and correlational studies of the WISC–R, and used that knowledge in reflecting on the testee's ways of approaching tasks.

_____ The assessor had developed an explicit working definition of intelligence, one that allowed integration of factor analytic studies and other research, but avoided static notions of "capacity," "native ability," traits, and the like.

References

Allport, G. W. *Personality: A psychological interpretation.* New York: Holt, 1937.

Allport, G. W. *Pattern and growth in personality.* New York: Holt, Rinehart & Winston, 1961.

American Psychiatric Association. *Diagnostic and statistical manual of mental disorders* (1st–3rd eds.). Washington, D.C.: Author, 1952, 1968, 1980.

American Psychological Association. Ethical Standards of Psychologists. *American Psychologist,* 1963, *18,* 56–60.

American Psychological Association. Psychological assessment and public policy. *American Psychologist,* 1970, *25,* 264–266.

American Psychological Association. *Standards for educational and psychological tests.* Washington, D.C.: Author, 1974.

American Psychological Association. *Standards for providers of psychological services.* Washington, D.C.: Author, 1977.

American Psychological Association. *Ethical principles of psychologists.* Washington, D.C.: Author, 1981.

American Psychological Association. *Specialty guidelines for the delivery of services.* Washington, D.C.: Author, 1981.

American Psychological Association. *Ethical principles in the conduct of research with human participants.* Washington, D.C.: Author, 1981.

American Psychological Association. *Publication manual* (3rd ed.). Washington, D.C.: Author, 1983.

Anastasi, A. *Psychological testing* (5th ed.). New York: Macmillan, 1982.

Appelbaum, S. A. Science and persuasion in the psychological test report. *Journal of Consulting and Clinical Psychology,* 1970, *35,* 349–355.

Arcaya, J. The multiple realities inherent in probation counseling. *Federal Probation,* 1973, *37,* 58–63.

Avila, D. L. On killing humanism and uniting humaneness and behaviorism. *American Psychologist,* 1972, *27,* 579.

Bakan, D. *On method: Toward a reconstruction of psychological investigation.* San Francisco: Jossey-Bass, 1968.

Baker, G. A therapeutic application of psychodiagnostic test results. *Journal of Projective Techniques,* 1964, *28,* 3–8.

Bandura, A. Influence of models' reinforcement contingencies on the acquisition of imitative responses. *Journal of Personality and Social Psychology,* 1965, *1,* 589–595.

Bandura, A. (Ed.). *Psychological modeling: Conflicting theories.* Chicago: Aldine-Atherton, 1971.

Bandura, A. Behavior theory and the models of man. *American Psychologist,* 1974, *29,* 859–869.

Beck, A. T., Rush, A. J., Shaw, B. F., & Emery, G. *Cognitive therapy of depression.* New York: Guilford, 1979.

Bem, D. J., & Funder, D. C. Predicting more of the people more of the time: Assessing the personality of situations. *Psychological Review,* 1978, *85,* 485–501.

384   References

Berger, P. L., & Luckmann, T. *The social construction of reality: A treatise in the sociology of knowledge*. Garden City, N.Y.: Doubleday, 1966.

Berger, P. L., & Kellner, H. *The homeless mind: Modernization and consciousness*. New York: Random House, 1973.

Bersoff, D. N. Silk purses into sows' ears: The decline of psychological testing and a suggestion for its redemption. *American Psychologist*, 1973, *28*, 892–899.

Binswanger, L. *Being-in-the-world: Selected papers of Ludwig Binswanger* (J. Needleman, Ed. and trans.). London: Souvenir Press, 1975. (Originally published, 1967.)

Blatt, S. J. The validity of projective techniques and their research and clinical contribution. *Journal of Personality Assessment*, 1975, *39*, 327–343.

Boelen, B. J. *Existential thinking: A philosophical orientation*. Pittsburgh: Duquesne University Press, 1968.

Boss, M. *Psychoanalysis and daseinsanalysis*. New York: Basic Books, 1963. (Originally published, 1957.)

Braginsky, B. M., & Braginsky, D. D. *Mainstream psychology: A critique*. New York: Holt, Rinehart, & Winston, 1974.

Braginsky, D. D., & Braginsky, B. M. *Hansels and Gretels: Studies of children in institutions for the mentally retarded*. New York: Holt, Rinehart & Winston, 1971.

Brown, E. C. Assessment from a humanistic perspective. *Psychotherapy: Theory, Research and Practice*, 1972, *9*, 103–106.

Brown, L. K. Family dialectics in a clinical context. *Human Development*, 1975, *18*, 223–238.

Buber, M. *I and thou*. New York: Scribner's, 1958. (Originally published, 1923.)

Bugental, J. F. T. Psychodiagnostics and the quest for certainty. *Psychiatry*, 1964, *27*, 73–77.

Bugental, J. F. T. *The search for authenticity: An existential-analytic approach to psychotherapy*. New York: Holt, Rinehart & Winston, 1965.

Bugental, J. F. T. (Ed.). *Challenges of humanistic psychology*. New York: McGraw-Hill, 1967.

Buss, A. R. *A dialectical psychology*. New York: Irvington, 1979.

Butcher, J. N. *Objective personality assessment: Changing perspectives*. New York: Academic Press, 1972.

Buttimer, A. Social space and the planning of residential areas. *Environment and Behavior*, 1972, *4*, 279–318.

Buttimer, A. Grasping the dynamism of the lifeworld. *Annals of the Association of American Geographers*, 1976, *66*, 277–292.

Camus, A. *The myth of Sisyphus and other essays*. New York: Knopf, 1955. (Originally published, 1942.)

Cantril, H. Toward a humanistic psychology. *Etc.*, 1955, *12*, 278–298.

Chein, I. *The science of behavior and the image of man*. New York: Basic Books, 1972.

Christophersen, E. R., Arnold, C. M., Hill, D. W., & Quilitch, H. R. The home point system: Token reinforcement procedures for application by parents of children with behavior problems. *Journal of Applied Behavior Analysis*, 1972, *5*, 485–497.

Christophersen, E. R., Barnard, J. D., Ford, D., & Wolf, M. M. The family training program: Improving parent-child interaction patterns. In E. J. Mash, L. C. Handy, & L. A. Hamerlynck (Eds.), *Behavior modification approaches to parenting*. New York: Brunner/Mazel, 1976.

Ciminero, A. R., Calhoun, K. S., & Adams, H. E. *Handbook of behavioral assessment*. New York: Wiley, 1977.

Colaizzi, P. F. *Reflections and research in psychology: A phenomenological study of learning.* Dubuque: Kendall/Hunt, 1973.

Cone, J. D., & Hawkins, R. P. (Eds.). *Behavioral assessment: New directions in clinical psychology.* New York: Brunner/Mazel, 1977.

Corn, W. M. *The art of Andrew Wyeth.* Greenwich, Conn.: New York Graphic Society, 1973.

Craddick, R. A. Humanistic assessment: A reply to Brown. *Psychotherapy: Theory, Research and Practice,* 1972, *9,* 107–110.

Craddick, R. A. Sharing oneself in the assessment procedure. *Professional Psychology,* 1975, *6,* 279–282.

Cronbach, L. J. *Essentials of psychological testing* (4th ed.). New York: Harper & Row, 1984.

Dailey, C. A. *Assessment of lives: Personal assessment in a bureaucratic system.* San Francisco: Jossey-Bass, 1971.

Dana, R. H. Eisegesis and assessment. *Journal of Projective Techniques and Personality Assessment,* 1966, *30,* 215–222.

Dana, R. H. *A human science model for personality assessment with projective techniques.* Springfield, Ill.: C. C. Thomas, 1982.

Dana, R. H., & Leech, S. Existential assessment. *Journal of Personality Assessment,* 1974, *38,* 428–435.

Delprato, D. J. The interbehavioral alternative to brain-dogma. *The Psychological Record,* 1979, *29,* 409–418.

de Rivera, J. *Field theory as human-science: Contributions of Lewin's Berlin group.* New York: Gardner Press, 1976.

de Rivera, J. A structural theory of the emotions. *Psychological Issues,* 1977, *10* (Monograph 40).

de Rivera, J. (Ed.). *Conceptual encounter: A method for the exploration of human experience.* Washington, D.C.: University Press of America, 1981.

de Rivera, J. (Ed.). (Special issue on qualitative analysis of emotional experience.) *American Behavioral Scientist,* 1984, *27* (6).

Dinoff, M., Rickard, H. C., Love, W., & Elder, I. A patient writes his own report. *Adolescence,* 1978, *13,* 135–141.

Dollard, J., & Miller, N. *Personality and psychotherapy.* New York: McGraw-Hill, 1950.

DuBois, P. H. *A history of psychological testing.* Boston: Allyn & Bacon, 1970.

El-Meligi, A. M., & Osmond, H. *The experiential world inventory.* New York: Mens Sana, 1970.

Erdberg, P. A systematic approach to providing feedback from the MMPI. In C. S. Newmark (Ed.), *MMPI: Clinical and research trends.* New York: Praeger, 1979.

Erikson, E. H. *Identity and the life cycle: Selected papers.* New York: International University Press, 1959.

Erikson, E. H. *Childhood and society* (2nd ed.). New York: Norton, 1963.

Erikson, E. H. *Identity: Youth and crisis.* New York: Norton, 1968.

Exner, J. E. *The Rorschach: A comprehensive system* (Vol. 1). New York: Wiley, 1974.

Exner, J. E. *The Rorschach: A comprehensive system* (Vol. 2). New York: Wiley, 1978.

Exner, J. E. But it's only an inkblot. *Journal of Personality Assessment,* 1980, *44,* 562–576.

Ferrarotti, F. *An alternative sociology.* New York: Halsted, 1979.

Fischer, C. T. Intelligence defined as effectiveness of approaches. *Journal of Consulting and Clinical Psychology,* 1969, *33,* 668–674. (a)

Fischer, C. T. Rapport as mutual respect. *The Personnel and Guidance Journal,* 1969, *48,* 201–204. (b)

Fischer, C. T. The testee as co-evaluator. *Journal of Counseling Psychology,* 1970, *17,* 70–76.

Fischer, C. T. Toward human research via a moratorium on IQ-testing. *Clinical Child Psychology Newsletter,* 1971, *10,* 4. (a)

Fischer, C. T. Toward the structure of privacy: Implications for psychological assessment. In A. Giorgi, W. F. Fischer, & R. von Eckartsberg (Eds.), *Duquesne studies in phenomenological psychology* (Vol. 1). Pittsburgh: Duquesne University Press, 1971. (b)

Fischer, C. T. Paradigm changes which allow sharing of results. *Professional Psychology,* 1972, *3,* 364–369. (a)

Fischer, C. T. A theme for the child advocate: Sharable everyday life-events of the child-in-the-world. *Journal of Clinical Child Psychology,* 1972, *1,* 23–25. (b)

Fischer, C. T. Contextual approach to assessment. *Community Mental Health Journal,* 1973, *9,* 38–45. (a)

Fischer, C. T. Intelligence contra IQ: A human-science critique and alternative to the natural science approach to man. *Human Development,* 1973, *16,* 8–20. (b)

Fischer, C. T. Exit IQ: Enter the child. In G. Williams & S. Gordon (Eds.), *Clinical child psychology: Current practices and future perspectives.* New York: Behavioral Publications, 1974.

Fischer, C. T. Privacy as a profile of authentic consciousness. *Humanitas,* 1975, *11,* 27–43.

Fischer, C. T. Undercutting the scientist-professional dichotomy: The reflective psychologist. *The Clinical Psychologist,* 1976, *29,* 5–7.

Fischer, C. T. Historical relations of psychology as an object-science and a subject-science: Toward psychology as a human-science. *Journal of the History of the Behavioral Sciences,* 1977, *13,* 369–378.

Fischer, C. T. Individualized assessment and phenomenological psychology. *Journal of Personality Assessment,* 1979, *43,* 115–122.

Fischer, C. T. Dilemmas in Standardized Testing. In J. Mearing (Ed.), Working for children: Ethical issues beyond professional guidelines. San Francisco: Jossey-Bass, 1978. (a)

Fischer, C. T. Personality and assessment. In R. Valle and M. King (Eds.), Existential-phenomenological alternatives for psychology. New York: Oxford University Press, 1978. (b)

Fischer, C. T. Privacy and human development. In W. C. Bier (Ed.), *Privacy: A vanishing value?* New York: Fordham University Press, 1980.

Fischer, C. T. Intimacy in assessment. In M. Fisher & G. Stricker (Eds.), *Intimacy.* New York: Plenum, 1982.

Fischer, C. T. Being criminally victimized: An illustrated structure. *American Behavioral Scientist,* 1984, *27,* 723–738. (a)

Fischer, C. T. A phenomenological study of being criminally victimized: Contributions and constraints of qualitative research. *Journal of Social Issues,* 1984, *40,* 161–177. (b)

Fischer, C. T., & Brodsky, S. L. (Eds.). *Client participation in human services: The Prometheus principle.* New Brunswick, N.J.: Transaction, 1978.

Fischer, C. T., & Fischer, W. F. Phenomenological-existential psychotherapy. In M. Hersen, A. E. Kazdin & A. S. Bellack (Eds.), The *Clinical Psychology Handbook.* New York: Pergamon, 1983.

Fischer, C. T., & Rizzo, A. A. A paradigm for humanizing special education. *Journal of Special Education,* 1974, *8,* 321–329.

Fischer, C. T., & Wertz, F. J. Empirical phenomenological analyses of being criminally victimized. In A. Giorgi, R. Knowles, & D. L. Smith (Eds.), *Duquesne studies in phenomenological psychology* (Vol. 3). Pittsburgh: Duquesne University Press/ Humanities Press, 1979.

Fischer, W. F. *Theories of anxiety.* New York: Harper & Row, 1970.

Fischer, W. F. An empirical-phenomenological approach to the psychology of anxiety. In A. de Konig & F. Jenner (Eds.), *Phenomenology and psychiatry.* London: Academic Press, 1982.

Fischer, W. F. Self-deception: An empirical-phenomenological inquiry into its essential meanings. In A. Giorgi (Ed.), *Phenomenology and psychological research.* Pittsburgh: Duquesne University Press, 1984.

Frankl, V. E. *The doctor and the soul: An introduction to logotherapy.* New York: Knopf, 1955. (Originally published, 1946.)

Frankl, V. E. *From death-camp to existentialism: A psychiatrist's path to a new therapy.* Boston: Beacon Press, 1959. (Originally published, 1946.)

Foucault, M. *Order of things: An archaeology of the human sciences.* New York: Pantheon Books, 1970.

Foucault, M. *The birth of the clinic: An archaeology of medical perception.* New York: Pantheon Books, 1973.

Freiberg, J. W. (Ed.). *Critical sociology: European perspectives.* New York: Halsted, 1979.

Freud, A. *Normality and pathology in childhood.* New York: International Universities Press, 1965.

Garfield, S. L. *Clinical psychology: The study of personality and behavior* (2nd ed.). Hawthorne, N.Y.: Aldine, 1983.

Garfinkel, H. *Studies in ethnomethodology.* Englewood Cliffs, N.J.: Prentice-Hall, 1967.

Gilberstadt, H., & Duker, J. *A handbook for clinical and actuarial MMPI interpretation.* Philadelphia: Saunders, 1965.

Giorgi, A. *Psychology as a human science: A phenomenologically based approach.* New York: Harper & Row, 1970.

Giorgi, A., Barton, A., & Maes, C. (Eds.). *Duquesne studies in phenomenological psycholgy* (Vol. 4). Pittsburgh: Duquesne University Press, 1983.

Giorgi, A., Fischer, C. T., & Murray, E. L. (Eds.). *Duquesne studies in phenomenological psychology* (Vol. 2). Pittsburgh: Duquesne University Press/Humanities Press, 1975.

Giorgi, A., Fischer, W. F., & von Eckartsberg, R. (Eds.). *Duquesne studies in phenomenological psychology* (Vol. 1). Pittsburgh: Duquesne University Press, 1971.

Giorgi, A., Knowles, R., & Smith, D. (Eds.). *Duquesne studies in phenomenological psychology* (Vol. 3). Pittsburgh: Duquesne University Press/Humanities Press, 1979.

Goldfried, M. R. Some views on effective principles of psychotherapy. *Cognitive Therapy and Research,* 1980, *4,* 271–306.

Goldstein, K. M., & Blackman, S. *Cognitive style: Five approaches and relevant research.* New York: Wiley Interscience, 1978.

Habermas, J. *Knowledge and human interests.* Boston: Beacon Press, 1971. (Originally published, 1968.)

Hammond, D. C., & Stanfield, K. *Multidimensional psychotherapy: A counselor's guide for the MAP form.* Champaign, Ill.: Institute for Personality and Ability Testing, 1977.

Harrower, M. Projective counseling: A psychotherapeutic technique. *American Journal of Psychotherapy*, 1956, *10*, 74–86.

Harrower, M. Changing roles and changing responsibilities. *The Clinical Psychologist*, 1966, *20*, 11–14.

Harrower, M. Research on the patient. In B. F. Riess (Ed.), *New directions in mental health*. New York: Grune & Stratton, 1968.

Heidegger, M. *Being and time*. New York: Harper & Row, 1962. (Originally published, 1927.)

Hersen, M., & Bellack, A. S. (Eds.). *Behavioral assessment: A practical handbook*. New York: Pergamon, 1976.

Hillman, J. An inquiry into image. *Spring*, 1977, 62–88.

Hobbs, N. (Ed.). *The future of children: Recommendations of the project on classification of exceptional children*. San Francisco: Jossey-Bass, 1975. (a)

Hobbs, N. (Ed.). *Issues in the classification of children: A source on categories, labels, and their consequences* (2 vols.). San Francisco: Jossey-Bass, 1975. (b)

Hollis, J. W., & Dunn, P. A. *Psychological report writing: Theory and practice*. Muncie, Ind.: Accelerated Development, 1979.

Holt, R. R. *Methods in clinical psychology: Projective assessment* (Vol. 1). New York: Plenum Press, 1978. (a)

Holt, R. R. *Methods in clinical psychology: Prediction and research* (Vol. 2). New York: Plenum Press, 1978. (b)

Hoving, T. *Two worlds of Andrew Wyeth: A conversation with Andrew Wyeth*. Boston: Houghton Mifflin, 1978.

Huber, J. T. *Report-writing in psychology and psychiatry*. New York: Harper & Row, 1961.

Husserl, E. *Ideas: General introduction to pure phenomenology*. New York: Humanities Press, 1969. (Originally published, 1913.)

Husserl, E. *The crisis of European sciences and transcendental phenomenology*. Evanston: Northwestern University Press, 1970. (Originally published, 1954.)

James, W. *Principles of psychology* (3 vols.). Cambridge, Mass.: Harvard University Press, 1981 (originally published 1890).

Janzen, W. B., & Love, W. Involving adolescents as active participants in their own treatment plans. *Psychological Reports*, 1977, *41*, 931–934.

Keefe, F. J., Kopel, S. A., & Gordon, S. B. *A practical guide to behavioral assessment*. New York: Springer, 1978.

Keen, E. *Three faces of being: Toward an existential clinical psychology*. New York: Appleton-Century-Crofts, 1970.

Keen, E. Studying unique events. *Journal of Phenomenological Psychology*, 1977, *8*, 27–43.

Keen, E. Psychopathology. In R. S. Valle & M. King (Eds.), *Existential-phenomenological alternatives for psychology*. New York: Oxford University Press, 1978.

Kelly, G. *The psychology of personal constructs* (Vols. 1 & 2). New York: W. W. Norton, 1955.

Koestenbaum, P. *The vitality of death: Essays in existential psychology and philosophy*. Westport, Conn.: Greenwood, 1971.

Korchin, S. J. *Modern clinical psychology: Principles of intervention in the clinic and community*. New York: Basic Books, 1976.

Lamson, A. *Guide for the beginning therapist: Relationship between diagnosis and treatment*. New York: Human Science Press, 1978.

Lazarus, A. A. *Behavior therapy and beyond*. New York: McGraw-Hill, 1971.

Lazarus, A. A. *Multimodal behavior therapy.* New York: Springer, 1976.

Leary, T. *Interpersonal diagnosis of personality: A functional theory and methodology for personality evaluation.* New York: Ronald Press, 1957.

Leary, T. The diagnosis of behavior and the diagnosis of experience. In A. R. Mahrer (Ed.), *New approaches to personality classification.* New York: Columbia University Press, 1970.

Leventhal, T., Gluck, M. R., Slepian, H. J., & Rosenblatt, B. P. The utilization of the psychologist-patient relationship in diagnostic testing. *Journal of Projective Techniques,* 1962, *26,* 66–79.

Levinson, D. J. *The seasons of a man's life.* New York: Ballantine, 1978.

Lieberman, D. A. Behaviorism and the mind: A (limited) call for a return to introspection. *American Psychologist,* 1979, *34,* 319–333.

Lifton, R. J., Kato, S., & Reich, M. R. *Six lives, six deaths: Portraits from modern Japan.* New Haven: Yale University Press, 1979.

London, P. The end of ideology in behavior modification. *American Psychologist,* 1972, *27,* 913–920.

Loo, C. M. The self-puzzle: A diagnostic and therapeutic tool. *Journal of Personality Assessment,* 1974, *38,* 236–242.

Lyons, J. *Psychology and the measure of man.* New York: Free Press, 1963.

Mahoney, M. J. Reflection on the cognitive-learning trend in psychotherapy. *American Psychologist,* 1977, *32,* 5–13.

Mahoney, M. J., Kazdin, A. E., & Lesswing, M. J. Behavior modification: Delusion or deliverance? In C. M. Franks & G. T. Wilson, *Behavior therapy, theory and practice.* New York: Brunner/Mazel, 1974.

Mann, L. Psychometric phrenology and the new faculty psychology: The case against ability assessment and training. *Journal of Special Education,* 1971, *5,* 3–14.

Marcel, G. *Homo viator: Introduction to a metaphysic of hope.* Gloucester, Mass.: Peter Smith, 1978. (Originally published, 1951.)

Marks, P. A., Seeman, W., & Haller, D. L. *The actuarial use of the MMPI with adolescents and adults.* Baltimore: Williams & Wilkins, 1974.

Maslow, A. H. *Motivation and Personality.* New York: Harper & Row, 1954.

Maslow, A. H. *Toward a psychology of being.* Princeton, N.J.: D. Van Nostrand, 1962.

May, R., Angel, E., & Ellenberger, H. F. (Eds.). *Existence: A new dimension in psychiatry and psychology.* New York: Basic Books, 1958.

McLemore, C. W., & Benjamin, L. S. Whatever happened to interpersonal diagnosis? A psychosocial alternative to DSM III. *American Psychologist,* 1979, *34,* 17–34.

McReynolds, P. M., & De Voge, S. Use of improvisational techniques in assessment. In P. McReynolds (Ed.), *Advances in psychological assessment* (Vol. 4). San Francisco: Jossey-Bass, 1978.

Mearig, J. (Ed.). *Working for children: Ethical dilemmas beyond professional guidelines.* San Francisco: Jossey-Bass, 1978.

Meehl, P. E. Wanted—a good cookbook. *American Psychologist,* 1956, *11,* 263–272.

Meichenbaum, D. B. *Cognitive behavior modification: An integrative approach.* New York: Plenum, 1977.

Mensh, I. N. *Clinical psychology: Science and profession.* New York: Macmillan, 1966.

Mercer, J. R. *Labelling the mentally retarded child.* Berkeley: University of California Press, 1973.

Mercer, J. R. Psychological assessment and the rights of children. In N. Hobbs (Ed.), *Issues in the classification of exceptional children* (Vol. 1). San Francisco: Jossey-Bass, 1975.

Merleau-Ponty, M. *Phenomenology of perception.* New York: Humanities Press, 1962. (Originally published, 1942.)

Merleau-Ponty, M. *The structure of behavior.* Boston: Beacon Press, 1963. (Originally published, 1942.)

Merleau-Ponty, M. *The visible and the invisible.* Evanston: Northwestern University Press, 1968.

Merleau-Ponty, M. *The prose of the world.* Evanston: Northwestern University Press, 1973.

Merluzzi, T. V., Glass, C. R., & Genest, M. (Eds.). *Cognitive assessment.* New York: Guilford Press, 1981.

Meryman, R. *Andrew Wyeth.* Boston: Houghton Mifflin, 1968.

Mischel, W. *Personality and assessment.* New York: Wiley, 1968.

Mischel, W. On the future of personality measurement. *American Psychologist,* 1977, *32,* 246–254.

Mruk, C. *Being pleased with oneself in a biographically critical way: An existential-phenomenological investigation.* Unpublished doctoral dissertation, Duquesne University, 1981.

Murphy, M. A., & Fischer, C. T. Styles of living with low back injury: The continuity dimension. *Social Sciences and Medicine,* 1983, *17,* 291–297.

Murray, H. A. *Explorations in personality.* New York: Oxford University Press, 1938.

National Education Association. *Style manual for writers and editors.* Washington, D.C.: Author, 1966.

Nay, W. R. *Multimethod clinical assessment.* New York: Gardner, 1979.

Newman, E. C. *Strictly speaking: Will America be the death of English?* New York: Warner, 1975.

Ornstein, R. E. *The psychology of consciousness.* New York: Harcourt Brace Jovanovich, 1972.

Palmer, J. O. *The psychological assessment of children.* (2nd ed.). New York: Wiley, 1983.

Piaget, J. *The psychology of intelligence.* London: Routledge & Kegan Paul, 1950.

Piaget, J. *Play, dreams and imitation in childhood.* New York: Norton, 1951.

Piaget, J. *The growth of logical thinking.* New York: Basic Books, 1958.

Piaget, J. *Six psychological studies.* New York: Random House, 1967.

Polkinghorne, D. *Methodology for the human sciences: Systems of inquiry.* Albany: State University of New York, 1983.

Pollio, H. R. *Behavior and existence: An introduction to empirical humanistic psychology.* Monterey: Brooks/Cole, 1982.

Pope, K. S., & Singer, J. L. *The stream of consciousness: Scientific investigation into the flow of human experience.* New York: Plenum Press, 1978.

Progoff, I. *At a journal workshop: The basic text and guide for using the intensive journal.* New York: Dialogue House, 1975.

Pruyser, P. W., & Menninger, K. Language pitfalls in diagnostic thought and work. *Bulletin of the Menninger Clinic,* 1976, *40,* 417–434.

Psathas, G. (Ed.). *Phenomenological sociology: Issues and applications.* New York: Wiley, 1973.

Psathas, G. (Ed.). *Everyday language: Studies in ethnomethodology.* New York: Irvington, 1979.

Rabin, A. I. (Ed.). *Assessment with projective techniques: A concise introduction.* New York: Springer, 1981.

Radnitzky, G. *Contemporary schools of metascience.* Chicago: Henry Regnery, 1973.

Rancurello, A. C. *A study of Franz Brentano.* New York: Academic Press, 1968.

Rapaport, D., Gill, M. M., & Schafer, R. *Diagnostic psychological testing* (revised and edited by R. R. Holt). New York: International Universities Press, 1968. (Original edition, 2 vols., 1945.)

Richman, J. Reporting diagnostic results to patients and their families. *Journal of Projective Techniques and Personality Assessment,* 1967, *31,* 62–70.

Riegel, K. F. *Psychology, mon amour: A countertext.* Boston: Houghton Mifflin, 1978.

Riegel, K. F. *Foundations of dialectical psychology.* New York: Academic Press, 1979.

Riscalla, L. M. The captive psychologist and the captive patient. *Professional Psychology,* 1972, *3,* 375–379. (a)

Riscalla, L. M. Is secrecy in the client's best interest? *Journal of Rehabilitation,* 1972, *38,* 19–20. (b)

Riscalla, L. M. A holistic approach to chronic illness. *American Archives of Rehabilitation Therapy,* 1975, *23,* 31–33.

Rogers, C. R. *Counseling and psychotherapy.* Boston: Houghton Mifflin, 1942.

Rogers, C. R. *Client-centered therapy.* Boston: Houghton Mifflin, 1951.

Rogers, C. R. *On becoming a person.* Boston: Houghton Mifflin, 1961.

Rogers, C. R. Contrasting bases for modern psychology. In T. W. Wann (Ed.), *Behavior and phenomenology.* Chicago, Ill.: University of Chicago Press, 1964.

Romanyshyn, R. *Psychological life: From science to metaphor.* Austin: University of Texas Press, 1982.

Rosenwald, G. C. Psychodiagnostics and its discontents. *Psychiatry,* 1963, *26,* 222–240.

Rosenwald, G. C. Physicalism and psychodiagnostics. *The Psychiatric Quarterly,* 1965, *39,* 1–16. (a)

Rosenwald, G. C. Training in psychodiagnostics. Preconference papers. *Conference on the professional preparation of clinical psychologists.* Washington, D.C.: American Psychological Association, 1965. (b)

Rosenwald, G. C. Personality description from the viewpoint of adaptation. *Psychiatry,* 1968, *31,* 16–31.

Ross-Larson, B. *Edit yourself: A manual for everyone who works with words.* New York: W. W. Norton, 1982.

Rychlak, J. F. *The psychology of rigorous humanism.* New York: Wiley, 1977.

Sarason, S. B. An asocial psychology and a misdirected clinical psychology. *American Psychologist,* 1981, *36,* 827–836.

Sardello, R. J. Hermeneutical reading: An approach to the classic texts of psychology. In A. Giorgi, C. T. Fischer, & E. L. Murray (Eds.), *Duquesne studies in phenomenological psychology* (Vol. 2). Pittsburgh: Duquesne University Press/Humanities Press, 1975.

Sartre, J. P. *Search for a method.* New York: Vintage Books, 1968. (Originally published, 1960.)

Sartre, J. P. *Being and nothingness: A phenomenological essay on ontology.* New York: Washington Square Press, 1975. (Originally published, 1943.)

Sattler, J. *Assessment of children's intelligence and special abilities* (2nd ed.). Boston: Allyn & Bacon, 1982.

Schafer, R. *A new language for psychoanalysis.* New Haven: Yale University Press, 1976.

Schafer, R. *Language and insight.* New Haven, Conn.: Yale University Press, 1978.

Scheler, M. *Man's place in nature.* New York: Farrar, Straus, & Cudahy, 1962. (Originally published, 1928.)

Schutz, A. *Collected papers* (Vol. 1). The Hague: Martinus Nijhoff, 1962.

Schutz, A. *Collected papers* (Vol. 2). The Hague: Martinus Nijhoff, 1964.

Schwartz, F., & Lazar, R. The scientific status of the Rorschach. *Journal of Personality Assessment, 1979, 43,* 3–11.

Seagull, E. A. W. Writing the report of the psychological assessment of a child. *Journal of Clinical Child Psychology, 1979, 8,* 39–42.

Seamon, D. *Geography of the Lifeworld.* London: Crooms Helm, 1979.

Seamon, D. The phenomenological contribution to environmental psychology. *Journal of Environmental Psychology, 1982, 2,* 119–140.

Sears, R. R., Maccoby, E. E., & Levin, H. *Patterns of child rearing.* New York: Harper & Row, 1957.

Severin, F. T. (Ed.). *Humanistic viewpoints in psychology.* New York: McGraw-Hill, 1965.

Shevrin, H., & Shectman, F. The diagnostic process in psychiatric evaluations. *Bulletin of the Menninger Clinic, 1973, 37,* 451–494.

Shostrom, E. L. *Personality orientation inventory.* San Diego: Educational and Individual Testing Service, 1966.

Smith, C. M. U. *The brain: Toward an understanding.* New York: Putnam, 1970.

Snyder, C. R. Acceptance of personality interpretations as a function of assessment procedures. *Journal of Consulting and Clinical Psychology, 1974, 42,* 150.

Snyder, C. R., Ingram, R. E., & Newburg, C. L. The role of feedback in helping relations. In T. A. Wills (Ed.), *Basic process in the helping relationships.* New York: Academic Press, 1982.

Snyder, C. R., Shenkel, R. J., & Lowery, C. R. Acceptance of personality interpretations: The "Barnum Effect" and beyond. *Journal of Counseling and Clinical Psychology, 1977, 45,* 105–114.

Snygg, D., & Coombs, A. W. *Individual behavior: A new frame of reference for psychology.* New York: Harper, 1949.

Strasser, S. *Phenomenology and the human sciences: A contribution to a new scientific ideal.* Pittsburgh: Duquesne University Press, 1963.

Strauss, E. L. The Rorschach as an encounter. *The Psychiatric Quarterly Supplement, 1967, 41,* 255–261.

Strunk, W., & White, E. B. *The elements of style* (2nd ed.). New York: Macmillan, 1972.

Sugarman, A. Is psychodiagnostic assessment humanistic? *Journal of Personality Assessment, 1978, 42,* 11–21.

Sullivan, H. S. *The interpersonal theory of psychiatry.* New York: Norton, 1953.

Sutich, A. J., & Vich, M. A. (Eds.). *Readings in humanistic psychology.* New York: Free Press, 1969.

Szasz, T. S. The myth of mental illness. *American Psychologist, 1960, 15,* 113–118.

Szasz, T. S. *Ideology and insanity: Essays on the psychiatric dehumanization of man.* Garden City, N.Y.: Anchor Books, 1970.

Szasz, T. S. *The myth of mental illness: Foundations of a theory of personal conduct.* New York: Harper & Row, 1974.

Tallent, N. On individualizing the psychologist's clinical evaluation. *Journal of Clinical Psychology, 1958, 14,* 243–244.

Tallent, N. Clinical communication and the psychodiagnostic process. *The Canadian Psychologist, 1966, 7a,* 197–208.

Tallent, N. *Psychological report writing.* Englewood Cliffs, N.J.: Prentice-Hall, 1976.

Tallent, N. *Psychological report writing* (2nd ed.). Englewood Cliffs, N.J.: Prentice-Hall, 1983.

Thinès, G. *Phenomenology and the science of behavior: An historical and epistemological approach.* London/Boston: G. Allen & Unwin, 1977.

Thomas, L. *The lives of a cell: Notes of a biology watcher.* New York: Viking, 1974.

Thorne, F. C., & Pishkin, V. The existential study. *Journal of Clinical Psychology,* 1973, Monograph Supplement No. 42.

Titelman, P. A phenomenological study of envy. (Doctoral dissertation, Duquesne University, 1976.) (University Microfilms No. 77-13, 608.) *Dissertation Abstracts International,* 1977, *38,* 383-B.

Towbin, A. P. Psychological testing from end to means. *Journal of Projective Techniques and Personality Assessment,* 1964, *28,* 86–91.

Tuddenham, R. The nature and measurement of intelligence. In L. Postman (Ed.), *Psychology in the making: Histories of selected research problems.* New York: Knopf, 1963.

Turabian, K. L. *A manual for writers of term papers, theses and dissertations* (4th ed.). Chicago: University of Chicago Press, 1973.

Tyler, L. E. *Individuality: Human possibilities and personal choice in the psychological development of men and women.* San Francisco: Jossey-Bass, 1978.

van den Berg, J. H. *The phenomenological approach to psychiatry: An introduction to recent phenomenological psychopathology.* Springfield, Ill.: Charles C. Thomas, 1955. (Revised version available as *A different existence: Principles of phenomenological psychopathology.* Pittsburgh: Duquesne University Press, 1972.)

van den Berg, J. H. *Divided existence and complex society: An historical approach.* Pittsburgh: Duquesne University Press/Humanities Press, 1974.

Vane, J. R. Getting information from school and clinical psychologists. *Professional Psychology,* 1972, *3,* 205–208.

von Eckartsberg, R. On experiential methodology. In A. Giorgi, W. F. Fischer, & R. von Eckartsberg (Eds.), *Duquesne studies in phenomenological psychology* (Vol. 1). Pittsburgh: Duquesne University Press/Humanities Press, 1971.

von Eckartsberg, R. The eco-psychology of personal culture building: An existential-hermeneutical approach. In A. Giorgi, R. Knowles, & D. L. Smith (Eds.), *Duquesne studies in phenomenological psychology* (Vol. 3). Pittsburgh: Duquesne University Press, 1979.

Walsh, J. M., & Walsh, A. K. *Plain English handbook: A complete guide to good English* (6th rev. ed.). Cincinnati: McCormick-Mathers, 1972.

Watson, R. I. A brief history of clinical psychology. *Psychological Bulletin,* 1953, *50,* 321–346.

Weiner, I. B. Approaches to Rorschach validation. In M. A. Rickers-Ovsiankina (Ed.), *Rorschach psychology* (2nd ed.). Huntington, N.Y.: Krieger, 1977.

Wills, T. A. (Ed.). *Basic processes in the helping relationships.* New York: Academic Press, 1982.

Witkin, H. A. *Cognitive styles in personal and cultural adaptation.* Worcester, Mass.: Clark University Press, 1978.

Wyeth, B. J. *Wyeth at Kuerners.* Boston: Houghton Mifflin, 1976.

Yochelson, S., & Samenow, S. E. *The criminal personality: A profile for change* (Vol. 1). New York: Aronson, 1976.

Zinsser, W. *On writing well: An informal guide to writing nonfiction.* New York: Harper & Row, 1976.

Name Index

Subject Index

Subject Index